EX LIBRIS

AMSTERDAM

Geert Mak

AMSTERDAM

Translated by Philipp Blom

Harvard University Press

Cambridge, Massachusetts

2000

Library of Congress Cataloging-in-Publication Data

Mak, Geert
[Kleine geschiedenis van Amsterdam. English]
Amsterdam / Geert Mak ; translated by Philipp Blom.
p.   cm.
Includes bibliographical references and index.
ISBN 0-674-00331-4 (alk. paper)
1. Amsterdam (Netherlands)—History.
2. Amsterdam (Netherlands)—Economic conditions I. Title

DJ411.A55 M3513 2000
949.2'352—dc21   00-039707

Contents

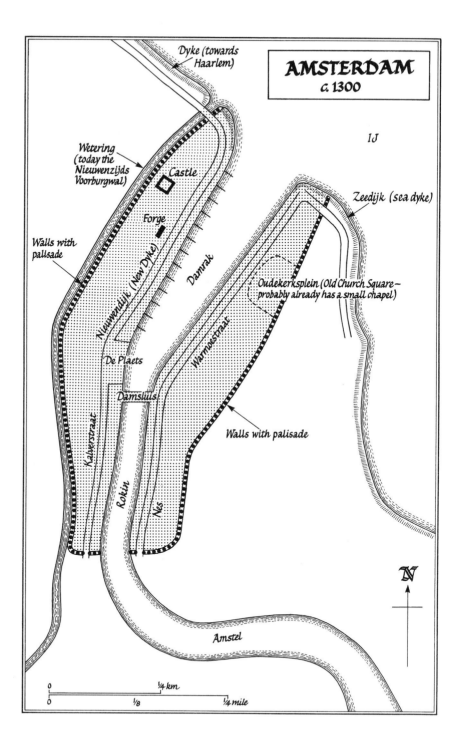

Dyke (towards Haarlem)

AMSTERDAM
c. 1300

IJ

Wetering (today the Nieuwenzijds Voorburgwal)

Castle

Zeedijk (sea dyke)

Forge

Walls with palisade

Damrak

Oudekerksplein (Old Church Square – probably already has a small chapel)

Nieuwendijk (New Dyke)

De Plaets

Warmoesstraat

Damsluis

Walls with palisade

Kalverstraat

Rokin

Nes

N

Amstel

0   ¼ km

0   ⅛   ¼ mile

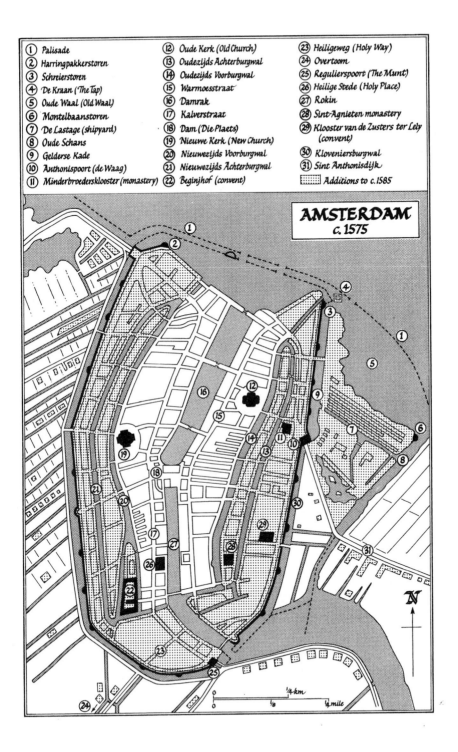

① Palisade	⑫ Oude Kerk (Old Church)	㉓ Heiligeweg (Holy Way)
② Harringpakkerstoren	⑬ Oudezijds Achterburgwal	㉔ Overtoom
③ Schreierstoren	⑭ Oudezijds Voorburgwal	㉕ Regulierspoort (The Munt)
④ De Kraan (The Tap)	⑮ Warmoesstraat	㉖ Heilige Stede (Holy Place)
⑤ Oude Waal (Old Waal)	⑯ Damrak	㉗ Rokin
⑥ Montelbaanstoren	⑰ Kalverstraat	㉘ Sint-Agnieten monastery
⑦ De Lastage (shipyard)	⑱ Dam (Die Plaets)	㉙ Klooster van de Zusters ter Lely (convent)
⑧ Oude Schans	⑲ Nieuwe Kerk (New Church)	
⑨ Gelderse Kade	⑳ Nieuwezijds Voorburgwal	㉚ Kloveniersburgwal
⑩ Anthonispoort (de Waag)	㉑ Nieuwezijds Achterburgwal	㉛ Sint Anthonisdijk
⑪ Minderbroedersklooster (monastery)	㉒ Beginhof (convent)	⬚ Additions to c. 1585

AMSTERDAM
c. 1575

N

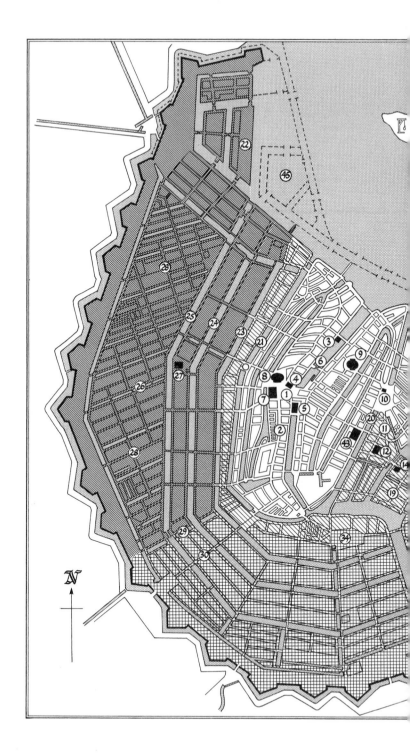

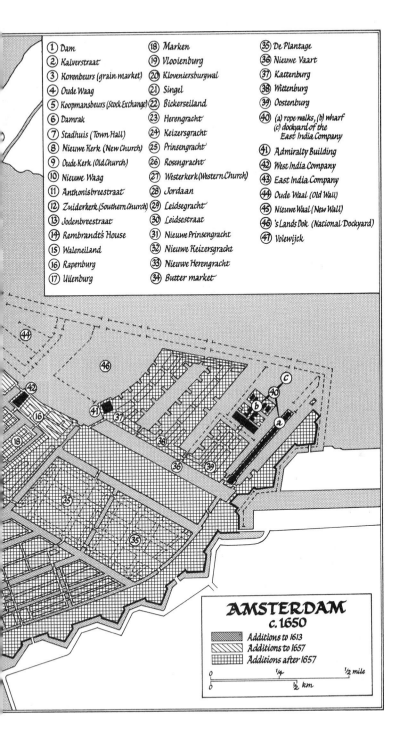

① Dam	⑱ Marken	㉟ De Plantage
② Kalverstraat	⑲ Vlooienburg	㊱ Nieuwe Vaart
③ Korenbeurs (grain market)	⑳ Kloveniersburgwal	㊲ Kattenburg
④ Oude Waag	㉑ Singel	㊳ Wittenburg
⑤ Koopmansbeurs (Stock Exchange)	㉒ Bickerseiland	㊴ Oostenburg
⑥ Damrak	㉓ Herengracht	㊵ (a) rope walks, (b) wharf
⑦ Stadhuis (Town Hall)	㉔ Keizersgracht	(c) dockyard of the
⑧ Nieuwe Kerk (New Church)	㉕ Prinsengracht	East India Company
⑨ Oude Kerk (Old Church)	㉖ Rosengracht	㊶ Admiralty Building
⑩ Nieuwe Waag	㉗ Westerkerk (Western Church)	㊷ West India Company
⑪ Anthonisbreestraat	㉘ Jordaan	㊸ East India Company
⑫ Zuiderkerk (Southern Church)	㉙ Leidsegracht	㊹ Oude Waal (Old Wall)
⑬ Jodenbreestraat	㉚ Leidsestraat	㊺ Nieuwe Waal (New Wall)
⑭ Rembrandt's House	㉛ Nieuwe Prinsengracht	㊻ 's Lands Dok (National Dockyard)
⑮ Waleneiland	㉜ Nieuwe Keizersgracht	㊼ Volewijck
⑯ Rapenburg	㉝ Nieuwe Herengracht	
⑰ Uilenburg	㉞ Butter market	

AMSTERDAM
c. 1650

Additions to 1613
Additions to 1657
Additions after 1657

0	¼	½ mile
0	½ km	

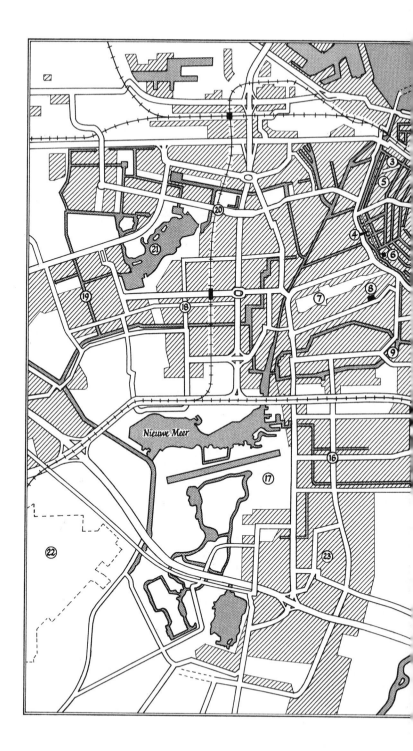

Nieuwe Meer

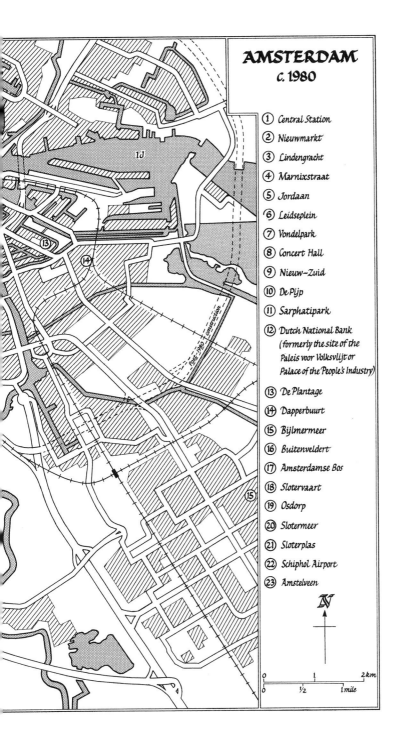

AMSTERDAM
c. 1980

1. Central Station
2. Nieuwmarkt
3. Lindengracht
4. Marnixstraat
5. Jordaan
6. Leidseplein
7. Vondelpark
8. Concert Hall
9. Nieuw–Zuid
10. De Pijp
11. Sarphatipark
12. Dutch National Bank
   (formerly the site of the
   Paleis voor Volksvlijt or
   Palace of the People's Industry)
13. De Plantage
14. Dapperbuurt
15. Bijlmermeer
16. Buitenveldert
17. Amsterdamse Bos
18. Slotervaart
19. Osdorp
20. Slotermeer
21. Sloterplas
22. Schiphol Airport
23. Amstelveen

N

| 0 | | 1 | | 2 km |
| 0 | ½ | | 1 mile | |

List of Illustrations

Prologue

AMSTERDAM IS A CITY, BUT IT IS ALSO A COUNTRY BY ITSELF, a small nation inside a larger one. Moreover, it is a city that spreads out progressively across the country. For a first impression it is best, as always, to drop in on the neighbours for a cup of coffee. Foreigners are often more interested in us Amsterdammers than we are in ourselves, decent and modest as we are.

Outsiders find themselves astonished by all sorts of things, too numerous to mention in detail. Certain observations, however, recur so often that something about them is bound to be true. Our political debate is as exciting as a wet sponge. Our culture of compromise – once a bitter necessity in order for us to be able to survive the next flood together – is now so refined that the concept of "feasibility" has begun to determine our entire way of thinking. Our avarice is legendary: the correspondent of Le Monde, Christian Chartier, has observed that Prime Minister Lubbers spoke about an "investment in the future" even during a debate about the Gulf War of 1991. Our spatial planning and drive for order are phenomenal. Our toleration and flexibility allow us to adapt to each new style that comes blowing across the border. The precocity of this region astonishes everyone: although it is a precocity which may also be called "guidebook effect" or "cosmopolitan trendiness", or defined as a "magpie culture". Levi's sends its trend scouts around the city at least once a year to find out what the women are wearing now; the music shops have all kinds of CDs and records which are not yet available anywhere else; McDonald's first tried out its vegetarian hamburgers in the Low Countries. As to business in Amsterdam, it is conducted in a pleasant sort of anarchism, a yielding order, a sober chaos.

In other words, we have a suburban culture which knows few

conventions, something which, according to some foreign commentators, has everything to do with the fact that Amsterdam (with the exception of the German occupation from 1940 to 1945) has never been ripped to shreds, never suppressed, that it has never stood in the surf, that it has never really known great difficulties.

For centuries Amsterdam – like the rest of the Netherlands – has been relatively safe. Yet its situation on the periphery of the great European trouble spots has led to what is, in the eyes of our neighbours, our most remarkable characteristic: complaining. The Dutch are not especially proud of their country, and this is doubly true for the Amsterdammers, whose lack of patriotism borders on the awful. The intense, aggressive nationalism of other countries is visible here only in the soccer stadiums. If Dutch people are nationalistic outside them, they are defensively so, in protection of their heritage and security – if they are not preaching, that is. The Dutch and the Americans (who have a considerable Dutch heritage) make the best religious ministers in the world.

All this, however, has nothing to do with our proverbial soberness. For centuries the Dutch have simply had no need for nationalism. They have come to take their achievements for granted; moreover, most of the miracles of their country are negative ones. Their greatest pride is perhaps that certain things did not happen: no appalling poverty; no large-scale racial unrest; no terrorism; and even the sea has not flooded the country for many years. Their aspirations beyond that are not very high. What more does a Dutchman want than, in the words of the retired civil servant Pieter Bas (the famous protagonist of a novel by Godfried Bomans), "freedom, old age, money, honour, fame, a dear wife, a lot of children, health, and my own little garden with a fence around it"?

One day, quite by chance, I saw our sovereign at the official departure, after a state visit, of the President of India, one of the largest nations in the world. It was a grey, rainy Amsterdam morning, a military band was playing, and only a handful of elderly people and truant youngsters turned out to watch this, an occasion for which any ordinary country would have drummed up a fleet of Jaguars, Cadillacs, or Mercedes stretch limousines. Instead, the convoy consisted of about ten modest-looking Fords and a little bus from a local tour operator.

The myth of Amsterdam is a myth of the spirit, where that of other European cities is, especially, one of monumentality. Many cities are distinguished by their engineering and their architecture, by a style of building that transforms the citizen into a subject. Monuments are the foremost carriers of a city's mythology, or, more precisely, of the mythology a city wishes for itself. The American city sociologist Donald Olsen once wrote: "A monument is meant to intimidate or to kindle admiration: to remind the onlooker of the age of the dynasty, the power of the regime, the wealth of the community, the truth of its ideology, or of a military victory, a successful revolution, which propagated such wealth, power and truth." Inwardness, he added, was in this context to be regarded as fundamentally wrong. "If a monument is to succeed in its aim, it has to be able to wrench the individual out of his daily life, away from the half-past six train which he has to catch, the driving licence he has to renew, the stamps he has to buy; it has to remind him that life contains more than these worries, that he may count himself lucky to be inhabiting such a glorious metropolis, to be subject to such a benevolent ruler and adherent to the one true faith."[1]

This is the song sung by every monumental building, the language spoken by the nineteenth-century villa suburb. Regent Street, Place de la Concorde, Stalin's Moscow skyscrapers, all make it clear that art and architecture are not merely concerned with themselves but with objects beyond them: politics, ideas, ethics, emotion, avarice, craft, institutions, history. In this way, the modern counterparts of the medieval city came into existence, places that fight chaos, no longer with walls and gates, but with a fantastical tissue of architectural construction. They are purely technical cities, suggesting unity in a fractured world, and clarity in a time longing for authority. Amsterdam, too, knows these bulwarks of technology, at least on its periphery.

Even so, Amsterdam is still an exception in this respect, for it is almost an anti-monument turned flesh. The city tried once to express its wealth and its power in a building, but that was bargained away to the royal court in the Hague. The architecture of prestige has largely passed Amsterdam by, apart from the Rijksmuseum and the Palace of People's Industry, although the latter burned to the ground in 1929. In the late twentieth century, the combination of Town Hall and opera house resulted in a massive, cumbersome building – the Stopera – born out of thriftiness and with all the grandeur of an Ikea chair. The modern business district, which lacks the least display of planning vision, is hidden away on the south-eastern outskirts of the city.

For some reason, monumental buildings do not work in Amsterdam. Whether such buildings are the result of the plan to lure the Olympic Games to the city, or of the plan to make the banks of the IJ (an arm of the Ijsselmeer) something that would be noticed abroad, or of the town-hall-and-opera idea which brought about the Stopera, the city's answer is nothing but mockery and sniggering. The monumentality of Amsterdam exists only in the heads of its inhabitants, not on the streets.

Amsterdam is not proud; indeed, it is even unproud in a proud sort of way. The wealthiest Amsterdammers have clung stubbornly to the sobriety of their seventeenth-century forefathers, with the result that a cityscape has emerged untouched by the grandeur of absolutism, and uncut by the broad avenues which might have been driven through the city in the nine-teenth century. Even the proud Amsterdam of the Golden Age was, in its time and according to the norms of the day, the very anti-image of a modern city: traditional in outlook, oriented towards individual citizens rather than a powerful aristocracy. Its wealth has always been quiet and discreet. There is a direct line from the eighteenth-century Widow Pels on the Herengracht, who, although the richest inhabitant of the Amsterdam of her day, employed no more than five servants, to the senior manager from the city who recently asked in a weekly magazine whether the KLM airline could not tone down the service in its Business Class a little: "A cheese sandwich and a glass of milk are more than enough as far as I am concerned."

The explanation for the modesty of this civic pride lies in the simple fact that Amsterdam has already existed for a very long time as a city state, and the quiet self-assurance our medium-sized European city derives from this fact is not to be underestimated. Amsterdammers, in other words, have for centuries felt no need of boastful tombs, palaces, statues, avenues.

The citizens of Amsterdam do not put on airs – which is one myth the Amsterdammers themselves believe. There has never been a royal court here to serve as a point of reference for the settled bourgeoisie, neither has there ever been an absolute monarch able to force through radical changes of the old structure, and with the power and the means to build on a truly monumental scale. Furthermore, the richest Amsterdam merchants were imbued with the conviction that money was, first and foremost, capital for business and the family, a basis for future generations to build upon, an idea considerably less important to the nobility in other countries, since they always had their lands to fall back on. Thus the culture that emerged in Amsterdam was one in which possessions were held to be more important than honour and where money usually counted for more than fashion, morality, social origin, and prestige, with all the advantages and disadvantages that this mentality brought. The lack of pride of modern Amsterdammers goes further, however. It is not only a character trait, it is a social norm. There is an unspoken ban on displaying high spirits, and the mowing machine is always on stand-by to chop off any heads that are raised above the parapet.

Commentators usually point to the old republican tradition of the city which, as early as 1581, permitted Amsterdam to abjure its prince. There seems to be rather more to it than that, however. We must not forget that for many centuries large parts of the Netherlands have been prey to catastrophes and near-catastrophes. It is a cliché, but none the less true, that people have worked their hearts out in this country in an effort of epic proportions to keep the place above water. This has given the Dutch, and therefore also the Amsterdammers, a natural feeling of ownership: the land was, literally, theirs. At the same time, however, there came about a curious coagulation of power relations, a culture of consensus and compromise which softened and eventually concealed even the fiercest generational conflicts. And yet every now and then, throughout history, the crowd broke through the fences, the quiet disturbed by a day of unheard-of rampaging and hysteria. Afterwards, however, the spiritual order was restored, and once more life carried on calmly and soberly.

Chapter One

The Beautifully Constructed House

HISTORY BEGINS BENEATH THE ROOTS of trees. That is certainly true of Amsterdam, a city that grew up on the IJ* and sank, only to rise again.

The people who lived through Amsterdam's history have vanished. Nobody can tell their stories; nevertheless, dumb witnesses to what happened still exist in their thousands. Time and again small fragments are released from this silent archive. Beneath the foundations of an old house in the Warmoesstraat, next to the red-light district of the Oudekerksplein, building workers found a barely deteriorated layer of fourteenth-century cow dung and straw, and a pair of bone skates, remnants of the time when the Warmoesstraat was still a dyke, and Amsterdam a little village on the IJ. Similarly, during work on a multi-storey car park at the Nieuwezijds Kolk, some walls were found that had once reinforced the early settlement and around which the city had grown. Again, by the Herengracht, close to the Leidsestraat, excavations for a new bank laid bare a bizarre combination of objects: the lower beams of an old mill; a silver medallion bearing a rose-shaped cameo; several skeletons in almost totally disintegrated coffins; a horn ointment press; smelling bottles; remarkable quantities of ointment pots; a medieval stone wall lamp; a single lady's shoe. The builders had chanced upon the site of the provisional

* A bay in the south-west of the Zuiderzee (now the Ijsselmeer), today largely reclaimed from the sea.

pesthouse from the seventeenth century, a place where thousands of victims of the Black Death spent their last days. The coffins, the ointment pots, the lady's shoe and the rose are a testament to their tragedy.

It must look like a battlefield under the surface of Amsterdam: beams, floor tiles, nails, grindstones, fishing hooks, riding spurs, pots, weights, bullets, scythes, compasses, scraps of wool and linen, coins, spindles, buckles, buttons, necklaces, shoes, keys, knives, spoons made from wood, pewter or bone, oil lamps, pilgrims' insignia, devotional pictures, dice, and, last but by no means least, purses. Little by little, enough objects have been found in the ground to keep a medieval town going, yet at the same time every single shoe in the mud holds its own little secret.

Thus the city has been leading a double life for centuries. Droning on in the streets is everyday existence, but behind the façades the city walls still stand, the gothic beams of monasteries remain in place, mills and chapels continue to creak, while, underground, the earth harbours treasures by the handful, thousands upon thousands of forgotten names. Not a week goes by in which an old bottle, the head of a pipe or a collection of pottery shards does not come to light somewhere in the city. During the 1970s, when the old houses around the Zuiderkerk were demolished to make way for an underground railway line, the bottom of the building pit was found to be strewn with skulls and bones: a graveyard had come to light again after two centuries. Underneath the Nieuwmarkt by the Lastage, the tools of the shipbuilders who had worked there around 1500 were found lying around: hatchets and hammers, workmen's gloves and an enormous iron cauldron, probably used for tarring and caulking. Then, too, there are all the things that have been found in the dark blue mud of the canals: thimbles, lace, hairpins, cloth seals, purse clasps, wooden plates (so-called telloren), eyeglasses, pens, forged coins, tobacco boxes, knucklebone dice, and even the visor of a knight's helmet.

Dig deeper still, however, and all of a sudden one encounters little but silence and the murmur of reeds along the banks of the Amstel. Where, around 1325, there was a solid city complete with harbour and fleet, houses and churches, workers, whores and burgomasters, only one and a half centuries earlier there had been nothing at all.

*

Amsterdam is young compared with most European cities. There is no prehistory of migrations, of military barracks or temples; emperors and kings have never held court there. "The origin and early growth of Amsterdam are hidden in a thick mist of doubtfulness and uncertainty," wrote Jan Wagenaar, one of the first historians of the city, in the eighteenth century. Not surprisingly, therefore, nobody really knows what to make of the earliest findings.

When the subway and the tunnel underneath the IJ were built, some Roman coins were dug up, much to everyone's surprise, and even a white marble bust of a Roman emperor has been excavated from the Amstel. During the sinking of a subway caisson, a Roman brooch was found, which the wearer must have lost in the area of the Weespeerstraat at the beginning of the Christian era. There were, therefore, certainly Roman passers-by – after all, Velsen, a considerable Roman garrison, was not far away; moreover, for centuries the windy IJ formed part of the northern border of the Roman Empire. But nobody has ever uncovered proof of Roman habitation in Amsterdam, and other indications of early human activity on the banks of the Amstel remain just as shrouded in mystery.[1]

One thing is certain, though: after the year AD 200, so many floods went over this low country that the banks of the Amstel and the IJ soon became unsuitable for all human occupation. For almost a thousand years it was to remain a deserted area of small lakes, rivulets, willows, rushes and moorland vegetation, not unlike the tiny nature reserves that still exist in Holland, now carefully guarded by conservationists. Such was the state of what was to become Amsterdam when the first university was founded in Paris and the Venetians were trading with the Emperor of China.

There are two legends about the origin of this city. The first is the tale of a knight, a Norwegian prince who, having been shipwrecked in a storm, was almost killed by the heathen Frisians until, at the last moment, he was saved by a Christian, a Frisian fisherman called Wolfert. Together they fled in Wolfert's boat, but on the Flevomeer they were caught in another terrible storm. The prince swore an oath that should they be delivered from their danger he would found a city on the exact spot where Wolfert's sheepdog lay down. Exhausted, they fell asleep, and awoke to find that their prayers had been answered: the boat sat high and dry on arable land, the sun was shining, and the dog was asleep under a tree. A whole new world awaited them.

The second legend is a peasant story. A hunter and a fisherman, wandering around in the desolate marshes along the Amstel, fell to worrying about their future, wondering where to go with their wives and children. A heron, taking pity on them, suddenly began to speak, advising them to build on the sandy corner where the Amstel flowed into the IJ: "Your houses will become a hamlet, the hamlet a village, the village a town, the town a city – and the city will one day rule the whole world!"[2]

So much for stories, now for the reality.

As far as we know, the first buildings to be erected where Amsterdam is now situated appeared at the end of the twelfth century, set on a layer of clay formed by the great floods of 1170 and 1173. Holland at this time was an inhospitable place, an area of marshland in the main, dotted with lakes connected to the sea, lakes which grew in size with every autumn storm. The land was habitable only in the sandy areas of the Gooi in the east and the dunes in the west.

A sort of Wild-West situation arose in the almost deserted Holland of around AD 1000. Families that had eked out a living on the sandy lands of the Gooi and in the dune strip along the IJ, began to venture into the wilderness like true-born pioneers. In some riverside spots these colonists would clear a piece of land of trees and reeds, then dig trenches around it to let the water drain away. All over the almost deserted Netherlands there sprang up isolated farms on which a little grain was cultivated and some livestock raised. The farmers made whatever they needed, with the result that these farmsteads were largely self-supporting. Trade was minimal and there was little money in circulation except for what was required to buy a few luxury goods and to pay rent and taxes. Work was strictly divided between the sexes: the women wove and spun, ground the grain, baked bread, dried salt, brewed ale, made shoes, candles and pots, and also concocted medicines. The men worked on the land, raised, tended and slaughtered the cattle, submitted to corvée* and built boats, which were vital on farms surrounded on all sides by water. This division of labour continued in the early Amsterdam.

---

* The practice whereby a vassal was required to give a day's unpaid labour to his feudal overlord.

During that same period, between 1000 and 1300, several pioneer villages sprang up: Sloten (1063), soon to be followed by Osdorp, Schellingwoude, Ruigoord, Spaarnwoude, Oud Diemen and Ouder-Amstel. Originally the land on which these pioneers lived was literally floating on the water. The canals they dug caused the bog to settle, but this had disastrous consequences, for every flood pushed the sea water further inland, creating large lakes – like the Purmer, the Beemster, the Schermer, the Bijlmer and the Haarlemmer – which threatened to engulf the entire area. The settlers therefore decided to build dykes, the first of which were constructed by the local count and his subjects. The tidal inlets leading to the largest lakes were closed and the whole south side of the IJ – then still a substantial area of water – was dammed by a dyke running for many kilometres all the way from the Gooi, along Diemen and the mouth of the Amstel up to the dunes near Haarlem. Today, the Amsterdamse Zeedijk and the Haarlemmerdijk are the visible remains of this project which was hugely ambitious for its time. In order to prevent the salt water from entering the river mouths, over the years the rivers were all equipped with dams and locks for shipping and for the draining-off of bog water – this was the origin of place names like Zaandam, Spaarndam, and even Amsterdam.

This delta plan *avant la lettre* was not imposed on the settlers by feudal overlords: for the Dutch back then it was literally a case of working on the dykes or drowning. Since the authority and wealth of the count were wholly insufficient for such a large project, and since the prince was far away, the fishermen and farmers had to save themselves, albeit with the Count's encouragement. The planning, building and upkeep of these dykes required good organization, which led to the setting up of a simple administrative system consisting of *dijkgraven* (dyke administrators) and *ingelanden* (landholders). Thus each had some say in the project, with the result that the system functioned reasonably efficiently. This was necessary because at stake was nothing less than the defence of the land against their greatest enemy: water. This tendency in the coastal areas to deal with problems privately, to tend towards decentralization and a rough kind of democracy, was to form the basis of the administrative tradition which, in the end, would determine Dutch political culture for centuries to come.

Officially, the area around Amsterdam, known as the Amestelle, was the property of the Bishop of Utrecht, a powerful man whose realm comprised a large part of the modern Netherlands. He was, moreover, a favourite of the Holy Roman Emperor, Henry IV, a regular visitor to Utrecht for the high holidays of the Church.

The administration of marshy Amestelle was hardly interesting for someone as important as the Bishop, however, and he therefore delegated it almost entirely to a trusted *villicus* or sheriff. A *villicus* was not always a nobleman. Documents from around 1100 mention for the first time a certain Wolfgerus, a serf, who was made a sheriff by the Bishop, and whose family had originally settled in a farmstead belonging to the bishopric, probably in Ouderkerk. Soon, however, Wolfgerus created a new position for himself by exploiting the discord that arose between the Counts of Holland and the Bishops of Utrecht.

In due course Wolfgerus was succeeded by his son, Egbert, who was followed in turn by a whole series of Gijsbreghts, grandsons and great-grandsons. In this way the office became hereditary, and while the colonization of the area was continuing, the family began to call themselves "squires of the Aemstel". However, the van Aemstels were freebooters rather than noblemen, quick to take advantage of the diminishing power of the Bishop and the problems facing the Count of Holland in his dealings with foreign countries. Steadily their influence expanded towards north and south Holland.

The farmstead they inhabited was converted into a simple castle. It was no luxury, for as soon as this no man's land started to develop, the Kennemers, who lived in the dunes, organized one looting expedition after another, the largest of which, as is related in the chronicles of the Egmond monastery, took place in 1204. These "hordes" – which in fact consisted of no more than some tens of men – breached the Amstel dyke, flooded the surrounding land and "burned the beautifully constructed house of Gijsbreght [van Aemstel II] to ash: the fruit trees standing by the house were wholly burned". This, however, was not to be the end of the van Aemstels by any means.

———

Every New Year's Day there was once a long-standing tradition in Amsterdam of staging a performance of the famous tragedy *Gijsbreght van Aemstel* in the city's main theatre. In this play, the seventeenth-century poet

Joost van den Vondel linked the rise of Amsterdam with the demise of the squires of Aemstel, and there was a great deal of truth in this notion.[3] The succeeding Gijsbreghts van Aemstel had between them established something of a dynasty in the wild wasteland of the Amstel region; indeed, by around 1290 Gijsbreght IV was even considered the most important nobleman in Holland.

Not unnaturally, Amsterdammers in later centuries found *Gijsbreght* a wonderful tale: a royal drama taking place in such, to them, familiar locations as Zwanenburgh, Slooterdijk, the Aemstel, the Dam, the Doelenburgh, the Haerelemmerpoort, and the Clarisse monastery. Later, romantic poets turned to the subject time and again.

> At last the hosts in heav'nly halls
> Have pitied my embattled walls,
> And my poor citizens, whose prayers
> And crying echoes with their terror.

So begins *Gijsbreght*, although it is, of course, pure fantasy. The central action of the play is the siege of Amsterdam in 1304. Such a siege did indeed take place, but its principal figure was not Gijsbreght at all, but Jan van Aemstel, and the motives behind his actions were considerably more trivial than those that infuse the tragedy. In 1304, the Count of Holland was so taken up with an invasion by the Flemish that Jan van Aemstel, seeing his chance to settle an old score with the Count, reinforced the then still small Amsterdam with stockades, moats and walls. Even so, when the Count's troops laid siege to the city, Jan was forced to capitulate after only two weeks. "Though it lies in ruins, the city will not tremble, it will rise again in greater glory out of ash and dirt," wrote Vondel, but the reality proved less dramatic. The people of Amsterdam were made to dismantle their own defences, their privileges were withdrawn, they had to pay special taxes, and that was that. Moreover, Vondel created for his play a prettified, if illusory, backdrop by setting it in a much larger city, similar to the Amsterdam of about 1550; as an extra attraction he put in a full-blown castle by the IJ in place of the Schreierstoren, where in reality there had been nothing but a little corner post in a city wall, and this was erected long after the events of 1304.

But Vondel had created a sparkling Greek tragedy on the dykes around the Amstel, a myth complete with angels, knights and virgins, love and duty, heroism and nobility of spirit, and the inhabitants of this grey little country were eternally grateful to him.

Nearly seven hundred years after the siege, in the winter of 1994, the little area behind the Nieuwezijds Kolk was cleared of squatters in a demonstration of strength by the police. The squatters had lived there for years and the houses were dilapidated; now a project developer wanted to tear them down and replace them with luxury apartments and a car park, a proposal to which the municipal authorities consented on condition that the city archaeologists were given access to the site first.

Every now and then I went to have a look at the enormous excavation, noticing how the dragline cut through the centuries like a knife through cake. Some cups from the nineteenth century, a layer of rubbish from the eighteenth, some bottles from the seventeenth; this is what a city looks like from underneath its contemporary surface. Sometimes the diggers displayed their daily harvest: ordinary fare in the main, coins and pottery shards, but also a shoe made from Turkish cork, some fabric, a medieval carnival sign and an iron drill used for shipbuilding.

One overcast day when I walked past, a whole stone hearth had appeared, a small open fireplace dating from the beginning of the fourteenth century. It was remarkable how ordinary it looked, as though it had been carved just a year ago – a little crude perhaps, the work of a cheap contractor – even the tree trunks beneath it might only have been felled the day before yesterday. The Inquisition, the Black Death, the discovery of America, the French Revolution, all these events had thundered over this fireplace and the tree trunks, without affecting them in the least. Now, after more than six hundred years, a machine stood there, rattling, while a man in a yellow plastic overall walked around.

Another visit, a few days later, and suddenly traces of a clay wall were visible. This had probably acted as protection not only against human enemies but also against the IJ, whose banks have receded by several hundred metres over the centuries (originally the IJ began at the Nieuwezijds Kolk and the Dirk van Hasseltway). Then, on 18 February 1994, after little more than a month's digging, the archaeologists decided to call a halt to their operations, for there is nothing to find in Amsterdam at a depth of more than five or six metres. Moreover, a stiff easterly breeze was blowing and the temperature stood at -3° C, making digging far from enjoyable. At this precise moment, at a depth of seven metres, they chanced upon the remains of a wall almost two metres thick. Such unthinkably massive walls could mean only one thing: that there had been a castle by the Amstel after all, just as the poet Vondel had described.

Some days after this discovery, all of history-loving Amsterdam came to have a look: elderly librarians, history teachers, genealogists, conservationists, art historians, and journalists; all stood beaming at this fragment of yellow and pink brickwork, as though this single find had not undermined all of their hypotheses and their archival research. Until then, the theory had always been that there had never been a castle in Amsterdam, that there had never been lords and servants, that this had been a city of independent burgers from the very beginning.

According to city archaeologist Jan Baart, the castle was built shortly after the sacking by the Kennemers of the first fortress of the van Aemstels in 1204, and judging by the worn tiled floors it was in constant use for many decades. It had stood on what was once a peninsula in the IJ, surrounded by a small settlement, measured a good 20 by 20 metres, and had four small corner towers.

The discovery explains certain things that had remained mysteries, among them the unearthing, some years earlier, of a twelfth-century shield in the vicinity, along with a smithy of almost the same age, from a period when there were only a few houses in the settlement. Little archival material has survived from the shadowy thirteenth century, although we do know that slightly later, in 1305, the bailiff still lived in, or had returned to, Ouderkerk, and that this was the centre of administration for the area during that time. Then, after the excitement of the find had abated a little, another opinion rapidly gained currency: the structure discovered was not in fact the castle of the van Aemstels at all, but a reinforcement built three-quarters of a century later, probably by Count Floris V. The timber used in the castle's construction was cut from trees still growing in 1273, as an examination of the rings in the wood proved. Moreover, such square castles were only introduced into Europe in the second half of the thirteenth century.[4]

But whatever the truth of such theories, they make little difference to the history of the development of Amsterdam. With or without a castle, the city has hardly known any feudal tradition. In many European cities the nobility kept their ruling position in society long after they had lost their commanding influence as a social paradigm. In Amsterdam, however, this was much less the case. The citizens observed their duties – until the middle of the seventeenth century the gallery of the Town Hall (the Stadhuis) was dominated by four wooden statues of the Counts of Holland, symbols of authority – but otherwise they simply went about their own business. This may have been due to the shortness of the period during which the van Aemstels ruled, but it may also have resulted from local power relations; besides, the van Aemstels themselves were freebooters at least as much as were the first pioneers to settle in Amsterdam. The original coat of arms of the city is telling: a cog (an early form of sailing ship) with two men and a dog. This is not a legendary image, but a rather prosaic one, translated into symbol. One man, a man of war on closer inspection, symbolizes the castle; the other, a merchant, the city; the dog is a symbol of loyalty; and together all three sail on the ship of the future.[5]

We know almost as little about the first settlement of Amsterdam as we do about the castle. The terrain was boggy marshland, full of alder thickets, hazelnut bushes, spindle trees, reeds and heather; this, at least, is what is suggested by the excavated seeds. Few trees grew alongside the Amstel. Around the year 1180, during the building of the first dyke or possibly even earlier, the settlers had raised artificial mounds on a solid layer of clay by the river and on these they built the first higgledy-piggledy assembly of houses. They were simple huts, each no larger than a sizeable living room of today, and were constructed from a few tree trunks, with walls of twigs covered with clay and a roof of reed or straw. A space for the fireplace was left in the back of the house, "a fire around which one can walk", and the clay floors sloped down from the centre towards the walls in order to prevent rainwater streaming into the house. Dwellings of this type stood in the city until the late Middle Ages. Their advantage was that they could be torn down very quickly in case of fire, it being the obligation of the owner of a burning house to pull down the walls with a hook as quickly as possible.

A row of such huts stood on what is now the Nieuwendijk and a part of the Kalverstraat, on the "New Side" of the city. Contrary to what most Amsterdammers think, the terms *Oude Zijde* (Old Side) and *Nieuwe Zijde* (New Side) have nothing to do with the origin of the city. They date from a later period, when Amsterdam was divided into two parishes, and should really be *Oude Kerks-zijde* (Old Church Side) and *Nieuwe Kerks-zijde* (New Church Side), the Oude Kerk dating from about 1300, and the Nieuwe Kerk from the fifteenth century.

It was mainly fishermen and farmers who lived in this fledgling Amsterdam, even if some discoveries around the castle indicate that there were also a few specialized craftsmen living there. This dyke village was extremely narrow, measuring less than 25 metres in breadth, although it would have taken a quarter of an hour to walk from one end to the other. It was soon broadened by filling up parts of the Amstel from one bank and building new houses on the reclaimed land. As a result the dyke became a street, with houses on either side. Only a few years ago, during excavations for the foundations of a commercial building by the Rokin,* the original bank of the Amstel was discovered. This clearly showed how the early pioneers had filled in parts of the river with mud and turf, alternating with layers of rubbish from the first houses. Although it was a difficult operation it proved successful, and the people of Amsterdam would repeat it several times in the following decades. All in all, about 60 metres were won from the original breadth of the Amstel during this early period. It was the first land that the city had won from the water, and once it had the taste it wanted more.

The dam that gave the settlement its name was probably built after the floods of 1170 and 1173, although some scientists believe it was erected some 50 years later.[6] It is traditionally assumed that the settlement was originally situated closer to the IJ, somewhere near today's Nieuwe Brug. By re-siting it a little further inland, the river mouth could be made to serve as a natural harbour. The settlers quickly began to populate the other side of the harbour, the site of today's Warmoesstraat, which probably derives its name from the vegetable gardens once situated there. In the area around the Oude Kerk a thriving quarter of textile merchants and craftsmen came

* A street, part of which runs alongside the river.

into being, as is evident from the finds there of seals and pieces of cloth.

This was the state of affairs on Sunday, 27 October 1275, when Amsterdam first appears in the archival sources. In the document in question, Floris V, Count of Holland, grants freedom from taxation "to the people abiding near the Amsteldam". The city has very carefully preserved this piece of parchment down through the centuries, and with good reason, for it was the first privilege granted to the young settlement by the Count. What is more, it was very valuable, for it meant that the first citizens of Amsterdam no longer had to pay costly tolls when crossing the bridges and locks that dotted the County of Holland.

This first document also tells us something about the situation in which early Amsterdam found itself. There is no mention of a real city; otherwise Count Floris might have been a little less vague about these "people abiding near the Amsteldam". At the same time, however, the settlement was obviously important enough for the Count to bind its inhabitants to him by the grant of a privilege. It may even be that the building of the walls, mentioned earlier, influenced his decision to treat the Amsterdammers so preferentially. Who can say?

The remainder of this episode in the city's history is indeed worth writing a tragedy about. Gijsbreght van Aemstel IV, seeing that the Bishop of Utrecht was losing his authority, decided to play off Holland and Utrecht against each other, just as his ancestors had done so successfully. Matters got so out of hand that in 1296 van Aemstel, together with other noblemen, even made an attempt to rid themselves entirely of Count Floris V. The coup failed, and the whole van Aemstel family was banished to Flanders for ever. The County of Holland confiscated the castle and set about demolishing it. Then, in 1304, as I wrote earlier, Gijsbreght's son, Jan, tried to seize power over Amsterdam. Although he conquered the city and fortified it with a wall, less than a year later he was chased out, this time for good, after a two-week siege by Floris V's successor as Count of Holland, William III. It seems likely that the headstrong, rebellious van Aemstels had the support of the population of Amsterdam, something which can at least be inferred from the fact that the city was initially punished severely by the Count. Since the people of Amsterdam had "taken in the murderers of Count Floris", they were stripped of all their privileges, the castle was pulled down, and the walls, too, were demolished – only to come to light again unexpectedly almost 700 years afterwards.

When the van Aemstel family was finally defeated in 1304, the city of Amsterdam had to relinquish its recently secured rights, only to have them restored a year later. Because it was during the same period of confusion, when the castle was pulled down, that Amsterdam must have been granted city rights. In a charter dating from around 1300, the new bishop, Gwijde van Avesnes, mentions for the first time "our burghers of Aemstelredamme". Thanks to these city rights, Amsterdam was removed from the authority of the Bishop, the Count, and the van Aemstel family and was in principle allowed to administrate itself through its own aldermen and councils and its own sheriff. Sheriff and aldermen had the power to decide whether to admit new citizens and were entitled to pass their own laws and administer justice, while, if a citizen was imprisoned beyond the city walls, all citizens were entitled to set out to liberate him. Apart from this, the charter also set down regulations about the treatment of serious crimes such as murder, wounding, and breach of the peace. This meant that the city could develop undisturbed, protected by its charter from the meddling of the nobility and by its walls from the uncertainties of the countryside.

Many European cities during this period became islands of commerce and progress in a sea of inertia, terror, superstition and oppression. This was not true of Amsterdam, however, for the interaction with the surrounding countryside was too strong, and the city was still relatively small. While Utrecht, Nijmegen and Dordrecht already had between one and two thousand houses, and Leiden almost a thousand, settlements like Hoorn, Medemblik and Amsterdam consisted of no more than a few hundred.[7] As to the city's spiritual needs, while there was already a small chapel on the square where the Oude Kerk now stands, "Amstelredamme" had to share a pastor with the churches of Ouder and Nieuwer-Amstel. Only on 5 May 1334, when the Bishop decided to appoint a certain Wouter van Drongelen as pastor of the Oude Kerk, was the young city apparently considered grown-up enough to provide enough work for a shepherd of souls. After this, however, things changed rather quickly.

What, within so short a period, transformed Amstelredamme into the city of Amsterdam? What was the dynamic force that drove a few fishing families that, around 1200, had paid the lowest fishery tax of the whole area but were to become a real power, conducting a veritable sea war in the Sound, only three or four generations later? And why did this all happen around the boggy mouth of the Amstel, of all places, when there were so many more suitable areas in the Netherlands in which to found cities?

When all is said and done, Amsterdam was an impossible city. Everything that was built sank into the mud, especially in later centuries when the harbour could only be reached by a complicated route made more difficult by sandbanks and headwinds. In addition, it was, when compared to other Dutch cities, something of a late bloomer: Dordrecht (1220), Haarlem (1245), Delft and Alkmaar (both 1246), among others, all preceded Amsterdam by many years. Yet the young city drew strength from the fact that it was situated close to so many important cities, at least by the standards of the day. Added to this were factors that so often lead to great success: (1) chance; (2) an invention that was to have momentous consequences; and (3) above all, the stupidity and short-sightedness of others.

Let us begin with the invention. Among the earliest inhabitants of the Amstel lands there were many Frisians. In the early Middle Ages they traditionally organized the transport links between the centres of commerce in the Netherlands such as Muiden, Staveren, the Ijssel towns and beyond, towards the Waddenzee, North Germany, Jutland and the Baltic. It seems almost certain that the little town of Amsterdam was part of this commercial route from the very beginning, if only because it is known that there were quite a few sailors living there (there is, for instance, a letter preserved from 1248 – before Amsterdam received its official name – in which Gijsbreght van Aemstel III protests against the confiscation of a ship from Amstelland by the city of Lübeck). During excavations, the remains of objects imported from strange and distant lands were found in the earliest Amsterdam houses: among these, a yellow earthenware jug which ended up in the river around 1200 appears to have been made in Belgium, while the seeds of dried grapes, currants and figs probably came from the south of France or Italy. Then, too, there was a curious strip of silk which came to light among objects dating from around 1225. Woven in Genoa, it had made a long journey on small boats through a complicated network of rivers and small channels, and thence by pathways and trading posts, eventually to arrive here.

The great invention was the cog: a large, broad-beamed wooden ship with a rounded prow and stern, like an enormous clog with a mast, seaworthy and able to transport large quantities of goods cheaply. Just as in the twentieth century the development of the jumbo jet caused a revolution in areas such as migration and international relations by offering relatively inexpensive mass transport between continents, so the cog suddenly made it possible to transport basic goods like grain, wood and salt across the seas in bulk.

Amsterdam was soon playing a part in all this: quays dating from the thirteenth century and designed for sea-going vessels have been excavated opposite the Central Station, and houses near by were found to have been built on the remains of decommissioned cogs. The cog had a capacity of about 100 tons, five or ten times that of its predecessors, and could sail on the open sea instead of taking the convoluted route through rivers and canals. Amsterdam's passive trade as part of a larger network soon turned into active involvement: the city began to go its own way.

As I have said, however, it was not this invention alone that propelled Amsterdam to prominence; it was also the stupidity and short-sightedness of others, and in particular of the Bishop of Utrecht. With the introduction of the cog, the merchants on the coast of the North Sea and the Baltic, especially those in Bremen, Hamburg and Lübeck, began increasingly to trade with southern Europe. They imported salt and wine from France, wool and cloth from England and Flanders, and silk, velvet and spices from Genoa and Venice, while also importing grain, wood and furs from the north. Brugge (Bruges) in Flanders was their entrepôt, an outpost from which they could transport their goods. Because of the treacherous nature of the North Sea, merchants preferred to avoid the open seas as much as possible. Their old route from the Baltic went by inland waterways right through the Netherlands, via the Waddenzee, Almere (the bay which would later grow to become the Zuiderzee), then via Muiden and up the Vecht, Utrecht via the Dutch IJssel to the Rhine, then onwards via the islands of Zeeland to Brugge.

During the thirteenth century the unstable equilibrium between the authorities, freedom and trade, the fine balance between coercion and promise which Amsterdam would exploit to rise to world power in later centuries, was ignored by the Bishops of Utrecht. Essentially, those who ruled mainly tried to make money from the merchants' route through the Netherlands, establishing tolls and building dams, and thereby slowly strangled the hen that laid the golden eggs. From the second half of the thirteenth century, the route along the Rhine through the province of Utrecht was as good as impassable. Under Bishop Jan van Nassau, the diocese sank into total chaos; merchants were robbed and murdered; while from his castle in Vreeland that noble lord Gijsbregt IV acted like a true robber baron.

It was as a result of this negative turn of events that Amsterdam began to grow so strongly after 1275. Merchants who sought, en masse, to avoid the old trading route soon found new ones which passed through Holland, and especially through the Amstel and Amsterdam. The route was by far the most advantageous, and what was more there was no toll to be paid to the Count. Unlike their rivals in Utrecht, the Counts of Holland had quickly understood that their increasing population could not sustain itself by agriculture alone on the boggy and sandy soils around the Amstel. They therefore stimulated and protected the trade, improved locks and bridges and lured merchants into their land with privileges and guarantees of safe passage, with the goal of making a second Brugge out of Dordrecht.

As Amsterdam grew, so it continued to cultivate its individuality; from then until today there has existed a contrast between the principal city and the rest of the country – or, if you will, between the mentality of the Counts and that of the Bishops.

The Bishops, relying on the feudal system of landowners and serfs, ruled over farmers who literally had nowhere else to go, and who were weighed down with taxes like old donkeys until they simply caved in. The Counts, on the other hand, understanding the importance of commerce to their lands, appreciated the fact that merchants were not serfs, and were at liberty to use other routes if they so chose. Furthermore, they understood what would later develop into one of the most important traditions of the Netherlands: the need to deal with the new and the foreign without smothering them with rules and restraints and cheap profit-hunting.

In Holland, people opened themselves to the sea and to everything that came from afar, while those on the sandy soil of Utrecht, Gelderland and Overijssel turned their backs on it. Holland looked towards the west and the north and the lands further to the east; a subtle divide which runs through the political and cultural landscape of the two Netherlands even today.

Chapter Two

Bread and Stones

THE SECOND HALF OF THE TWELFTH CENTURY — THOSE UNKNOWN
years between 1150 and 1200 — must have been an extraordinary period.
Marked by revolutions great and small, it was arguably one of the most
important ages in the history of northern Europe, a time like the nineteenth
century, when events seemed to suddenly hurtle down the rapids of history.

Cogs came into their own, making it possible to carry even more goods
for increasingly greater distances. The great Christian pilgrimages to the
Holy Land began, thus giving people a taste of the strange and the exotic.
Mills and large looms rendered many domestic tasks redundant, shifting
the balance of the division of labour between men and women, and thus
altering the roles of the sexes. In place of bartered goods, money was
increasingly used for payments, the beginning of a market economy.
Moreover, in Holland great floods submerged such vast areas of the country
that they necessitated enormous water-regulation projects. Added to this,
the farming population continued to grow, forcing more and more people
to look for means of making a living outside agriculture. All these developments took place during a few decades, and it was exactly at that turning
point that Amsterdam came into being.

The growth of a village settlement around a river dam into a small town
was a process that certainly lasted a century — about three generations. The
precise border demarcating the end of the village and the beginning of the
town, the "threshold value of urbanity", as the French historian Fernand
Braudel calls it,[1] is impossible to determine for settlements dating from the
Middle Ages. For French towns in the sixteenth century, a lower population
limit of "six hundred hearth-steads" is assumed, which translates into about

two thousand inhabitants. Others, however, believe this figure to be far too high, certainly for medieval towns. Be that as it may, the settlement of Amstelredamme, with its tens and then hundreds of hearths, is likely to have made the lower limit very quickly.

The best indicator of Amsterdam's rapidly developing urban characteristics is the kind of people who lived there. It was not only farmers, fishermen and sailors that had settled. From the very beginning this community on the dykes displayed an important trait in urban life: variation and specialization.

One of the oldest houses of the settlement of Amstelredamme to have been excavated dates from 1225, half a century before the first surviving written reference to the town. Digging in the plot of an old cinema at the Nieuwendijk, a fireplace was found at a depth of four metres, together with some household items and part of a fence belonging to a property. "A large amount of refuse also made clear which profession this pioneer followed," city archaeologist Jan Baart would later write in one of his reports. "Thick layers of ash, a certain amount of coal, a cache of iron waste and some tools tell us that we are dealing with a blacksmith." From different fragments and half-finished items it was possible to deduce that the blacksmith had manufactured not only his own agricultural and horticultural implements, but also carpenter's tools, iron utensils for shipbuilding and fishing, reinforcements for shoes, eating instruments, horseshoes and several weapons. The proximity of the so-called castle would certainly have had a connection here. Moulds and remnants of copper sheets also indicated that the blacksmith knew how to work with copper and pewter. His smithy vanished around 1275, after a good two generations of smiths had lived and worked there.

The remains of the oldest house but one tell of another artisan. It was discovered deep below ground in 1980, near the Kalverstraat, on the site of what had once been a bank of the Amstel, dates from 1250 and was almost certainly inhabited by a shoemaker.[2] Among the remains of the building were found woven willow branches, structural timbers, and stones; in addition, numerous fragments of leather and cow hair mixed with quicklime came to light. Apparently the hides were stripped clean of hairs using lime mixed with river water, the tanning process followed, and then the shoes were made.

There are bound to have been other craftsmen. Among the earliest

Amsterdammers we know by name a certain Lambrecht the Baker from around 1310. This means that the town already had its own bakery, where people could bring the dough they had kneaded themselves to be baked. Around 1307 a windmill was established by the Zeedijk – the grain having previously been ground by hand – and later a second one was built by the Nieuwendijk (which, incidentally, used to be called Windmolenstraat or Windmill Street). With the help of archaeological finds and archives, Jan Baart has been able to list the crafts practised in fourteenth-century Amsterdam. He arrived at about 50 professions, varying from goldsmith, crossbow-maker and brewer, to cooper, whore, and even a female hermit. Clearly by then Amsterdam was nothing less than a city.

This specialization of trades must have had momentous consequences, especially for women. Until the thirteenth century, they ground the grain by hand at home, made bread, wove garments and baked pots in the fire. By the end of the twelfth century, however, looms and potteries were beginning to be introduced, and soon these female tasks were taken over by male weavers and potters. This transition is clear from fingerprints found on earthenware dating from this time. With the help of fingerprint experts from the municipal police, Amsterdam city archaeologists were able to establish that the earliest pieces of earthenware were almost always handmade by women. Later, however, the pieces show the prints of men's fingers.[3] During the thirteenth and fourteenth centuries, the same thing happened with grinding grain, brewing beer, and medical care. At the same time, these new professions were protected by the emerging guilds, which were, almost without exception, exclusively male organizations. It is clear that this transfer of roles must have had significant consequences for the balance of power between men and women, and probably also for the moral order that went with it, even if we can say little about this for certain because of the dearth of written sources.

How should we imagine the village of Amsterdam? Wet and muddy, undoubtedly. During excavations by the Nieuwendijk it was clear from the strata of soil that the family of blacksmiths had to raise the level of their yard almost every two years because it kept sagging into the boggy ground of the marshland on which it was built. Nor did our shoemaker have any more luck with his lodgings. The building, like all the others, was made of wood and stood on the ground without separate foundations. The smoke from the fire curled upwards freely through a few holes in the roof and the clay floor was covered by a woven willow mat. The discovery of these items allows us to deduce that half a century later, around 1300, another house was built on the same spot, with a small cobblestone street adjoining it. In the Amstel, behind the house, a quantity of domestic waste was found, including a wooden vat and some fragments of pots originating from Germany and from Amsterdam itself. At the same site, a century later, about 1400, the first stone house appeared.

Nevertheless, Amsterdam did not turn to stone overnight. Large areas of the city were burned to ashes in 1421, then again in 1452, and after each fire the building regulations became stricter. Reed roofs were prohibited, house fronts and side walls had to be built from brick. On the first map of Amsterdam, dating from 1544, however, it is clear that at least half of the houses still had wooden façades, and there were entirely wooden areas of the city until well into the seventeenth century – wood is, after all, an easy material to work with. A street of wooden houses always offers variation, as can be seen from the oldest drawings of the Warmoesstraat, the Damrak and the Ouderzijds Voorburgwal, so reminiscent of Norwegian and German towns, full of little extensions and architectural frills. That is how the city must have looked around 1350. Two of those wooden houses have survived today, but there are probably more: pretty façades sometimes hide foundations, walls and beams twice as old, and it was a common practice in Amsterdam, in the seventeenth and eighteenth centuries especially, to fix a "modern" façade on to a medieval house. Only recently, during demolition of buildings to make way for the Scandic Crown Hotel Victoria, opposite the Central Station, an almost pristine wooden skeleton of the house of a medieval merchant came to light, complete with the usual rigging construction. Dating from the fourteenth century, it is probably the oldest surviving house in Amsterdam. Because the building of the hotel could not be delayed, the remains quickly vanished into store.

Just as the first cars were no more than carriages in which engines took the place of horses, so the first stone houses exactly followed the building techniques of wooden ones, a construction recognizable today wherever one goes. Wooden beams still carried the roof and stone was used to fill in the walls. The form of the roof was rarely very inventive either. The

town houses tended either to look like castles in miniature, or they were
built with pointed, stepped gables in order to emulate the steep roof of
a wooden house.

Each succeeding storey of a medieval wooden house came out further
into the street, something that can still be seen in old timber-framed homes.
The advantage of this is that the façade and frame of the house encountered
far less strain from wind and rain than would a building with vertical walls.
Thus the gable ends of the houses in any street always inclined towards
each other, making the already narrow streets and dykes appear even more
cramped, and shutting out a good deal of daylight. The advent of stone
façades changed little; the new houses, too, were built "on air", with their
slightly inclining façades staying in alignment with the old wooden houses
of the street. This was done in the first place because a perpendicular façade
among other leaning houses in a street was considered ugly; indeed, it
would appear to be toppling backwards, an optical effect that also enhanced
the beauty of a façade slightly inclining forwards. As merchants came to
build more and more attics for their wares this stepped construction also
offered the advantage that hoisting goods up and down was much easier,
without the constant risk of collision with the façade and the glass windows
of which the master of the house would have been inordinately proud.
The house fronts of Amsterdam's inner city still incline forwards, a tradition
which has survived to this day thanks to that curious mixture of old-
fashionedness and pragmatism which is so characteristic of this city.

Initially, the great revolution that came about with building stone houses
was mainly noticeable in the famous interiors of Amsterdam houses.[4]
Stone made it possible to erect chimneys, so that the fire was displaced
from the middle of the room into a fireplace in one of the stone walls. This
was not a quick process, however, and for almost another two centuries,
until 1492, the city edicts continued to speak of the "open hearth". Even
so, a chimney had considerable advantages. Because the upper part of the
house was no longer full of smoke, it was now possible to lay planks
over the structural beams beneath the roof and thus gain another floor: the
attic. After that, some Amsterdammers began to build little rooms around
the fireplace, as a protection from draughts and to keep in the heat more
efficiently. This cubicle became an established phenomenon in traditional
Amsterdam houses, and was called in Old Dutch the "binnenhaert" or inner

hearth. While the rest of the house maintained its relationship with the open street, this internal fireplace became the germ of a private space. In order to make even better use of its warmth, the ceiling of this little room was lowered, thereby creating a small additional floor above. This new room, in turn, was gradually extended in height and even gained its own chimney. Thus two separate rooms, one on top of the other, grew out of the inner hearth, one becoming the living room, the other the kitchen.

Quite early on, this development led to a clear division between the private and the public in the Amsterdam house itself. We know the "voorhuys" or front house well from the paintings of Vermeer, Jan Steen and other seventeenth-century artists. It was high, light and open, and normally used as a shop, merchant's office, or workshop, and also as a living space. In the summer, the shutters and the door would be left open at all times, although the lower half of the door might be kept shut on account of the many stray dogs roaming the city. The inner hearth, however, was intimate and enclosed. Here Amsterdammmers hid themselves away from the cold and from their hard lives. Such drawings and paintings of these inner rooms as have come down to us breathe an air of blissful indolence: pipe-smoking men and knitting women. The dual nature of this domesticity was to characterize the city for centuries to come: on the one hand the cordial openness of the merchant who meets his customers in the front house and will close neither shutters nor curtains at night, on the other, the contained, private life of the inner hearth, that curious atmosphere which the Dutch delineate with the word *gezelligheid*, the snugness which is soft on the inside and hard on the outside.

Despite the growth of the city, Amsterdam maintained its rural image for a considerable time. As was true in most other European cities around that time, the majority of Amsterdammers were only part-time city dwellers. Sheep, goats, geese and pigs were kept everywhere and were left to roam freely to find their own food; almost every excavation in the city today will hit upon a layer of medieval manure at some point. The areas by the city walls served as communal pastures for cows and horses. In the city archives one finds, for example, decrees forbidding the building of pigsties against the city wall, and there still survive many contracts between citizens regulating the ownership and use of land on which hay was grown. In the city statutes of 1342, I even found a clause under which watchmen at the city gates were allowed six weeks' absence during spring and autumn "in order to go about working on their fields". As late as 1500, the city administrators were forced to forbid owners from letting livestock run freely "on proper roads, on the Holy Way, in gardens and on bleaching fields". The people of Amsterdam were certainly not only occupied with fishing, sailing the high seas and trading – for centuries they combined this existence with a farming life.

Still, it was mainly trade and everything connected with it that led to the rise in the city's fortunes. After the death of the Bishop of Utrecht, Gwijde van Avesnes, in 1317, William III, the Count of Holland, took the opportunity to draw Amsterdam definitively into his county. From that point onwards the city belonged to Holland. Shortly afterwards, the Count introduced a duty on beer, which meant that all beer imported into Holland had to be declared in Amsterdam and tax paid on it there.

In these times, beer was easily the most popular drink in the Netherlands, and most of it was imported, mainly from Hamburg. Amsterdam quickly became the centre of this trade.[5] The preserved tax registers also show that the Hamburg merchants began to bring in other goods as well, which they had bought in Germany and in the Baltic region: wood, grain, beans, nuts, mustard seed, tar, herring, ash, honey, cloth, leather, wire, furs, iron, hops, bacon, meat, grease, and hides. Beer, however, was still their principal export. Around 1365, a remarkable 2,500 tons was shipped into Amsterdam each month, a third of Hamburg's total beer export. The unloading of the beer took place on the Oudezijds Voorburgwal, the "beer quay", between the Oudekerksplein and what is the Damstraat today.[6]

Commercial sailing was by no means an activity exclusive to Amsterdam. The customs registers list the home ports of 120 ships, of which, although all but eight actually came from the Netherlands, by far the greater number hailed from Hindeloopen (31) and Terschelling (17). Nine ships came from Wieringen and another nine from Enkhuizen, six from Stavoren and six from Harderwijk, and only seven from Amsterdam. This is not as strange as it may seem: even in later centuries ships from Amsterdam transported only a fraction of the goods that landed in their harbour. Until the eighteenth century, for instance, sailors from Hindeloopen played an important role in Amsterdam, and later the city recruited many other sailors from the poor flatlands north of the IJ, especially for risky voyages such as whaling expeditions. Villages like Ransdorp and De Rijp were fruitful recruiting grounds for Amsterdam ship owners.

From the very start, Amsterdam was the port to which most of the trade came, a situation that was reinforced by another development in the fourteenth century: the sailors slowly transformed themselves into merchants.

It began when sailors returning to Hamburg started to take goods back with them; first typically Dutch products like cheese, butter, and fish, then other goods from further afield. In the course of this process Amsterdam literally found itself in the wake of the famous trading cities, first as mercantile ally, then as competitor, and later still as enemy.

The stubbornly independent course of the Amsterdam merchants was, to put it mildly, remarkable. After all, this was the heyday of the Hanse, a young, uncommonly energetic league of North German mercantile cities whose members supported and gave preferential treatment to one another. For little Amsterdam, the Hanseatic League would have been a very attractive ally. Other Dutch trading towns were members already, and there is nothing to indicate that Amsterdam could not have followed the example of Nijmegen, Kampen, and Groningen. By doing so, it would immediately have gained access to a network of connections and facilities in a large number of foreign harbours between Novgorod and Brugge. Amsterdam, however, went its own way, retaining its independence. As it turned out it was the protected and spoiled Hanse cities that were to be left behind and underdeveloped.

In the middle of the fourteenth century, however, none of this was apparent. Today, it is almost impossible to outline the nature of trade and power relations in these years. However, a decent indication of the city's success survives in the archives: the number of war cogs that Amsterdam contributed to the joint expeditions, skirmishes and wars of the period.

The first real war in which the city was involved took place around 1368. In Denmark there had risen to power a veritable beast of a prince who, on account of his permanent swearing, was called King Atterbag (King Quarrel). When this king dared to block the Sound, the passage to the Baltic, the Hanse cities dispatched a punitive expedition. The preserved records show that Amsterdam participated in this, but only with one ship: "the peace cog of Amsterdam", as the documents so neatly put it. Kampen, at the mouth of the Vecht, sent no fewer than three cogs, a fact that says something about the relationship between these two cities.[7]

The expedition broke the power of King Atterbag; his capital, Copenhagen, was occupied, and in the subsequent peace conference Amsterdam was granted by the King of Sweden the right to maintain a *fitte*, an outpost, on the island of Schonen. Such a *pied-à-terre* was of enormous importance to the city. In the summer months, large schools of herring migrated to the region, which meant that fishermen and merchants from all corners of the Baltic congregated there. Amsterdam was now allowed to build its own offices and storehouses on Schonen, even its own chapel; furthermore, the island enjoyed a special status under which it was subject not to Swedish law but to Amsterdam city law.

The extent to which relations had changed within a few decades is clear from the records of another common expedition 30 years later, this time against the Frisians.[8] The Hollanders had had designs on Friesland for some time, if only to secure their trade routes. Their Count, William IV, had died in Warns in 1345 during an attempt to invade Friesland, but at the end of the century his successor, Albrecht, saw new possibilities by exploiting the fact that the Frisians were locked in a desperate civil war, a conflict to the death over issues nobody knows any more. In 1398, a large expedition from Holland assaulted Friesland, providing us with quite an accurate image of the extent to which each city in the county contributed to the war effort. The most highly populated cities had to provide the bulk of the soldiers, those with the most shipping the majority of the vessels.

Dordrecht and Haarlem put up most of the men, 600 each, but only 25 and 40 transport ships respectively. The relatively small but very active Amsterdam, however, supplied only 300 troops, but put 50 ships in service. In addition to this, the city sent four large vessels to be used as floating bakeries, each equipped with five bread ovens, while five flour ships accompanied these baking vessels. The expedition was a success, even if the Hollanders had to surrender the area five years later.

It is not known where in Amsterdam all these cogs were constructed, but there are indications. Taking advantage of building work on the Barbizon Hotel, Jan Baart and his fellow archaeologists found to their great surprise the remains of a substantial wharf, which must have been in operation around the end of the fourteenth century, one of the first large wharves of the town. Baart's team unearthed the remnants of at least four workshops, and also floor matting made from strips of peat. The matting was soaked with pitch and covered with tarred tow, as though the shipwrights had simply downed tools and walked away. Behind the workshops, the remnants of a 30-metre-long wooden construction were uncovered, probably a ropewalk, used to twist innumerable ropes for ships. Even the pit of a peach was found in the latrines, a miraculous fruit in Amsterdam at the time.

By the beginning of the fifteenth century the Amsterdammers had less and less need of any contacts with the Hanse. They did everything for themselves. They sailed past Hamburg, circumnavigated Jutland, left Lübeck by the wayside, and took whatever they could get from the harbours of the Baltic. The land route from Lübeck to Hamburg, until then the busiest Hanseatic trading route, was of no interest to them. Thanks to the quality of their ships and of their navigators, the sailors from Amsterdam were increasingly untroubled by the risks of the Ommelandvaart, the sea route.

The merchants of Amsterdam also faced greater dangers, with the result that they developed, quite early on, the habit of spreading the risk among themselves. Traders would never load a large cargo on a single ship; almost always it would be spread over several vessels, belonging to different colleagues, so that even if one ship should sink unexpectedly, only a part of the cargo would be lost. This form of collaboration among the merchants was to extend from trade into several other projects and expeditions. It was because of this habit of spreading risks that, in later centuries, the city of Amsterdam could dare to attempt the impossible: expeditions to the East Indies; a voyage around the world; the finding of a new route via the North Pole; the establishment of a permanent settlement in icy Spitzbergen; the draining of the North Holland seas by means of dykes, channels and hundreds of windmills. Each of these projects cost enormous sums of money and had questionable chances of success because nobody had ever attempted them before.

To the Hanse this "wild" sailing of Dutch ships around their shores, especially ships from Amsterdam, was a considerable irritant. Instead of engaging in coastal shipping and making use of the new trade routes themselves, the Hanseatic League closed like an oyster, its members seeking to protect their near-monopoly in several ways. On Hanse Day, the gathering of the cities in the federation, Lübeck even proposed closing the Baltic entirely to the Dutch. Blind to new possibilities, the Hanse stagnated – Kampen and Brugge became the towns we know today: picturesque and quiet.

Amsterdam, however, blossomed. We have a reasonable idea of how merchants of around this time worked because two account books have survived.[9] These belonged to Symon Reyerszoon and his nephew Reyer Dircszoon, both of whom traded with Danzig, now Gdansk, in Poland. They bought ash, potassium, thread, hemp, wood, pitch, tar, rye, wheat, and talcum, and exported herring, cloth, wine, exotic fruit and salt. Together they formed a family association, a type of company common in the Middle Ages. Since information travelled very slowly in those days, exported wares were frequently accompanied by an associate of the merchant, at the most a close family member, in order to oversee the selling and buying of goods on the spot. But because it was impossible to have family members resident in all harbours, merchants also made use of local representatives, so-called factors. The family concern employed a factor in Lübeck, but the trade with Danzig was conducted by Reyerszoon and Dircszoon themselves, one of the partners staying in Amsterdam, while the other established himself in the Baltic harbour for several months of every year. They conducted a busy correspondence, because something like a rise in the price of grain in Amsterdam could mean that the associate would have to buy more of it, or less if the price fell.

Uncle Symon was clearly the more experienced man, as the surviving papers show, and it was he who usually stayed in Danzig. In 1485 he sailed to the Baltic with a sum of money, having left Reyer with instructions to send him salt, oil, herring, and more money. Symon would then sell the goods in Danzig, buy in products from the Baltic and dispatch them back to Amsterdam. From the correspondence we can see that a change of guard took place within the family in 1487. In that year both uncle and nephew went to Danzig, and a year later Symon stayed in Amsterdam, obviously trusting his nephew with the business abroad.

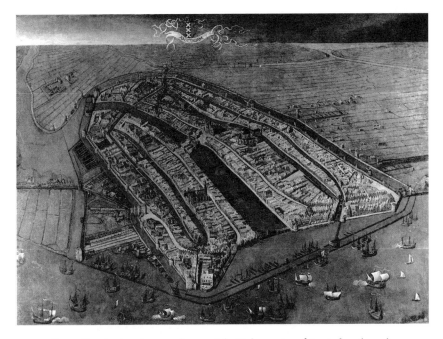

Cornelius Anthoniszoon (1507–61), Birds-eye view of Amsterdam (1534).

Everywhere in the city, people were busy weighing and counting, wheeling and dealing. Of all ships passing through the Sound during the fifteenth century, almost 60 per cent came from Holland, those from Amsterdam playing by far the most important role. This increased trade also had significant consequences for the cityscape of Amsterdam.

The original harbours, the Damrak and the Rokin, had become too small, so that ships were having to moor side by side at the quays. A basin on the south bank of the IJ, the Ouderzijds Waal (now the Oude Waal), served as a harbour for overwintering and "resting" ships, and even the city canals were used more and more as places for loading and unloading goods. Most of the large vessels, however, remained anchored in the IJ in front of the city. During the fourteenth century there was a double row of poles hammered into the ground as protection for the city against flood, in the location of today's Central Station, and most large ships were moored here. Especially when the Baltic fleet was home, this harbour was full of grain vessels, with their high prows and sterns rolling on the waves next to one another. The channel between these two enormous rows of poles was closed every night with thick floating beams, and until the nineteenth century in the evenings the modest "beam bell" was sounded over the silent waters of the IJ when the city was closed to the sea.

Amsterdam grew quickly after 1380. Areas of land were raised and new canals dug: the Oudezijds Achterburgwal and the Nieuwezijds Achterburgwal, today the Spuistraat. At that time the population of Amsterdam numbered no more than three to five thousand souls, and projects of this kind and on such a scale must have been an enormous effort for a city that was still quite small. Yet within only a few seasons tens of thousands of tons of clay had been dug out, loaded and tipped into the moorland, and this with the few and primitive means available in the Middle Ages. Making the land suitable for construction must have required almost more effort than the building itself.

In spite of all this, in 1425 the city had to be enlarged again. Now a broad canal was dug on the east side, today's Geldersekade and Kloveniersburgwal. A quarter of a century later, a similar canal was looped around the west side of the city like a piece of rope: the Singel.

By then the centre of the town was already the Dam. Here the Amstel was built over and closed off with locks, although ships could pass with lowered masts. Eventually, houses were built over the supporting arches, and a square developed on the left bank of the river, the Plaetse, although this also soon became known as the Dam. Over the years, the whole area was built on, and it was only later that these houses were to be demolished to make place for a square again. Until the demolition of the locks in 1675, vessels could pass through the Dam from the Amstel to the IJ, and vice-versa.

The administration of the town was situated there as well. For centuries, Amsterdam's highest authority consisted of four burgomasters or mayors; a sheriff; seven (later nine) magistrates; and a town council. The burgo-masters were elected on 1 February each year and had the right to make everything that happened in the city their concern during their year in office, with the exception of the administration of justice, which fell to the sheriff and aldermen, who were also elected for a year. The city council was a college of 36 "free" citizens who, after 1400, represented all of the citizenry. In practice, they were recruited from the elite of the city: merchants who had made good by trading in the Baltic. They elected the burgomasters and aldermen, but had to be consulted for important decisions. In addition to this, a number of citizens' guards emerged, militia groups consisting of armed citizens whose task it was to defend the town during emergencies. Each group practised in its own building, and over the centuries, as there has never been a great deal of warfare in this city, these developed into something like gentlemen's clubs.

Thus far, all these administrators had worked in an assortment of rooms and houses, their important documents, including those detailing their privileges, being housed in the so-called Iron Chapel, a primitive safe hidden away in the upper reaches of the Oude Kerk. This could go on no longer. The expansion of the city and other major projects were not the work of amateurs any more, and around 1400 the burgomasters bought a house at the Dam, which was to serve as a Town Hall. This was quickly replaced by a purpose-built building, Gothic in style, with a tower and, on the first floor, a large assembly room measuring at least 25 metres long by nine wide.

A large new church was built at the Plaetse, too. By now Amsterdam was divided into two parishes, one on either side of the Amstel, and although the Oude Kerk had been enlarged and added to during the fourteenth century, it finally became too small as the population steadily increased. Thus it was that, early in the fifteenth century, the citizens of Amsterdam began to build their first prestigious building, a purely Gothic cathedral modelled on that at Amiens. The merchant and banker William Eggert, the first rich citizen to find his way into the history of this city, owned an orchard behind the Dam which he offered as the site, and in addition paid a substantial part of the building costs. Thus the picture which characterized so many cities in Western Europe also came into being in Amsterdam: a large agglomeration of small, usually wooden houses with, in the centre, a gigantic stone structure, slowly growing, a sanctuary built with the sacrifice of almost all of a town's money, energy, and expertise, an eternal symbol of piety and sense of community in this city of individualists, bankers and traders.

Let us take a short walk around the medieval Amsterdam, a stroll of no more than half an hour. Southwards along the Warmoesstraat, the houses back on to the Amstel, built in the same manner as must have been common at the very beginning of the city's life. Past the Oude Kerk, the last unspoiled medieval building in the town, still preserving inside the silence and smell of an ancient French village church. Turning west into the Grimburgwal: the opposite side, today the Binnengasthuisterrein, the city's first extension. Through to the Kalverstraat, running northwards to the Dam. Here the medieval houses lie some three or four metres under street level, although that yellow earthenware jug from Belgium was found at a depth of about twelve metres. Walk across the Dam, buried under the square, and the vaults of the old locks are still extant beneath the National Monument. Continuing northwards, along the Nieuwendijk, there are still a few steps to climb in the pedestrian zone around the modern C&A building, because the bulk of the structure of the Nieuwe Dijk has never entirely vanished. On the left, behind the former Royal Cinema, are the foundations of the van Aemstel castle. Finally, back to the Warmoesstraat again, via the Onze-Lieve-Vrouwesteeg, left, underneath numbers 6 and 8, some beams and floor tiles were found that belonged to the Onze-Lieve-Vrouwekapel, the Chapel of Our Lady, in the wall of the Chinese restaurant, Fook Hing.

We now have some images. But can we restore more? Smells? Sounds? During the winter there would have been a smell of wood fires between the houses, and of peat and manure, a little like an Eastern European village. The first city dwellers lived mainly on self-baked bread, a porridge of boiled buckwheat, barley, oats, and some fruit. In the latrines of the oldest houses, archaeologists have found the pits of several different fruits: apples, pears, wild strawberries, imported figs, and mulberries which must have been grown here. Roaming geese and pigs would have determined the image of the Dam, the Nieuwendijk, the Warmoesstraat and the Kalverstraat. In the autumn they were slaughtered, and Breughel-like scenes must have taken place on the muddy streets of the town, full of people and animals running, screaming, and crying out.

And the other sounds? From our vantage point at the end of this millennium, the Middle Ages are a strange and remote reality, one which we can only see as in a broken mirror. Far and away the loudest noise known then was that of church bells, but people knew more than enough about singing, praying and wailing too – Heaven and life, Hell and death, were just around the corner. From documents we know that the city employed bands of musicians "with shawms, trumpets and other musical instruments". They had to play "a song, maybe two or three" every evening from the tower of the Town Hall at the Dam, and also in the mornings "when the watch comes from their duty, and also on all holidays and on all celebrations held by the city, such as may be required."[10]

Dice have been found from every century of the city's existence, the oldest dating from its very earliest years. Even a chess piece from the latter days of Uncle Symon and his nephew Reyer has come to light, as well as spinning tops, toy swords and a children's bow from the years of William Eggert. Then, too, there is a rusty Jew's harp from the time of Lambrecht the Baker; a simple instrument that would have entertained a few people sitting around a fire in the evening. It is a vibrating piece of iron held between the teeth, using the mouth as a resonating body, and emitting almost African sounds: poi-oing, poi-oing, poi-oing.

Chapter Three

The Enemy

IT IS SOMETIMES SAID THAT EVERY PERSON DIES TWICE: THE first time when he dies, and the second when he is forgotten by the last survivor from his own time, an old man or woman. Thus a number of the dead vanish for ever when the last living memory of them dies. By the same token, most of the life of a city dies in a single generation; after that, faces, smells, sounds and atmospheres can only be reconstructed with the help of fragmentary sketches or the occasional preserved picture. Our collective memory, whether or not it is receptive to the written word, is as loose as dry sand; apart from the most essential facts, the rest is guesswork.

Not a single face survives of those who called themselves "Amster-dammers" during the first three centuries of the city's history, and the first to make a personal appearance are mainly seen *en passant*, walking along a road in a city panorama; spectators at a memorable execution; or donors painted into this or that altarpiece. There is the meagre, hard face of a female bread seller, captured at some time between 1555 and 1560 in Amsterdam by the painter Pieter Aertsz. There are some group portraits of citizen's militia societies, the oldest, by Rot H, is *The Company of the Crossbow Militia of St Joris at Dinner*: seventeen serious, heavy-set men wearing black clothes, their hair cut short, a kind of wide French beret on each head. On their plates one can see baked duck and fillets of fish arranged in intricate patterns. One of the marksmen is holding a sheet of music; it is just possible to decipher the text accompanying the notation: "*Discantus.* In my soul I have chosen for a girl . . . " The Amsterdam Historical Museum has had the melody of this love song reconstructed. It sounds as heavy as a psalm. At the top of the painting is the year: 1533.

Among the very earliest faces to come down to us there are also those of a couple, probably the merchant and burgomaster Egbert Gerbrandzoon and his wife Gerrit Janszoon Peggedochter, painted in 1541 by Dirck Jacobszoon. Egbert has a round face and worried eyes; his wife, looking from beneath her cap, is smaller and finer. They stand behind a table on which we see objects heavy with symbolism: an hourglass, an accounts book, a handful of gold coins, an inkpot, penknives, a ball of spinning thread. In the background we look through a window on to a landscape in which Christ hangs upon the Cross, and in the foreground there is a chapless skull. On the right-hand side of the painting are two more symbols of domestic industry: a shelf full of business letters on which one can read, just, the name of the man, and on the wall the woman's broom.

In order to accentuate even more the transience of our existence, the couple are pointing demonstratively to the hourglass and the gold, for work one must, time is running out, and one should not indulge in vanity. *Cedit Mors Nemini*, death spares no one, is painted on the wall behind the merchant, while behind his wife is a maxim for later generations that can be summed up as: life is short; live honestly and as Christians;

and if you are rich, you are duty bound to share your possessions – on pain of the fires of Hell.

The portrait of the couple is curious in several respects, not least because it continually invites the viewer to step behind its content. On the most obvious level, two people have chosen to have a portrait painted of their outer selves, yet at the same time they are anxious to turn themselves inside out on the canvas, to demonstrate their relationship to God and eternity. In doing so, they are giving us a glimpse, however formally, of the driving force behind the history of this city, its mentality.

Amsterdam was never a truly medieval city. No king has ever held court here, the Church has never played a truly all-encompassing role, the social and political structures were never determined by the relations between ruler, vassal, and serf. From the very beginning it was a modern city, its citizens were independent and stubborn enough to take care of themselves.

At the same time, however, Amsterdam was a child of its time, with medieval houses, streets and squares in which, as the historian Johan Huizinga has described it in his timeless manner: "all of life's situations had outer forms more accentuated than they are today".[1] "Everything people experienced had that degree of immediacy and absoluteness which joy and sorrow still have in the mind of children [. . .] There was less protection from catastrophe and illness, which struck more horrifically and more painfully. Illness was more obvious than health; the barren frost and the terrible dark were more substantial evils. Honour and riches were enjoyed more fervently, since their power to hold at bay the terrors of poverty and exclusion was more apparent." To which he adds that "everything in life had an ostensive and horrifying manifestness." Lepers made a noise with their rattles, beggars exhibited their desperate state in churches, every profession and rank was recognizable from the apparel of its members, and no gentleman moved through town without the accompanying demonstrations of reverence as befitted his position. Justice, the buying and selling of goods, weddings and funerals – everything was accompanied by processions, shrieks, wails, singing, bell ringing, and drumming, by cheers and cries.

All of which was true of Amsterdam. From 1492 there was a cattle market in the Kalverstraat, a dairy market on the Dam, and vegetables, fruit, wood, and medicines were sold along the Damrak. Sea and river fish were offered for sale on the locks, sometimes even a seal or a porpoise. The annual free market was the climax of the year; there was even an elephant there in 1484.

Every year, too, the so-called "miracle procession" was held, a colourful display which drew the entire city out on to the streets. First came the members of the guilds carrying lit candles, each group with its own banners and pictures of its patron saint. This was followed, according to a description of the occasion,[2] by a small group of "girls and young boys", who performed, among other works, the short play *St Joris and the Dragon*. More children followed: little angels with wings on their shoulders, and little devils carrying pitch-black sticks and smeared with soot, "with terrifying grins on their faces", as though they had just leapt from Hell. These always succeeded in making the smallest children among the spectators cry when they saw them coming. Behind them walked the archers in full accoutrements, with drums and banners; then the singing students of the Latin school in white surplices; the monks of the city monasteries in their black, grey, and brown habits, with crosses and images on their backs; then the clergy with their banners; a group of penitents going through the streets barefoot and almost naked because of this or that vow; and, at the end, underneath a magnificent baldachin carried by the four burgomasters, the priest, holding the monstrance with the holy Host inside. Meanwhile, the city band played "very finely and beautifully on pipes and shawms".

Traditionally the procession started by the Nieuwe Kerk, went round the city via the Kalverstraat, then back to the Nieuwe Brug and thence to the IJ, where it halted to bless the ships and guarantee their safe passage. Then the route continued to the Oude Kerk, where the Holy Sacrament was exhibited for worship.

The patron saint of the Oude Kerk, Saint Nicolaas, the "water saint", was also very popular, as he protected the sailors and those living on the polders* from the dangers of the sea. Later he was to have something of a second career as a friend of children, riding his horse over the rooftops of Amsterdam on the eve of his name day, 6 December, and distributing presents by dropping them down chimneys.

---

* Land reclaimed from the water.

The Oude Kerk and the Nieuwe Kerk were no longer the only places of worship, however. In fifteenth-century Amsterdam all hospices and monasteries had their chapels, and there were small chapels on bridges, one in the Town Hall, several scattered about the city's different boroughs – in short, the 10,000 or so Amsterdammers of the time had a surfeit of consecrated places. There is even a decree surviving which forbids children to play ball games or make too much noise in a street called the Nes, as this would disturb the devotions of the sisters in a nunnery close by.

Nevertheless, the City Fathers often did their utmost to curb the growth of cloisters in the city. In 1498, the masters of the carpenters' and brick-layers' guilds were ordered not to make any repairs or undertake any building works in a certain monastery, no matter how trivial the job. Convents and monasteries took up space: each one had to have its own chapel, vegetable garden, bakery, churchyard, stables, bleaching fields and workshops, and on top of this they were usually rich enough to buy up the entire surrounding area. In the year 1500, Amsterdam had no fewer than 20 convents and monasteries, roughly one for every 500 inhabitants. All but four of them were situated around the Oudezijds Achterburgwal, and the street names still remind us of the fact: the Gebed zonder end (Perpetual Prayer), the site of at least five nunneries; the Monnikenstraat (Monk Street), named after the monastery of the Franciscans; the Bloedstraat, named after the Holy Blood; the Bethaniënstraat, after the Bethany nunnery; and the Koestraat (Cow Street), the Bethany sisters being famous for their fattened oxen.

The religious life of the city received a powerful boost on 15 March 1345, when a miracle occurred in a house on the Kalverstraat. A sick man, "in danger of dying", had received the Holy Sacrament from a priest; but, as he was ill, he had vomited it all up again immediately afterwards. The women looking after him threw the vomit into the fire, which was kept burning throughout the night for the suffering man, without looking to see whether there was anything left of the Host. The following morning, however, when one of the women raked the ashes, she found to her great astonishment "among the flames a clean white Host, whole and unharmed". Fearlessly she reached into the fire and took the Host, without being burned in the least, finding that it was quite cool; later, it changed colour several times, and even began to move on its own. After the priest had been notified all the clergy of Amsterdam came to the house where this miracle had occurred.

The Holy Sacrament was returned to the Oude Kerk in a great procession, with banners and flags and songs of praise and thanks.

Few miracles have been so precisely documented. There is even an account of the episode by the bailiff of Amstelland and the government of Amsterdam, written just three weeks after the event. The site of the miracle soon became a popular place of pilgrimage, with the result that a chapel was built in the Kalverstraat for pilgrims; and by 1347 there is already an account of a procession of believers who went around this Holy Place in silent prayer. In order to facilitate the journey of the pilgrims, a special path was built from Sloten called the Heilige Weg (Sacred Way). Parts of it later became the Overtoom and the Leidsestraat, but the very last surviving piece, now a busy shopping street between the Singel and the Kalverstaat, still bears that ancient name.

Many other miracles were ascribed to the Holy Place. In 1476 a nun who had been paralysed by a stroke was gripped by supernatural powers when visiting the Holy Sacrament: three times she walked around the Oude Kerk and then returned to her convent healed. A similar incident happened to a nun of the Bethany convent in 1514. According to her own testimony, she had suffered from dizzy spells: "And then my heart jumped so terribly and my body shook and the bed on which I lay began to shudder".[3] A woman from Hoorn, who had been travelling on the market barge with her children and who almost drowned when the vessel capsized as too many people pushed on to it, saved herself and her family by vowing to visit the Holy Place. When Archduke Maximilian of Austria (later, as Maximilian I, to be Holy Roman Emperor), had fallen mortally ill in The Hague, he was promptly healed when he made the same vow. Even the oldest known literary work in which Amsterdam features, a naive text by the court minstrel William van Hillegaersberch dating from about 1380, deals with nothing but the miracle of the Kalverstraat, the miracle "bright and clear" which "occurred in a place called Amsterdam in Amsterlant."[4]

The remarkable blossoming of Amsterdam after 1350 was not due simply to trade. Almost certainly it also had a religious stimulus – even if that is often forgotten. The city was an extraordinarily popular place of pilgrimage, hailed as the "Eighth Wonder of the World", something no foreign traveller should miss, as one sixteenth-century author wrote. The merchants who came streaming into the little town on holy days, in such large numbers that special regulations had to be made for them, must have given additional zest to it's economic life, and the solemn visits by the great and the good such as the Holy Roman Emperors Charles IV, Maximilian I and Charles V, would have lent special prestige to the then small Amsterdam. In short, it was not only a trade centre but was also a focus of religious life over two centuries, a Canterbury of the Low Countries.

In medieval Amsterdam, secular authority was just as embedded in countless forms of ritual as the spiritual life. Initially quite open, the city was soon surrounded by ramparts and eventually by a wall. This latter developed into more than a physical barrier: gradually it became a political, economic, and social border, and every evening for centuries the city closed itself off hermetically from the outside world. At 9.30 p.m. the city gates slammed shut. Soldiers brought the keys to the Town Hall, placed them in a special box and then carried the key of that box to one of the burgomasters. At sunrise the whole ritual took place in reverse.

As was the case with all medieval cities, there was in Amsterdam a marked difference in status between burghers and non-burghers. A crime against a burgher was perceived as a violation of the whole city community.

Punishments were meted out in the open, and were often directly linked to the nature of the crime: thieves had their hands hacked off, blasphemers had their tongues pierced, and those sentenced to death frequently had the instrument of their crime exhibited next to their corpses. Until halfway through the seventeenth century – by which time Amsterdam had grown into a fully fledged metropolis – three concentric circles were visible on the Dam, which probably had once served as a ceremony of expulsion, an almost magical ritual carried out around the navel of the city. If a burgher of medieval Amsterdam had incurred too many debts, and if every attempt to resolve the situation had failed, he was led around these circles three times (in earlier days, probably around the little town itself), during which it was asked of the assembled populace whether there was anybody left who was prepared to vouch for him. Only after it had been established that there was no one to answer for him could the burgher be evicted from the city, or even cast into debtor's prison.

The public nature of medieval city life brought human existence on to the streets in all its colour, a colour heightened by the abiding contrast between rich and poor, life and death, health and illness. By virtue of this the life of the city gave rise to, in Huizinga's words, "a teasing, passionate suggestiveness, which revealed itself in the fickle moods of rowdy abandon, absolute fury, and intense mortification between which the life of the medieval city moved".

It is not always easy, therefore, to identify with the thinking of the Amsterdam of 500 years ago. What, for instance, was the course of the city council's discussion in the great hall of Amsterdam's small Town Hall in 1398, when it had to be decided whether the city would join the great punitive expedition which Holland was mustering against the Frisians? Economic motives may well have played a part in the decision-making process in this city of merchants, but it is too simplistic to assume that the actions of the city council were based on rational grounds alone. It is equally possible that loyalty, pride and the idea of divine justice all played their part. Even revenge could be a powerful motive: the Count of Holland had, after all, been murdered on an earlier expedition against the Frisians. This was the style of reasoning of the relatively sober administration of Amsterdam, and it was similar to most other cities at that time.

Illness, death, plague, wars, all were at close quarters. Storm and flood threatened human life every day. The sailors and fishermen especially, and all the Amsterdammers living just behind the dykes, must have been filled with an awareness of the omnipotence of nature, the unpredictability of the elements and a fear of God. Heaven, Hell and the Last Judgement were never far away. The penitence preacher Johannes Brugman, who in 1462 established himself in the Franciscan monastery in Amsterdam, was so popular that even now, after more than five centuries, persuasive talkers are referred to as people who "talk like Brugman". His friend and brother in spirit, Dionysius the Carthusian described Hell thus: "Let us imagine in our mind's eyes the hottest and most intensely glowing oven, and lying inside it a naked man who is never to be relieved from such suffering. Let us think how this man will toss back and forth in the oven, how he will scream and howl, how he will live, what terror will oppress him, what pain will pierce him, especially when he notices that this insufferable punishment is never-ending."[5] Against the heat of the fire or the terrible cold, the worms, the wailing and screaming, there was only one thin shield: the excellence of virtue, the charitable work of Gerrit Janszoon Peggedochter.

———

Sometimes this fear assumed a human face. The people of Amsterdam lived in the same terror of witches, devils, and wizards as anywhere else in Europe, although there were never any comprehensive witch hunts in the city, and even heretics were not pursued with any great fanaticism. Clearly this kind of persecution was already, even then, not in the population's nature.

Thanks to the assiduity of one eighteenth-century historian of Amsterdam, Jan Wagenaar, there has survived a complete record of an interrogation, in 1555, of a maid accused of practising magic.[6] The narrator, who tells her own story, is Meyns Cornelis, originally from Purmerend, a woman who perceived human existence through a veil of madness. Out of that perception she created a detailed picture of what befell a woman who had lost control of her mind in this sixteenth century city, with all the terror and confusion that accompanied her misfortunes.

During the first interrogation, on 8 November 1555, Meyns gave the sheriff a broad outline of her spiritual life story. She had become aware of strange phenomena at least 20 years before. While she was sitting alone by the fire one evening, ten or twelve cats had suddenly come in and had begun "to dance for about half an hour, paw in paw". When she retired to bed, she discovered one of the cats lying under the covers. Grabbing the beast by the scruff, she threw it out of the upper door into the canal, but when she crept back to bed it was lying there again, now dripping wet. Fearing for her life, she had asked her master and his wife to allow her to sleep downstairs for a few nights.

The next occurrence was not until about a decade later. Meyns had meanwhile moved in with a certain Jacob Roel, with whom she later had a relationship. One night, she suddenly saw four women in strange clothes standing in front of her. One of them was carrying old bricks in her skirt and proceeded to pelt Meyns with them, repeating over and over: "Your face shall catch flies!" The following morning, Meyns found that her body, in her own words, had turned "as blue as a lung". Neighbours carried her downstairs and sat her on a stool by the fireplace; then, in order to ward off witches, they hung "a pot full of new needles into which she had pissed" over the fire.

After this incident, she was sent to an exorcist, Master Simon in Medemblik, who recommended that she marry and also sewed several bags of gunpowder into her clothes. Some weeks later she returned to Amsterdam and the problems returned with her. She had taken lodgings with a man named Adriaan Klaassen, but when she tried to enter the mezzanine room of his house, she was repeatedly thrown downstairs by unseen forces, and early one morning her skirt was ripped to shreds by a strange man who appeared on the threshold. There was also an incident involving her savings which, according to Meyns, had been stolen from a little box; the money was then offered to her again by several strange figures. Among these was a "young fellow with a Spanish cap lined with black velvet on his head", who called out to her when she was cleaning out barrels: "Lovely one, don't you want a lover? Here I stand – a young man!"

Several weeks afterwards Meyns married a certain Cornelis Willemszoon, and lived with him in peace for about seven years, untroubled by apparitions. One day, however, when Cornelis came home drunk and yelled to her that "she needed a thorough going-over" and threatened her with his sword, ten or twelve women in strange clothes appeared, streaming in through the front door and calling: "Break the knife, he cannot treat you so ill!" The women helped her to do just that, according to Meyns's increasingly confused account, but afterwards they grabbed her and "threw her into the street over the lower door, from where her husband dragged her back into the house". Since then, the mysterious women had regularly reappeared, had abused, kicked and punched her and again thrown her out into the street; even while she was being interrogated, she said that three of them were sitting next to her, and were occasionally "pinching her in the body".

Cornelis enlisted as a mercenary and promptly vanished from the scene, leaving Meyns pregnant. She moved in with a Jacob van Marken, gave birth to a daughter, and stayed with him for another two years. While she was expecting, the ghostly women had returned and had tied her to a roof window, with the upper half of her body thrust outside. Again she went to the exorcist, who read to her from books and sewed magic formulas into her clothes, but all to no avail.

After this, the delusions of poor Meyns took an even stranger turn. One day, around midday, one of the ghostly women, whom Meyns described as "a beautiful young woman with a cap from Overijssel on her head", came to her to ask her forgiveness for all the terrible things she had done. This was followed by a walk through the old streets of Amsterdam, a route which, even today, one can easily follow. First they went to the Nieuwe Kerk, where they knelt and prayed together for forgiveness, and where Meyns also prayed for the woman's salvation. Then they went on to the Dam, and while they were sitting on the steps of the Town Hall to rest, her companion said to Meyns: "If there were a pole standing there and I were chained to it with iron chains, and wild beasts were to tear my flesh from my body, piece by piece, I would still not receive the punishment I deserve." From there they went to the Holy Place, walked three times around the Holy Sacrament on their knees, and then went along the Rokin and over the Langebrug. On the Lommertsbrug the ghostly woman suddenly pulled something from her skirt and threw it into the water, saying: "There goes all my wickedness and mischief." The two women then parted for good.

The following day, 9 November 1555, Meyns was interrogated again. Now she spoke of four women, as well as a number of strange men, who pestered her at night, but that, wanting no part in such goings-on, she had "stayed with her Lord and God". On 15 November, however, she admitted that what she called "The Enemy" had taken from her, after much torture, "her Christian faith, from in front as well as from behind" and, while continuing to harass her, had told her: "Now thou art mine." Three days later she admitted that while "she was deprived of her Christianity," she was restrained by "women in white". The Enemy had also twice "lain on top of her without clothes".

The councillors of Amsterdam now ordered Meyns to be put to the rack and whipped with rods in order to make her confess what she had done to her child. Even from the old documents, it is clear that Meyn's confusion was rapidly increasing. First she admits that the name of The Enemy is really Satan, the same who betrayed Christ, but soon afterwards says that his name is Roeltje. She had at first resisted him, but had given herself to him "since the month of blossoming" and after that he had spent every night with her. Later the same day she describes how she had been sitting on the privy one evening, worrying over some financial problem, when a young man with a red beard had suddenly appeared and had "lusted for her body". She had refused him. She also said that Roeltje the Enemy had stuck something into her body from underneath and had removed it only after several weeks.

Meyns was questioned again on the morning of 19 November, and now she was telling her inquisitors whatever they wished to hear. She claimed to have been in the countryside near the Carthusian monastery – now in the middle of an area of western Amsterdam known as the Jordaan – with two other women, one apparently called Femmetje, the other Grietje Willems, and with them to have attempted to bewitch the cattle grazing there by plucking grass from underneath them and muttering the word "tierius". She also says that she later tried bewitching the sheep pastured outside the Reguliers Gate (of which today's Munt is a remnant), this time in the company of Roeltje the Enemy and a female greengrocer named Machteld, among others. When the interrogation was continued in the afternoon, Meyns offered the information that Roeltje the Enemy had married her with a golden penny and 22 stuiver (penny) coins. Ordered to be bound with a rope prior to torture, she then confessed that she had bewitched two cows on the Monnickendam by pulling hairs from their bellies and whispering the words "inturius" and "fugita"; that she had also put a spell on the servant of a physician, but had later made him better again; that, near Edam, she had put a spell on two cattle; that she had taken part in a witches' sabbath with a woman called Griet Pieters; and that, with Roeltje the Enemy, she had flown out of the chimney three or four times.

A little over a week later, on 27 November 1555, Meyns was sentenced to the stake for the crime of witchcraft by the Amsterdam magistrates, and subsequently "burned to powder" on the Dam.

She was neither the first nor the last to die a cruel death there. In the same year a certain Anne Jans was "doomed to the fire" in Amsterdam, together with her daughters Lijsbeth and Jannetje Pieters, because they had "hurt, pestered and bewitched several people and also beasts, and had been in alliance with Satan".

In Amsterdam in the sixteenth-century the teachings of the True Church only assumed importance when they were threatened by the new and the unknown. Here and there, followers of Martin Luther were already congregating in secret, and several years before the execution of Meyns there had even been a small religious uprising that had claimed many lives. By now, however, the increasing wealth of the city's merchants was slowly beginning to triumph over the good works enjoined by the old motto "Charitate". The magistrates of Amsterdam burned Meyns Cornelis because they were afraid, even if they did not know of what. They had good reason to fear.

Chapter Four

Towards a New Jerusalem

THE DRAMA OF MEYNS CORNELIS WAS ENACTED AGAINST A VERY
different backdrop to that of the little town of merchants, sailors, fishermen
and farmers of a century earlier. The city had freed itself from the shadow
of the early Middle Ages, and now stood in the light.

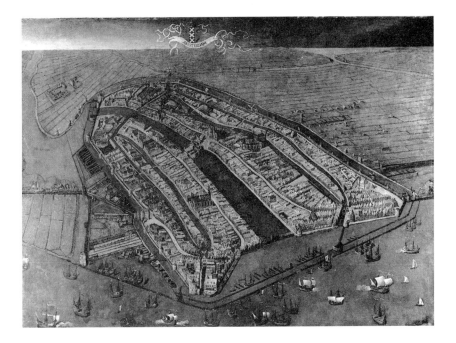

In the Amsterdam Historical Museum there hangs a painting by Cornelis
Anthoniszoon, dating from 1534. Commissioned by the Emperor Charles V
for his collection of city paintings, it is the first work to depict a complete
view of Amsterdam. For some imponderable reason it never reached the

Emperor's palace – happily for the people of Amsterdam, because there is much to be seen in this birds-eye view of the city. A fresh wind is blowing; ships ride the waves of the IJ; here and there a shadow of cloud lies over the city, and everything breathes the atmosphere of a fine spring day. Cornelis Anthoniszoon also made a woodcut from this panel in 1544, in twelve blocks, and offered the prints for sale in his workshop behind the Nieuwe Kerk. He had, it seems, measured up and drawn his scenes house by house, canal by canal, ship by ship, but just how precisely he went about it has only now become apparent, as excavations begin to uncover the buildings he depicted: length, breadth, sometimes even height, everything is meticulously recorded in the map of 1544.

By this time the city had not only increased in size, it had also become both richer and busier. Contrary to what is sometimes thought, Amsterdam houses of this period had warm and cheerful interiors. Only recently, city archaeologists uncovered the remains of a sixteenth-century sitting room on a demolition sight: the walls, which are decorated with a motif of red flowers and delicate black foliage, appear to have been painted with considerable craftsmanship.

Amsterdam also established a reputation, becoming "so famous that many people in faraway lands did not think it a city but a country and wanted to make alliances with it," as a chronicler was to note in 1493. Four years earlier, Emperor Maximilian of Austria, son of the Holy Roman Emperor Frederick III, had granted the city the right to incorporate the imperial crown in its coat of arms – or Amsterdam bought the right, who can tell? Not a single other Dutch city had been honoured in this way, and even the mighty Hanseatic city of Lübeck had to make do with an imperial eagle. The crown was much more than just an ornament on the West Tower (which, incidentally, dates from much later); it was also an important visiting card for foreign trade, a kind of hallmark of trustworthiness, a proud emblem at the stern of every Amsterdam ship and on the head of all waybills carried by sea and on land.

According to customs documents preserved down the years, some 700 Dutch ships passed the Sound at the beginning of the sixteenth century, a number that had quadrupled by the end of the century. The lion's share of this increase can be ascribed to Amsterdam. This had everything to do with the fact that Amsterdam merchants could transport bulk goods such as rye, wood, tar, flax and hemp significantly cheaper than their foreign competitors. Wages in Holland were low – the large land-reclaiming projects were over, which meant that there were more people in the countryside than were needed to work the land. Moreover, the large quantities of timber and hemp (used for ropes) coming into Amsterdam meant that ships could be built there more easily and more cheaply than elsewhere. For the first time in history it was possible to transport mass goods on a large scale over great distances. Also for the first time, an international division of labour was becoming apparent in this part of Northern Europe: agriculture in the Baltic; commerce, shipping, and dairy farming in the coastal regions of the Netherlands and in England.[1] These areas acquired quickly some of the characteristics of modern urban areas: one of the first drawings of Amsterdam, made from a point on the Amstel and dating from 1589, shows a lively traffic of coaches and carriages, rowing boats, barges and sailing ships, all making their way to or from what was then still a small city. In 1514, more than half of all Holland's inhabitants lived in towns. At that time, Amsterdam had about 11,000 citizens, as is clear from the census conducted by the city administration and by the priests of the Oude and Nieuwe Kerk. By 1554 this number had doubled, and it had doubled again by 1600, with the city's inhabitants by then about numbering 50,000.

The area of the city had also expanded over the centuries. About 1380, a broad strip of new ground around the city was reclaimed which is now the red-light district, along the Oudezijds and Nieuwezijds Achterburgwal. Amsterdam expanded again about a century later, which left its boundaries lying along the Kloveniersbrugwal in the east, thence via the Munt, and along the Singel and towards the IJ.

Just how large sixteenth-century Amsterdam appeared in the eyes of contemporaries coming from elsewhere is made obvious by the failure of one of the few attempts to storm the city. The attackers, a group of Protestant rebels called The Beggars (*Geuzen*) had forced their way into the city via one of the gates, but in the general confusion their captain, a man named Helling, mistook the Nieuwezijds Voorburgwal (then still a canal) for the Damrak, and the Nieuwezijds Kolk for the Dam, which led him to conclude that the Koornmetershuisje was the Town Hall. Precious minutes were wasted before the attackers understood that they had occupied the wrong building. Captain Helling did not survive his error.

*

The city had not been spared its own share of disasters; unusually, however, it was ravaged more by fire than by water. On 23 April 1421, Easter Sunday, about a third of the mainly wooden houses went up in flames; the Dam and the Kalverstraat, among much else, being swiftly transformed into a stinking, smouldering mess. But worse was to follow, which is also the reason why there is very little of the medieval city left. On the night of 23–24 May 1452 another fire broke out, this time near the Oude Kerk. The ships lying in the Damrak caught fire and were driven by the north wind to the opposite bank like blazing torches, where everything was transformed into an inferno within minutes. The flames raced the full breadth of the city until the last houses had been consumed. Only the streets along the IJ were spared. Three quarters of Amsterdam was burned to cinders that night, including an enormous quantity of commercial goods, often worth more than the houses in which they had been stored.

Amsterdam could not survive such a blow without outside aid. The city was fortunate in its ruler – and ardent supporter – Philip, Duke of Burgundy, who even then was of the opinion that this was the most important trading city in Holland, and who saw in it great opportunities for the future. He therefore granted its ruined citizens an exemption from all taxes for a number of years, on the condition that the rebuilt city was to be enclosed by stone walls on at least two sides.

The citizens of Amsterdam were not, however, greatly enamoured of this idea, and managed to postpone it for several decades. First of all, they did not see the need: in any emergency, it would be enough to block the few approaches to the city, while anyone who dared try another route would soon become mired in the shallow waters or the boggy land around the remainder.[2] Secondly, because of the marshland upon which the structure would have to be built, and which would first have to be reclaimed, the erection of a complete city wall was a project that would be comparable in cost and effort only to the draining of the river delta. Thirdly, such a project in any case ran counter to the mentality of Amsterdammers.

Initially Amsterdam was not a very closed city. It was not a "miniature country", as the French historian Fernand Braudel once called it,[3] a typical medieval city in which the walls encompassed not only the territory, but the entire existence of its people. Amsterdam did not, at least in its early years, live apart from the land behind it but in symbiosis with it. Just as, during the Peloponnesian War of the fifth century BC, farmers had retreated from their land and sought refuge in Athens, so the streets of Amsterdam would be thronged with hay carts when an enemy was sighted. This was still true in 1575, when Amsterdam was already a true city.[4] Fortifications and massive walls did not fit in with this concept of interdependence between city and countryside. It is not altogether surprising, therefore, that Philip and his successor, Maximilian of Austria, had to admonish the people of Amsterdam many times to improve their defences. Nevertheless, it was not until they had experienced a taste of war themselves that they began to realize that their city was too fat a prize to be left lying in the clay for anyone to claim.

In 1420 a troop of armed men from Utrecht had appeared beyond the ramparts by the Amstel, roughly where today's Rembrandtplein stands, obviously planning to raid the city. The people of Amsterdam were faithful followers of the Count of Holland, relations were far from smooth with the rebelling Duchy of Gelre and especially its main rival, the Bishopric of Utrecht. It was therefore only to be expected that Utrecht would attempt such a raid against Amsterdam. However this first attack on the city was repelled by the citizens, who had placed a large cannon on the Amstel dyke. Unfortunately, this failed to go off when the city's master gunner tried to fire on the Utrecht troops, but when two Amsterdammers rolled a second cannon in front of the first, the recalcitrant gun suddenly fired, apparently spontaneously. A man named Tideman Simonszoon lost his arm in the accident, but the Utrecht soldiers took to their heels.

In 1480 tensions between the cities rose to dangerous levels again, and a veritable maritime battle took place on the Zuiderzee between Amsterdam fishermen and Gelderland barges from Harderwijk, Elburg, and Hattum. In December 1481, a force of about 600 Utrecht troops assaulted Naarden, a fortified outpost of Amsterdam some twelve miles to the east, "and did many wanton and cruel things". Within two days, Amsterdam's soldiers, aided by men from the cities of Weesp and Muiden, succeeded in retaking the stronghold. The prisoners of war, a hundred or so, were led in triumph through Amsterdam and the captured Utrecht banner was displayed in the Oude Kerk. Again, in September 1482, ships from Amsterdam seized two Utrecht barges, one of which was full of "saltpetre, gunpowder, stone bullets, arrows and other instruments of war". It was only after the troops of the new ruler, Maximilian of Austria, had conquered Utrecht in 1483 that a peace treaty was signed.

During that mini civil war, Amsterdam's administration finally decided to begin building a city wall. Traces of this gigantic project are still visible today; for instance, De Waag, on the Nieuwmarkt, was once one of the city's three gates until, in 1617, it was converted into the city weighing-house. When the high middle roof, a later addition, was removed during this century the contours of the late-medieval Sint-Anthonis gate were clearly revealed. Another example is the Schreierstoren – the name is commonly thought to translate as "wailing tower", though in fact it has nothing to do with sobbing sailors' wives waving goodbye and everything to do with the schreye, the sharp angle on which it is built – the Munttoren, and the Montelbaanstoren, which was later equipped with an elegant pointed roof, but had originally been intended as an artillery tower. These were impressive defences, especially if we take into account the low height of most of the city's buildings then, and the flatness the land surrounding it. The Schreierstoren stood into the IJ like a "fortified fist", and by the Amstel, near today's Doelen Hotel, there stood a similar tower, appropriately named Swijgt Utrecht, or "Utrecht Silenced".

The city wall was built from brick on a foundation of stone. As one can still make out from old maps, there were arched embrasures on the inside of the wall from which an enemy could be fired upon in time of war – and since there hardly ever was war, these became shelters for pigs, goats, and paupers.

The financial pressure resulting from the building of the wall is mirrored in the rulings of the courts preserved from this time. To anyone delving into the archives it soon becomes apparent that, from around 1500, many penalties took the form of deliveries of stones instead of financial or physical punishments. The Widow Trude, for instance, was given the choice of three punishments for arguing with and insulting a tax collector: a pilgrimage to Rijssel, a fine of 90 stivers (pennies) or 6,000 stones for the city wall. Claes and Florys, who supervised the unloading of fish in the harbour, had to contribute 5,000 stones after being found guilty of accepting bribes from a few fishwives and turning a blind eye when they started selling their wares earlier than was permitted. A man called Jan van den Burch, who had sold salmon above the maximum price allowed in the city, had to pay three Flemish pounds within three days "for the purpose of the walling of the city".[5]

The wall was finally completed in 1508 – just in time to see off another enemy. During the spring, Karl, Duke of Gelre, suddenly went on the offensive. He moved through the Gooi, took Muiden and Weesp and, on 25 May, appeared in front of Amsterdam. The Amsterdammers had prepared themselves thoroughly for a lengthy siege, but after a few skirmishes on the Diemerdijk the Duke's troops retreated. In December 1512, some 1100 men from Gelderland advanced across the frozen water from Ouderkerk towards the eastern wall, near today's Geldersekade. Encountering heavy fire from the Sint-Anthonispoort, now the Waag on the Nieuwmarkt, they retired, although not before they had – on Christmas Eve, no less – set fire to the ships that lay icebound on the IJ and the Lastage. The latter was then a chaotic part of town, lying just beyond the city walls to the south-east, full of warehouses and little wharves, economically important but extremely vulnerable to attacks from the outside. The city fathers therefore decided to put an additional defensive wall around this area, now the Oude Schans, with an artillery tower at the end, the Montelbaanstoren.

In the summer of 1508, the Emperor Maximilian was at last able to inaugurate the finished towers, gates and walls of "his" Amsterdam, finally completed after years of work. Amid cheers and the sound of tolling bells, the Emperor rode slowly through the streets. The nuns in all the convents had received instructions to stand by the windows and applaud their august visitor, who did indeed stop at two cloisters, where he gave the nuns wine, as well as money to pay for prayers for the good fortune of his empire. Thus money was once again mingled with devotion, the worldly with the spiritual. In retrospect, this pageant proved to be the last opportunity for medieval Amsterdam to reveal itself in all its splendour. The proud city wall, built for all eternity, would be demolished only a hundred years later, and would become a superfluous curiosity for all but the scores of homeless who had found shelter beneath its arches.

The first fissure separating the old Amsterdam of God's Blessing from the new Amsterdam of Good Fortune was to enter the history books as the

Women's Uprising. It all began with a wool depot. In 1531 the town magistrates decided to erect a building for the storage and taxation of wool in the courtyard of the Holy Place. Amsterdam was becoming increasingly crowded and the location was, technically speaking, ideal: by the Rokin, and close to the waters of the Amstel. A number of pious women took great exception to this plan, however. In their eyes, such a worldly project was a desecration of the Holy Place; furthermore, pilgrims would find it more difficult to walk or crawl around the Holy Sacrament, as had been the custom for two centuries. Nevertheless, the burgomasters were unimpressed by these arguments, with the result that in May 1531 workers began to dig the first holes for the foundations of the wool warehouse. One spring evening, however, after darkness had fallen, a crowd of at least than 300 women assembled in the courtyard. They were carrying spades, with which they proceeded to fill in the holes again.

Not surprisingly, it quickly came to light who had been responsible for this, the first engagement between the two parties. A fortnight later the four richest women who had stood in the first row of the pious diggers were banned from the city for four years unless they paid a fine of 50 guilders each. The women, however, did not give in that easily. They travelled to Brussels to complain to the Emperor Maximilian in person about a city "that would build on sacred ground, bequeathed to the honour of the Holy Sacrament", according to the anonymous chronicler of this dispute.[6]

Maximilian, however, had no intention of burning his fingers by meddling in this affair. Much as he respected the Holy Place, he was financially dependent on the rich Amsterdam merchants and magistrates. Other members of the Brussels court were no more amenable to the plight of the women – even the Pope's envoy and the father confessor to the Emperor declined to give them any support. Having failed in their mission the women returned to Amsterdam after six weeks' absence, although, rather shrewdly, they decided to ride into the city "and raise their hands into the air", as though in Brussels they had won their case against the city. Meanwhile, however, the ban remained in force, and the city lost no time in depositing the rebellious ladies outside the city walls, where they had to pass the time at an inn until their fines had been paid. The other women who had participated were also punished. Some were sentenced to a year's house arrest and a fine of six Carolus guilders, but the majority pleaded guilty, asked the court for clemency, and were discharged without sentence.

All the women would have belonged to the Guild of the Sacrament of the Holy Place, a fellowship consisting entirely of women, and of which the four leaders who were punished especially severely were almost certainly *overwiven*, that is, superiors or guild mistresses. The surviving lists of names demonstrate that women like these were invariably recruited from the best Amsterdam families; it is understandable, therefore, that the rebellion should have upset the entire city, and ruined several families.

It also has to be understood that the insubordination of the women of the city was more than mere recklessness – it is a testimony to the collision between, on the one hand, the new worldly orientation and business sense of Amsterdam's administration, and, on the other, the world of medieval devotion which was still exercising a considerable influence on the life of the city. This devotion placed a heavy emphasis on morals, on an unsullied life before God and a simple and sober life in this world. We have already met one of these women who ranked their religious sisterhoods and ties more highly than their social status. She is Gerrit Janszoon Peggedochter, the wife of Burgomaster Egbert Gebrandszoon, whom we encounter ten years later in the old painted tableau with its omnipresent proverbs and symbols: "Therefore let us accomplish what God has elected us to do, which is all the works of *charitate*."

The Women's Rebellion was only one sign of the confusion of the times. On 31 October 1517, a Saturday, the Augustinian monk Martin Luther nailed his 95 theses against the Catholic powers to the door of the church at Wittenberg in Germany, a deed that was to mark the beginning of a landslide change in the relations between Church and society, man and God.

Luther's movement for religious reform, particularly reform of the Church of Rome, quickly found its way to Amsterdam. Despite the threats of hellfire and damnation issued by the Emperor Charles V against the heretics who supported Luther, the first sentences meted out in Amsterdam were significantly mild: the merchant city had no taste for religious disputes. In 1524, eight people accused of having been present at a Lutheran gathering were sentenced to nothing more than being compelled to proceed around the Oude Kerk with burning candles in their hands.

Aagje Arents, who had organized such a gathering, had to supply 10,000 bricks and make a pilgrimage to Rome. A statute was made against the posting of "infamous libel and dishonest writings against our most Holy Father the Pope". The advent of the printing press, only recently invented, ensured that the issue was primarily one of censorship. The first stake to be erected in Amsterdam at this time was used to burn a book, a heretical volume sold, unwittingly, by the verger of the Oude Kerk.

One striking characteristic of this first series of trials is the unheard-of, almost gleeful rebelliousness apparent in the behaviour of the heretics.[7] Jan Goessens was ordered to make a pilgrimage because he had been heard to say of the Virgin Mary: "If Our Lady is so holy, how holy is the ass that carried her?" A shoemaker, Jan Ijsbrants, stood up in the Saint Olaf Chapel halfway through a sermon and loudly interrupted the chaplain by saying: "I shall go home. I have heard enough twisters of God's Word" – he was banned for six years. Albert Dirkszoon, a man from the Gelderland who had been brought before the court for openly eating meat during a fast, was sentenced to flagellation and ordered to make a pilgrimage to Naples. Hillebrand van Zwol had his tongue pierced with a bodkin because he had maintained that the Host consecrated in the Eucharist was nothing more than ordinary bread. A baker, Jacob Klaaszoon, was sentenced because he had obstructed a procession of the Holy Sacrament on the Oudekerk bridge and had not even bared his head. In the summer of 1534, a basket weaver and his friend were sentenced because, in protest against the avarice of the monasteries, they had painted on the door of their house little devils in monks' garb fishing for money, cheese and other goods. In 1539, the 14 year-old Joriaen Benthuyzen was seen in a garden reading Martin Luther's translation of the New Testament, a crime punishable by death. When Joriaen explained that he knew of no such law as he had come to the city only recently and had been given the book by his father, the aldermen and burgomaster showed mercy on him. He was merely sentenced to take part in a procession on the following Sunday with the heretical work around his neck, and a placard bearing, in large letters, the inscription: "This is Martin Luther's book."

"The world is evil," wrote Huizinga. "The fire of violence is still burning, injustice rules and with his black wings the Devil is covering a dark earth." Let us try to visualize the townscape of late-medieval Amsterdam once again, to imagine what such romantic little towns − today, with their Disney-like restorations − really looked like in their own time. It is as well not have too many illusions, however. The streets were full of carts and horses and were strewn with heaps of dung. Everywhere breweries, dyeing shops, tanneries, and scores of other little businesses caused constant stench, smoke, and noise in among the houses in which people lived. Much of the rubbish was thrown into the canals, which led to enormous waves of foul air rolling over the city, especially in summer. Amid all this, men, women, and children tried to get by the best they could.

It is possible to deduce the average standard of living of Amsterdammers at this time from surviving documents: the bills of monasteries and the wages of masons and carpenters, and from the total rents and prices of grain. At the beginning of the sixteenth century the economic situation was not all that comfortable. There was no slack in the budget of an ordinary household. More than three quarters of a family's income was spent on food and the rest on rent, clothing, heat and light. Prices were rising because of the steady influx of gold into Europe from the newly discovered America. According to some sources rye, the main food of the masses, rose in price by a third during the first decade of the sixteenth century. Wages, however, remained stagnant, with the result that great numbers of craftsmen and their families fell on hard times. There was unrest in the cloth industry, and food riots, known as "cheese-and-bread games", could only be contained with difficulty.

During this time, the first accounts reached Amsterdam of a new religious community founded by followers of the Swiss reformer Ulrich Zwingli in Zürich. This movement propounded a number of remarkable ideas, seeking to establish the Kingdom of God on earth by dividing Church and State, sharing all property, refusing to carry weapons, and rejecting the baptism of infants. Only when followers were old enough to have learned to tell good from evil were they allowed to be baptized and the members of this community let themselves be rebaptized as adults, hence the name Anabaptists. Their ideas, a kind of communism *avant la lettre*, fell on fertile soil in Amsterdam, especially among the petty bourgeoisie. Later, in the sentences passed on them by the courts, it is shoemakers, coopers, makers of cloth, glass, harnesses and brooms, bargees, bookbinders, carpenters, goldsmiths, tailors, weavers, and locksmiths whom we encounter again and again, and who supported this rebel movement.

The Anabaptists first came to the attention of the authorities in Saxony when, around 1530, there was a popular uprising of some 30,000 farmers and workers in and around the silver mines and quarries. When the rebellion was crushed, its participants fled throughout Europe, the tolerant Amsterdam proving an especially attractive port of call for the refugees. Here their following grew fast. They claimed, among other things, that they alone were holy and immaculate, that it was right according to natural law to have many wives, and that it was given into their power to destroy the ungodly magistrates with the sword.

The revolutionary nature of this new community was sufficient reason for the magistrates of Amsterdam to tackle them harder from the very beginning than had been the case with, for instance, the Lutherans. The Anabaptists' ideology not only threatened the position of the Church, it menaced the magistracy itself; moreover, their credo was diametrically opposed to the trading mentality of the emerging Amsterdam. Tolerance was in this town not a mere principle but a practical necessity: the open merchant city, being the meeting place of all sorts of different cultures, could not allow itself to indulge in the large-scale prosecution of those adhering to different beliefs. Nevertheless, if this function of the city as a meeting place, and with it the idea of tolerance, were to be threatened by any group, the city fathers would crush the interlopers mercilessly.

In November 1533 the first nine Anabaptists to be arrested in Amsterdam were seized in their beds and sent to The Hague to be tried by the High Court of Holland. The court, unable to make up its mind about the new heretics, sent a messenger to Charles V in Brussels for instructions as to how to deal with them. When the Emperor answered, the nine men were beheaded, their bodies buried in The Hague, and their heads sent to Amsterdam in a herring barrel to be publicly impaled.

All this did little to help the authorities' cause, however. Everywhere along the streets pamphlets and booklets were sold in which God's wrath was called upon those refusing to give up their goods and turn their backs on this Babel. In January 1534, the Anabaptists came to power in the

Westphalian town of Münster and proclaimed the thousand-year Kingdom of Zion; their leader was a Dutch tailor, Jan Beukelszoon, from Leiden, a town south of Amsterdam. Münster would be the beginning of a world revolution, and Amsterdam was second on the list.

In May of the same year, five Anabaptists charged, swords drawn, through the streets of Amsterdam in broad daylight, shouting: "In the name of the Lord, the left side of the city is blessed and the right side damned!" Shocked, many citizens congregated on the Dam and the company of the civil militia was put on alert in the Doelen, the shooting gallery.

On the same day, scores of Anabaptists abandoned their homes and all their belongings, came together in the harbour with their wives and children and, embarking in a dozen ships, set out across the Zuiderzee for a country which, they said, God would lead them to. A short time later, there was a second exodus of men, women, and children. Both groups went to Münster, only to meet a terrible death there a year later in a bloodbath by the troops of the Bishopric of Cologne, after months of siege.

In June, Amsterdam was again plunged into turmoil when news came that a group of Anabaptists were on their way from Friesland, bent on taking the city by force. The militia was put on high alert, and several imprisoned Anabaptists were beheaded or burned at the stake by way of warning. The city remained in a state of considerable tension during the ensuing months, not least because even within its walls the religious revolutionaries remained active.

What happened at meetings of the sect was well documented by the city historian Jan Wagenaar, who gives as an example an incident on the Zoutsteeg, probably drawing on the record of interrogations. On the night of 11 February 1535, several Anabaptists, led by their prophet, a certain Dirk, had come together there in the house of a draper. During their prayers the house began to shake. When the prophet had opened his eyes, he said to those around him: "I have seen God on His throne face to face and have spoken to Him. I was carried up to Heaven and then sent down to Hell and I have seen all. The great Day of Judgement is nigh." Then, "Thou art condemned in all eternity" he said, pointing to one of those standing around him, "thou art not worthy to be taken down to Hell and shalt therefore sink into the abyss below it." The man cried out for forgiveness and was promptly readmitted into the circle: "The Father has had pity and has accepted thee as a son."

The following night the community met again, some of the women having clandestinely left their sleeping husbands in order to attend. After they had spent four hours talking and praying the prophet removed his helmet from his head, took off his harness and, throwing the rest of his clothes into the fire, stood stark naked before his followers. He exhorted them to do the same, because everything that was made from earth had to be committed to the fire, as it would be "a pleasing burnt offering for God". The lady of the house, Aagje Jans, who knew nothing of these happenings and was asleep, was awakened by the stench of the smouldering clothes and ran up to the attic thinking the house was on fire, only to find eleven brothers-and-sisters-in-spirit, seven men and four women, without a stitch on. The prophet ordered Aagje to take off her clothes and throw them into the fire like the others, and she obeyed him at once.

After this, the prophet and his followers, ran out of the house, shouting "Woe, woe, woe, the wrath, O heavenly Father!" Hearing this noise, which carried throughout the town, the citizens immediately took up arms and came together on the Dam. Like Aagje, the neighbours on the Zoutsteeg had also been woken up by the smell of burning cloth, but had had to shoot down the door of the house with a blunderbuss because the excited Anabaptists had closed it very securely before leaving. Inside, the palliasses were aflame, alongside the smouldering heap of weapons and clothes, with two dishes of meat on top.

The small group of Anabaptists was quickly apprehended, but all refused to put on any clothing: "We are the naked truth," they said. A sheriff, seeking to put his coat around one of the women, was roundly sermonized with the statement that "The image of God does not need to be ashamed." The prophet's acolytes also refused to eat and drink out of earthenware, throwing the vessels to the ground and dancing among the shards. One of the men declared that he was a child, and said that he would eat only if the food was pre-chewed. A few weeks after their arrest, the men were beheaded, and the women sewn into sacks and thrown into the IJ from the Haringpakkerstoren, near today's car park opposite the Central Station. Aagje Jans was hanged from the doorframe of her house in the Zoutsteeg.

Nevertheless, the unwavering conviction of the Anabaptists made a considerable impression on their contemporaries. In 1535 an eye witness recorded the last words of nine condemned men just before their execution.[8]

The first, after climbing the scaffold and being blindfolded, said, "Rejoice in the Lord," and then, kneeling down: "O power of the Highest of High, be with me."

The second talked a lot, "but he was faint and his words incomprehensible".

The third was similarly impossible to understand, apart from crying, while kneeling down: "O Father, have pity on them, they know not what they do."

The fourth said: "Praise and thanks to Thee, O Father, now and for all eternity, Amen."

The fifth spoke but could not be heard.

The sixth said: "O Lord, I will sacrifice my soul unto Thee, as Abraham did with Isaac."

The seventh: "O Lord, I will hold out my neck here for Thy sake."

The eighth cried: " O Lord, I beseech Thee, receive thy poor servant; open their eyes, for they are blind; forgive what they are doing and do not count it as a sin against them!"

The ninth spoke "very freely" and ended: "O Lord, here I offer Thy servant as a burnt offering, and ask that Thou be not mindful of the sins that I have committed before."

In May 1535, the simmering rebellion finally reached its climax. Münster was by then under siege, and as the situation there grew increasingly precarious, a number of Anabaptists in Amsterdam decided to stage a local coup in order to establish the Kingdom of Zion in the city. On 10 May 40 rebels occupied the Town Hall on the Dam. The moment was well chosen, as most city administrators were "wel bij drancke", that is, well into their cups, it being the day of the annual feast of the company of the crossbow militia. One of the burgomasters led some of his men in an attempt to storm the Town Hall, but the attack failed and he was killed.

Meanwhile a notorious drunkard, Klaas Pieterszoon van Aken, appeared at the Town Hall and declared himself to be the city's envoy to the Anabaptists, shouting out that he would "restore the peace". Hendrik

Goedbeleid, the rebel leader, intervened and told him that he must go home, as "a dangerous issue was being negotiated", but when Klaas "kept on standing and gawking, as was his custom," he was stabbed to death without mercy. By now, the Dam was closed off with boats and guarded by armed citizens who kept the Town Hall under constant fire.

At first light the following morning the Town Hall was stormed. There was a severe exchange of fire, but the situation was soon resolved. Of the Anabaptists, 28 were killed in this action, as well as 20 of the attackers. Other groups of armed Anabaptists in and outside the city quickly took to their heels. Hendrik Goedbeleid, the leader of the rebellion, was killed in the Town Hall, but his lieutenant, Jan van Geel, had climbed to the top of the building's tower, from which he roundly abused the good people of Amsterdam. He was shot at and finally hit, falling to his death on the pavement of the Dam.

The hearts of the twelve surviving Anabaptists were "cut from their living bodies and thrown in their faces", their bodies were drawn and quartered and one part displayed at each city gate, and their severed heads were impaled. The women were drowned in the IJ or hanged from the doorposts of their houses. Even the Anabaptists that had been killed in the rebellion were punished, their naked corpses strung up from the gallows. Their bishop, Jacob van Kampen, was found hiding in a stack of peat after a large-scale raid. He was displayed on the scaffold, wearing a tin mitre with two horns and the coat of arms of the city painted on it. First his tongue was cut out, then the right hand with which he had baptized his flock was chopped off, before he was finally beheaded and his body burned.

On 12 April 1537, two more men – "ordinary" Lutherans, this time – were decapitated on the Dam because of their beliefs. Then, at the end of 1543, Anabaptists were again put on trial, in this case seven of them, albeit from the so-called "silent", non-violent wing. Their leader admitted having printed 600 copies of a book by a leading Anabaptist, Menno Simons, the founder of the Doopsgezinde Kerk, the Dutch Mennonite Church. In 1546, two members of the sect were tied to ladders erected over a pyre on the Plaetse and thrown into the flames face first. Three years later, eight stakes stood next to one another on the Dam. From this point the Anabaptists ceased to trouble the authorities in Amsterdam. The Mennonites, who were to take their place, would stay well clear of official dealings and public life for centuries to come. Even so, no group of reformers was prosecuted more severely: between 1536 and 1576, a total of 29 Mennonites were burned at the stake on the Dam, while a further twelve were beheaded, six hanged, and four drowned in the IJ.

In 1544, the silver shrine that housed the Sacrament vanished from the Holy Place, and with it the Sacrament itself. When the thief was arrested the silver had already been melted down and sold, while the crystal vase containing the Sacrament, he claimed, had been thrown into the Ouderzijds Achterburgwal. A search was immediately instituted, with barges, nets and dredgers, and the news that "they are fishing for our dear Lord" went round the city like wildfire. The miraculous Sacrament, however, which had withstood all fire, was never to be given back by the water.

Chapter Five

The Joy of God's Wrath

Adieu lads and lasses all,
Adieu Amsterdam, so beautiful,
Adieu, I write, for the present time,
Adieu pleasure and laughter's chime,
Adieu dancing and jumping and melodious strings,
Adieu to flute and trumpet rings,
Adieu to all that may please the ear,
Adieu – I am to depart from here.
Adieu talking and courting and also fooling,
With young maids in the Doelen strolling,
In May or by the sweet moon's shine;
Adieu! O clear wine from the Rhine,
Adieu Sint-Anthonisdijck and Outewael,
Adieu – I know it all too well.
Adieu Anneken's house and Reguliers Hof,
Adieu . . .

ROEMER VISSCHER, 1572[1]

ON CHRISTMAS EVE 1572, WOUTER JACOBSZOON, AN
Augustinian father living in the Sint-Agnieten monastery by the Ouderzijds
Voorburgwal, his mood lonely and sombre, noted in his diary: "Who would
not be forced to screaming, howling, and crying?" Desolate times, he wrote,
had settled over Amsterdam and the rest of the country: "As if [they] had
been overrun by the Turks. The sacraments are no longer dispensed, there
are no church services any more, everyone born in these days remains

without lawful christening, and the dying are dealt with like beasts." After this lament, however, he collected himself, remembering "how happy the *invitatorium* of this feast day had sounded: 'Today thou shalt know that the Lord will come, and quickly shalt thou see Him in His glory.'" Thus did Wouter Jacobszoon console himself by writing, and by happy chance these thoughts, fears, and experiences, many folios of them, have been preserved, the first real diary to come down to us from Amsterdam history.[2]

The internal world of Wouter Jacobszoon (1522–95) is a rare source, a survival from a time when such individual testimonies hardly existed. Most authors of medieval memoirs and chronicles valued their anonymity, so that not only did they not record their names, they also strove anxiously to keep everything personal out of their works. Wouter Jacobszoon thought nothing of committing his loves and fears to paper for a reason other than personal vanity. His preserved papers were probably never intended as a diary, but as a memorial, a record in which the monks following Saint Augustine privately noted down everything that occurred to them during their meditations. As Wouter Jacobszoon recorded his thoughts during one of the darkest periods in the history of Amsterdam, his writings are today a priceless source for anyone wanting to know what a Catholic citizen experienced during the Eighty Years War of 1568–1648, what he heard, what he felt and, most of all, what he feared. And that, it appears, was almost everything.

A popular rebellion was raging throughout the Low Countries, a desperate attempt to shake off the autocratic rule – and the high taxes and religious oppression that went with it – of the remote Philip II of Spain. The war in the Netherlands was not a conflict between Catholics and Protestants, however, even if it seemed to be. Rather it was a rebellion of burghers against feudal rule, of merchants against nobles, and of a new era against the Middle Ages. The pattern of this struggle, too, did not follow the old rituals of battles in the open, of winners and losers and peace negotiations. It was more like a bush fire, a conflict which, erupting in different places, would burn itself out or be put out, only to flare up again somewhere else a little later. In 1572, when Wouter Jacobszoon wrote of desolate times, the Protestant rebels, who had given themselves the honorific title the Beggars, had not yet taken Amsterdam. The capital was still ruled by a

Artist unknown, *The Schreierstoren*, drawing, seventeenth century

network of old, Catholic, merchant families, but there was a new elite in
the ascendant, and there were few who did not feel that the transition of
power was only a matter of time.

Meanwhile, young rebels who were active in Amsterdam hunted down
monks, nuns and priests throughout the city, and Wouter Jacobszoon
records one terrible story after another: an elderly cleric from Leiden who
was thrown into a canal, pulled out again, run through with rapiers, and
pushed back into the water; another priest who was crushed on a chair
in such a manner that his head was forced into his body; nuns who
were stripped naked; a "pious gentleman" in Delft who had his loins
smashed and his genitals cut off. "O Lord, how long wilt thou sleep?"
wrote Jacobszoon. "Wake up at long last and condescend to revenge
the blood of your saints." During the night of 12 January 1573, the
monk suffered an attack of sheer terror so severe that he was quite unable
to find any sleep – "I tossed and I turned, but whatever I did, I did not
close an eye."

It seems that Wouter Jacobszoon wrote in his diary almost every day,
densely covering the pages in a fine hand, the letters only becoming larger
when the quill grew blunt and, being almost used up, could no longer be

sharpened. The diarist had been abbot of the Stein monastery near Gouda, but when that town chose to side with the Beggars in 1572 he clandestinely made his way to Amsterdam. First he found hospitality in the Sint-Agnieten monastery, before he assumed the pastoral care of the nunnery of the Nieuwe Nonnen ter Lely, near today's Binnengasthuis. In Amsterdam, though, peace could not be taken for granted any more than it could in Gouda. On 10 November 1572, Jacobszoon recorded, in between his notes about the goings-on in house, garden, and kitchen, that the Beggars had been seen across the IJ, on the Volewijk, threatening the citizens of Amsterdam from afar with bloody swords and shouting "You servile papists! Come over, god eaters [a reference to the Sacrament of the Eucharist], come and get us, for tomorrow we will come over and take a look what you have got to eat!" On the following day the monk wrote: "On St Martin's day around four o'clock in the morning we heard from our bedroom a great noise of firing from heavy guns, over and over again; we did not know what was happening, but around eight o'clock we were told that the Beggars had filled five ships with tar, pitch, reeds and suchlike, had set them alight and sent them against our warships in order to set them ablaze as well. But it was all futile work, effort, and cost. The ships were seen driving past the city as if they were being steered, and one of them came to run into the poles, turned around and went in the opposite direction, against our enemies, without anyone having lifted a finger." That same day, the Holy Place was filled with people thanking God for His deliverance of the city and the miraculous steering of the ships by His hand.

Refugee peasants roamed outside the city, having lost house and home to the plundering and marauding of the Beggars. An entire herd of cattle was said to have broken through the ice of the Diemermeer – according to some versions of the story more than a hundred animals – and the very next day countless "shabby folk" went out from cold and hungry Amsterdam, each bent on securing a piece of meat from the drowned beasts. Near the Huis ter Hart on the Amstel, a woman was found frozen to death by a dyke, with a live infant on her lap "still with milk in her breasts, and the child still sucking on them". On 23 March 1573, at half-past seven in the morning, the monks saw a miraculous sign above the ravaged town: the sun darkened and became red as blood. "We perceived this apparition as a warning, and were possessed by hopes and fears."

In September that year, Wouter Jacobszoon notes that corn has now become so expensive that "it is most surprising that people can still find nourishment". Outside a bakery on the Dam he saw a large, pushing crowd that had gathered because it was the only place where bread was still available. According to the rumours, people had to wait for three hours in order to get a single loaf. "One woman started to cry, another one made desperate movements when they heard that bread was nowhere to be had any more."

On 6 November, the abbot saw a woman who had starved to death in the street "to the horror of many good people". Even the blanket and the cloth with which the corpse had been covered had been immediately stolen, "so that one saw her lying there entirely naked". Three weeks later, on 25 November, a woman threw herself from the Oudebrug into the Damrak: "If nobody was there to help her, she simply had to help herself, she said, and jumped into the water." A little later, Jacobszoon chanced upon the body of a "stout man of war" in a small annexe, dead from cold and hunger. "Initially, we were shocked when we saw him, but we got over our fright when we understood that this sort of thing is an everyday occurrence in this time."

On the 27th, our monk records that several people lay dead either on or close to the Haarlemmerdijk, "without anybody covering them up with earth or even shoving them off the pathway . . . As if they were the corpses of animals, they were just lying there rotting away, and were eaten by dogs and birds." Later he writes with disgust of a nun who was so desperately poor that she had taken to going around the streets at night singing pious songs, begging for a piece of bread. "She only went on her way in the evenings after dark, because during the day she was too ashamed and in her heart she was still a respectable woman."

Several months later Jacobszoon paid a short visit to a monastery in Haarlem, then only recently recaptured by the Spanish. "Along the way, I saw many people hanging from trees, gallows and other horizontal beams in various places," he noted. Houses had been burned down, churches ransacked, the land lay uncultivated and devoid of any cattle. "In between the many corpses of animals which I saw here and there, I also saw a human corpse, lying naked on the roadway, directly in the track of the carriages. It was entirely dried out from the sun and so flattened that it was a horrible sight for ordinary eyes." It is indeed a desolate landscape he describes, a landscape of murder, fire, gallows and crows, as in a film by Pasolini.

———

"This war was unlike any other ever fought in Europe," the Polish author Zbigniew Herbert was to write about the Eighty Years War two centuries later. "It was a clash of two different ideals of life, two sets of values and, it would be no exaggeration to say, between two civilizations standing diametrically opposed to each other: the military aristocracy of the Spaniards and the world of burgherdom and peasantry of the Dutch."[3]

It was understandable that this struggle between ideologies should assume the characteristics of a religious war; in particular, the teachings of the French Protestant reformer John Calvin, a refugee from religious persecution in Geneva, contained all the elements the rebellious Dutch sought by way of justification for their actions. In contrast to the Anabaptists, who relinquished or shared all worldly goods, the Calvinists enjoined strict obedience to God and to worldly authorities. There was, however, a limit to such obedience, since God's Word stood above that of emperors and kings. Thus Calvinism acknowledged the right to rebel against worldly authority if that authority required its subject to act against their consciences. Even so, Calvinism forbade the individual citizen to rise up; only properly consitituted organizations, the lesser worldly authorities, as it were, were permitted to take up arms against prince or State. "Calvinism has its roots in the free city and has never betrayed this beginning," wrote one of the historians of Amsterdam, H. Brugmans. "It originated among a citizenship freed from noble authority and has never denied its birth."[4] In contrast to the Anabaptists, who found followers particularly among the lower strata of society, people from all social backgrounds became Calvinists.

There were significant democratic elements in Calvinism, as well as strict rules governing morality, standards, values, and conduct. It "does not demand freedom to serve God according to one's own understanding," Brugmans opined. "Since it holds itself to be absolutely true, it wants to fight to win, to win in order to rule. It does not tolerate any power next to itself, but seeks to be above everything else, because it is eternal, absolute, just as absolute as the Catholic Church." The latter element of Calvinism found less favour with the merchants of Amsterdam, and even centuries later a tension was to remain between dogmatism and freedom, although by then there were no Catholic priests to defend dogma, but Calvinist preachers instead. They, too, were never quite able to tip the balance in their favour, for this merchant city's urge for freedom was to prove stronger than any religious doctrine.

During the Dutch Revolt, however, Calvinism was the "strong, immutable and unconquerable belief of the insurrection", the ideal banner under which the good fight against Spain could be fought. In the stories of the Old Testament, the rebellious Dutch citizens recognized a world of symbols and signs: the corrupt power of Babylon; David's triumph over Goliath; the struggle of the Children of Israel against the oppression of mighty Egypt, God's hand leading them out of the land of the pharaoh, the parting of the Red Sea for God's people and its closing again over the enemy's great armies. The parallel between the Children of Israel and the people of God in the Low Countries by the sea was unavoidable. It was a message that was to be repeated and reinforced in thousands of works of art and tens of thousands of writings and sermons until well into the seventeenth century. In addition, Calvinism, with its discipline, strictness and sobriety quickly offered a firm structure and organization for the insurrection.

Laurens Jacobszoon, grain merchant "In de Gouden Reael", near today's Damrak, and one of the earliest of Amsterdam's Calvinists, tells in his memoirs how it seemed during the secret meetings that those assembled were going to a happy feast.[5] To judge by what we hear about them, the assemblies themselves also resembled feasts: the psalms were sung to the melodies of popular songs of the day. By and by this practice was rapidly gaining popularity. A horrified Father Wouter Jacobszoon, returning from a visit to Utrecht, records in his diary that those gathered on the roof of his canal barge "freely sang the praises of the Prince" – William of Nassau, Prince of Orange, the leader of the revolt against Spain – after "a ditty that had been composed for His glory long before". What the Augustinian heard was almost certainly the original form of the Dutch national anthem, "Wilhelmus van Nassaue":

> William of Nassau –
> I am of German blood;
> Faithful to the fatherland
> I am unto death;
> A Prince of Orange
> I am, free and unfettered;
> The King of Spain
> I have always honoured.

In the context of the rebellion, it is necessary to dwell for a while on the manner in which Amsterdam's administration reacted to dissident groups over the centuries – something which was characterized by an ambiguity that has frequently, and erroneously, been confused with an attitude of toleration. The grain merchant Laurens Jacobszoon, for instance, records that there was a coded warning among the Calvinist minority of Amsterdam: "Joseph took mother and child and fled to Egypt." On hearing this, everyone knew that a raid was about to be carried out. The all-clear signal was: "They are dead who threatened the life of the child." Nobody knew where these messages originated, but it was thought that the sheriff himself was involved. While it was that officer's task to implement the strict penal codes against other faiths without mercy, he apparently did not think that raids and other forms of repression against heretics were worth his while, especially as they usually sparked widespread unrest in the city.

Several centuries later this attitude was to grow into a typically Dutch way of using the law, a *modus operandi* governed by civic opportunism: the state is entitled to prosecute a crime, but it is not bound to do so, especially if the means of prosecution is deemed to be worse than the crime – as, for instance, in the case of prostitution, or the use of soft drugs. There are instances of this benevolent duplicity even in the fifteenth century. Convicted brothel keepers were supposed to be punished by being "buried in the earth alive", according to Amsterdam city law. In practice, however, brothels were tolerated on the Pijlsteeg and the Halsteeg, today's Damstraat. There, many of the "women of loose morals" lived in the houses of the under-sheriffs, who were therefore in effect brothel keepers themselves. In 1495, the city administration even toyed with the idea of establishing what they called a "comprehensive school" – in other words, an Eros centre (an official house of pleasure) – on the Halsteeg, although this plan was never brought to fruition.[6]

In political matters, too, the city administrators gave priority to the avoidance of potential unrest. Battling it out for the sake of principles was left to others. For a good deal of the fifteenth century the rest of the Low Countries was plagued by a curious civil war, or rather a war between rival nobles and their adherents, the so-called "Hook and Cod Wars". Amsterdam tried – successfully, as it turned out – not to get involved in this dispute by simply forbidding its citizens to talk about it. By an order of 26 December 1481, it was officially forbidden for anyone to say: "Thou art a hook" or "Thou art a cod".[7]

This relatively mild attitude extended to the first Lutherans living in the city, despite pressure from the Bishop that they should be dealt with as heretics. We know from the archives that after 1518 there were repeated incidents between the Procurator-General at the Dutch Court, the notorious heretic hunter Reynier Brunt, and the moderate Amsterdam sheriff Jan Hubrechtzoon. In 1534, Brunt finally saw a chance to deprive the sheriff of his post by accusing him of arresting innocent people and letting real heretics go. Five years later, Hubrechtzoon himself was accused of having participated in the activities of "the sect" and fled after enduring an interrogation. Just over 20 years later, in 1555, a similar conflict erupted around another Amsterdam sheriff, William Dirckszoon Bardes, "a man of wise reasoning and admirable manners, if somewhat stammering in speech". He was wrongly accused. Inspired by the Spanish Inquisition, the priest of the Oude Kerk had reported the sheriff, supporting his charge with false testimonies. The affair became a huge political scandal, although in the end it was the priest, not the sheriff, who was convicted and sentenced. It is assumed, incidentally, that Bardes was indeed well disposed towards religious reforms, and that he clandestinely tipped off heretics to "flee to Egypt".

The relative tolerance of Amsterdam's authorities did not, however, prevent the mood in the city from hardening appreciably after the Anabaptist uprising of 1535. Not only Lutherans, but also other reform-minded people retreated into their hiding places for the next 30 years. Many prominent Amsterdam citizens, who had previously been indifferent to religious matters, now came out strongly in favour of the Catholic camp. In the

Town Hall, the old group of moderate city fathers was swept aside after the uprising by a new generation which did not show any inclination towards lenience. When the new list of aldermen was submitted to the government in 1536, the year after the rebellion, a note was appended to it which read: "These aldermen have all been elected anew, something that has never happened before."[8]

This hardening of attitude within the city was mirrored in the international situation. In 1555, the Emperor Charles V handed authority over the Low Countries (the Netherlands and Belgium were still one entity at that time) to his son Philip II; Spain and her colonies abroad also formed part of this inheritance. In the aftermath of this handover, everything in the relations between the Low Countries and their new prince that could possibly go wrong, duly did.

While Charles V had taken an active interest in the fortunes of the Low Countries, Philip II showed no affinity with these provinces. He had been educated entirely in Spain, thought like a Spaniard – indeed, was a Spaniard – and regarded his new lands in the same feudal manner as he did his colonies and other adjuncts to his dominion. This approach might have been tenable, even understandable, some centuries earlier, but at the end of the sixteenth century the Low Countries were already so strongly urbanized, and the power, independence and wealth of their inhabitants so great, that this model of medieval serfdom proved entirely impracticable. In this way, within a decade, Philip II managed to antagonize just about every group in the Netherlands.

Cities that had been rich were brought close to the abyss by the ever-increasing burden of taxation; the governors-general were angered to find that they had lost their tax-raising power to the Crown, which introduced another tax, the so-called "tenth penny". The southern Netherlands, especially, found themselves in an increasingly precarious economic position. Ordinary citizens were hit by huge price increases, and the zealous hunt for heretics that was carried out under the auspices of the deeply pious Philip was more and more strongly opposed. The local nobility, too, quickly turned against him, as he ignored their ancient rights and with increasing frequency gave important posts to foreign Spanish noblemen who had his trust.

Looking today at the small monk's cell in the Escorial Palace from which

Philip II ruled his immense empire, one recognizes in the hard, Spanish sobriety a parallel with the moderation and discipline that were so dominant in Calvinism. Yet neither Philip nor his Calvinist opponents ever understood how strongly they resembled one another in their restraint and asceticism, and especially in the inclination of each to perceive its own faith as absolute. Because of this similarity, their confrontation was all the more forceful, prolonged, and violent.

———

In Amsterdam, it all started exactly according to the rules. Around 1564, a group of rich and progressive merchants banded together to end the domination of the old and exclusive city administration that was barring them from high office. In a letter of petition to the authorities in Brussels, these 70 notables listed a succession of complaints against the ruling families of Amsterdam: trade was hindered; jurisdiction was biased; much of the business coming to the city was channelled into the pockets of the city council or of the firms its members favoured; the burgomasters did everything they could to appoint their sons, brothers-in-law, nephews and other appendages to the city administration; the canals were dirt-ridden and water from them was flooding cellar dwellings around the Achterburgwallen; the fire hazard presented by the Lastage was almost completely ignored; tax money was misused. The petitioners assured the authorities that they all were pious Catholics and that they had frequently helped the King, willingly and with pleasure. Such a letter could not be ignored in Brussels. After an investigation by the Governor of Holland, the Prince of Orange, the authors of the petition were largely vindicated. During the following elections to the magistracy, the Governor decided to change the law by appointing a new city council, thereby openly contravening the privileges of the city; in the event, however, the council was chosen from among those same old families, since the unrest in the city was too great to allow of any other changes.

Throughout most of the sixteenth century, a silent war raged between the ruling families of Amsterdam, a situation reminiscent of the bitter inter-family feuds in some medieval Italian cities, such as the famous war between the Montagues and the Capulets in Verona. In Amsterdam, this conflict initially took place independently of the problems connected with the rise of Calvinism, but soon the two converged. The merchants' petition of 1564 marked an important moment, therefore, not because of the effect it had on the city, which was negligible, but, as is often the case, because of the group of people connected with the document who came out into the open. Among the signatories of the petition were men who, only a short time afterwards, would find themselves up to their necks in the revolt; some would have to flee the city. Others joined the Beggars before being sentenced in *absentia* by the Duke of Alva, whom Philip II sent to subdue the Netherlands in 1567. Many of them would be the first leaders of what was to become the free, Protestant Amsterdam. They would again form family cliques and thereby partly repeat the mistake of their predecessors, as is the way of things. Even so, if there is one group of men who can be called the grandfathers of the Amsterdam of the Golden Age, these were they, the men who, in 1564, first let themselves be heard.

Two years later, the time bomb finally exploded and Amsterdam was engulfed by an indomitable people's uprising. Hordes of citizens ran amok in a cataclysm of hysterical rage and destruction, something this sober and orderly city was to experience again in later centuries. The wave of violence started in the south of the Netherlands, where furious mobs stormed churches and monasteries around Ghent, destroying religious images and church altars. On the night of Tuesday, 23 August 1566, several merchants from Antwerp arrived at the Amsterdam fair – then still held in the open air around the Warmoesstraat – with the first news of what went down in history as the "Iconoclastic Fury". They showed little pieces of marble and alabaster to the surprised Amsterdammers, fragments from statues destroyed by the raging mob. When the news reached members of the city administration they became very nervous, particularly because they had been unable to prevent several thousand Amsterdammers from attending a Calvinist open-air service, a so-called *hagepreek* – literally, a "hedge sermon" – outside the Haarlemmerpoort, near today's Vinkenstraat. Five or ten dissidents could be burned at the stake, but not a thousand.

As soon as the news from Antwerp came, priests, monks and nuns were ordered to remove the most precious items in their possession from the churches, monasteries and convents, and hide them. With this precaution, intended to limit public unrest by removing temptation, the city fathers in fact lit the spark that would explode into a raging blaze. Workers, coming home for their lunch break around eleven o'clock, saw to their great surprise "priests and monks running along the street, loaded with silver, chalices, sacrament boxes, bowls and ecclesiastical robes, among which also were the precious items belonging to the embellishments of the altars of several guilds."[9] This sight caused such a great stir that bands of workers went to the churches in order to find out what was happening. Arriving at the Oude Kerk at around two o'clock in the afternoon, they found vespers just starting and a number of baptisms being carried out. When the officiating chaplain began to recite the conventional formula for exorcism used at baptism, some of the assembled workers began to shout: "You papist! Stop calling the Devil out of little children! You have cheated the world for long enough!" Street urchins began to throw stones at the altar, a boy named Wijntje Ottens threw a shoe at the head of the statue of the Virgin Mary, and there were other small acts of destruction.

Fearing an escalation of the unrest, the city administrators made some important concessions to the Protestants: the Catholic churches were closed after the removal of all religious images; the Calvinists were permitted to hold their hedge sermons, albeit only outside the city; and the sick were granted the right to choose whether a Catholic priest or a Protestant preacher should attend them. An angry letter arrived from Brussels almost immediately, demanding a tough line against the rebellion, the reopening of the churches, harsh punishments for those who had desecrated them, and for preachers and other heretics. It will always be the task of the authorities in large cities to reconcile the orders and plans of the high administration with the reality of the street. With regard to the Iconoclastic Fury, the course advocated by Brussels was wholly unrealistic, for it would have been difficult indeed to arrest half the population of Amsterdam.

The tension in the city erupted in a second rampage two weeks later. After a burial by the Nieuwe Kerk had ended in a riot, the agitated masses ran to the seat of the hated Inquisition, the Friar Minor monastery, close to the Nieuwmarkt (where the Albert Heijn supermarket stands today). Here objects were broken and a certain amount of looting took place. "The beef and other monastic food" was taken to the orphanage, although the monastery's library was saved by a whisker.

As a result of the unrest, the Amsterdam of the year 1566 remained a kind of political and religious no man's land. The city knew neither where it wanted to go, nor where it ought to go. Its strong feeling for independence resisted the widespread persecution of heretics and the extremely high taxes of the Spanish. Its sober mercantile spirit, however, shied away from open conflict with one of the greatest powers of the day. For a time the city hung suspended between these two sides, a state of affairs that proved to be just the stillness before the storm.

Meanwhile, behind the scenes, several different political factions – or, perhaps more accurately, family networks – were struggling for power within the city administration. First among them was the network of old Catholic families that had firmly ruled the city council for decades. They were loyal to Philip, as long as their loyalty did not come into conflict with their commercial interests or with the freedom of the city. Next to them, another group was vying for influence: the "new entrepreneurs", the merchant families that had been signatories to the petition of 1564 and still found themselves excluded from power. Many of these had close trading relations with the north of Germany, the bastion of the Reformation. Some of them had become Calvinists, others thought along Christian-Humanist lines, others still remained faithful to the spirit of Catholicism while undoubtedly seeking power, which meant attempting to sweep away the old Catholic elite. Ordinary citizens and craftsmen, too, formed part of the opposition to Spanish, Catholic hegemony, although their opposition was mainly motivated by the disastrous economic plight in which the country found itself through Philip II's ill governance.

Another important factor in the struggle for power was the attitude of the citizens' militias. The militiamen, mostly from wealthy families, were entrusted with defending the city in times of need and with maintaining public order. Many of them had slowly drifted towards the opposition. On 4 August 1566, for example, Sheriff Pieter Pieterszoon found that he was unable to take action against a preacher because he was suddenly confronted by a group of militiamen, all of them Calvinists, who taunted him by asking whether he was intent on bringing about a bloodbath.

In the vacuum that resulted from this struggle for power, the Beggars saw an ideal opportunity to take over the city without bloodshed, and supported by the enthusiasm of the people. One of the Beggars leaders, the popular

Hendrik van Brederode (who seems to have been a very witty man), had come to Amsterdam expressly for this purpose. Under pressure from a great number of people who had assembled on the Dam, the city council saw itself forced to appoint him "captain of war supplies", a position that effectively put the military control of the city into his hands. "Heer Heinderik Kapiteinderik", as Bredenrode was quickly apostrophized, resided in an inn on the Dam called The Prince of Orange, where he received the leaders of the new movement, among them Laurens Jacobszoon Reael, thereby reinforcing the latter's position.

In April 1567, the fortunes of the reformers turned. Hard-liners dedicated to the service of the King and of Catholicism had gained the upper hand at the court of Brussels, and as a consequence William of Orange refused to maintain his allegiance to Philip of Spain and went abroad. A considerable part of the nobility followed him. Moreover, the Duke of Alva, a merciless hunter of heretics, was leading a large army towards the Netherlands in order to bring the rebellious province back into line. Yet although the Calvinists were by now in the majority in Amsterdam, it was still thought unwise to risk an out-and-out confrontation. The preachers were forced to leave the city, taking with them thousands of reform-minded followers. Then, on the evening of 27 April, Brederode departed. The city council held a large banquet in his honour, speeches were made, and then he was "led to his ship with great ceremony" and sailed for the North-German city of Emden, where a lively exile community of Amsterdam merchants was rapidly springing up.

After this exodus, Amsterdam itself rapidly went downhill. With the departure of so many merchants, the city had lost a large part of its capital and trading contacts. Heretics were now prosecuted more severely. Wijntje Ottens, the boy who had thrown a slipper at the statue of Mary in the Oude Kerk during the uprising, was publicly drowned in a wine barrel on the Dam. The terror of the Duke of Alva's Council of Troubles – called the "Blood Council" by the people – and the counter-terror of the Beggars, drove tens of thousands of Amsterdammers away from hearth and home. At the same time the city was flooded with thousands of refugees, among them Wouter Jacobszoon. On top of all this, trade was hampered by Protestant pirates, the so-called Sea Beggars. After 1572, as more and more Dutch cities adopted the cause of the Sea Beggars, Amsterdam became increasingly isolated. When Haarlem and Alkmar were besieged by Spanish troops, the enemy even received provisions and reinforcements via Amsterdam, although the city did refuse unequivocally to let the occupying forces within its own walls. In the years following 1574, by which time the rebellion had triumphed throughout the rest of Holland, the rebel cities threw a cordon sanitaire around Amsterdam in order to prevent the Spanish using it as a base from which to reconquer Holland. The city's engine, trade, ground almost completely to a halt, and hunger once again ruled Amsterdam.

This was the situation when, in the monastery by the Ouderzijds Voorburgwal, Father Wouter Jacobszoon set down his observations for later generations. On 20 April 1573, there was a new sign of impending doom, for, suddenly and miraculously, it began to snow over Amsterdam. "The roofs of the houses were covered with snow as if it were winter," Jacobszoon wrote. All the religious houses had brought their cattle within the city walls for fear of the marauding hordes, "and these beasts lowed so mightily that it would have softened a heart of stone".

Meanwhile our monk tried to do as much of his ordinary work as he was able. He buried a child that had not survived the journey to Amsterdam from Beverwijk: "And I saw that nothing could be done but to bury it like a little dog. The uncle of the child carried it to the grave himself, put it into the earth and closed the grave himself." At another burial, he noticed that a second-hand coffin was used. "The gravedigger had simply dug up the coffin from the earth and had tipped out the other corpse, which had been buried in it first, just as one would throw rats and other vermin on a rubbish dump."

From the monastery, he could see the villages around Amsterdam burning, set alight by gangs of Beggars pillaging the countryside: Westzaan, Sloterdijk, Diemen, even the Carthusian monastery was not exempted, barely escaping capture by the soldiers. One night Jacobszoon hears noises around the city "in between waking and sleeping". "First I thought that it was a brewery putting beer into barrels, but then I understood that it was a drum." Unable to fall asleep again, he spends the rest of the night "sighing and crying" about the terrible times in which he lives. The following morning he is told that the drumming he heard during the night came from a troop of Walloon mercenaries making their way around Amsterdam towards Haarlem.

Fear of betrayal and of an attack by the Beggars dominate the daily life and thoughts of Wouter Jacobszoon. He knows for certain that he and his brothers in the monastery would be slaughtered. In one of his notes he regrets not having any clothes apart from his monk's habit: "At one time I was determined to get myself normal clothes, but until now I have not done so. This was pure negligence, hoping that there would be enough time should an emergency arise, but also fearing it might cost too much and because I thought that I should put the money I had into things more essential for getting through the world."

He regularly notes a strange turmoil among the children of the city. They fight each other, coming together in great numbers; the citizens regard all this as a bad omen. One day, Jacobszoon records, the corpse of a boy is brought to the sheriff. It transpires that the child was mortally wounded whilst playing at "Beggar and Cardinal" – that is, rebel and loyalist – with his little friends. "They attacked one another as if they were real fighting parties, they charged, shouting 'Hoar! Hoar!', and did not stop wickedly throwing stones."

Gradually the pressure that the Beggars exerted on the half-besieged Amsterdam increased. Again and again our diarist tells us of exchanges of gunfire close to the city – near the Overtoom, or on the Sint-Anthonisdijk, or by the Amstel. Now and then the Beggars can even be seen within the city's walls.

8 April 1577

Yesterday at night a Beggar entered uninvited a house in which two nuns took their evening meal, and sat down at their table and ate their food as if he had been their guest. And he spoke there, to the distress of these maidens, most coarsely and blasphemously about the most Holy Sacrament, even so that the pious ones did not dare to stay but got up and ran out into the street, leaving their lodgings behind, and they stayed away until the rascal had left.

23 November 1577

In the morning around eight nobody was thinking of anything untoward and at half-past about forty Beggars were on the Dam, two of them already standing on the steps of the Waag in order to occupy it. By the Sint-Luciens monastery, too, the drums of the Beggars were beating and they were marching around the Nieuwe Kerk with them, shouting: "Hoar! Hoar! The city is ours!" They also shouted: "Come out of your hiding places, you prince-lovers," and "Kill! Kill!", and "We will kill monks, priests and nuns!"

As already mentioned in the last chapter, the Beggars' captain, Helling, had managed to trick the guard at the Harlemmerpoort, but his troops lost their way in the city, reinforcements failed to arrive and, two hours later, after some fierce fighting, the intruders were thrown out again.

1 January 1578
Many Catholics assembled before the gentlemen of the Town Hall [. . .] One of them said that he would rather be burned on the Dam together with his good wife and seven children than fail to do his best to keep the town out of the clutches of the Beggars. Many folk left the city hurriedly, and a great terror descended on our community.

6 January 1578
An old spinster killed herself by cutting her own throat. At the same time, many priests began to keep watch at night in order to help reinforce the guards. The Beggars are spreading more and more around the city.

23 January 1578
It is almost impossible to get to the area of the Regulierspoort, so many people have assembled there to leave the city. Across the street, I saw sacks and packs, beds and palliasses being moved, just as in May, the month in which people usually move house. If one went further into the city, one heard nothing but sighing and moaning.

20 February 1578
And now matters have come so far that the lovely and pious city of Amsterdam, after waiting all this time and after such great loyalty to the King and so much sorrow and courage, is in the hands of the Beggars. [In fact, at this date, it was only part of Amsterdam.] One hears people, even the devout ones, saying openly: "Ah, be merry with me, because now we will live well again. All sorts of foodstuffs will come into the city again."

23 February 1578

We heard that many of those who fled and lived in exile have come back into the city.

16 March 1578

In Amsterdam there is a great hubbub in celebration of the peace that they have now made with the Beggars. Each evening, all the bells are rung from seven until eight. Every gun is fired, so that there was a terrible noise, painful to hear, the simultaneous clamour of bells and thunder of guns. There were many exuberant celebrations, lit by the flames of pitch torches and suchlike. Many good people, thoughtful people, saw all this and were so distressed that they did not know to contain themselves and cried and shouted, frightened of further oppression.

22 April 1578

I myself, writer of this, have been warned that I should prepare myself to leave, otherwise I shall be expelled from the city tomorrow, as − or so I was told − I had not appeared with the other priests in front of the commissioners [in order to swear allegiance to the new administration].

3 May 1578

The soldiers ran through the town like wild animals, behaving in the strangest, most mindless fashion. Many busied themselves around a maypole that they had planted on May Day, drenching it with English beer, as if the beer were water and the maypole needed watering.

On 26 May, the city was finally taken over in its entirety by the Beggars. Almost immediately, a great number of Protestants, among whom were many who had returned from exile, demanded that a church of their own should be established. When the burgomasters and the City Fathers refused, they were ousted from the Town Hall and taken prisoner by the Beggars. Meanwhile, the hated Friar Minor monastery was once again stormed and plundered. As Wouter Jacobszoon relates, the brothers "were terribly maltreated, made prisoner, driven along the streets to the accompaniment of shouting and shameful language, and thrown one upon the other into a ship. As most of their clothes had been torn off, and because they had been so severely beaten, they no longer had any inclination to change their position or to turn around. Among the brothers who were brought on to the ship were the priest of the Nieuwe Kerk, the provisor and also the entire city administration and the councillors, and many others, very good Catholics. And all these were sailed out of the city together and landed on a dyke, from where everyone was able to go away on foot." A few days later, Jacobszoon himself was clandestinely brought out of Amsterdam with the help of some friends and finally found refuge with fellow Catholics in Montfoort. In one of his last Amsterdam notes he writes that, as soon as the warships had left the city, "the Damrak lay full of ships as had been the custom earlier, before this time of upheaval."

This virtually bloodless revolution, during which the city literally put the Middle Ages out on the dyke, was later to enter the history books as the so-called "Alteration". Amsterdam became the economic centre of the world's first modern republic – the Republic of the Seven United Provinces – under the direction of a governor, a predecessor of today's royal family, and of a representative body, the Estates General. A new generation of city administrators came to power. They were men who had suffered hard times during their exile and were ready to take chances and even to risk their entire fortunes for their principles. They had, of necessity, looked beyond the horizons of their predecessors, and had built up new business networks and trading contacts during their almost ten years in foreign countries. These men thought in terms of a new political and religious order. The Catholics had to relinquish their churches and offices, but their lives, their trade and their firms remained untouched. Calvinism became the new official religion, although it was never to overtake the unofficial religion of the city: the freedom of trade and of capital and, to a certain extent, of thinking and writing. The Alteration marks the beginning of an almost limitless growth of the city, and (according to some historians, at least) 26 May 1578 is the exact moment at which the real Amsterdam was born.

In 1592, not even 15 years after Wouter Jacobszoon had left the city, an English traveller called Fynes Moryson would describe Amsterdam: "Near the port there is a field, rather than a marketplace, called Campplatz [he

means the Plaetse] where the burghers bid farewell to their family and
friends who are sailing off. In the summer the numerous merchants gather
on the bridge. In the winter they do so in the Nieuwe Kerk, where they
proceed up and down the nave in two lines. There is no possible way out
other than joining one of the lines and being carried away with the people
up to the doors. East of the city, there is a beautiful stone wall on which a
walking path has been laid out." [10]

Artist unknown, *The City of Amsterdam*, 1611, detail.

More than ever, Amsterdam was a hubbub of activity. Aside from this, the
city was increasingly assuming the function of a storehouse for goods in
transit. In particular, timber and grain imported from the Baltic waited
here for transportation to Western Europe. Warehousing was vital in a
time when storms, poor harvests and wars made supplies unreliable.
Amsterdam was, and still is, full of storehouses, lofts and cellars, and all
sorts of other storage places, and old maps also show the so-called "timber
gardens" for storing wood.

The quantity of goods flowing into and out of the city was also
substantially increased by the opening of new trading areas. In the north,
ships now went as far as the White Sea, while to the south contacts with
the Mediterranean grew in importance. Amsterdam also earned large
amounts from trade with the enemy. Spain had a great need for grain,
and Amsterdam merchants, ignoring isolated voices of protest, felt no
compunction in feeding their opponents. The Spanish fleet, which had been
destroyed by Amsterdam ships, was rebuilt with Amsterdam timber. The

wages of Spanish soldiers were financed with Amsterdam loans, and the cannon and muskets with which the Spanish hoped to bring the Low Countries back under the rule of their king, were delivered in large numbers via the most important city of that same king's enemies. It is still possible, for example, to see on the so-called Trippenhuis, on the Kloveniersburgwal, how the Trip family made its fortune: the chimneys are designed to imitate the bores of mortars. National sentiments had not yet come into play; if anything, one was loyal to one's city. Above everything, however, stood the requirements of the trade.

An important catalyst for Amsterdam was the fall of its largest competitor, Antwerp. In 1576, Spanish mutineers instituted an horrific bloodbath in that city, and in 1585 Antwerp was finally occupied for Philip II by the Duke of Parma. In response to this, the gateway to the sea, the river Schelde, was blocked by a pirate from Zeeland, bringing about a complete collapse of Antwerp's trade. Within a few years, the number of its inhabitants dwindled from 100,000 to 49,000. By contrast, Amsterdam managed to remain aloof from the cruelties of the continuing European struggle – the Eighty Years War, as it would be called – and was therefore able to take over, and to build on, Antwerp's function as the international marketplace for the Low Countries.

With the fall of Antwerp, tens of thousands of immigrants came to Amsterdam from the southern Netherlands, bringing with them their trading expertise, their capital, and their goods, as well as their appreciation of art and culture, their verve, and their language. In total, almost half of the newcomers to Amsterdam between 1585 and 1600 came from the southern Netherlands.[11] Once established in the city, they initiated, among other things, the silk industry, sugar refining, the trade in diamonds; they also brought new techniques of painting, while it was largely by their efforts that Amsterdam's publishing trade acquired its international reputation.

Even the language of the citizens changed under the influence of the colourful influx of "Spanish Brabanters". During the time of Wouter Jacobszoon, old Amsterdam dialect was spoken, which is likely to have sounded more like Afrikaans than today's Dutch. By about 1600, however, a third of the population spoke Antwerp dialect, while the wealthy bourgeoisie spoke French; the harsh old Amsterdam dialect quickly vanished with the establishment of the new immigrants. It is only through the surviving texts of the early seventeenth-century petition writer, Bredero, that something of the original Amsterdam tongue can be reconstructed.

Walking through the City Militia Gallery in the Amsterdam Historical Museum, one can see in succeeding group portraits how quickly this revolution took place: the stiff, dark clothes of the militiamen of the mid-sixteenth century become increasingly colourful towards the end of the century; little collars and modest berets turn into enormous displays of white linen and huge hats; and, by around 1625, sombre groups of farmers and fishermen have, within one or at most two generations, been transformed into elegant assemblies full of colour.[12] Almost nothing of all those magnificent costumes is preserved today. In the museums, the few surviving items are cared for with great attention: a collar, a single glove, a hat, a velvet purse.

Amsterdam's soil yields some of the luxuries of those days: exquisitely decorated drinking glasses, spools of lace (during the sixteenth century, lace collars and cuffs became increasingly fashionable), "ironing glasses" (the forerunner of the flat-iron which served to tighten and gloss the lace), coat brooches, purse clasps, rings (so-called "love-rings" were especially popular, representing two clasped hands holding a heart), spectacles, whistles, and even toys such as a little wooden play sword and several spinning tops, which appeared around 1375.

Another wave of immigrants arrived from Portugal: Sephardic Jews who had lost their livelihoods there because of the Inquisition. These laid the foundations of the tobacco trade and the diamond industry, and also made Amsterdam famous as a centre for Hebrew typography. The new republic was an ideal refuge for them: religious observance was not controlled by the state; there was no oppression by the Inquisition; there was freedom to marry within the community; no one was compelled to live in a ghetto; and Jews could acquire property freely. Such freedom was unheard-of elsewhere.

Many of these Portuguese Jews had converted to Christianity under the pressure of the Inquisition, and did not dare live openly as Jews even in Amsterdam. Initially, the city administration refused to give its consent to the building of a synagogue, and a change in this attitude came about only in 1614, when the Jewish community was granted permission to maintain its own graveyard in Oudekerk aan de Amstel. As a social group, however, the Jews remained isolated; movreover, they were forbidden "to gain carnal knowledge of Christian women or their daughters in or out of wedlock, even if they are women of light morals." To become a member of a guild was, with few exceptions, impossible for a Jews, something which restricted their economic base mainly to trading.

That some Portuguese Jews were wealthy should not create a false impression about the lives of the immigrants in Amsterdam. Most of the newcomers were poor or very poor. They had been uprooted by hunger, war, and epidemics, and were among the hundreds of thousands who strayed through Europe at this time, alone or in groups, looking for refuge. For them the city was the last port of call. A line from the verdict of an Amsterdam court against a certain Cateleyne de Vos, 31 years old, from the South Netherlandish Hoboken, speaks volumes for the plight of many of the immigrants: "She claims to win her bread with spinning and also that she was forced by need and desperation to become a whore."[13] Thousands of Cateleynes were walking the streets of the city, making what living they could through begging, prostitution, and stealing. Within less than 50 years the population of Amsterdam had increased from about 30,000 inhabitants to 105,000.

A bird's-eye-view map made by Pieter Bast in 1597 is significant: there is not a single spot of green to be seen. Each each piece of ground is a commodity; countless huts are appended to the city wall; whole families live under its arches. While the total area of the city has remained about the same as a century earlier, the population has quadrupled. There are also some quite tall houses to be seen, three and even four storeys high, and the process of extending existing buildings upwards would continue for centuries to come; the roof was simply – and literally – raised and another floor, or even more than one, built into the gap as long as the foundations would support the extra load.

During this period, Roemer Visscher, a grain merchant on the Geldersekade and member of the chamber of ship owners, wrote a poem in his In Liefde Bloeiende (Blossoming in Love) about "the girls on the Nieuwendijck":

Those by the Water are happy, 'tis true,
In the Warmoesstraat they are of high mind,
In the Kalverstraat they won't dance with you,
Those on the Burgwal I would like to woo,
On the Dam they have rosy cheeks
But in my arms they will entertain me most.

Without intending to, Visscher's poem also demonstrates the village atmosphere that still prevailed in Amsterdam. For almost a century, the old city government had refused to extend the area of the city. To make matters worse, many merchants had had the good sense to invest in the surrounding land, driving the prices of property there sky-high. Only after the Alteration in 1578 did the new city administration begin in earnest to extend the area of the city. First, shallow areas of the IJ were reclaimed from the sea and converted into land, thus avoiding the need to buy the property of speculators. In this way, the islands of Uilenburg, Rapenburg and Marken came into existence; later they were to become a part of the Nieuwmarkt area of the town. Here the newcomers, in particular the Sephardic Jews who had fled from Portugal, built their houses, yards and storehouses. This was also true of a fourth island, Vloonburg, which was claimed from the Amstel, and would later become Waterlooplein. Four centuries after this, when the metro was built, the remains of three sixteenth-century ships were excavated here, filled with boulders and probably sunk there as a foundation for the landfill.

To the west and south-west, on the other side of the city, the old wall was replaced with a modern system of earth walls and ramparts, while at the same time the city limits were extended by about 150 metres. The area around the original city canal, the Singel, became a residential district; immediately to the west were houses and small businesses, then the wall, and west of that the new canal, later to be called Herengracht. The entire works were completed by about 1591.

Amsterdam was ready for a new age. In the paintings from these years one can feel the tension in the air: many massacres, corpses, dissected bodies, a past world of wars, all had to be painted away. There is also a strong fascination for the falling body, and Icarus, the young man who flew towards the sun and who, in doing so, forgot all sense of proportion, is a recurring image.

Between such images there stands the portrait of Laurens Laurenszoon Reael, the son of the Beggar Laurens Jacobszoon, vice-admiral of the fleet. Painted by Cornelis van der Voort in 1620, it now hangs in the Rijksmuseum, right in the middle of that new Amsterdam which Reael's Calvinist father would never have recognized. We see a man leaning over a stick with a hard, active expression on his face. He is dressed in black, like his father, but his collar and cuffs radiate a rich sobriety, as do his watch chain and gold shoe buckle. He stands ready to issue a quick order, one hand on the stick; equally, he might also suddenly start lashing out with it, and both he and the onlooker know this.

Here stands a self-made man, possessed of the fighting spirit that was characteristic of the new wealth, a man who is at once both quick and solid, with features that make one think of the owner of a cattle-feed factory or a restaurant chain. "Thus let us complete what God has destined," Burgomaster Egbert Gerbrandszoon and his wife, Gerrit Janszoon Peggedochter, had had inscribed on their portrait, not even 80 years earlier. Laurens Laurenszoon Reael, however, had other thoughts in his head.

Chapter Six

Insiders and Outsiders

THE YOUNG GIRL HUNG FROM A POLE LIKE A LIFELESS DOLL, swaying in the wind, the IJ below her feet as she faced the city. To left and right of her were two horizontal beams; a rope ran beneath her armpits and others around her baize skirt; the right-hand side of her body was lifted slightly by the scaffold; a hatchet lay on the ground beside her. When the old painter saw her for the first time, she had been dead for several hours. She had been strangled on the Dam on this day in early May, then her body had been brought up the IJ to the Volewijk, where the pontoon is now, and left there to slowly rot away in the rain.

The artist drew everything precisely. With great attention to detail he recorded the fall of her clothes, the ropes around her slightly rounded belly, the dangling feet, the hem of her skirt moving in the wind, her the crooked mouth and closed eyes which gave her face a childlike quality. When he was finished, he stood to her right and began to draw her again, from the side. He drew nothing of her surroundings or the other bodies hung there; just her, in a close-up uncharacteristic of him, as though he wanted to preserve something of her innocence for all eternity.

Now they hang in the Metropolitan Museum of Art in New York, two drawings by Rembrandt Harmenszoon van Rijn, and thanks to the detective work of the Amsterdam archive specialist Isabella van Eeghen we even know the identity of the girl.[1] "Elsje Christiaens, of Spouwen in Jutland, aged 18 years, claims to have been in the city no longer than 14 days" – thus begins Case 84 before the Aldermen's Court on 28 April 1664, documented in the city's confession books, which are themselves preserved in the municipal archives.

It is easy to see from the manuscript what happened in the short time during which Elsje Christiaens lived in Amsterdam. She had arrived halfway through April, in search of a position as a maid. Temporarily, she had taken a room on the Damrak, hoping to be able to pay for her lodging from her first wages. After two weeks, the landlady suddenly demanded a part of the rent money from her, money which Elsje did not have. At around half-past eight the following morning, the woman again insisted on payment and threatened to impound the girl's meagre possessions. Elsje refused and the landlady began to beat her with a broomstick, whereupon Elsje, "in her fury", took up a hatchet lying on a nearby chair and attacked her assailant. Knocked over by the blow, the woman fell down a flight of stairs and lay there, dead. After this, Elsje broke open the travelling chest of another lodger with a hammer and took out some linen, then put it back again and took a cloth coat from another chest. Telling the neighbours, who had been alarmed by the screams, that her hands were bloody from a nosebleed, she then made her escape. However, the neighbours, having discovered the corpse in the cellar, pursued her through the streets. In panic, Elsje jumped into the Damrak, but was swiftly captured and led directly to the Court.

The notes from her interrogation now lying in front of me record what was said from that very moment on. "She says that she was very frightened because the landlady did not want to give her any more credit. She says that the man had left the woman 14 days ago." Many of these so-called landladies were in reality brothel keepers, a factor that might have lain behind the terrible quarrel between Elsje and the woman she killed.[2] The confession book, however, does not record anything of the kind. During a second interrogation on the following day, Elsje admits everything, as she had when questioned the day before, and in the entry for 1 May, I find a note to this effect: she admits to having taken the linen and the coat from the other lodgers' chests, but claims to know nothing of other missing items – money and an earring. In the margin, the verdict is recorded: "To be garrotted on a pole until death ensues, and then to be beaten upon the head several times by the hangman with the same hatchet with which she killed the woman."

It is not clear on which day Elsje Christiaens died. It may even have been on May Day itself; if not, then no more than one or two days later.

Rembrandt must have gone to the gibbet almost immediately after the execution: in the drawing the corpse of the girl is still fresh.

When Rembrandt was rowed across the IJ in order to draw the body of Elsje Christiaens, he had long ceased to be the successful painter established in the Jodenbreestraat, today's Rembrandthuis, with a court of apprentices. He was old. His second great love, Hendrickje Stoffels, had died shortly before and he had moved to a little house on the Rozengracht, number 184. Like most of his fellow painters, he now lived in the immense area in the west that had been added to the city at the beginning of the seventeenth century. Carel du Jardin also lived on the Rozengracht, Govert Flinck had a wonderful house on the Lauriergracht in which there was an impressive room for displaying his paintings; Pieter de Hoogh, Gabriel Metsu and the poet Joost van den Vondel lived just around the corner. They had all followed their rich patrons to the new areas around the old city.

Within one generation Amsterdam entirely changed. The number of inhabitants rose from 50,000 in 1600 to 150,000 in 1650. Together with the original inhabitants of the city, the tens of thousands of immigrants from Antwerp, the Portuguese Jews and, later, the Huguenots from France and itinerant workers from Germany, formed a metropolis that must have exerted the same attraction in people's minds then as New York does in ours.

A large painting of the Dam by Johannes Lingebach, dating from 1652, depicts the people of Amsterdam at that time: merchants from all quarters of the earth, three even in eastern dress, sailors and bargemen, drummers, female pedlars, notables, beggars, and behind this busy scene the row of façades of the Warmoesstraat and the tower of the Oude Kerk. The marriage registers, which provide a good representative cross section of the city's population, show that for many years more than half of the newlyweds of Amsterdam came from outside the city; indeed, the figure was as high as 73 per cent between 1611 and 1615.[3] The vast majority of immigrants, more than five thousand, came from what are now Poland and Germany: farmers from Schleswig-Holstein and East Friesland who hoped to find employment as workers or seamen, craftsmen from Bremen, Jewish shopkeepers from Poland, all cast adrift by the Thirty Years War.[4]

Amsterdam had thus acquired the dynamics of a city of outsiders, of people who had shaken off the Middle Ages and who were intimately bound up with their new city, while at the same time maintaining their bonds with countless cities in Europe via a network of letters, trading contacts, friendships, and family ties. It was a city of the here and now. "In this city there is nobody who does not trade in something," wrote the French philosopher René Descartes around 1635. "Everyone is so preoccupied by his own profit that I could live here for all my life without ever being noticed by anyone."[5] There were few palaces and churches or imposing buildings here, and it was noticed by every visitor that this city existed for financial gain alone. The Amsterdam of the "golden" seventeenth century was, to all intents and purposes, one enormous slot machine. Each available piece of earth, every skilled hand, was turned to this end.

From a train passing between the buildings on the south bank of the IJ it is still possible to catch a glimpse of the cityscape as it must have been then. For someone sailing into seventeenth-century Amsterdam, the first impression was of a forest of masts, flags, and towers. Windmills stood on the walls, cranes jutted high into the sky, and close by it was squirming with sails and rowing boats. Behind the harbour, stiff and stately, stood the quarters where the sea captains lodged, the Zandhoek and the Buitenkant, now the Prins Hendrikkade.[6] Bargemen and merchants walked the pontoons, and on the quays there was a lively trade in milk, eggs, straw, burned lime, and whatever else came in from the flatlands of North Holland. Such cargoes were rowed ashore from the larger vessels, but the smaller ships went up the Damrak, where the lodgings of Elsje Christiaens had been, and unloaded their wares there. The bigger merchant ships of the seventeenth century could not get there; they had to anchor in the deeper waters by the poles in the IJ, now the island on which Central Station stands, and unload with the help of smaller craft.

Alongside this slowly curving bay, which stretches out over some three kilometres, a complete waterscape had come into being, subdivided by pontoons, in which some large and countless small ships rose and fell with the waves.[7] This waterscape had a structure of its own, and there were even a number of buildings on stilts seemingly lost amid the ships: shipping offices, a platform on which there were two wooden cranes, guardhouses, dredging mills, the "tree bell" which was sounded each evening when the booms were lowered to close the city's access to the sea (the booms were the trunks of substantial trees, hence the name), and finally a special inn, a substantial wooden building catering to those foreigners who were not permitted to enter the city. The atmosphere of this strange, sloshing, half-rotting world is recalled in prints from the period: crooked, mossy poles; fences, pontoons and short ladders, the silent water, rowing boats, a few seagulls. For centuries this scene would define the transition from city to water, until the Central Station definitively closed Amsterdam off from the IJ.

Elsje had lived in one of the busiest parts of Amsterdam. It was, and still is, the point of arrival for most travellers, which may also be the reason why she ran into trouble there. Ship's captains congregated in a round building at the head of the Nieuwe Brug in order to pay their harbour dues and to pick up new passengers and cargo. Notices were posted up in a nearby room documenting the times of arrival and departure of all ships in the harbour. There was an ingenious system of barges operating around the city, and throughout Holland, which departed and arrived punctually to the exact minute, day and night. The hourly service between Amsterdam and Haarlem alone transported about 250,000 people a year, most of whom had to transfer to other craft to continue their journeys. The departure points therefore always attracted porters, merchants, people seeking to rescue lost souls, and others hunting for customers for lodgings and other services.

A German, Philip von Zesen, who visited Amsterdam during the same period as Elsje, found himself simply unable to describe in enough detail and with sufficient amazement the busy atmosphere which pervaded the Damrak.[8] First he saw the Corn Exchange, built above the water in the form of a square and with a colonnade running round all four sides. The traders would take handfuls of grain out of the boxes and, facing north in order to catch the right light, examine it very slowly and carefully, because the profit lay in the details. Everyone, however, knew that the trade was concerned not with handfuls, but with tons of grain, with storehouses full of it, with ships and whole areas of cities, and sometimes with war and famine.

A little further on was the Dam, and, audible from far away, shouts from the fish market there. In those days, the Damrak ran through the spot where the National Monument now stands, and it, too, was full of ships. In front of it was the Waag, the Weighing House, where the militia had its head-quarters, always a busy place as all wholesale goods had to be weighed there for the city tax before they could be sold on. The building was demolished in 1808, because the then king found it spoiled his view from the palace.

On the other, south, side of the Dam there was the merchants' exchange, built over the waters of the Rokin. It was a large stone building with galleries, an open court for the merchants, and a top floor of shops in which almost every imaginable luxurious item or curiosity was sold. "It almost seems as if the whole world were assembled here in order to trade," von Zesen remarks. Dutchmen, Germans, Poles, Hungarians, Frenchmen, Spaniards, Muscovites, Persians, Turks and even Indians came and went. The noise was deafening, and by every column particular kinds of wares were traded: tobacco, silk, jewels, bills of exchange, shares, real estate, foodstuffs, hides, altogether about 400 different types of goods or services. Everyone had access to everything, including art collections or loans with which to build palaces; princes could even order whole war fleets here. The destinations of the ships written up on the boards covered the entire known world.

The City Exchange Bank had been established in a side wing of the Town Hall, on the west side of the Dam, since 1609, an initiative of the city administration which made trading in Amsterdam considerably easier. As trade was carried out in innumerable cities and innumerable different currencies, when it came to payments, international trade was disorganized, even chaotic. Through the Exchange Bank the city assumed the role of general cashier. Here it was no problem to obtain a value for the most obscure or *recherché* money, and to get good local currency in exchange. A bag full of English guineas, a handful of French *louis d'ors*, a gold ingot from the West Indies, all would be converted by the City Exchange Bank into a fixed *bona fide* currency: the *banco florine*. A bill of exchange from this bank, really an early kind of paper money, was accepted by every merchant in Amsterdam. The city guaranteed absolute discretion and total availability of the banked monies on demand. Famous all over Europe, the Exchange Bank was seen as the lubricant of trade in Amsterdam.

There were also several early newspapers sold around these centres of trade: they published lists of prices, trading letters giving information about the position of fleets and the cargoes of commercial caravans, and reported on the quality of harvests around the world. As early as 1618, Amsterdam had a regular newspaper, the first in the world, the *Courante Uyt Italien, Duytschlant, etc.*, owned and edited by Gaspard van Huten. Later, Broer Janszoon's *Tydinghen uit Verscheyde Quartieren* would grow into the first real press centre, for merchants all over the world were only too glad to read these reports.

The power of this whole complex of capital, trade, and information lay mainly in its thoroughness and speed. The merchants in the city administration watched, hawklike, over the quality of the service sector. Immediately after landing, a shipper knew where to bring his cargo, while a merchant could work even with foreign currencies without any problems and, given the information available in Amsterdam, could ensure that reports from abroad were viable and impartial. Continuity, efficiency and absolute trustworthiness were the key elements of this economic miracle.

Presiding over all of this, markets and bank, trade and shipping, was the brand-new Town Hall (later to become the Royal Palace) on the west side of the Dam, the last part of which was completed in 1662. During these years Amsterdam grew into a world power, the modest medieval Council

Hall had remained the centre of all plans and activities. On 7 July 1652, however, a fire put an end to the old building, with its tower and its arches and its large sculptures of the Counts of Holland.[9]

Gerrit Adriaensz Berckheijde (1638–98), *Dam square with new Town Hall* (1673).

The new building was designed, on a scale unknown at the time, by the painter and architect Jacob van Campen (1595–1657), who was strongly influenced by Italian Classicism. The power and wealth of Amsterdam shone from every detail. It rose high above the houses, rivalling the nearby Nieuwe Kerk. Sober, even stern, on the outside, the lavishness of the interior decorations was unprecedented: beautifully worked galleries and courts, an enormous Citizens' Hall in the Venetian style, surrounded by dozens of offices, official apartments, and halls for the burgomasters and magistrates.

This splendour, however, was not allowed to go unchecked. There was no sculpture and no painting that did not wag a raised finger of morality. Above the entrance to the Desolate Boedelskamer, the Desolate Bailiff's Chamber where bankruptcies are heard, there is still a fresco depicting the fall of Icarus. Reliefs in the aldermen's hall displayed biblical scenes and pictorial reminders of the duties of a good and honest government. The paintings all depicted those rulers of biblical times and of antiquity who were in every way beyond reproach. There was no room in which a burgomaster would ot be reminded that he was the descendant of a sailor or a trader in, say, woollen goods, that good fortune was nothing but God's grace and could just as easily turn against him.

In this building full of sermons, Elsje Christiaens came to her end. Her death sentence was pronounced in the Hall of the Vierschaar with its great bronze doors. The execution took place, like all other executions of the day, on a wooden scaffold in front of the Town Hall; the façade still bears the square holes which were used to anchor the beams. She spent her last hours in the cells underground, next to the torture chambers and the dungeons used as whipping rooms.

How strange this dyke's course, how many ships abroad,
How noble these men sailing high on their yachts so proud,
How splendid is this town with all its new houses.
The whole country has, I hear, been built on dykes and sluices.

These are the words of one of the peasants in Bredero's *Klucht van de Koe* (The Cow's Complaint, 1612) as he walks one morning past the Ouderkerk and on along the Amstel towards Amsterdam.

'Tis a miracle, is it not? The Zuiderkerk so fair,
With towers of white stone, a work beyond compare!
How shines the sun with reflections and light's gleam
On the glazed roofs, on many a new beam.

The seventeenth century was the century of the city. At its beginning, there were in the world scarcely more than 40 cities with a population of more than 40,000 inhabitants. Six of these were in France, seven in Spain and seven in the Netherlands, even though, of these three countries, the latter had by far the smallest land area.[10] By the end of the century, many other such cities had appeared.

Amsterdam was at the forefront of this process of urbanization. Thousands of people seeking work lived on the periphery of the city in virtual slums; in 1609, someone counted 3,000 illegal dwellings just outside the city walls. Small, disorganized areas mushroomed alongside the paths and canals, especially what are now the Herenmarkt and the Raadhuisstraat, full of little houses, barns, workshops, vegetable gardens, pigsties, windmills, and small refuges for sufferers from the plague.

Only 20 years after the completion of the Herengracht canal, plans for another expansion of the city were put in hand. With this third enlargement, a start was made to the half-onion-shaped layout of the Amsterdam canal belt. It was a bold and ambitious project: the Herengracht was widened; another canal, the Keizersgracht, was dug around it, then another one, the somewhat less exclusive Prinsengracht; and beyond that a large area was developed for the petty bourgeoisie and the working class, which quickly came to be called the Jordaan for reasons still unknown (perhaps from the French *jardin*, or possibly a biblical reference invoking the Promised Land beyond the river Jordan); finally, near what are today the Nassau and Stadhouderskade, a fortification was constructed, as befitted a city like Amsterdam.

The canals were intended for the new wealth which was beginning to colonize the city, and were accordingly given noble names. The houses there were designed with ample space behind them for gardens and greenery, and all trades liable to cause rubbish, smoke, stench or noise were banned from establishing themselves there. Two churches were built: a Calvinist cathedral, the Westerkerk, for the rich canal belt, and a more simple house of God intended for the population of the Jordaan, the Noorderkerk, one of the first churches in the world to be designed and built especially for Calvinist worship: simple, spacious, with excellent acoustics, and with the pulpit in the centre – the Word in the centre, surrounded by the people of God.

The construction of the canal belt was actually started in 1613. It must have been an enormous enterprise, giving work to thousands of people: the building of the roads for the works, the digging of the canals themselves by an army of workers, the heaping of peat between the canals by labourers using pushcarts, the draining and pumping of the water that enabled the work to continue, the ramming in of thousands of piles on the canal banks, the erection of many miles of quays, the building of the first 40 bridges, and the delivery of enormous quantities of sand in ships and wagons from the dunes and the Gooi in order to prepare the ground for building. And after all this, not a single house had yet been put up.

The widening of the Herengracht and the digging of the other two canals did not begin from the centre outwards; in its full breadth, however, the development resembled a kind of gigantic windscreen wiper starting in the north-west and arcing south and then east. The wiper got stuck at roughly a third of the way round, at roughly eight o'clock: the first wave of building stretched only as far as today's Leidsegracht. The bare building ground beyond it was slowly to be developed up to the Amstel during the rest of the seventeenth century, but the project ground to a halt when the wealth of the city declined. The land on the opposite, eastern, side of the river, the last area marked for development, was allocated at the end of the seventeenth century to charitable organizations for housing for the elderly. The remainder was to be fashioned into a park, De Plantage, a sort of Tivoli Gardens *avant la lettre*, with theatres, beer gardens, playing fields and abundant green spaces. The Artis Zoo still serves as a reminder of this time.

"Among people of the seventeenth century, Amsterdam was famed as the stock exchange *par excellence*, the temple of trade," writes the French historian Henri Méchoulan in his book about the mentality of seventeenth-century

Artist unknown, *Amsterdam as seen from the IJ*, engraving, seventeenth century.

Amsterdam.[11] "But," he continues, "it has to be seen, in the first place, as the cradle of freedom," for although Genoa, Venice and Antwerp were also important trading cities of the day, they never managed to bring about a revolution in European consciousness. The new Amsterdam that had emerged after the peaceful revolution of 1578 was dominated by a formula for success which, until then, had been unknown: the pursuit of wealth in combination with a new conception of liberty. Money and freedom pushed aside, for the first time, the old medieval combination of "honour" and "heroism". With these vanished another idea, the belief that the greatest virtue lay in conquest, in war, and was embodied in the knight, the king, and his court. "The merchant, the new hero, vanquishes war every day by means of his trade, a fountain of power, of life, which can only flourish in an environment of freedom," Méchoulan writes. And the first freedom is undeniably that of "remaining oneself".

After the toppling of the last medieval regents, the city paradoxically grew into a realization of a medieval utopia: the safe, enclosed space in which the non-citizen could cast off the yoke of serfdom. "This church consecrated to God knows not enforced beliefs, nor torture, nor death," the Jewish immigrants, full of trust, wrote above the door of their Portuguese Synagogue. They called Amsterdam the Jerusalem of the West.

John Locke wrote his *Epistulae de Tolerantia* in Amsterdam, among other works. Baruch de Spinoza and René Descartes found the leisure and freedom here to conduct their researches, just as did the painter and inventor Jan van der Heijden and the composer Jan Pieterszoon Sweelinck. Jan Swammerdam laid the foundations for the science of biology and of entomology. Among much else, the architect and sculptor Hendrick de Keyser built the Zuiderkerk, the Westerkerk, the Beurs (the Amsterdam stock exchange of its day), and the famous Bartolotti Huis by the Herengracht. The master builders Jacob van Campen and Daniel Stalpaert enriched the city with a new kind of grandeur, the latter even managing to complete the building of the Admiralty (today's Dutch Maritime Museum) within nine months of work starting.

Painting was the most popular art form in seventeenth-century Amsterdam. There was neither Court nor nobility in the city, the Church barely commissioned works of art, and artists therefore had to look to the well-situated middle classes, who loved to have "something on the wall" more than anything else; something not too expensive but that still enhanced one's status. Portraits, landscapes and biblical scenes were all produced en masse, often by anonymous painters for an anonymous market. Painting had become less detailed than in previous centuries, and the new, sweeping style made it possible for some artists to finish one, and sometimes several, works in a single day. Paintings became increasingly cheap and were sold on markets alongside chairs, tables, even chickens. "Everyone strives to embellish his house with precious pieces, especially the room towards the street," the Englishman Peter Mundy wrote during a visit to Amsterdam in 1640, adding that he had even seen paintings in bakeries, butcher's shops, and the workshops of blacksmiths and cobblers.[12]

The migration of the Amsterdam painters' colony clearly demonstrates both the growth of the market for art and the slow movement of the elite from the centre of the city towards the periphery. The latter process would continue in later centuries, and would eventually reach the area around the Vondelpark and Amsterdam South, and even Buitenveldert, Amstelveen and Bloemendaal.

Around 1600, however, the majority of Amsterdam's painters still lived in the centre of the city, in a small area around the Pijlsteeg, close to the Dam and near what was to become the Damstraat. There were always paintings sold here, especially by the bailiffs and second-hand shops which were concentrated there. The Pijlsteeg was also the location for many of the brothels, which served to supply the painters with models. A whole group of boys who grew up in this area were later to become painters, among them Pieter Lastman.

At the beginning of the seventeenth century the entire art trade of Amsterdam moved towards the broadest part of the Sint-Anthonisdijk, later the (Joden-) Breestraat, which still offered enough space for the regents of Amsterdam and rich immigrants from Antwerp to build houses fit for kings. The street quickly grew into an "industrial area for painting".[13] The painters Pieter Potter and his son Paulus moved into a house near the new Sint-Anthonispoort, today's Daniel Meijerplein, and Pieter Lastman had his studio opposite the Zuiderkerk; Rembrandt spent six months of his apprenticeship there under Lastman. Cornelis van de Voort, he who painted Laurens Reael, lived by the lock on the corner of the Zwanenburgwal, while the entire workshop of the art dealer Hendrick Uylenburg (who himself could hardly tell at which end one was supposed to hold a brush) was situated there.[14]

In 1631, Rembrandt was entrusted with the management of this workshop, which was in effect a factory for paintings, and here he and his apprentices produced or copied one canvas after another. In the four years he worked for Uylenburg, Rembrandt painted more than fifty portraits of well-to-do burghers, and his popularity increased further when he started to use his young Frisian wife, Saskia, a niece of Uylenburg, as a model. The charming Floras, the shepherdesses and courtesans were whisked off his easel before the paint was dry. The relationship with Uylenburg cooled, however, and in 1635, a year after his wedding, Rembrandt ended his collaboration with the art dealer.

The area in which he lived exerted a considerable influence on Rembrandt's work. One of his biographers, Gary Schwartz, has demonstrated that many of the painter's most important patrons, clients and dealers lived within a 600-metre radius of his house: Pieter Lastman, the religious minister Joannus Uytenbogaert, Hendrick Uylenburg, Rembrandt's friend and patron Jan Six, and the Trip family, also patrons, whose wealth mainly came from armaments.

In January 1639, Rembrandt bought the imposing house next to the Uylenburg studio, now known as the Rembrandthuis. For his apprentices, he had also set up a studio in a storehouse in the Bloemgracht, close to the Westerkerk in the Jordaan, as an extension of his workshop. In doing so he thereby followed the elite to the Jordaan, a move other painters were making as well. All activity banned from the exclusive canal belt was concentrated here and the area was therefore very lively. In 1658, by then greatly reduced in circumstances, Rembrandt went to live there himself.[15] The Jordaan, with its small streets, had been born at the same time as the two imposing new canals, the Herengracht and the Keizersgracht. The quarter of the grubby fingernails thus came into existence with those of the perfumed hands. Now, however, they did not flow into each other. They were set apart. The Prinsengracht lay between them like an impassable river, and that was quite intentional.

The segregation of the canal belt from the Jordaan was indicative of the changing social relations within Amsterdam's population. In the time of Wouter Jacobszoon, a typical merchant had mostly stored his goods in his own attic. His life was played out between shopkeepers and artisans and he did his work at home or on his private grounds. While there were several rich merchants in Amsterdam even then, the average income of such men was not high. According to the tax registers of 1585, Dirck Janszoon Graaf, burgomaster and iron merchant, with a fortune of 140,000 guilders, about £600,000 in today's money, was the richest citizen of Amsterdam. There were no more than five other citizens who also possessed more than 100,000 guilders. By 1631, however, this group was twenty times as large.

Within one generation, a new kind of merchant had emerged in Amsterdam, hoarding large amounts of capital. Such merchants traded mainly on the stock exchange in goods they had never seen and which sometimes had not yet even arrived in the harbour; furthermore, they invested enormous sums in enterprises of which they themselves had no expertise whatsoever. The polders of North Holland and the large-scale reclaiming of land were typical products of seventeenth-century investment. The merchants also put large amounts of money into expeditions to the unknown worlds of India, America, Tierra del Fuego, and the North Pole. They had developed not only a new status, but a new kind of intellect.[16]

The silent social change in Amsterdam took place during the first decades of the seventeenth century. As the historian Ed Taverne was to write in his study of the canal belt: "The merchant regent, who eventually ceased to be fully aware of the origins of his authority and power, became alienated from the general population, moved away from the overcrowded inner city and ensconced himself in an exclusive outer part, the canal belt, which had been established since 1615."[17]

Amsterdam had created for itself only one urban monument. No large squares, parks or palaces, but something else, typical of a rich, independent and somewhat stubborn bourgeoisie: their own separate residential area. Regarding this grand project, it still remains unclear to what extent beauty was of more concern than practical necessity. Since most of the original plans have been lost, it is now impossible to shed any light on the motives of the architects. There are indications that they were strongly influenced by the ideal of the Italian Renaissance, the circular "perfect city", while the symmetry and proportions make it clear that the canals were intended to be the "jewel of this city". In 1609, however, the first sketches made by the city carpenter Hendrick Jacobszoon Staets, were in the main based on plans for fortifications, and the city council was in the following years to speak chiefly about bulwarks, gates, walls, and moats. For them, Amsterdam was principally a large and rich fort; everything else took second place.

For the projected area that was to house the petty bourgeoisie – the district that was to become the Jordaan – it was deemed enough to fill in several ditches, to broaden others and make them into canals, and to straighten some of the small paths into proper roads. The strange, crooked streets of this characteristically compact part of the town still testify to the pattern of medieval ditches that had run throughout the city. In September 1614, by which time the work was already progressing at full pace, some of the councillors involved came up with an entirely new idea: to build a boulevard in the place of the Keizersgracht, a long, narrow avenue to rival the Voorhout in The Hague. This plan was, however, abandoned almost as soon as it was articulated. Meanwhile, the people in charge made a healthy profit from trading and speculating in the building land.[18]

The construction of the canal belt was unquestionably an imposing project, and the regents who dared to undertake it were several centuries ahead of their time. Beside the grandeur of the city, the project also reflected the narrowmindedness and avarice of the merchant regents. "The mathematical, uncluttered relation between streets and canals in the area of the belt, with its extremely spacious waterways, quays, streets, and plots of land, is in marked contrast to the method of adjusting and broadening existing streets and canals that was practised elsewhere," concluded Ed Taverne after meticulous research in the city archives. "This led to a city which, because of its divided aspect, is unique to urban development during the Republic."[19] The canal belt, in short, is the result of a policy of city improvement that was designed by its implementers to provide themselves with the best possible accommodation. As such, the plan also heralded the end of the city as a place in which people could live and work in the same location. From then on, citizens would increasingly go about their business in different parts of Amsterdam.

In this respect, Rembrandt was still an old-fashioned Amsterdammer who maintained strong ties with his local area. He could, for instance, literally find his biblical characters on the street in the Breestraat, for the Jewish quarter began just around the corner from his house. A contemporary described him as constantly walking in the markets, looking on the Nieuwe and the Noordermarkt for harnesses, medals, Japanese daggers, fur and lace collars, which he deemed worth painting.[20]

Such objects were meant for his studio, where he would often stage whole scenes like a theatre director. In his famous Prodigal Son, he himself plays the lead, beautifully dressed and with a goblet in his hand, while his wife Saskia takes the role of the woman of easy virtue. He is radiant and exuberant, she somewhat more hesitant, sitting on his knee and turning towards the spectator. In the past, Rembrandt experts tended to see a moral finger being wagged in this picture, but in truth it seems here that the painter is holding a mirror up to himself. He kept this canvas, a fact which encourages the interpretation that he did indeed play himself in all the charades and disguises which he chose to paint, and that he used them to provoke his audience.[21]

Half a century later, the painter and art historian Arnoldus Houbraken, who had been an apprentice to several of Rembrandt's students, would describe how the Master had created separate compartments in the studio, using partitions of paper and cloth, so that each of his apprentices could draw from life undisturbed. On a warm day in summer, both the model and the draughtsman in one of the compartments were as "naked as their mother had given birth to them". As the other apprentices stood watching the scene through a hole in the fabric, Rembrandt entered. At first, he just watched with the others, but when the apprentice told his model that they were now "like Adam and Eve", Rembrandt beat on the door with his painter's baton, shouted "And now – out of Paradise!" and chased them, still naked, down the stairs.

It will have become clear by now that Rembrandt was a true craftsman, as well as an artist. His business was the focal point of his existence, but it was also a considerable commercial enterprise. Several of his own studio canvases from his "factory" have been preserved: groups of apprentices sitting in a circle and drawing a model, an apprentice with two models and the Master, come to inspect his work; a magnificent genre piece depicting the private studio in Rembrandt's house – an easel in the foreground, light streaming in from a high window, in front of that a table with a lectern used for showing etchings and drawings, to the right a cradle with opened canopy and, next to that, the fireplace and a half-dressed woman, probably Hendrickje Stoffels.[22]

Rembrandt had more than fifty apprentices and collaborators in the course of his working life, one of the reasons why so many canvases have been wrongly attributed to him down the years.[23] Once he had become fashionable he set about building on his reputation and converting it into hard currency, even visiting auctions and bidding for his own pictures in order to drive up the price. It is said that he once bought his own etching of the *Preaching Christ* for the enormous sum of 100 guilders in order to keep his pictures rare and thus more expensive.[24] It was a strategy with which he had considerable success. A portrait from his hand, for instance that of Andries de Graeff, later a burgomaster, cost 500 guilders for each figure depicted. This made Rembrandt one of the best-paid artists in the city.[25] His etchings, which were spread throughout many collections in Europe, made him famous internationally. For much of his career, therefore, he was no "lonely genius", but a painter who knew how to position himself in the very centre of events, and who determined what was fashionable in the canal belt for many years.

In the spring of 1664, when he drew Elsje Christiaens, all that was over. In the self-portraits from these years we see a heavy man with a painter's cap, grey hair, and tired, puffy features. His gaze is more detached, more observing than assertive. Especially after Saskia's death in 1642, he had taken to making sketches during his wanderings through the city. The centre of his work, however, was still his studio.

When he was rowed to the Volewijk on that day in May, he ventured beyond the ways usually described by his routine. Not only did he produce finished work, rather than sketches, outside his studio, but the drawings he made of Elsje differ from his other work during this period.[26] It seems that he intended to capture the dead girl as realistically as he could, as though he wanted to freeze her death, to stem her inevitable decay. At the same time, both drawings have about them an air of rest and of pity, a memory of her youth which would transcend the end that she had met.

Several weeks later, the body of Elsje Christiaens was immortalized once more, this time by the painter Anthonie van Borssom. He painted the gallows of the Volewijk with all the corpses hanging or sitting there at that time: two men suspended from a large stone gibbet (we can glean from the court records that one of them had been hanging there for a year, the other for three); an impaled body with an iron spade next to it; the remains of a murderer who had been broken on the wheel, a pistol nailed up above him; and on the right-hand side, clearly visible, the pole with the hatchet and the body of Elsje Christiaens.[27] We can now see the colours of her dress as well. We can see that Elsje had been wearing a red skirt and a grey jacket, but her body has slumped a good deal, the head especially, which has sagged by about two feet.

As can be read in the book of confessions, Elsje had been sentenced to be "eaten up by the air and by the birds of the skies . . . tied to a pole with a hatchet above her head", and this is exactly what happened. From the same confession book we also know which men interrogated her and eventually decided upon her death: the aldermen Burg, Blaeu, Rochus van de Capelle, van Loon, Spieghel and Bronckhorst. Without much difficulty we can find the ancestors of most of these men.[28] Dirck Spieghel came from one of the oldest Amsterdam families. He was the grandson of a herring merchant and son of a soap-boiler on the Nieuwendijk, and himself a director of the Westindische Compagnie (the West India Company, chartered by the Republic in 1621) and captain of the crossbow militia. Nicolaas van Loon was a merchant on the Keizersgracht and administrator of the House of Correction. Vincent van Bronckhorst came also came from a rich merchant family. Coenraad Burg, former ambassador to the Russian Court, was also a director of the Westindische Compagnie and administrator of the Amsterdam colony New Netherland, in North America. Blaeu was no less than the famous cartographer Jan Blaeu, the publisher of the magnificent nine-part *Grooten atlas ofte werelt-beschrijving*, better known as the *Grote Atlas van Blaeu*.

Those who determined Elsje's fate were therefore perfect examples of the patrician families ruling seventeenth-century Amsterdam, members of an elite that set the tone in all areas of city life, the new family network which controlled both trade and shipping and which had a firm grip on power in the city. We know their self-satisfied faces from hundreds of portraits, including those by Rembrandt: the captain of *The Night Watch*, Frans Banningh Cocq, who was later to be Mayor; Dr Nicolaes Tulp from *The Anatomy Lesson*; the burgomaster Andries de Graeff; the Trip family; Jan Six; the Bicker brothers; and many other such worthies.

Take Vincent van Bronckhost, for example. He himself was a widely respected merchant on the Keizersgracht, but the real money had come from his father, who was one of the group of entrepreneurs who, in 1595, had equipped the sea captains Cornelis Houtman and Pieter Keyser with four ships and had sent them on an expedition to discover their own trading route to India, independently of the Portuguese and the Spanish. India was already known; in 1592 the enterprising preacher Peter Plancius had managed to acquire twenty-five Portuguese maps of the continent showing "all sea shores of the entire face of the Earth", the heights of cliffs and the depths of the waterways and harbours, as well as the secrets of the routes to the East and West Indies and the habits and principal trading goods of foreign peoples. These facts were immensely valuable for the merchants of Amsterdam. They even sent a secret delegation, probably Cornelis Houtman himself, to Lisbon, to gain further information about the Indian routes.

On 2 April 1595, the small fleet sailed from the IJ. A little over two years later, 14 August 1597, three of the four ships reappeared in front of the poles by the Schreierstoren. Of the 240 members of the expedition who had sailed, only 87 had survived, and the whole enterprise had proved to be not that profitable after all. Nevertheless, the sailors were brought into the city as heroes: now the route to India was known. The greatest trade venture the city had ever known was ready to begin.

Bronckhorst *père* was a director of the Nieuwe Compagnie op de Vaart op Oost-Indie, the New Company for the Passage to East India. The companies were powerful establishments, comparable to today's limited-liability companies, through which the Amsterdam merchants financed high-risk projects. Since the risk was spread, they were more daring. In 1602, the companies grew to form the world's first multinational in the world, the Verenighde Oostindische Compagnie (United East-Indian Company), the VOC, which was to control Dutch trade and shipping in Asia for the next two centuries. The head office was situated in the Oostindisch Huis, the East India House, in the Oude Hoogstraat, now a part of the University of Amsterdam, and according to contemporary accounts the smell of cloves and nutmeg permeated the building and its surroundings.

A company like the VOC was little less than a state within the state. Its governing body, the omnipotent "Heren Zeventien", seventeen gentlemen, had the power to negotiate with Indian rulers on behalf of the Dutch Republic, and was entitled to build forts and recruit soldiers for its own military formations.

In 1621, a second company was established in a bid to wrest supremacy over the Atlantic from Portugal and Spain: the Westindische Compagnie (WIC). It was the WIC which, under the command of Governor Peter Stuyvesant, Director-General of the Dutch colony of New Netherland (the present-day states of New York and New Jersey) since 1647, established a small trading post near the mouth of the river Hudson, on the east coast of North America. "The meadows are rich with grass and flowers and strong trees, and lovely fragrances are wafted around," as the first reports from the island of Manhattan had it. It was the beginning of the settlement of Nieuw-Amsterdam, later New York City.

The WIC traded mainly in sugar, tobacco, pearls, furs, tropical woods, and ivory. It also earned large sums from transporting black slaves from West Africa to the plantations of America, about seventy thousand between 1626 and 1650 alone, of which only one in five survived the passage.[29] All these activities were directed from the Westindisch Huis in the Haarlemmerstraat, which is still standing, although it is now used for receptions.

There was a third powerful trading company, the Noordse of Groenlandse, founded 1614, which specialized in whaling. Initially, the merchants tried to overcome the dangers of the normal Indian route via the Cape of Good Hope by seeking a new route through the polar regions – the so-called North-West and North-East Passages – but this idea was finally abandoned after three failed expeditions; one of these, under the command of Willem Barentsz, had to spent the entire winter of 1596 on the polar island of Novaya Zemlya, off the north-eastern coast of Russia. These expeditions, however, had shown that there were large numbers of whales in these waters, and this in turn meant meat and whale oil, soap, lamp oil, and, above all, a new source of income.

The driving force behind this was more than mere avarice. To the Dutch explorers and navigators, and the merchants who backed them, the maps of Jan Blaeu, with their strange forms, faraway islands and vague coastlines were no longer frightening; rather, they presented a challenge. The large white areas asked to be discovered; the entire world was begging to be explored, the microcosm within a drop of water just as much as the *terra incognita* of North America. Jan Blaeu made all this palpable, knowable, and possible. The activities of the great trading companies were therefore also a national adventure of which everyone could partake, even if the centre remained in Amsterdam. Their registers are inscribed with the names of more than a thousand shareholders: patrician merchants, of course, but also craftsmen, preachers, schoolteachers, and servants.[30] Above all, the way they went about their business was an expression of the courage and dynamism of a city population that felt itself to be on the threshold of a new era.

Artist unknown, *Amsterdam as seen from the IJ*, engraving, seventeenth century.

It was this dynamism that attracted outsiders like a magnet. For Elsje Christiaens, Amsterdam had been an obvious choice in order to find a position in service. While real earnings were falling in the rest of Europe, they were rising in Amsterdam. In Cologne, a worker earned about 15 stivers a day, 22 in Arnhem, and 27 in Amsterdam. There was little evidence here of the extreme poverty and hopelessness that were besetting the European proletariat during this period. Bread prices were stable because the city held a key position in the grain trade. A three-pound rye loaf during that period cost about four and a half pennies, which in turn meant that even ordinary people had money enough to afford the luxury of a varied diet: fresh greens, butter, cheese, eggs, and fish.[31] Everything was there in plenty on the markets of the city, and it was cheap.

As a newcomer from Leiden, Rembrandt quickly found employment here. Thanks to Hendrick Uylenburg he gained access to the highest circles in the city. He painted pastors and burgomasters and shipping magnates, became a member of the Sint-Lucas guild of painters, and moved into that spacious merchant house in the Breestraat, while his marriage to Saskia van Uylenburg brought him additional status and income. His extensive collection of stones, coins, Roman statues, helmets, drawings, prints, and other rare items stood comparison with those of the richest merchants. That Rembrandt, a craftsman, was so readily accepted into a higher social circle, at a time when painters did not yet have the aura of an artist, is indicative of the relative openness of seventeenth-century Amsterdam society.[32]

Rembrandt's painting The Company of Captain Frans Banning Cocq. later came to be known as The Night Watch, because of the darkening effect of dirt on the varnish. It was considered a daring piece in its time, for the members of the militia are arranged in what was, then, a very unconventional way; however, it was also thought by many to be the pinnacle of the genre of militia portraits.[33]

Rembrandt was a stubborn man and a perfectionist, something which his clients had to accept when they commissioned him. Houbraken later heard his apprentices tell of how their master would sometimes spend two days "putting on a turban according to his liking". He could be particularly careless about other details, however, and he would fling them down on the canvas "as though with a tar brush", so that some paintings looked "as if smeared with a mason's trowel". When visitors wanted to look at these paintings close to, Rembrandt would prevent them from doing so, saying that they would find the smell of the paint too unpleasant. "And concerning the women," adds Houbraken, "the most wonderful subjects for an artist's brush, [as depicted by Rembrandt] they are too pitiful to make a song and dance about."

Another contemporary complained that the painter never took a "Greek Venus" as his model, but a washerwoman "or a turf-treader from the barn".

For his part, Rembrandt paid not the slightest attention to his critics. One of his satirical drawings (now in New York) shows fashionable gentlemen in a studio admiring his latest works. One visitor wears a hat from which sprout two enormous ass's ears, while next to the canvas is the artist himself, laughing and shitting in a chamber pot. The Amsterdammers took such evidence of contempt in their stride. His freedom as an artist was seen as a form of freedom of conscience. Nobody in Amsterdam argued against the right of a citizen to do whatever he pleased within his own four walls, so long as he did not step out of line socially.

Despite the exotic fragrances emanating from the East India and West India Houses, it should not be forgotten that Amsterdam was and remained a typically Dutch trading city. As greatly as the VOC and the WIC and the Greenland Company may have appealed to people's imaginations, they did not determine the urban economy. Most of the money was made, less spectacularly, from the shipping trade within Europe. The Dutch owed their success largely to their technological superiority in shipbuilding. The fluit, for instance, which was developed in the 1590s, was a revolutionary type of ship in its time, half as expensive to build as other ships of comparable size, and capable of being sailed by ten men, where other vessels of similar displacement required crews of at least thirty.

In the middle of the seventeenth century, the Dutch had more than 700 ships at sea, a fleet larger than the English, Scottish, and French fleets combined. Between 1600 and 1800, a total of 9,641 ships sailed from Europe to Asia. Almost half of these, 4,720, came from Holland. As has already been mentioned, Dutch crews were cheap, not least because many seamen lived in the countryside of North Holland and frequently kept small farms in addition to their work at sea.[34] The cost of materials was a third lower than elsewhere because of the profusion of imported wood and hemp; furthermore, there was plenty of capital in Amsterdam with which to fund new ships or commercial voyages. There was also little competition within Europe. England and France had a great many internal problems which adversely affected their trade, while Spain and Portugal concentrated on South America and Asia.

By the early 1600s Holland found itself in a very peculiar position. For a few decades it held the hegemony, as economists would put it, utterly dominating the emerging world economy. According to the American economic historian Immanuel Wallenstein, seventeenth-century Holland enjoyed a role later followed only by Great Britain and the United States. All three held their positions only for a short period. The Dutch hegemony, he asserts, is the most difficult to explain, as it was not backed by a strong military power. Wallenstein believes that apart from trade, fishing and the early industrialization of the Netherlands also played a significant part in establishing the country. It was the invention of the Dutch windmill, an early example of technical innovation, which allowed the area around Amsterdam to grow into a centre of the "era of wood mechanization". These windmills also enabled the Dutch to drain the polders and to develop farming of a hitherto unparalleled intensity.[35]

With the benefit of hindsight, it is easy to point to the combination of circumstances which was the key to the success of Amsterdam. For most contemporary commentators, however, this economic boom was nothing short of a miracle. "In the conversations of wise men," wrote the English scholar William Aglionby, "almost no topic features so frequently as the wondrous ascent of this small State, which has risen within no more than a hundred years, to a height which does not only infinitely exceed the standing of all the old Greek republics, but in some ways is not even shamed by the greatest monarchies of our times."[36] Within that small, miraculous nation, Amsterdam had absolute dominance.

The city carried the greatest part of the defence costs of the Republic, and determined to a large degree the nation's foreign policy. When, in 1638, the treacherous Marie de'Medici, widow of King Henry IV of France and mother of the ruling monarch, Louis XIII, was received by the city, the regents of Amsterdam displayed such grandeur that they might themselves have been sons of noblemen. The city's gift to the newborn Henry, Prince of Wales, son of King James I and VI (of England and Scotland), consisted not of diamonds or pearls, but of a chest made of solid gold and filled with bonds drawn on the Amsterdam stock market – "pure gold", as a Dutch diplomat remarked.[37]

Coins issued in Amsterdam were so highly trusted that for more than a century even the English were compelled to buy ducats there, as their Asian trading partners preferred not to accept any other currency. Even as late as the end of the eighteenth century, Polish grain producers wanted to be paid in this currency.[38] In 1645 it was sufficient to send a fleet to the Sont in order to guarantee free passage for Dutch trading vessels. "The keys to the Sont are lying in the IJ," as the city's diplomat, Coenraad van Beuningen put it to the Swedish king. An entire area populated by Dutch people sprang up near Copenhagen, so that it must have been relatively easy, as well as quite understandable, for a young Danish girl who wanted to see the world to wind up in Amsterdam.

Unsurprisingly, in the light of all this, Amsterdam considered itself more than a city, and not without reason. It was not omnipotent, but was nevertheless quite capable of blocking the whole administrative machinery of the Republic. Little could happen without the city's assent, especially with regard to foreign affairs, for every conflict could cause the blocking of a harbour or a sea passage and thus damage the trade. A city of such power, however, is seldom loved by those beyond its walls, and for several centuries, perhaps even to our day, that power was the source of tensions between the proud Amsterdam and the rest of the country.

Indeed, initially, Amsterdam had even attempted to prolong the war with Spain. In 1617, a fierce theological conflict had erupted among the Calvinists between the liberal Remonstrants and the orthodox, zealously anti-Catholic contra-Remonstrants. The Amsterdam regents supported the contra-Remonstrants, not because of their strict teachings but because this allowed them to obstruct the peace negotiations of Jan van Oldenbarneveldt, the Councillor-Pensionary. There were already far-reaching plans in Amsterdam to establish a West India Company expressly to exploit the gold-rich countries of South America and to wrest part of the trade with those areas away from Spain. Peace with Spain, therefore, was the last thing the Amsterdam regents wanted to see.[39]

At first, the merchant elite of the city supported the new Governor, the "city vanquisher" Prince Frederik Hendrick, with a golden hand, and he repaid their favour by taking one city after another from the Spanish: Den Bosch, Venlo, Roermond, Maastricht, Breda. These triumphs brought the governor considerable political momentum. Frederik Hendrick began to surround himself with a court, adopted more and more the mannerisms of royalty, and even arranged the succession of his son, the young Prince

William II of Orange. Frederik Hendrick proved to be a man bent on converting the Republic back into a monarchy, and that ran totally counter to the interests of Amsterdam. The merchant regents saw themselves as dyed-in-the-wool republican magistrates, while their self-regard was aroused by the grandeur of the new town; as a result, they wasted not so much as a single thought on handing back a proportion of their power to a new dynasty of the House of Orange. Relations between that princely House and the city of Amsterdam therefore cooled, and over the years developed into an out-and-out opposition.

In addition to this, most of the Amsterdam merchants came to understand that a continuation of the war was, in the long run, liable to harm the welfare of the city. Increasingly the conviction gained ground that a complex trading city like Amsterdam had no interest in conquests and chaos, but in a status quo that was opposed to any notion of war or disorder. When finally the Stadtholder decided to reconquer Antwerp, matters came to a head. The mere thought of new life being breathed into their old rival city made the regents of Amsterdam foam at the mouth.

Frederik Hendrik's most determined opponents were the burgomasters Cornelis and Andries Bicker, their brothers Jacob and Jan, and that same Andries de Graeff who bears the distinction of having been painted by Rembrandt. Under their auspices, the city administration had been transformed into a kind of family firm of "crude, haughty, unbearable, avaricious and power-hungry manipulators", as their detractors apostrophized them. The Bickers were rich beyond even the dreams of Amsterdam merchants; They had had a part of the IJ filled in especially for their wharves (the still-existing Bickers Island), had brazenly built a fleet for the Spanish, and had organized a silver shipment in order to finance the Spanish troops defending Antwerp, thereby angering Frederik Hendrik.

Under strong pressure from the Bicker-de Graeff faction, the Republic entered into peace negotiations with the Spanish, and in 1648 – ironically just a year after Frederik Hendrick's death – the Peace of Münster was signed. The King of Spain, Philip IV, recognized the Republic as an independent power, the southern Netherlands remained Spanish, the lands annexed and settled by the VOC and the WIC were recognized, and the competing city of Antwerp remained cut off from the sea. The Eighty Years War of the Low Countries had been a resounding success for Amsterdam.

The regents' pragmatism – or opportunism, if one wants to call it that – had borne rich fruit.

The tensions between Amsterdam and the House of Orange had not been resolved, however. They reached their climax in a bizarre incident in the margins of the city's history: the storming of the city by Stadtholder William II, Prince of Orange.

This William was a young man of twenty-four who, having succeeded his father Frederik Hendrick in 1647, had hit trouble right from the start. After the Peace of Münster, Amsterdam and other Dutch cities wanted to reduce the expensive mercenary armies by half, but the Stadtholder vehemently opposed this. He still dreamed of conquering the southern Netherlands, including Antwerp, in order to gain a royal position in the Low Countries. First of all, however, he wanted to impose his will on the intractable Amsterdam. During the night of 29 July 1650, therefore, he sent his troops to Abcoude and Ouderkerk with orders to overpower the Amsterdam city guards by daybreak, when the gates were opened, and to occupy the city itself. With this accomplished, the Prince would throw the various members of the Bicker family out of the administration and replace them with his allies.

Matters worked out rather differently, however. A fierce storm broke out on Hilversum Heath in the middle of the night, and William's troops lost their way and reached Abcoude only at nine o'clock in the morning. The mail courier from Hamburg had spotted the soldiers wandering over the heath and had warned the Amsterdam administration. Cornelis Bicker had the city's gates closed, had the cannons loaded and run out, stationed musketeers and foot soldiers at the ready, ordered some low-lying areas to be flooded and had ten warships sail into the mouth of the IJ. The enthusiasm for the defence of the city was considerable: even the pacifist Mennonites were willing to serve as watchmen against the prince.

The ambush had failed, but Amsterdam had no mind to be besieged, either. At noon an armed yacht was dispatched to the commander of the Prince's force, William, Count of Nassau, who had set up his headquarters on the Amstel. The Amsterdam delegation exhausted themselves in polite phrases, before tactfully indicating that it might be wise for the Count to depart quickly, as "the city is full of all manner of folk and strange people who could easily get it into their heads to do something which could be damaging to you, and very unpleasant." When the young Prince of Orange heard that his attempt had failed, he shut himself in and, according to Wagenaar, "stamped around his room with rage and threw his hat to the ground".

William did at least get a part of what he wanted: after this episode, the Bickers were deposed. To a certain extent, these fabled military actions restricted Amsterdam's independence. The city could ill afford to be continually at war with the Stadtholder and the rest of the country. At any rate, the Prince was to die a few months later of chicken pox.

After this it seems that both parties, the House of Orange and the city, realized that they coexisted in a delicate balance, a fragile construction which could only withstand the pressures put upon it if each side tried its utmost to accommodate the other. This was the origin of a form of government that was judged weak by many, which was interconnected and dependent on compromises, but which also proved to be both adequate and flexible. It did not set itself against its citizens, as tended to happen in absolute monarchies, but made allies of them. It combined a degree of central power with a great deal of autonomy for the cities and regions, and thus placed decision-making where the loyalty of most citizens lay: in their own cities. Among ordinary people, the concept of national states hardly existed, so that during the seventeenth century a man did not call himself a Dutchman, but an Amsterdammer or a Leidener, or whatever. People thought in terms of cities and city elites. The rest was secondary. Recognition of local city authority gave the Republic its own almost democratic energy, allowing the nation to expand unimpeded, unhindered by royal bureaucracy.[40]

Sadly, poor Elsje Christiaens would hardly have done more than stammer and stumble before the mighty masters of Amsterdam. In the confession book it is noted that she came from Jutland, from a place apparently called "Sprouwen". Yet when I tried to reconstruct something of Elsje's life, at the very least the place she had come from, I came to an immediate dead end. There does not appear to have been a Sprouwen at any time in the whole of Denmark.

A Danish-speaking friend suggested that there had possibly been a small, unfortunate misunderstanding. "Sprog", "sprow" derives from the verb "to speak" and the chances are that Elsje Christiaens simply did not understand what Messrs Bronckhorst & Co. were saying to her from behind their table. If asked where she came from she would have replied something along the lines of "But I can't speak your language, sir!", which might easily have been noted down as "Sprouwen". According to them, Elsje simply came from the place "What-do-you-call-it". Later on, through some friends, I found a description of a tiny Funen island called Sprogø, which was also mentioned in a hand-written text from the Middle Ages as Sprowae. The island was a notorious robbers' den and moreover had been home to mainly Dutch people for years. But whether she came from Sprogø or "What-do-you-call-it", her place of origin did not make much difference to Elsje's destiny.

For Rembrandt, relations with the city elite were more complex. Like Elsje, he was a newcomer, a simple miller's son from Leiden. Because of his talent he was noticed at an early age, but socially he was never really to succeed. Just as the militiamen of his Night Watch – rich cloth merchants who played their part in the welfare, as well as the defence, of the city – were church-wardens and trustees of orphanages but had little further influence, so Rembrandt never made it to the top of the ladder. During almost 40 years as one of the city's most outstanding portrait painters, he did not paint more than three members of the city council, and never painted either a serving or a former burgomaster. "He was never addressed as 'Sir', a title reserved for the ruling class. He remained a painter-merchant, trading in art," concludes S. A. C. Dudok van Heel in his study on the miller's son and Amsterdam's social life.[41] Elsje Christiaens' attempted immigration was literally strangled at its inception, but Rembrandt, too, was to remain an outsider.

Not that the city was closed. There were immigrants who did achieve high positions, even if this might sometimes take a generation or even two. Vincent van Bronckhorst, for instance, one of the judges of Elsje Christiaens, was just such a one. His grandfather had been a brewer in Weesp, his father a grain merchant in the Warmoesstraat, while he himself belonged to the topmost echelon of Amsterdam society, had an immense fortune, and was later even to become a member of the Supreme Court of Holland.

The city went further than merely tolerating strangers, however, for it pursued an active immigration policy from quite early on in its development. As the economy continued to grow and the lack of certain skills in the city became noticeable, the administration did not hesitate to import this missing know-how. In 1597, Amsterdam made a contract with the Venetian glassblower Anthony Obisy, prompting him to move to the city in order to introduce the art of making crystal glass. A short time afterwards, the Portuguese merchant Manuel Rodrigues de Vega received 120,000 guilders from the city coffers in order to establish a silk industry there; the Republic had captured two Portuguese silk ships and it was anxious not to miss out on yet another lucrative trade. Hans le Maitre, from the southern Netherlands, was subsidized to the tune of 2,000 guilders and furnished with a workshop in order to teach Amsterdammers the craft of making gilded leather wall hangings. Even French Huguenots, the group of Protestant refugees who, fleeing persecution in their own country, established themselves in the city after 1685, received incentives to spread their knowledge of different trades. The silk weaver Pierre Baille benefited from several cash injections of between 10,000 and 40,000 guilders in order to set up a factory with 60 looms, partly staffed by apprentices from city orphanages. French hatters, gilders, silk and brocade weavers, ribbon and lace makers, were even allotted their own little neighbourhood, in which the houses were equipped with spacious ground floor workshops – remains of which are still to be seen today in Weteringstraat, near the Spiegelstraat and the Rijksmuseum

The phenomenon of immigration, in short, dominated to a considerable extent the life and mentality of seventeenth-century Amsterdam. In the period from 1601 to 1800, 174,874 immigrants came to Amsterdam from Europe, and another 153,490 from the Dutch provinces. In 1600, the city had about 50,000 inhabitants, in 1622 105,000, in 1630 120,000, in 1650 about 160,000, and after 1700 the number stabilized at around 220,000. Such a massive influx must have given Amsterdam something of the quality of an American city of today, a society in which a person might rise quickly, and fall just as fast. Both were to be the lot of Rembrandt, as it happened.

Elsje Christiaens died, to the incessant ringing of the bells of the Town Hall on the Dam, under the eyes of the assembled masses, but there is no eyewitness account of her death. Without a doubt, Messrs Burg, Blaeu, Rochus van de Capelle, van Loon, Spieghel and Bronckhorst would have been present in a prominent place. The executioner received his usual fee, six guilders, and there were no burial costs since "she was not permitted the earth", as it was called in those days. And that, as far as the city was concerned, was that.

Rembrandt had a different fate. His masterpiece, *The Night Watch*, was taken to the Town Hall some decades after his death, together with other large-sized group portraits of the city's militia. There it was allotted the smallest space, between two doors, and in order to make it fit it was cut on all four sides. Two militiamen vanished on the left, and the drummer on the right was cut in half so that only his head, an arm and the drum remained. The canvas then darkened slowly under generations of dirt and dust.

Rembrandt's decline had little to do with the commonly held picture of poverty and lack of recognition. When Saskia died in 1642, he was a rich and famous artist. Houbraken has calculated that he earned about 2,500 guilders a year from his apprentices alone.[42] For years he had had an outstanding relationship with a young merchant, writer, patron of the arts and, later, burgomaster, Jan Six. He had made etchings for him, plates for the family album, sold him three of his paintings, borrowed money from him, and painted his portrait. Six even tried, without success, to integrate Rembrandt in Amsterdam society. Then, in 1654, the friendship suddenly cooled. The merchant sold Rembrandt's debt, and when he married in 1656, the official portrait was painted by Govert Flinck.[43] We can only guess at the reasons for this breakdown in relations.

In retrospect, however, the steps that brought about the painter's fall from the social ladder were most probably social *faux pas*. The same cheek that had led him to paint *The Night Watch* in the way he did eventually sealed his exclusion from the city's upper crust.

The first problem was Rembrandt's character. He was, to put it mildly, not especially polite. The few anecdotes about him that have come down to us also illustrate his greed: as a practical joke, his apprentices would paint coins on the floor in order to make him stoop. Stories also relate his bad humour, his moodiness, his coarseness and his falseness. Gary Schwartz has pointed out the silent witness borne by the surviving documents about the painter.

Nobody ever asked him to be godfather to a child, or called him as witness, or even asked him to value a painting as an expert.

Rembrandt also lacked a solid political base in the city. The Amsterdam socio-political system was founded on patronage and protection, with the result that the status of a painter depended only in part on the quality of his work. Far more important was the question of which circles patronized him, something akin to the importance which museums and art critics place upon the "value" of a piece of art today. In this Rembrandt did not exactly prove himself adept. The most powerful family in Amsterdam, the Bicker dynasty, never commissioned a single painting from him. When the painter, for reasons unclear today, fell from favour at the Orange court after the death of Saskia, his prestige in the Amsterdam salons declined as well. The commissions for portraits quickly tailed off. After 1650 several people who had been among his clients came to power: Frans Banningh Cocq in 1650, Jan Huydecooper in 1651, Nicolaes Tulp in 1654, and Andries de Graeff in 1657, but his most highly placed sitter was a mere alderman, Joan Jacobszoon Hinlopen. In no respect could he equal the success of his former student, the then celebrated Amsterdam painter Govert Flinck, an artist with excellent connections to the House of Orange, the Court of Brandenburg and other regents, but whose fame today rests on little more than the name of a run-down street in an area of the city known today as De Pijp. There was, however, more to Rembrandt's comparative lack of success than a failure to cultivate the right patrons. From the surviving documents it is clear that he violated two unwritten rules of the Calvinist ruling class, the first being the perceived immorality of his domestic arrangements, the second the questionable nature of his business dealings.

Disapproval of the painter's domestic arrangements revolved around his unedifying affair with his housekeeper, Geertje Dircx. She had been employed as a nurse for Titus, the only one of his four children by Saskia to survive, but soon after Saskia's death in 1642 Rembrandt began a relationship with Geertje. There are indications that Saskia's uncle, the upright Baptist Hendrick Uylenburg, was upset at this. At the same time, as I have mentioned before, his relations with the Court cooled and the stream of portrait commissions began to dry up from one day to the next.

Five years later, the 22 year-old Hendrickje Stoffels, a farmer's daughter, "small of stature, but well proportioned in her features and with an ample womanly body", as Houbraken describes her, joined the household as a maid. Complications were inevitable, and in 1649 Geertje Dircx left the house on the Breestraat. An unsavoury wrangle ensued: Rembrandt had agreed to pay her an annual alimony of 60 guilders, but she found this too little. After a stormy scene in his kitchen, she had him summoned before the commissioners for marital affairs for a breach of his alleged promise of marriage. Since a formal union was impossible because of the differences in station between the two, she settled for an alimony of 200 guilders a year. In the records of the proceedings of the matrimonial court we find the following notice: "The plaintiff denies having made promises of marriage but claims not having to admit that he slept by her."[44] Rembrandt, however, retaliated in kind. He bribed Geertje's brother and nephew, who came to collect the alimonies, and also a certain Cornelia Jansdochter, to gather testimony from Geertje's neighbours about her moral conduct. Using this information, he succeeded in having her locked up in the woman's prison at Gouda, from which she was only released in 1655, after several friends had interceded on her behalf.[45]

In 1654 a new scandal had erupted when Hendrickje Stoffels became pregnant and was summoned before the Church Council because, as the documents put it, she had lived "like a whore with Rembrandt the painter". The painter himself escaped unpunished; since he was not a member of the church, the priests had no power over him. Even so, he could have prevented much misery by marrying Hendrickje Stoffels, and the reason he did not do so was probably that he could not afford to. In the event that he should marry again, he would have to pay out Saskia's legacy to their son Titus, the – to him – wholly unattainable sum of 20,000 guilders.[46]

In this way Rembrandt also breached the second article of faith of the Amsterdam elite: financial solvency. He had what would seem today a somewhat curious method of financing his extravagant lifestyle: for a long time his work was so greatly in demand that patrons were happy to advance him money in order to have at least a moral claim on him to finish a commissioned painting. There was even a small market in these Rembrandt promissory notes, a trifle speculative, perhaps, since nobody knew whether the Master really would finish the promised painting.[47] In about 1654, however, it all began to go wrong. Rembrandt could no longer honour his old promises, and he was lent no more money, not least because most of the merchants had been forced to trim their outgoings during this period: Holland was at war with England, which in turn meant that many ships could not reach the city, and the spectre of unemployment and bankruptcy loomed. The people of Amsterdam suddenly understood how vulnerable their economy really was.

In an inn on the Kalverstraat, De Keizerskroon, in December 1655, Rembrandt held an auction of his belongings. The sale included his paintings, but the takings were small. Six months later he was forced to declare himself bankrupt and the Desolate Boedelskamer, the bankruptcy court, initiated proceedings. One of the creditors who proved particularly troublesome was Geertje Dircx, who had by now been released from prison. She even threatened to have him arrested if he would not cough up the 200 guilders alimony which was her due. As it turned out, however, she died a short time after making this threat.[48]

Rembrandt was now confronted with the power of the Church for a second time. In bankruptcy cases the Church Council assumed the role of moral judge, deciding whether the case before it was simply a matter of an honest merchant who had been unlucky but who had at least made efforts to make good the damage, or one of deception, perhaps involving an attempt to hide goods from the bailiffs. The former case would be treated as a liquidation, the latter as a bankruptcy – and an undischarged bankrupt could kiss goodbye to any thought of a commercial future in the Calvinist city.

As the documents show, Rembrandt employed every trick in the book in order to retain as many of his possessions as possible. First he tried to keep his house on the Breestraat out of the proceedings by making it over to his son Titus; then he had himself formally employed by Titus and Hendrickje Stoffels in order to keep his creditors at bay. While theoretically free of the clerics, socially he had been branded a bankrupt because of his ducking and weaving. Not Jan Six, nor any other patron, wanted to have his official marriage portrait painted by someone like that.

The house on the Breestraat was sold, and the furniture went to the pawnbrokers on the Oudezijds Voorburgwal (the building is still standing), to be sold from there. Titus, then seventeen, managed to use his savings to buy a precious mirror with an ebony frame which his father had used when

H. J. Baden, *Interior of the Nieuwezijdskapel, during a service* (1658).

working on his self-portraits. After he had it carried back to the house, it fell and shattered.[49]

Rembrandt's last works have an atmosphere different from his earlier ones. The contours are less distinct, foreground and background mingle, spaces become vague and seem to flow into infinity. The largest commission of these times, to decorate the interior of Amsterdam's Town Hall, was awarded to Govert Flinck. When Flinck suddenly died in 1860, Rembrandt was allowed to undertake only a small part of the project: the conspiracy of Claudius Civilis. In 1662 Rembrandt's enormous canvas was removed by order of the council; instead, Govert Flinck's sketch was finished by a little-known painter. By then, Rembrandt had moved to the Rozengracht, supported only by a few members of the Amsterdam elite, among them the arms dealer Trip. In 1664, the year in which he drew Elsje Christiaens, the painter was obliged to sell even Saskia's grave in the Oude Kerk. Plague epidemics were rampant at this time, especially in the middle-class areas like the Jordaan where thousands of people would die in a matter of weeks. "The day before yesterday 27 deceased were counted in the Bloemstraat," wrote a woman during one of these outbreaks. "Today 22 in the Anjelierstraat; and yesterday three people living in the same house on the Barnde canal were buried."[50]

In the same year, a "pale fiery flame" came down from the skies one evening at half past eleven, as if "a burning torch was dropping down to the earth". A few months later, a ball of fire showed itself above the city, shining in short, broad rays, "emitting a very pale light, a face of flames".[51] Almost 30,000 victims were claimed by the plague epidemic of 1663–4, one in seven of the population. Among them was a woman "of ample body", Hendrickje Stoffels. Five years later Titus, 27 years old and only recently married, also died. The next year, at the age of 60, Rembrandt himself succumbed. He was buried in an unmarked pauper's grave in the Westerkerk.

When the church was renovated more than three centuries later, it was thought for a while that the painter's remains had been found when a body was uncovered during the work. The skull, however, crumbled to dust in front of the television cameras.

Chapter Seven

The Ice Age Explained

THERE ARE IN AMSTERDAM — JUST AS THERE ARE IN EVERY CITY
of a certain size — some houses that are better not talked about. One of
these strange places is the old and imposing building on the Amstel
canal, number 216, between the arched bridges of the Herengracht and
Keizersgracht. On a dull afternoon in 1992, I looked at the graffiti which
have amassed on the façade over the years. A few letters and a coarse,
light blue *tag* was sprayed on to the façade, but underneath is some older
material, drawn in red: stars, a sailing ship, some strange signs, part of
a name, "Van Buenige . . .", and if one looks closely one can make out a
squiggle reading "Jacoba". The marks seem to have been smeared on to the
stone during the 1960s. But they weren't.

The inscriptions, faint but still legible, were almost certainly written
some 300 years ago by the Amsterdam diplomat and burgomaster Coenraad
van Beuningen during the last years of his madness. Some say he used red
chalk, others maintain that he wrote them in his own blood, an assertion
not entirely improbable considering the extent of his insanity.

It has always been said of the "Bloodstained House", as the property
has been called for centuries, that it carries inscriptions which cannot be
eradicated; on the contrary, they are said to stand out more clearly with
every attempt to clean them off. Not much of them remains visible today,
however. It was only in 1937, when the façade was cleaned using what
was then modern technology, that it became clear how much was written
there: Hebrew letters, ships with masts and flags, a pentagram and an
octogram, the name Van Beuningen and the first name of his wife, Jacoba.[1]
The Hebrew name "Magog" is just decipherable, the biblical symbol
for all heathendom in the last struggle between the Kingdom of God

and the kingdoms of the world.[2] However faint, these marks have proved impossible to remove, despite all the efforts of council workers and high-pressure pumps.

Coenraad van Beuningen has already been mentioned in passing in the previous chapter. He was the diplomat who told the Swedish king that the keys to the Sont lay in the IJ; subsequently he lent money to the King of Denmark so that the latter could arm a fleet against his Swedish rival. Van Beuningen was, to translate his position into a more or less contemporary equivalent, the Henry Kissinger of seventeenth-century Amsterdam, a brilliant, international-class administrator and negotiator. Born into a famous family, he was secretary to the renowned poet and statesman Constantijn Huygens at the age of 19, secretary to the city of Amsterdam one year later, was the Republic's Ambassador to France and Sweden, councillor to the Stadtholder William III, a councillor of the city of Amsterdam, a director of the VOC, and six times burgomaster. A bachelor for almost all his life, he was known to be a little eccentric at times; even so, he was undoubtedly a star in the firmament of European diplomacy.

It is not entirely clear what went wrong with him, but there is little doubt that the year 1672 played some part in his decline. This was the so-called "Year of Catastrophe", the year in which the young Republic was not only torn apart by internal conflicts, but also attacked from four different sides: France, England, Münster, and Cologne.

After the death of Philip IV of Spain in 1665, the King of France – the Sun King himself, Louis XIV – who was married to Philip's daughter, had laid claim to the "Spanish Netherlands". In 1667, the French army invaded and occupied the southern Netherlands, making light work of the Spanish troops, but had been stopped by an allied army comprising men from England, Sweden and the Republic. A brief conflict, referred to as the War of Dutch Devolution, ended in 1668 with the Peace of Aachen, at which France declared herself content with a portion of Flanders. Four years later, however, the treaty notwithstanding, the Sun King decided to march against the Republic once more. This time, England, seeing an opportunity to rid herself of a rival maritime power, attacked the Dutch fleet while marauding bands of soldiers from Cologne and Münster exploited the Republic's chaos by marching into Groningen and other parts of the country.

These unexpected attacks were motivated largely by economic rivalries, but there was also an important ideological element: the absolute monarchies of Europe had had enough of the Republic's freedoms of speech, ideas and religion, the satirical prints and forbidden books, suppressed elsewhere in Europe, which streamed forth from the tolerant Holland.

The Dutch mentality, at once chaotic and prosaic, was diametrically opposed to the order and subjugation demanded by the monarchies that surrounded it. Beyond that, however, it was feared that anarchy would spread across Europe "as a poisonous weed", for the Dutch, or so it was believed by many, were "nurturing the parasites of rebellion" while thinking of nothing but their own profit.[3]

Above all else, however, Louis XIV was intent on humiliation. Apart from his harsh territorial and economic demands, he wanted to see an annual delegation from Holland in Versailles with a letter expressing their deep regret at their insubordination, their complete obedience to the will of the King, and their eternal gratefulness for his goodwill and mercy. In addition to that he wanted to create a different kind of Netherlands, under the direction of the Stadtholder William III, Prince of Orange, ruling as a puppet king. In this, however, Louis underestimated the republican spirit of his puppet-to-be, who knew full well that the governorship of the Netherlands under such terms would be very different from the King of France's conception of absolute power. The prospect of being crowned a king was no doubt alluring to William, but he felt that a disruption of the fragile balance of power within the Republic would prove fatal to everything for which the Dutch had worked and fought.

Meanwhile, the population of the United Provinces was in a state of panic. Priests were preaching that the seven-headed monster and the Whore of Babylon had risen again. Coenraad van Beuningen, then Ambassador to Paris, had a vision in which he saw Louis with the features of Nebuchadnezzar; as the earth spewed forth smoke, the King shouted: "Death! Death! The hunt is good!".[4] The two most powerful administrators of the Republic, the brothers de Witt, were lynched at The Hague, all rivalries were forgotten, and everyone of influence flocked around William III, among them Van Beuningen, who had also dropped the de Witt brothers, his former friends, and sided with the Prince.

The French troops were almost within shooting distance of Amsterdam

and were only prevented from reaching the city because large parts of
Holland were flooded along the so-called "Hollandse Waterlinie", the Dutch
water line. Meanwhile, using all of his considerable diplomatic skills, Van
Beuningen managed to bring together a coalition against France, allying
William III with Spain, Austria, Denmark, and a number of German princes.
Charles II of England gradually withdrew from the war, his hand forced by
public opinion in his own country.

Once the immediate danger had passed, however, the undying conflict
between Amsterdam and the House of Orange re-emerged. William III
wanted to continue the war against France in company with his new-found
allies, but the Amsterdam opposed this plan: merchants rarely love wars.
It was not to be the last time that the city traders were to drive princes
and generals and admirals to distraction. "Ces coquins d'Amsterdam", the Prince
called them, adding that Burgomaster Van Beuningen's life was forfeit,
and that he, the Prince, would never succumb to the diplomat's "caprices".[5]
It would take more than two years of negotiations before the House of
Orange and Amsterdam had effected a reconciliation.[6] But Coenraad van
Beuningen had earned the disfavour of The Hague for good.

Was it this shameful treatment that marked the beginning of the end of
a top European diplomat – or was it love? In 1686, Van Beuningen, then 64
years old, suddenly decided to marry, despite the dark moods from which,
by then, he was already suffering. His bride-to-be was from a leading
patrician family, with a reputation that left something to be desired, the 46
year-old Jacoba Bartolotti van den Heuvel, who lived on the Herengracht,
just around the corner from Van Beuningen's house on the Amstel. Jacoba
seems to have been a viper (even the simple inventory of their possessions after Van Beuningen's death bears testimony to the fact that she
made trouble for the men who had come to estimate the value of her late
husband's estate), and the marriage brought nothing but grief.

In the same year in which he and Jacoba married, Van Beuningen asked
to be released from his posts as burgomaster and member of the city
council. This was unheard of and everyone was very surprised. No decision
appears to have been made. At the same time he began to speculate – disastrously – in VOC shares, and yet the more he lost the more he became
convinced that he would win, thereby dissipating his fortune under the illusion that he was increasing his wealth. The city, he decided, was to share in

his new-found, and entirely imaginary, fortune, and he was therefore deeply disappointed to find that nobody was interested in his offer. He interpreted this indifference as a sign of the times, an indication of the impending Apocalypse. Increasingly distanced from reality, he foresaw the coming of Christ, and had pamphlets printed about the combination of consonants in the Masoretic Bible (which incidentally showed that he wrote Hebrew fluently) and other such august topics.

In the winter of 1689 he announced news of the following:

> "a strange light and fire, which has been observed, and a great number of huge, fiery rocks, red as artificial light and glistening like stars, which have displayed themselves higher than the highest houses. Furthermore, and at the same time, an object has vanished from a stable on the Reguliersgracht, by the Botermarkt [the butter market], which had been described by all witnesses as a coffin in the colours of the rainbow, this object having shrunk together and then launched itself into the air in a fountain of fire."

His wife left him. Around this time he must have painted his message on the wall of his house – in blood, according to some sources, having cut his arms with a scalpel. One midwinter night, he got up and ran past the silent houses along the Amstel, raging and shouting, knocking and ringing at his neighbours' houses, in order to break the "incomprehensible lethargy of the inhabitants of the city". At last, on 12 May, he addressed a cri de cœur to the Church Council of the Mennonites in Amsterdam "from the depth of his downcast soul". In response, he was forced to leave his large house, had a custodial sentence assigned to him, and was more or less locked up in a back room of a small apartment on the Amstel. He died two years later, on 26 October 1693, leaving "a cloak and two Japanese robes", a bedstead, some chairs, a reading stand, an oval mirror, four old stools and a portrait of a man by Rembrandt, valued at seven guilders.[7]

Coenraad van Beuningen was a remarkable man. Before he began to suffer from his delusions, he was the very embodiment of the ideal Amsterdam merchant, the mercator sapiens, as Barlaeus had described him in his opening speech to the Amsterdam Athenaeum Illustre, the precursor of the University of Amsterdam. This ideal of a "wise merchant" was a model for

Amsterdam society, rather than the "clever merchant" or the "preaching merchant". The "wise merchant" had to be of good extraction, which would ensure that he knew best how to maintain the tradition of good service to the city from one generation to another; he had to be rich, or to marry a rich girl from a slightly lower class; and he had to participate in the culture of the elite, which involved speaking mainly French, with the odd Latin word or phrase thrown in, a world which knew well the Greek and Roman classics and which displayed a wide appreciation of poetry and painting.[8]

In Dutch vernacular, the words "regent" and "regent-like" are associated mainly with the authoritarian abuse of power. This perception, however, does no justice to the regents of the city of Amsterdam. Despite scandals and a degree of corruption, with the benefit of hindsight it cannot be denied that during the seventeenth century the city was administered exceptionally well. In particular, merchant–regent combination proved to be especially beneficial. Like a merchant, a good politician had to be able to run a large organization, to gauge the mood of his negotiating partners, to keep his nerve, to build up an efficient network, to evaluate information quickly, to understand the motives of his adversaries and to recognize hidden agendas; above all, he needed the skill to strike at the right moment, and to seek the best possible compromise.

During the seventeenth century this high school of trading supplied Amsterdam with several outstanding administrators. They organized the entire financial infrastructure of the city, kept foreign relations active, oversaw the digging of the canal belt, arranged for grain to be stored in order to alleviate famines, and established a system of orphanages and other charitable institutions without equal in Europe.

"The regent is a good citizen who takes on responsibilities", thus, the French historian Henri Méchoulan defined this phenomenon so characteristic of Amsterdam. A regent could stand at the helm of companies such as the VOC or the WIC, administrate an orphanage, be a magistrate or a burgomaster: at all events belonged to an all but silent elite which formed, in the words of Méchoulan, "the soul of the city".

The requirements asked of such a man were high. A good regent had to be Protestant, trustworthy, level-headed, intelligent, and well educated in the classics, the model of the virtuous and incorruptible Roman magistrate being the ideal. Wealth was an indispensable prerequisite, the best guarantee against a man succumbing to the great temptations of money and advancement.

Most Amsterdammers understood this in one way or another. If they had not, it would be impossible to explain how, over many years, the city administration was based on an elite network of wealthy men and this system was accepted without protest. The four burgomasters and 36 members of the council held in their hands the entire administration of Amsterdam, and had a great deal of power within the Republic. Moreover, their families had agreements, called "contracts of harmony", which allowed them to regulate the allocation of posts to an even greater degree. Once a regent had been appointed he rarely left the corridors of power, for there was always another position open to him. Naturally this nepotism led at times to excesses, but it had one great advantage: within the city there was a high level of administrative continuity, and the pool of potential candidates was of the highest calibre.[9]

Job Berckheyde (1630–93) *The Inner Courtyard of the Stock Exchange after Renovation* (1668).

All this notwithstanding, the system had slowly begun to change in the Year of Catastrophe, 1672, and the bloodstained scrawls of the *mercator sapiens*, Van Beuningen, are illustrative of this hiatus. The population understood that the war with France had been touch and go both for the Republic and for the existence of Amsterdam. Indicative of this loss of confidence is the collapse of the art market, especially painting, after 1672. Both Jan Vermeer and the art trader Uylenburg went bankrupt as a consequence of the cataclysmic events of that year. In truth, the zenith of the city's blossoming had passed, the unusual had become ordinary, the miracle of Amsterdam merely routine. What one might call "city nationalism", the great force that had allowed Amsterdam to oppose any foe during the Golden Age, became moderate. The elite began to look for new inspiration and new allies.

Unusually, in view of her antagonism, France became a new point of reference. Literature, theatre and architecture increasingly followed the fashion of the French Court. The younger members of the Amsterdam patrician class began to behave like minor courtiers: they wore wigs *à la mode*, spiced their language with French expressions and developed a "gallant" style of greeting others, promenading and making conversation. Coarse language was taboo, even at home.

These trends increased the gap between the ruling class, powdered and bewigged according to the taste of the international courts, and the rest of the population, which remained old-fashionedly Dutch. Some historians speak of an "aristocratization" of the patrician class, especially as it became increasingly difficult to gain admission to their circle. The process of segregation which had begun with the building of the canal belt became even more established during the eighteenth century. The city was partitioned into different cultures, and the administrative ethics preached on the Dam were inverted, for it was no longer a common language, religion and moral outlook shared with the population of the city that gave the regents the right to rule, but the very fact that they were different. Their legitimacy was derived not from their being identified with the responsible citizenship, but from their dissimilarity. It was no longer *citoyens* who ruled the city, but the *bourgeoisie*.[10]

In the city's power game, the clergy were the direct opponents of the regents, and nowhere was this opposition more clearly in evidence than in

Amsterdam's only theatre. The social life of the elite was concentrated within this building on the Keizersgracht, while outside, the preachers fulminated.

On the evening of Monday, 11 May 1672, there was a performance of *De kwalijk bewaarde dochter* (The Ill-Protected Daughter) before an audience of exquisitely dressed Amsterdam notables. At times during the second act, which was set in a dark dungeon, a smell of burning had been noticed. When the lights came on again for the third act and the blackout cones were removed from the burning candles, flames suddenly engulfed the stage. A terrible panic broke out in the auditorium. People jumped from the boxes and galleries, the scenery collapsed with a horrific thundering sound, the stairs and doors were soon blocked with a mass of bodies, one of the chandeliers fell from the ceiling into the crowd. Within half an hour the flames had broken through the roof, burning pieces of curtain flew through the air. The fire could be seen from well beyond Amsterdam, even from as far away as the island of Texel in the North Sea.

Eighteen people were killed in the fire, a surprisingly modest number under the circumstances. Among the dead were the enormously rich Jacob de Neufville van Lennep and his wife, and also a wealthy lady called Texeira de Mattos. "Considerable treasures such as jewels, gold, and other precious objects went missing," the Amsterdam merchant Jacob Bicker Raye noted in his diary, adding that "it was said about Lady Texeira that she had worn jewellery worth more than 20,000 guilders."

The disaster made an enormous impression on Amsterdammers, and the preachers seized their chance. In their eyes, the Year of Catastrophe was God's punishment for the immorality that was nightly displayed on the stage. On the following Sunday, one of the ministers preached Ezekiel (24: 10 and 11) presaging the destruction of Jerusalem: "Heap on wood, kindle the fire, consume the flesh, and spice it well, and let the bones be burned. Then set it empty upon the coals thereof, that the brass of it may be hot, and may burn, and that the filthiness of it may be molten in it, that the scum of it may be consumed." [11]

Relations between the city's merchants and religious elites were not good, that much was clear. Although preachers had started to play an important role in Amsterdam after the Synod of Dordrecht and the conflict between Remonstrants and contra-Remonstrants, they were never able to transform it into the theocracy they would have preferred. Moreover, the fanaticism and internecine feuds of the orthodox church leaders were widely suspected as serving first and foremost their own interests. During the period when the new Town Hall on the Dam was being built (it was started in 1648 and completed eight years later), the city administration had also planned to give the Nieuwe Kerk an impressive new southern façade. In doing so, they were seeking to bring the authority of the town magistrates in line with that of the church – at least in architectural terms. The clergy, however, wanted more: they demanded that the tower of the Nieuwe Kerk be raised high above the cupola of the Town Hall, thereby demonstrating the supremacy of God's power on earth, and that was how the plans were drawn up in the end. That the mighty tower was never actually built speaks volumes.

While Calvinism was the recognized religion of the State, that was the extent of its power in Amsterdam, for the city's merchant mentality was still diametrically opposed to any form of religious coercion. Rembrandt was allowed to choose not to be a member of any church at all, and, uniquely in Europe, marriages contracted other than in church were recognized by the city administration as legally valid and regarded as quite normal. "Apart from Jews, Anabaptists are living here in all freedom, as well as Mennonites, Sozinites, Arrians, Borelists, Enthusiasts, Libertines, Sceptics, and Spinozists", wrote the Swiss military man Stoppa in a French pamphlet.[12] A comment which Amsterdammers took as a compliment. Officially the "papal mass" was seen as "a cursed ungodliness", but in practice nobody opposed, and far less persecuted, the Catholics in any way, provided they paid their annual "demonstration of politeness" to magistrates and bailiffs.* While again, officially, the Catholics were in hiding and held masses in clandestine chapels with poetic names such as "Our Lord in the Attic" (the building, now the Museum Amstelkring, can still be visited), these buildings had large organs installed in them and the singing of mass and vespers was audible from a good distance away, as recorded by several contemporaries.[13] It was also widely known that a number of prominent Amsterdammers were Roman Catholics,

---

* Catholics would pay sweeteners to the authorities to persuade them to turn a blind eye to their religious meetings.

among them the poet Joost van den Vondel, the sculptor Rombout Verhulst, and the architects Philip Vingboons and Hendrick de Keyser; the latter, incidentally, had designed the city's three most important Protestant churches.

After 1650, the power of the clergy within the city somewhat increased. Under the influence of economic depression, the Anglo-Dutch Wars of 1652–3 and 1664–7, a terrible plague epidemic, and other things commonly perceived as God's wrath, Calvinism enjoyed a sort of renaissance. The struggle against immorality in general, and the stage in particular, was once more being vigorously fought, and it was during this period that Hendrickje Stoffels was arraigned before the Church Council and Vondel had big problems on account of his play, Lucifer. In 1655, the well-known surgeon Dr Tulp succeeded in pushing through a "luxury law" against excessive wedding celebrations, although this was not exceptionally draconian: the number of guests could not exceed 50 and festivities were not allowed to last longer than two days. In December 1663, Tulp and his camp went one step further: they prohibited the selling of the traditional Saint Nicholas gingerbread figures as "idolatry" and "papist perversion". The result was a small children's riot, and the ban was hastily lifted.[14] Amsterdam remained first and foremost a trading city, not a religious one, where there was only one creed that was regarded as universally valid: negotiation.

Let us return to the place where most of these disputes took place: the typical Amsterdam house. It was a textbook example of the principle that limitations always offer new possibilities. As the ground on which the city was built was so soft, the stone side walls of town houses had to rest on solid foundations. The façades, however, had no separate foundation and were, so to speak, hung from the timber framework that supported the house. Given the small plots into which the city was divided, combined with the fact that good building ground was a rare commodity, the Amsterdam house was, of necessity, a curiously flexible entity. Even now, after three or even four centuries, these houses are very much sought after, something which cannot be said of many types of accommodation.

The external appearance of a house could be changed radically, while by and large the interior stayed the same. Over the centuries, countless new façades have been appended to houses, invariably according to the ruling fashion of the day. The stepped gable was superseded by the so-called neck or bell gable, and in about 1700 the horizontal gable became fashionable, often embellished with ornaments and balustrades. During the second half of the seventeenth century, windows became larger, broader, higher and different in style. Shutters vanished. Roof-trees came and went. Sometimes, as has been said, the roof of a building was simply pushed up and another floor added in the space beneath.

All these changes, and many others, left their mark on the city. Neither the proportions nor the colours of the Amsterdam of today are in any way those of the city during the eighteenth century. The brick façades were not black or left in natural colours, as so many are now, but were painted red, while unrendered stone façades were of yellowish colour. Doors were usually red, later ochre or brown. As to the proportions, it was especially the heightening of the houses that changed the character of the city, for it left streets seeming both smaller and darker. Squares like the Dam and the Rembrandtplein, which in old prints can be seen to have been rather grandly proportioned, are now out of proportion because of the higher houses, and as a result appear smaller and more hemmed in than they were earlier.

Inside, the high, spacious front room of medieval times had contracted into a very small space. A side chamber was built next to it, making it possible to live adjacent to the street. The front house would shrink even further, becoming a hall, from which a long corridor led to the inner room or salon, a large reception area at the back of the house. Behind the house there was usually a garden which, especially by the canals, was often large and of very elaborate design.

The Amsterdam canal house has long been a beacon of shining, polished orderliness in a chaotic world. From the late sixteenth to mid-seventeenth centuries, furnishings were typically Dutch, just as we know them from the paintings of Rembrandt, Vermeer, Jan Steen, and others. Rooms were furnished sparsely and in dark colours, the floors downstairs often tiled with stone slabs, the pine planks upstairs strewn with sand, the walls plastered.

After 1672, French fashion also began to gain a hold over Amsterdam interiors. Plasterwork was hidden behind gilded leather wall hangings, floor tiles by marble or thick rugs, the first stucco made its appearance on ceilings, walls were painted, increasingly expensive wood was used, and more and more pieces of furniture came into the house.

The country house also gained in importance. Rich Amsterdammers would now retreat from the noise and stench of the city to their estates on the banks of the River Amstel and Vecht, on the coastal dunes or around the Beemster, de Purmer and Watergraaf lakes. In 1742, the number of summer houses had reached about 600, and those who could not afford a house would try at least to have a small *pied-a-terre* or a tea pavilion by the Buitensingel (later the Stadhouderskade), or by the Gein or the Haarlemmertrekvaart. Eventually it became customary among the patrician class to move house by barge twice a year, taking with them all their staff and a large part of their possessions. Thus each May Day the wealthy left for their summer houses, returning to the city in September. Out of town, they spent their time in outings, visits to friends on nearby estates and breeding different sorts of plants. At the end of the seventeenth century a society lady succeeded in rearing a pineapple plant, and an administrator of the VOC had growing in his conservatory a coffee bush and a real banana tree.[15] Exotic birds, brought from the colonies, stalked the lawns, and Dutch literature began to spill over with arcadian scenes, poems about shepherds and bowers and suchlike.

Adriaan Artmann, *River Scene* (1755).

Some people even went so far as to connect their names with their country estates, in imitation of the nobility. Most patrician Amsterdammers regarded this as going a step too far, however. They remained typical townspeople, and never forgot that they were citizens of a republic.

"The image presented by eighteenth-century Amsterdam is more one of refined consolidation than of vigorous development," writes Brugmans. "Continuous effort was not required in order to rise in society. People who felt that they had reached the top could choose to devote themselves to the conservation of the fruits of their labours." [16]

The city had reached its limits.

Hendrick Dubbels (c. 1621–76), The Amstel River in Winter with Blockhouses (c. 1650).

The eighteenth century was the century of cold and of the Great Frost. A remarkably large number of winters were severe and lasted for long months, so that today, climatologists even speak of a little Ice Age. It was no coincidence that every rich Amsterdam family kept a horse sleigh, or that so many panoramas of the city in winter were painted during these years. The icy cold regularly swept across the canals, and on the IJ the moored ships froze to the pilings. In drawings and prints we see the quays under ice, the roofs of shops and houses thick with snow. In one by Reiner Vinkeles, *De Amstel bij de Berebijt*, a peasant girl walks a tow-path, her shawl flapping in the stiff easterly wind.[17] It is afternoon, and the birds flying above the bare trees presage another flurry of snow.

On 8 January 1767 the Amsterdam merchant Jacob Bicker Raye noted in his diary: "It is bitterly cold, and freezing so strongly that, even as I write and despite the large fire blazing beside me, the ink is freezing in my pen." By no means badly off, Bicker Raye was, one could say, a prototype of the well-situated middle classes during the eighteenth century. He did not belong to the patrician class, but was close enough to it to have a few lucrative posts pushed his way, positions that involved very little work. He was an auctioneer at the fish market on the Dam, a job which he paid a locum to do for him, but for which he raked in a certain percentage. He was captain of one of the militias, the collector of taxes on coal and peat, and a bookkeeper for the grain register. He lived for some time on the Herengracht, and then later on the Keizersgracht, near the Hartenstraat.

His diary, which he kept between 1732 and 1772, is full of daily news:

— Johan Dusard became blind because of a playful lady to whom he offered some tobacco and who hit the snuffbox so hard that the tobacco flew up into his eyes. If he wasn't completely blind after this incident, he was after seeing the doctor.
— In one of the work houses the chimneysweep accidentally fell into a pot of boiling water. They ripped off his clothes and brushed his whole body with rape seed oil.
— The secretary of the town magistrate, Nicolaas van Strijen, has eloped with the wife of a wine merchant.
— A girl of 17 fell out of the window on the Niewendijk. She lost her balance as she was pulling up the laundry, fell, and was smashed to pieces.
— Lady De Haan, who had taken leave of her senses ever since her husband died, was "trepanned" – "an abscess was extracted success-fully" – and when the operation was complete, she was dead.

— At the Botermakt [butter market] fair, a young "rhinosteros" was exhibited, a novel attraction, "an enormously heavy-built beast".

— A Spanish sailor emasculated himself with a razor out of despair, when "after having visited the prostitutes, he came back unhappy".

— In the Nes area, an old woman on her way back home was hit by a falling beam and killed, leaving her husband in a deadly state of sorrow. "These old folks loved each other so much; he threw his arms around her so violently that the gathering crowd had to pull him away."

— Lady de Marquette was taken to her grave at the Oude Kerk with a six-horse coach after a very strange illness which had "left her without stool for 35 days, and thus she had to get rid of her food through her mouth".

— A Jew sentenced to death would not listen to the minister, and thus he died like a beast, "crying horribly on the scaffold".

Bicker Raye led the life of a gossiping civil servant, lived with his mother for many years, complaining about his gout, and had little interest in science, literature, or the arts; to him, not even the visit of the ten-year-old prodigy Wolfgang Amadeus Mozart to Amsterdam in 1766, a great sensation, was worth the ink. One of his few entertainments was visiting public executions. Most of his little snippets of news were probably picked up from his drinking comrades in the civic militia house on the Singel, the Garnalendoelen (today the University Library), and in his diary we can still read of the rumours and backbiting of his day.[18]

Here, for instance, is a description of the partial collapse of a house on the Haarlemmerplein during a funeral dinner, orators and drunken guests alike crashing through the floor and "rolling helter-skelter like a pot of pears, the table and glasses and bottles all broken". Or the story of the cobbler who drowned in the Nieuwezijds Voorburg behind the Town Hall because he had been "wanting to relieve himself. He took off his trousers and fell into the water as he was suffering from dropsy quite badly." Here too are details of a curious early case of euthanasia: a child bitten by a rabid dog had been declared beyond help by doctors and "smothered with permission of the government".

Elsewhere, Bicker Raye writes of a man's head, wrapped in a white napkin, that had been fished out of the Amstel near the Hoedenmakerspad. An 86-year-old Swedish sea captain was arrested, convicted for the crime and sentenced to be broken on the wheel. Death held no fear for him, however: at his execution he jumped on to the cross and helpfully stretched out his arms and legs himself. Bicker Raye also tells the story of the mad wife of a wig maker in the Kalverstraat who had been locked in the attic, as "naked as her mother had given birth to her". One day the corpse of a newborn baby was discovered with her. It transpired that she had been pregnant without anybody noticing, and had murdered the child immediately after its birth. The wig maker had later declared that "he had not been with her for many years, and that she must have got the affliction from a servant". Other scandals and yet more gossip abound. The wine merchant Paling, for instance, was notorious for the vast quantities of food he would put away: "He could eat with great appetite a piece of fried beef of seven or eight pounds, a whole leg of mutton was nothing to him, thirty smoked herrings from the IJ baked in a pan with a large plate of apple cake was like a child's game, and even when he had eaten well he could still devour three poults, while six bottles of red wine meant little to him." Eventually, Paling would stagger drunkenly into the Leidsegracht one autumn night, and thereby meet his maker.

The Amsterdam of Bicker Raye was no longer a booming international centre but a large, self-satisfied, bitching, pipe-smoking provincial town. The "incomprehensible lethargy" against which Coenraad van Beuningen had ranted and raved by night along the Amstel and the Herengracht had increasingly enveloped the city after 1672. England, France, Prussia, and Austria had developed into absolute monarchies with effective administrations and strongly directed economies. The Republic was too divided and chaotic for an organized State system. There was no suggestion of solid economic and military policies. For decades, no stadtholder who would counterbalance the power of the Amsterdam regents had been appointed. Hence the latter carried on giving posts and positions to family, friends, and business contacts who were prepared to pay for the privilege. This in turn threw the rest of the administration off balance. The most modern state in Europe had been arrested in its development, and after one and a half centuries of blossoming much of seventeenth-century Holland was atrophying, besides being superceded.

Business life was ailing. Holland's great advantages – its outstanding waterways, cheap labour and energy, a large fleet, and a never-ending stream of basic materials and half-finished goods –had been acquired or otherwise neutralized by other countries. The once superior Dutch technology became more and more antiquated: during the seventeenth century England had still been glad to copy the fast and manoeuvrable *fluits* of the Dutch, but a century later, shipbuilders in Holland had fallen hopelessly behind the times. By then, English shipyards were much more advanced, especially in the building of three-deck ships and in the cladding of hulls with copper.[19]

For Amsterdam, all this was compounded by the problems of its harbour. Quite apart from anything else, this had always been difficult to reach. Ships approached the city through the Zuiderzee and the IJ, but, depending on the direction of the wind, they sometimes had to lie off for days if not weeks in the shallows near the small island of Pampus. In addition, land reclamation and the building of pilings in the water had caused the IJ to silt up with sand, and it was only thanks to several ingenious inventions, such as horse treadmills powering dredgers, that sufficient depth for seagoing vessels could be maintained near the city.

Amsterdam's pre-eminence during the seventeenth century had not been based on a large and strong land base, but on the fact that its position was advantageous for international trade. This, however, left the city vulnerable, so that when London and Hamburg developed harbours that were more easily accessible, they took over Amsterdam's role. Both had large hinterlands which increasingly began to produce goods for export, something Amsterdam had always been without. The change in the international streaming of goods meant that they were more and more often brought directly from the place of production to the place of consumption, depriving Amsterdam of its value as a transit harbour. The market spread, and as it did so the city lost its key position.

Furthermore, this economic decline was compounded by the fact that many nations closed their borders to foreign produce, a factor that especially affected agriculture and fishing. France, the southern Netherlands, Prussia, and Denmark stopped the import of Dutch herring, causing not only fishermen to lose their livelihoods but also herring packers, shipbuilders, sailmakers, ropemakers, and many others.

All this does not mean that Amsterdam did not remain an important trading city during the eighteenth century. It was, albeit now in competition with London and Hamburg, still a vital focus for international trade, a place in which enormous sums of money circulated and where merchants of many countries could meet one another. What had changed, however, was the character of trading. During the economic boom of the seventeenth century the capital sums amassed in the city were such that it became much more lucrative for merchants to lend money than to bear trading risks themselves. Princes and governments, the Emperor of Austria and even the Bank of England borrowed from Amsterdam on a grand scale. By the end of the eighteenth century about 500 million guilders had been invested abroad. When the economy of the country went into recession many of Amsterdam's leading regents continued to invest abroad, nor was any authority in a position to stop them doing so. The Amsterdam merchant had metamorphosed from an active trader into a passive broker; in short, he became a banker. The nature of trade had shifted, veering towards a culture of living off interest, so that the middle classes began to regard consumption, rather than production, as central to their lives.

Hendrick Cornelis Vroom (1566–1640), *The IJ* (1608).

Although the rich, sober Laurens Laurenszoon Reael, with his heavy stick, differs from the bewigged, powdered Jacob Bicker Raye as night does from day, only a century divides the two men. Details listed in the "Personal Tax Contributions" from 1742 show that among the taxpayers of Amsterdam, "investor" is the profession most frequently given. Further, the register holds 1,111 merchants, 760 publicans, 472 bakers, 392 wine merchants, 327 tobacco shops, 220 greengrocers, 209 joiners and carpenters, 199 surgeons, 198 book keepers, and 184 simple shopkeepers.

Those who paid most tax, the wealthiest group of citizens, consisted of 23 shareholders (rentiers), 30 merchants, 30 city administrators, and only three brewers and one manufacturer.[20] For all its wealth, however, the shareholding Amsterdam sought a quiet existence. The rich kept themselves occupied with politics, literature, painting, science and music, founded clubs and societies, and spent a great deal of time complying with a complicated set of social obligations: visits, meals, parties, the theatre, walks, journeys.

As in every moneyed culture, its members found themselves more or less obliged to do nothing; after all, one had to be able to demonstrate that one could live off one's interest and yet still be both able and willing to spend a lot. Language, manner, and dress were used in such a way as to differentiate oneself from those who were unlucky enough to have to work for a living. It is therefore not surprising that the literature of the century that followed the advent of this culture is obsessed with acquiring a fortune by marriage or inheritance in order to be able to join this group of the privileged unemployed.

There remains, however, the question of the extent to which the rentier culture influenced the life of the city. In their novel De historie van mejuffrouw Sara Burgerhart (The History of Miss Sara Burgerhart), the eighteenth-century female writers Bertje Wolff and Aagje Deken portrayed Amsterdam merchant families as they found them. Their characters, Jan and Hendrik Edeling, however, do anything but live off unearned income: they labour away in their offices, often travel to Papist lands, and their colleague, Abraham Blankaard, is a hard worker, "a fine negotiator, a lover of the fatherland and very keen on his own church".[21] In many respects, Amsterdam had remained a dynamic city. Towards the end of the seventeenth century,

Commelin described the hustle and bustle by the Hoge Sluis in the Amstel, near today's Amstel Hotel. He saw a river almost too narrow "to let the bobbing market barges from the neighbouring villages through, which came laden with butter, cheese, eggs, chickens, ducks, river fish, and other goods, depending on what the season would yield". There were other boats, too: pleasure craft, peat barges, boats "bringing all manner of vegetables, milk, and other refreshments", as well as "a constant toing and froing of vessels carrying travellers, coming from and going to Muiden, Weesp, Naarden, Utrecht, Gouda, Delft, The Hague, and Rotterdam". In Bicker Raye's century this scene had changed little: some 800 boat services left every week from Amsterdam alone, carrying passengers and goods to 180 different destinations.

The archives hold countless pieces of evidence from the day-to-day life of the city which also serve to put into perspective the image of the sedate period of wigs and indolent luxury: ships were continually laden with cargo and equipped with provisions, the stock exchange worked overtime, and Amsterdam's merchants busied themselves trying to retain their city's central position, and to broaden it if possible. It was typical, for instance, that Amsterdam should have so energetically pursued a connection with the newly founded United States, in search of fresh trading links. The risk, a new war with Britain, was cheerfully accepted; something that one would not have expected of a group of merchants who had mothballed their ambition.

There were excesses, or course. With so much capital amassed in the city some strange surges of speculation occasionally gripped its traders, although this was not peculiar to the eighteenth century alone. Famously, in 1636, the trading index of tulip bulbs had rocketed in Amsterdam and throughout the rest of Holland. Originally imported from Turkey, tulips had suddenly become all the rage, and though the average bulb sold for about three guilders, the price for a particular species might easily soar to two or even three thousand guilders. After a while, it was no longer the bulbs themselves that were sold, but an image, an ideal; the names and colourful pictures that went with them: the "Image of Perfection", the "Royal Agate", the "Admiral van Enckhuysen", and the absolute prize, "Semper Augustus". Thanks to old drawings we know how sophisticated this tulip looked: impeccably white petals with small veins of a fiery ruby-red running through them, the base of the bloom as blue as the skies. The price of this transient joy? 5,000 guilders, equivalent to the cost of a house with a large garden.[22]

Jacob Marrell, *Four Tulips and an Anemone*, drawing on parchment (c. 1640).

A century later another speculative craze seized Amsterdam. In the coffee houses people began to buy shares in spurious companies trading in the most strange and fantastical wares. This so-called "wind trade" resulted in a number of bankruptcies, workers were laid off, and an angry crowd stormed the most important trading centre after the stock exchange, the Quincampoix coffee-house in the Kalverstraat. Indeed, the situation became so threatening that the authorities had to step in to restore order and normality to the city's commercial life.

Despite these incidents, the behaviour of the average *rentier* was not characterized by extravagance. The richest woman in Bicker Raye's Amsterdam, the widow Pels on the Herengracht, kept no more than five servants, although her fortune exceeded those of many princes or dukes. While a good number of the houses alongside the canals displayed considerable pomp and splendour on the inside, they maintained their sober façades. The wealth of Amsterdam was a banking wealth, in which the display of luxury was turned in upon itself, something that has not changed much even today.

Excessive flamboyance was never – and is still not – highly regarded by the Dutch bourgeoisie. Money was first and foremost capital for business and family, a basis for later generations to build on. The amassed fortune had to be maintained or enlarged in order to allow children and grandchildren to remain part of the elite. Moreover, the trading tradition of Holland was not one of fighting financial battles. In general, investors were quite content with low but long-term profit, which was repeated and followed by new activities. The trading capital of the Dutch Republic was essentially the result of an accumulation of countless little advantages, rarely ever the fruit of a grand gesture.

Without fail, foreigners professed themselves amazed at the frugality of Amsterdam. In the canal belt during the eighteenth century, it was required to live in a certain style, but to throw money about was absolutely not done. Life was lived within strict rules; thus, Sunday would entail a promenade in the afternoon, perhaps another small walk in the evening along the Hoge Sluis and across the Amstel. Here, the Dutch lover, at least according to the Marquis de Sade, who visited Amsterdam in 1769, "portenteously declares his love after having smoked a little pipe. And the object of his affections is likely to be glad about it, for how would she know that such matters can be any different?"

As I have already mentioned, the eighteenth century was the century of the Snow Queen. Take the winter of 1740. On 5 January Jacob Bicker Raye noted that the frost was so severe that people had taken to skating on the canals. On the 22nd, it was possible to drive a coach and four across the IJ, and the diarist himself went for a spin in his carriage across the Amstel to Ouderkerk. By now the ice was so thick that the ice-breaker could no longer get through. The ice-breaker was an enormous contraption which was pulled along the canals, with much groaning and cracking of ice, by 20 horses in order to free a passage for the barges which delivered fresh drinking water to the brewers and the remainder of the city, the water in the canals being practically raw sewage. Faced with this difficulty, the brewers planned to have freshwater ice sawed by hand at Weesp and the blocks transported back overland. Meanwhile, the most water-rich city in Europe was suffering from an acute shortage of drinking water. If any was to be had, people would pay as much as two *stivers* for a bucket of it. There was even a small-scale rebellion against the high price of drinking water.

On 23 January, Bicker Raye records that it is so cold that Master Hendrik de Veer, watching the fruitless attempts to get the ice-breaker going on the Amstel, had caught a chill so severe that his bowels became blocked and he died the following day. A few days later, an entire house burned down because it proved impossible to keep open a hole in the ice so as to draw water and extinguish the flames. In February there was a brief thaw, but then the bitter cold returned. Bicker Raye writes that letters from South Holland had reached him far too late because the post horse had fallen on the way and had frozen to death. Even as late as 3 May it was still bleak and cold. Vegetables and grass were nowhere to be seen, the hay was almost used up. Hay prices were at 30 to 40 guilders for 100 pounds, and a week later they had tripled. The wind kept blowing from the north, everywhere the ground remained frozen and barren. Hundreds of cattle starved to death – for a time they had been fed on rye bread, but that soon proved too expensive as well.

Poverty was especially severe in the countryside during these years. The slump affecting trade, agriculture and fishing resulted in the exodus from the smaller cities of a large proportion of their inhabitants; a quarter in the case of Gouda and Delft, one third in Leiden, almost half in Haarlem. Hoards of beggers roamed across the north Holland flatlands, while decommissioned soldiers and seasonal workers joined forces and plundered farms by night. The most famous of these master thieves, known as Sjakoo (Shako), was a popular hero comparable with Robin Hood in the poorer districts of Amsterdam. Even a century and a half later people would reverently point out his house on the Elandsgracht, saying "This is Shako's fort". His working methods were legendary. Extremely professional, he was said to fly through the land like a phantom, striking once in, say, Groningen, then in Gouda, then in Amsterdam. In addition to this he was, as his neighbours would attest many years after his death, "a noble man who would only steal from the rich".

His apartment was in a large building, a "fort" as the Amsterdammers put it, a structure full of secret passages and exits, which, two centuries later, its inhabitants would proudly show off to visitors. Several times Shako managed to stage spectacular escapes, but in Amsterdam in 1717 he was finally caught, "lying in bed with his accomplice, Griet Lammers", in an inn called De Gulden Wagen on the Haarlemmerdijk. He was sentenced to be "broken on the wheel from the feet up and so to remain alive one half-hour, whereafter his head is to be severed from his body."[23]

In Amsterdam poverty was also on the increase, though probably less severely than elsewhere. In 1654, only one in eight beggars in the workhouse came from the city itself, a hundred years later it had risen to one in three. The number of foundlings rose from 15 in 1691 to almost 500 in 1800.

Bicker Raye relates an incident in which an unknown woman, "very heavily pregnant but still doing hard work", had given birth in the street on the Rokin and would have simply walked away, had not some street children forced her to return to her baby. In the cold January of 1738, he writes of an inn where some 40 corpses were stacked up, all people pulled out from underneath the ice. He also notes a number of suicides, people who had fallen on hard times and despaired of ever being able to make a living again.

The Jewish community was especially heavily hit by poverty. The stagnation of trade in the city caused great hardship among the Sephardic Jews, and in 1799 more than half of them lived by begging. At the same time, thousands of Ashkenazic Jews had come to the city, fleeing pogroms in Germany and Poland. While at the beginning of the eighteenth century the Jewish community formed less than three per cent of the Amsterdam population, by the end of the century it accounted for almost ten per cent. The new arrivals from Eastern Europe, who quickly came to form the majority of Amsterdam's Jews, did not have the same trading contacts as the Sephardim, and most professions were closed to them; many found themselves compelled to deal in second-hand goods in the local markets. At the end of the eighteenth century, two in three German Jews in Amsterdam lived off Jewish charity, a figure twice as high as among non-Jews.

The only branch of commerce in which Jews were able to work in any great numbers was the diamond industry, as diamond workers did not have to be members of a guild. In 1748, when the diamond trade was going through a period of recession, Christian diamond workers attempted to found a guild for themselves in order to eliminate the Jewish competition. The city administration, however, could not muster any enthusiasm for such a plan. The Jews "had established the trade in diamonds in this city", they wrote; moreover they feared that the industry would quickly die off without Jewish skill. Large Jewish families were indeed in a better position to import Brazilian diamonds on a grand scale, and to have them split and cut, even though they were paid a pittance and working conditions were terrible.

Hermanus Petrus Schouten, *The Portuguese Synagogue* (1770).

The majority of the Jews lived on the islands of Uilenburg, Rapenburg and Marken, the area we know today as Niewmarkt area. After the wharves had moved to the newly reclaimed islands of Kattenburg, Wittenburg and Oostenburg during the seventeenth century, the Ashkenazim in particular established themselves on these abandoned industrial areas. Rich Jews eventually moved towards the newly continued canals on the eastern side of Amsterdam, the Nieuwe Prinsengracht, Nieuwe Keizersgracht and Nieuwe Herengracht, which were not as sought after by non-Jewish Amsterdammers because of their location.[24] Most of the Jews, however, stayed behind in the passages and alleyways of the "old" islands.

This was the beginning of the Jodenbreestraat, the half-voluntary ghetto, a "labyrinth of narrow, filthy streets with ancient houses which look as if they would collapse at a single kick against their walls", as one traveller was later to describe it.[25] All around, torn shirts, ripped trousers and mended skirts dangled from washing lines between the damp walls. Merchandise was laid out in front of the house doors: "fragments of furniture, parts of weapons, devotional objects, scraps of uniforms, the remains of tools, and remnants of toys, old ironwork, broken earthenware, frills, rags, all sorts of things that do not have a name in any human tongue." The area seemed to be one large oriental market in which everything happened openly on the street. "Women bake fish in small ovens, girls cradle small infants, men mill around in their old things." It was a "Babel of filthiness", our traveller found, and was so glad to leave the quarter that, having returned to one of the canals, he recorded his enjoyment of breathing in the "invigorating tarry air" of Amsterdam.

For the poorest Amsterdammers there were always two means of escaping their lot, both quite common, although tantamount to suicide. Men could enlist on one of the VOC ships bound for the East Indies, women could sell their souls as prostitutes.

The recruiting of hands for the Dutch East India Company's ships was usually carried out by so-called *zielverkopers* or "soul merchants". These plucked men off the streets and provided them with food and shelter until such time as the VOC made it known, amid much drumming and trumpeting, that it needed men. The soul merchants then put down the names of their "guests" as crew and pocketed most of the premium as payment for their lodging. Large sums of money were earned in this way, and most of the seamen were kept in a state of constant debt, no matter how hard they worked. The governors of orphanages and workhouses also regularly supplied additional manpower to the VOC.

On the voyage to Asia, the sailors died in their hundreds. They would fall from the masts, be swept overboard, murdered by pirates, contract scurvy, malaria or dysentery, or would go down with their ships. Between 1701 and 1800, a total of 671,000 paupers, sailors, bankrupt sons of wealthy merchants, fugitive farmers, and adventurers set sail from the Montelbaanstoren for the East Indies. An unknown Amsterdam author described how a *bak* — one of the eight-man units into which the crew of a VOC ship was divided — was assembled, and how its members ate together, bought provisions together, and often developed a strong personal bond among themselves. The ship was due to set out on its voyage in 1751. Among this *bak* were the sons of a silversmith, the son of a tailor, the son of butcher, the son of a baker, and the son of a debt collector for the Van Lening bank, "and each one told of a misfortune which compelled him to leave". During a great storm they had to go up into the rigging in order to secure the sails, something which so frightened the author of the memoir that he "shivered like a lady's dog in the cold . . . I thought to myself: 'Had I only known that, I would have taken care to stay by the old home fire'." [26]

One in ten deck hands would not even survive the outward-bound journey. One in every 25 ships would sink on its way back from the West Indies. Of the 671,000 men who travelled out from Amsterdam, only 266,000 were to return.

Whaling, too, was extraordinarily risky. Amsterdam merchants had built train-oil boilers near Spitsbergen in the Barents Sea, but because of the severity of the winter temperatures, hunting ships could operate there only in spring and summer. An experiment to set up a permanent settlement on the island had met with fatal results. When the ships had returned in spring, they had found the winter crew of seven men frozen to death. Their last log entry had been: "We are lying in the bunk with four men, the only ones left alive. We want to eat, but nobody has got the strength to light a fire. We cannot move because of pain. We implore God with faithful hands to rescue us from this terrible world." [27]

In 1980, the skeleton of a Dutch whaler, probably a harpooner, was found on the island. He had died aged 68, and his body displayed astonishing injuries, including fractures, with which he had survived for many years. Both his legs had been damaged, the right being stiff, most likely due to a fall from a mast, he had broken ribs on both sides, broken (and more or less mended) shinbones, a wrist which had been fractured and had healed at a strange angle, and several broken bones in his hand. Accident after accident, danger after danger had been survived by this man who had been as tough as a wild animal.

Then there was the woman's way out of poverty: prostitution. There is no traveller's account of the Amsterdam that does not mention its loose morals. In 1634 an English officer noted to his surprise that he was greeted by many of the ladies on the Haarlemmerstraat as if they had been old friends. He was patted on his shoulder and tugged by his jacket, and asked in a very seductive way whether he wanted to pop upstairs with them. The French comedian Jean François Regnard wrote in 1681 that after Paris there was probably no place on earth that showed less restraint than Amsterdam,[28] and when Prince Eugenius of Savoy, the Governor of the Southern Netherlands, visited the city in 1722, he did not rest until, together with a Sir Renard, he had visited the pleasure house of Madame Traëse. Once there, he let all the ladies pass by in a grand parade, and found it "the greatest pleasure to look at them thoroughly from behind and from in front". A drawing of this scene is still preserved: Sir Renard and the Prince (wearing a tricorn hat and smoking a long clay pipe) are on the right, laughing. On the left, seven women are walking by, their skirts gathered up high, baring their buttocks, some slim, others plump and more curvaceous, processing in a circle.

In its morals, the city had a unique character, a hint of freedom about it, so that even the sophisticated hedonist Casanova was surprised to see the independence with which women walked about in Amsterdam unchaperoned. Around the turn of the year 1759, he stayed with Burgomaster Hooft and was lost for words when he was sent to the theatre with the burgomaster's beautiful daughter – alone and in a closed carriage. "I know that it is not customary elsewhere for a girl to go out with a man unaccompanied," the 14-year-old Hester Hooft remarked, "but here we learn to be independent." When Casanova attempted to kiss her hand she asked "Why my hand?" She instead offered him her lips and, as he wrote in his memoirs, "she gave me a kiss that went straight to my heart. However, when she told me that she would do the same in the presence of her father, should I enjoy it, I did not pursue the matter any further."[29]

Still, most of the evident easy virtue in the city had nothing to do with freedom and everything with poverty, despair, and powerlessness.

Somewhere in his diary, Jacob Bicker Raye mentions the death of a certain Jan Standent, a "great and accomplished cotton printer" who left, apart from money, "more than 25 bastards, which he had manufactured with several cotton printer's maids among others."[30] Apart from this, Bicker Raye also records a little problem in a charitable orphanage, where 13 of the girls had all fallen pregnant at the same time. They were immediately sent to the spinning house.

In his book *The Embarrassment of Riches*, Simon Schama sketches the profile of the Amsterdam prostitute using court records of the time.[31] Most were aged between 18 and 30, many from villages and towns in Holland, others from Friesland, Germany, Denmark, or the Southern Netherlands, and had often come to town to work as seamstresses or maids. All too frequently they had lost their positions because they had fallen pregnant, and afterwards they tried to keep themselves and their children alive by prostituting themselves. Most of them quickly acquired nicknames: Catryn Davids from Copenhagen was better known as "The Northern Cat", Annetje Hendricx was nicknamed "Anna in the Stall", and 50-year-old Madame Catalyn Laurens was better known as "Sweetie Cunt". In the context of the Amsterdam flesh trade, Simon Schama speaks of a "sexual commodities market", a mirror image of the more legal financial trading. The vendors of sexual services followed the same patterns as their mercantile colleagues: the staple income came from the trade with the Baltic and with the hinterland of the German river plains, and there were seasonal, albeit unreliable, highs when the East India fleets returned from their trips, bringing with them their celebrating "six-week gentlemen", who blew their wages in no time at all and then had to go back to sea. "In the moral economy of the Dutch Republic, the whorehouse, with its own family hierarchy, language and habits, was a kind of anti-home, one in which the control functions of domesticity had been turned on their head," writes Schama. "Instead of home filtering out the dirt of the world, as all true burghers endeavoured to guarantee, the *bordeel* was a place where the world (and its devil, said the preachers) made the comforts." [32]

Like the sailors, most prostitutes had run up debts in order to be able to afford to "kit themselves out" in expensive clothes and jewellery, debts which most of them would struggle to pay off for the rest of their lives. Such a situation all too often displayed the characteristics of genuine slavery, as, for instance, when one madam sold a prostitute, debts and all, to another.

All over Amsterdam there were music halls, or *musicos*, where many of the prostitutes plied their trade, people danced to the sound of hurdy-gurdies, reed organs, and Jewish fiddlers, and the hits of the day were dances or songs like "Haagse Kermis" (Hague Fair), "Koolslaatje" (Cabbage Salad), and "Een Posje met een Pietersijltje" (A Parsley Posey). The girls here did "what could be expected of a Venus who had accepted gifts". There was even a gay equivalent of the *musico* trade: the so-called *Lolhuizen* (fun houses), although often under the guise of agencies for male domestic servants.[33] The unknown Amsterdam author who has already been quoted describes with gusto the "Jewish warehouses" of about 1750, where young and old came together to sing "the most light-hearted songs like nightingales" and which were full "as if church were about to begin". The music halls on the Jordaan also held a great allure for him. In the Huis van Mirakelen (House of Miracles) near the Franse Pad – now the Willemsstraat – he was picked up one evening by a woman who took him along to a shelter for the homeless called De Gekroonde Naarheid (Crowned Misery), where he learned many things: "There were those who went on crutches when on the street, but who here walked without. Lame or crippled or blind people who played the fiddle for money were the musicians for the dance. There were also flute players, oboists, and womenfolk who went out into the street at night to make a little money. They all had their meal here. One had pig's knuckles with white bread, another smoked meat with salmon, others again ate boiled meat. They all had as much to drink as they could have wished." He adds, with some pardonable exaggeration: "I was not surprised any more that the city had so many beggars. I believe that if everyone knew that so much was being eaten here, we would have as many again." The day's adventures were recounted by the fireside and information swapped about the best places for begging: the Herengracht and the Keizersgracht, the Buitenkant, where the North Hollanders and the travellers were usually generous, and in the thoroughfares, but "there one really has to be blind, lame, or a cripple, and not just apparently, but genuinely so," and one had to cry out loud "that God will repay you ten times over."[34]

So began the year 1763, the year of the Great Frost. The early months brought a winter during which it was almost possible to see the bottom of the canals through the ice, the rime clung to peoples faces and everything froze that could possibly freeze – a substantial amount in a city like Amsterdam, so rich in water. Jacob Bicker Raye lived through the Great Frost, and I have mainly followed his diary in reconstructing this time, along with a few other sources.

On the first day of January, he records a "very severe" frost "making, in a very short time, the water suitable for lovers of skating". The frost continued, and on the 10th "people were riding with hundreds of horse-drawn sleighs through all the canals and the ice was one and half a metre thick." The ice-breaker proved useless.

On the same day, a woman was found with her children in a room in the Hoogstraat, frozen to death. "She was lying with three children in a box-bed on some straw and one child was sitting on its potty, dead. There was nothing in the room except the potty and the straw bedding, on which the dead woman lay with her children."

On 11 January drinking water had become so scarce in the city that three bucketsful sold for eight to ten stivers. It was therefore decided to saw open the waterway to Weesp by hand. Work began on the 12th, with more than 250 men, later as many as 350, every one of them earning 24 stivers a day, plus half a loaf of bread, a quarter pound of cheese, beer and two ladlesful of jannever (gin) against the cold. Ten days later and the way was free. The ice-breaker could try again. Initially, it was planned to tow it with 160 horses, a record number, but as it was not possible to find as many as that, they had to settle for trying with 84. In the event, however, the ice-breaker could get no further than Schulpbrug, near today's Amstel Station. Panic was beginning to take hold of Amsterdam. An emergency meeting of everyone who worked with water was called, but nobody could think of a possible solution.

On 23 January Bicker Raye writes: "The harsh frost continues, and one can read in the papers from different places that many people have perished from the cold, even several soldiers, who have frozen to death in their sentry huts. As the ice-breaker cannot get through, water is now so rare that one has to pay 50 stivers for an oxhooft, water that is brought all the way from Muiden and Weesp on hundreds of sledges. That is why many people are using melted ice from the IJ and the Amstel for drinking water, which causes many diseases." Four days later, he notes: "There was a fire on the Rapenburg, caused by a warming bedpan which an old woman had taken to bed. She was asphyxiated, then burned to death."

On 27 January three men submitted plans for the improvement of the ice-breaker. The reward promised each of them by the city administration is an indication of the prevailing despair: a pension for life of 300 guilders annually. The improvement, however, proved to be yet another failure. At a trial held on 1 February between ten in the morning and half past one in the afternoon, 46 horses could only move the ice-breaker about 400 metres.

Finally, on 3 February, the ice-breaker was at last able to take up its work again, and a convoy of barges arrived in Weesp on the following day. They had to search for clean drinking water for several days, but on 8 February, the ice-breaker ended the long wait by leading more than 30 barges full of water back into the city. Amsterdam, which had then about 200,000 inhabitants, had been without water for almost six weeks.[35]

At the end of February, the weather suddenly changed and temperatures became almost summery. It was a false spring, however, for at the beginning of March an icy storm raged across the land for three days, freezing the water once more "so stiff that one can walk across the IJ again".

The Great Frost marked the beginning of the city's slow decline, a decline that would accelerate towards the end of the century. During the same month of February 1763, the Seven Years War between Britain and Prussia on the one side, and France, Sweden, Russia, and Austria on the other ended. German, Swedish, and English bankers, especially, who had been obliged to finance their own countries' efforts, had borrowed heavily from their Amsterdam colleagues. Now, however, the time of war profits was over. Not only that: for, as some of the bills of exchange were not honoured, the mood of the city's financial community became noticeably tense.

Some months later, Jacob Bicker Raye records that the large banking house of the brothers De Neufville had gone into receivership, "causing the ruin of at least 25 decent merchants, and the downfall of hundreds of people, who have all suffered considerably". Leendert Pieter de Neufville, the most important of the brothers, was a typical "young urban professional" of his day. Between the ages of 20 and 30 he had worked his way up to become one of the most powerful bankers in the city. He had five large ships on the seas, held shares in the VOC to the value of 40,000 guilders, and owned a cotton-printing workshop, as well as a glass blower's and a silversmith's. His office, three rooms in his house, equipped with 19 desks and a staff of 23, traded with more than 70 firms in England, France, and Sweden, and over a hundred firms in Germany. He dealt in grain, sugar, spices, French wine, textiles, silver, non-precious metals, Saxonian porcelain, and black slaves. Almost a hundred paintings were hung in his house, the walls were covered entirely in silk hangings, and gilt gaming tables stood in the bedrooms, but there was not a single book to be found anywhere.

The fall of De Neufville dragged a great number of other houses down as well. All in all, more than 360 merchants became the victims of this bankruptcy, with total losses of almost ten million guilders.[36] Even so, the collapse was limited to a single trading network, and in time the sober merchant community of the city found its feet again.

Ten years later there was another crisis of trust, this time brought about when the well-respected banking house, Clifford, suddenly ceased making payments. This time the problems had been caused by speculation with shares in the East India Company (the British equivalent of the VOC), and again several houses, their banker's support withdrawn, went to the wall. The burgomasters of the city and the bank's commissioners behaved very much like a modern central bank: they intervened with the simple economic tools at their disposal in an attempt to contain the catastrophe.

Both these financial crises were short-lived, but that was not the case with the feeling of slow stagnation that was evident in the city. Amsterdam stank. It was rotting away. Poverty was on the increase. The city was still rich, but money changed hands rather than goods. Thousands of porters, loaders and warehouse staff became surplus to requirements, and there was little work to be had in the ailing manufacturing sector.

A good indication of the poverty at the time is provided by the number of patients admitted to the Binnen and Buitengasthuis, the city hospital. Between 1785 and 1796, the weekly figure increased from 500 to 800. This was not because of any epidemic, nor was it because more people had come to live in the city; the reasons were simply hunger and deprivation.

The lowest strata of Amsterdam's population could no longer withstand the pressures of subsistence.

More and more citizens also began to complain about the blue haze of mist, smoke and decay which now hung almost permanently over the city, especially during the summer. The English traveller, Fell, described the Amsterdam canals in 1800 as a stinking sewer of animal remains, rotten fish and rubbish from the markets: "Uncounted dead dogs and cats are floating there. In one canal I even saw a horse in the most horrifying state of decay." His countryman, the writer and engraver Samuel Ireland, opined that the Dutch smoked so much only to drive away the stench from the canals, thus fighting one evil with another.[37] The city stank in other respects, too. Because of the weakness and frequent absences of the stadtholders, the regents had enjoyed a free hand in the city for several decades, and they had given the most important of the more than 3,000 official posts to their friends and relations. Aptitude did not enter into the equation, for the holders were nominated only to be able to draw their salaries, while the work was done by someone else whom they paid to do it.

Our own chronicler, Jacob Bicker Raye, had taken over the position of auctioneer at the Grand Fish Market on the Dam from his brother. He received 2½ per cent of the market's turnover, which could amount to as much as 500 guilders a month, and sometimes double that. The man whom Bicker Raye engaged to do the real work received 400 guilders a year. The rest was there for the taking.

Bicker Raye's diary abounds with stories of this sort of cheating, the wheeling and dealing that surrounded lucrative appointments. It was clearly a regular topic at the Garnalendoelen, his local watering hole and club. He describes that burgomaster Bicker gave the post of city auctioneer, which carried an annual salary of 6,000 guilders, to his 14-year-old son, Hendrick. The son of Burgomaster Jan Corver Rip, could trump this early career, however: postmaster of Rotterdam, Delft, and The Hague at the age of five, he became postmaster of the Hamburg post comptoir when he was eight, and at 18 was deacon of the Nieuwe Walenkerk. He died a year later, having tightened a leather strap, which he wore around his body to conceal his fatness, to such a degree that "his best pieces, lungs and liver, had grown together". He left a fortune of 2,000 guilders.

It was known of Burgomasters Sautijn, Six, and Gillis van Bempten that they never gave posts to anyone without demanding something in return. Moreover, Gillis van Bempten was a notorious rake. He was so fat that he had to be supported by manservants when entering the Town Hall. He eventually died in 1748 "of dropsy, whereby the water left his body from the legs and from other places of the body through great holes in the flesh".

It is significant that the nepotism that characterized the city took place quite openly and was more or less accepted by the rest of the population. Here and there insurrectionary pamphlets were in circulation, but there was little indication of any coherent rebellion against this rule by a handful of rich families. Posts were seen as favours, gifts that could be granted and received, lent and withdrawn, a tradition of government dating back to the Middle Ages.

In addition to this, the burgomasters themselves were obliged to keep large houses and to live on the grandest canals without being paid for their work in the administration. Their position and rank therefore functioned as a substitute for salaries, the only problem being that this system had got completely out of hand.

To a certain extent even normal Amsterdammers profited from this trade in official posts and corruption, which took place, albeit on a smaller scale, throughout the entire population. Those who went too far could always find a way to accommodate themselves with the magistrates and their bailiffs. This was common, especially in cases of moral misdemeanours, usually with the "collaboration" of the prostitute in question. The sums with which the more highly placed would pay to buy themselves free from accusations ran into hundreds, and sometimes thousands, of guilders.

Meanwhile, the ministers preached in their churches, the services were well attended but nobody was ashamed to earn a fortune from the slave trade, or from forcing women into prostitution, or from ripping off their fellow man. The moral allegories depicted in the Town Hall had long been forgotten.

Around the middle of the eighteenth century the first cracks began to appear in this system of self-satisfied corruption. The costs of posts and favours were paid mainly by means of consumption taxes and were there-fore passed on to the population, rich and poor. Especially the high taxes on bread, meat, and peat pushed up the cost of living considerably. When, in 1740, food prices rose throughout Europe because of a succession of poor harvests, the first signs of civil unrest began to appear. There were violent incidents on account of the price of bread, buckwheat flour, apples, and, as we have seen, drinking water. There had been widespread plundering during the so-called "Wailer's Revolt" of 1696, when the issue had been the limitation of the "free profession" of funeral directors. Now there were strikes, of which the most serious occurred in 1744 among the cotton printers, who even organized a strike fund and issued printed leaflets outlining their wage demands.

"A hungry people is beyond government," Vondel had observed a century earlier, something that Amsterdam's city administration knew all too well. Once again, the principle of opportunism was applied. In order to forestall public-order problems, the administration subsidized foodstuffs. There was always enough grain in Amsterdam, and the authorities kept a close watch on the quantities in storage in order to maintain a surplus which could be used to head off any riots. When bread became expensive, the poor of the city received coupons enabling them to buy below price. In 1700, the city administrators even quelled an imminent revolt by ordering back into the harbour two ships loaded with grain from Danzig and Helsingør. [38]

Yet it was not merely opportunism that drove the Amsterdammers. The *charitate* advocated by the pious merchant Egbert Gerbrandszoon and his wife Gerrit Janszoon Peggedochter had developed over the centuries into a comprehensive system of workhouses and other charitable institutions, a source of endless amazement for foreign visitors. Food and shelter in these institutions were remarkably good compared with neighbouring countries; inmates were taught a craft, young adults were apprenticed with a master, in short, the strict regime of these almshouses and orphanages often succeeded in reintegrating potential paupers into society.

This should not be taken to mean that the social care of eighteenth-century Amsterdam should be idealized, even if it was imitated all over Europe. Most workhouses were inhabited by a motley assemblage of people who were in any case liable to be taken into care or simply locked up, for one reason or another: the insane, petty criminals, widows, orphans, the old, the ill, even children of rich families whose behaviour had put them beyond the pale. Those who were able to do so quickly got out again.

Although these houses were intended to provide a means of moral improvement through work, praying, preaching and heavy punishment were closer to reality. Nor were they what their founders had meant them to be: shelters for those poor people who were fit to work, providing them with both something to do and a strict schedule.[39] Instead they functioned more like asylums, and in practice these almshouses were very close to being houses of correction. Mostly, these alm houses had the function of an asylum, a closed institution for those who had no other place.

Artist unknown, *The Tuchthuis*, engraving, seventeenth century.

The city's true penal institutions were the Rasphuis for male prisoners, where brazil wood was ground down ("rasped") to make pigment, and the Spinhuis (Spinning House) for women. Both were attractions on the itinerary of every traveller. The people of Amsterdam also came to look, especially during the fairs when admission was free, or when they had a mind to jeer at the whores, "these pretty animals", who were locked up in the Spinhuis. Still, even these places were modern in comparison to jails in other European countries, where prisoners were often literally left to rot in dark dungeons, written off and expelled from society. There was at least an attempt at "moral improvement" in the Republic, even if it was largely theoretical.[40]

Another way of effecting this so-called moral improvement was not easily forgotten by those who came into contact with it. Whippings and floggings, among other forms of physical punishment, were a fixed part of internal discipline in jails. Bicker Raye and several others even write about the existence of a "water house", a drowning cell, although its existence is not confirmed by any historical records. Those who refused to work were cast into a cellar which was then allowed to fill up with water. The cell was equipped with a pump. If the convict standing there did not use it, or did so with insufficient energy, he or she would inevitably drown.[41]

Did any of this help? The French traveller Guillaume Daignan, who visited the Spinhuis in 1777, found that the women and girls there did not look unduly remorseful. They had decent manners, the building was clean and the girls were pleasant to look at. An unknown Englishwoman, however, found the Rasphuis to be a hell on earth: "All the men were half naked and entirely black with dust from sawing the wood. As they sweat heavily during their work, the sawdust runs over their faces and bodies like a black sauce. One cannot look at all this without shuddering with horror."[42]

This system of repression, moderate for its day, eventually proved insufficient to keep the ruling class in its position of power. In 1747, when there was a threat that Holland would be dragged into the war over the Austrian succession, and when France annexed parts of the Southern Netherlands, the population, fearing another Year of Catastrophe, began to demand the restoration of the House of Orange, and open rebellion erupted in the streets of Amsterdam. At first, on the instigation of the porcelain merchant Daniel Raap, who proved himself a truly popular leader, a petition signed by a large number of citizens was handed in, urging the city to recognize the hereditary rule of the House of Orange and that the sale of all lesser positions should go to the highest bidder. It seems that the people of Amsterdam did not feel that it was quite time to break away from this system entirely, but nepotism had to come to an end.

While the city's administrators were still in session debating the petition a spontaneous rebellion erupted on the streets. The Town Hall was stormed, and the only burgomaster present, Nicolaas Geelvinck, was so scared that he ran straight home. A group of Amsterdammers climbed into the Town

Hall and sat down at the council table, on the cushions of the councillors, while others opened the windows, waved their hats at the assembled masses, hung a broom out of the window as a mock rod of justice and called out: "The Government has changed! *Vivat* Orange!" Although the militia cleared the Town Hall on the same day, the anger of the people created a profound impression. Daniel Raap even got his way, if only partly: Amsterdam recognised the Orange governorship as hereditary, most of those who held positions in the administration were no longer allowed to have their work carried out by deputies, and it was entirely forbidden for them to "sublet" their posts at a profit.

Six months later another rebellion occurred, this time against the taxation system. The post of tax collector was still leased out, and since there was always something to be creamed off the amount collected, it was one of the most lucrative positions around. As a result, tax collectors were among the most hated people in the city.

In Friesland, where the trouble started, the unrest spread like wildfire, and it was not long before the anger of the people came to be directed not only at tax collectors but also against the corruption of the regents in general. From the north, the revolt spread to Amsterdam, where popular rage reached such proportions that, as one observer put it, "people had not been so confused and shocked in living memory".

On 25 June 1748 there were disturbances in the Butter Market, today's Rembrandtplein, where the butter excise was located. The excise clerks were manhandled, rubbish was thrown, and suddenly, unable to control the crowd, the militia opened fire. A "rude female", so a contemporary relates, "several times hitched up her skirts, smacked her bare buttocks and told the militia that this was for them". In response, "the woman was shot in her bared nether regions" and died hours later. After that, the powder keg exploded.[43]

During the riots, Jacob Bicker Raye was sitting at home nursing a severe attack of gout, but he still managed to collect enough information to write a fairly detailed account of events. At least 30 houses, not only those of tax collectors but also those of several wealthy citizens, were plundered by "the beast", that is, the raging mob. According to Bicker Raye, the horror at seeing "the most beautiful furnishings destroyed and then thrown into the water" was indescribable. Bands of plunderers prowled the city, equipped with a list of the addresses of tax collectors, working their way through, house by house. Porcelain, wardrobes, mirrors, harpsichords, everything was hacked to pieces and thrown into the street; cushions were cut open, giving the effect of a heavy snowfall, and rising from the canals, just above the water, there were piles of furniture, bed linen, books, crockery, clothes, carpets, and all sorts of ruined artefacts.

W. Streelink, *The Pachtersoproer*, drawing (1777).

In the house of Christoffel Lublink, on the Keizersgracht, some women had put on Miss Lublink's clothes and were dancing, screaming, and tearing down everything in sight. Once the fine interior had been torn to pieces, the rioters turned their attention to the roof, which they smashed. Banners made from rags were hung from the windows. An aviary was broken up and a colourful cloud of canaries, goldfinches, chaffinches, and siskins fluttered to freedom.

One of the most significant facts about the riots, however, is that very little was actually looted. It was a case of people running amok, a madness that swept through the streets of this Calvinist city for days, a second iconoclastic fury. When the raiders found a bag of money, they cut it open and tipped the contents into the canal. Bicker Raye writes that "even iron chests, partly full of money, were carried by groups of people, 30 or 40 strong, to the canals and thrown over the parapets of bridges into the water". Elsewhere, a collection of paintings was cut to shreds, including a painting by Melchior Hondecoeter, which was "as beautiful as one might ever hope to see". An eyewitness tells of one of the chief pillagers, known as The Burgomaster, who beat a painting by Flip Wouwerman over the post of a banister which was carved like a lion, "with his own great terrifying paws".

The orgy of drunkenness and destruction reached its apogee on the Singel, in the house of a wine merchant called Van Aarsen. 32,000 bottles were laid up in his cellars, and most of them were smashed. In one room that had a particularly high threshold the spilled wine was so deep that the revellers could swim around in it like animals. Some of them lost consciousness because of the strong wine fumes. According to Bicker Raye the plunderers spent the night "guzzling and fornicating", and all this immorality took place in the open, in the house, on the pavement, even on the street and down by the canal. "Some of them had drunk themselves to death and one woman, among others, was pulled from the cellar, stark naked, having died from excess and from drink."

The members of the militia, who also had a bone to pick with the tax collectors, barely intervened in this chaos. Only when the pillaging threatened to spread to other houses that did not belong to taxmen did they consent to restore order.

After four days the rampage ended. The three most important ringleaders, among them a "deranged female", Mat van den Nieuwendijk, and The Burgomaster, Pieter van Dord, were hanged at the Waag on the Dam, as recorded by Chaim Braatbard in his *Yiddish Chronicle*. When the condemned were led outside, he writes, drummers began a loud drum roll in order to drown out the screams of the fish wife, Mat. "But she was wailing horribly: 'Revenge! Revenge, dear citizens! Come to my aid! You let me perish now so shamefully while I did not fight for myself! I did it for the whole country, against the oppression of the tax collectors who tortured the citizens so much and who took away our goods and our money by force!' But neither shouting nor pleading could help her – she had to hang. Immediately the pulley moved. It was difficult to heave her out of the window, and it was painful to look on. When she finally emerged outside, one could hear her shouting 'Revenge, revenge!' and nothing else, for as long as she could. And so she was hanged out of the window, and dangled there until she was dead."[44]

When Pieter van Dord was pushed out of the window, the crowd surged forward, pressing closer so as not to miss any detail of the spectacle. As a result, the whole mass of people appeared to be in uproar and the guards, thinking they were being attacked, shot into the crowd. A great panic ensued, and according to Bicker Raye many hundreds of people fell into the Damrak. About 60 were drowned. Others, he writes, "were crushed so terribly that they gave up the ghost standing up, whole mountains of people lying one on top of the other, some dead, some injured by the trampling." Another hundred Amsterdammers lost their life in this madness.

As in earlier centuries, the ordinary people of Amsterdam had pinned their hopes on the House of Orange without understanding that there was little left of this noble house apart from its myth. For years an embittered William IV had waited for the restoration of his governorship, but when power fell into his lap in 1747 he was taken entirely by surprise. Though he relished his newly-acquired influence, he had no conception of how to exercise it, lacking both the vision and the decisiveness necessary to forge the situation into a concrete advantage for himself and his followers. During the second half of the eighteenth century Holland and Amsterdam were therefore ruled by a balance between two equally weak opponents: on the one hand the competent but on all fronts degenerated regent elite, on the other hand a dull William IV and, from 1751, his successor William V, neither of whom seized the initiative, even once, in order to repay the trust that the people had placed in the dynasty. In 1748, however, those citizens who took an interest in politics did not yet understand that.

In Amsterdam, it was the so-called Doelists who saw the House of Orange as a means of curtailing the power of the burgomasters. This was a real citizens' movement, with delegates in all districts of the city, who met in the shooting house of the Kloveniers militia (the Kloveniersdoelen, hence their name). Its members soon came to regard themselves as an alternative government, an elected representative of the burghers, a sort of Jacobin club *avant-la-lettre*, with almost revolutionary goals: free elections of burgomasters, sheriffs and officers of the militia, abolition of excise duties, the administrators of the VOC and the WIC to be elected by the citizens, and much more. These demands were to reverberate throughout the Low Countries and France, and these radical Doelists were perhaps simply too far ahead of their time.

Led by Daniel Raap, the movement soon adopted more moderate aims, limited to the re-establishment of the old guilds, an end to the abuse of positions and official appointments, and the nomination of militia officers by the citizens. Under pressure from Raap, who was engaged in a kind of shuttle diplomacy between the Prince of Orange, the city administration, and his own followers, the burgomasters decided to relinquish their posts "if it is in the national interest". This is when Jacob Bicker Raye lost his post as captain of the militia.

Thus the election of the city government was now the exclusive right of the Governor, and William IV was asked to visit Amsterdam in person. On 2 September 1748 he arrived with a large entourage. Carpenters from the Kattenburg area, the Bijltjes,* known for their loyalty to the dynasty, accompanied the coach to where the Prince was awaited by two trumpeters, a large ship's flag inscribed *For Orange and Freedom*, and a vast cheering crowd. It was hoped that the Prince would look after their interests and channel their wild revolution in a positive and fruitful direction.

As it turned out, however, William IV did not understand the movement that had gained such power in Amsterdam. He had given rise to, if not encouraged, the expectation that he would do something for Daniel Raap and his supporters, and as a result power was presented to him on a platter, there for the taking. He did nominate a new government, but all four of the new burgomasters came from the ruling elite of regents, and he made it understood that he let the previous administration go with a heavy heart. Hendrik Fagel, the Secretary to the States General, who was present during the ceremony, later recounted in his diary that he had heard the Prince tell Burgomaster Corver, a well-respected magistrate: "I am more

---

* Literally, "little axes", workers who were fierce Orangists, mainly from the dockyards on the IJ and the Amstel.

sorry than I can tell you that I have to dismiss you, but I have no choice." Corver answered that he understood that the Prince's hands were tied and both men "had tears in their eyes and embraced each other in the most touching way".[45]

The radical Doelists, meanwhile, were utterly confused about the manner in which their revolution had been suppressed by the regents and the royal court, and decided to make one last blundering attempt at convincing their former idol to adopt their cause. In the middle of the night a small deputation of "free Kattenburgers"* forced their way into the Prince's lodgings in the Oudezijds Herenlogement in order to speak with him personally. William did not understand the situation. He was curt and high-handed, and decided to have no more dealings with the group. Shortly afterwards he left the city.

The citizens felt abandoned, while the democrats among them now knew that they had nothing to hope for from the House of Orange. They turned away from William and founded their own societies and militias, which were eventually to become the patriotic movement. With hindsight, it is obvious that William's visit in September 1748 caused a breach of trust between the city and that princely house which was not to be mended until 1818.

As so often happens, the anger of the betrayed population turned against its own hapless leaders rather than against its enemy. The extent of that fury can be gauged from the people's reaction six years later at the funeral of Daniel Raap. When he died of dropsy in 1754, nobody could be found to carry him to his grave. At the official beginning of the funeral, two o'clock in the afternoon, hundreds of Amsterdammers had assembled in front of Raap's porcelain shop. They destroyed the bier that was already standing in front of the house, and would certainly have taken the corpse from the house by force in order to rip it apart had not the militia prevented them. In the end, so our chronicler Bicker Raye tells us, Raap was buried in the dead of night "with a white horse which was normally used for taking the corpses of the executed from the scaffold to the Damrak, escorted by 20 servants, two undersheriffs, and many guards with rattles, brought to the Oude Kerk, and there thrown into a grave like a beast". It was freezing

---

* That is, inhabitants of Kattenburg, an area of Amsterdam.

cold that night, but still the streets were lined with people and there was a great crowd on the Oudekerksplein hoping to snatch away the body and take it to the gallows fields. Daniel Raap, populist and negotiator, the first social democrat of the city, was dumped unceremoniously in grave number 45 of the Oude Kerk, while his friends, "fearful of the wrath of the people", ran away.

In January 1771 it snowed again in Amsterdam. Jacob Bicker Raye, now grown old and stiff, could only watch from his window the fun people were having on the frozen Keizersgracht in front of his house. Out of sheer boredom he counted the horse-drawn sleighs that passed by his window. "It being 11 January, between the hours of ten and half-past two, and then again in the afternoon from three to half past four, counted by myself 357 horse-drawn sleighs on this side of the house alone, on this beautiful, soft sunny day, perfect for the ladies riding out with their grand coiffures, mostly in magnificent sleighs drawn by splendid horses." For the poor, however, it was another terrible winter, and the middle classes now found their economic base flattening out as slowly and irreversibly as Amsterdam harbour.

Three distinct groups had emerged in the stagnating city: the top layer of the regents, the large class merchants and bankers, which was slowly shrinking, an underclass of paupers and workmen, who were increasing both in numbers and in the wretchedness of their condition; and a middle class of citizens who found the ineffectiveness of the House of Orange and the mismanagement of the city oligarchy more and more intolerable, but who lacked the political means to bring about change.

The intellectual horizon of the Amsterdam middle classes now embraced a new philosophy, one that was rapidly gaining ground throughout Europe: the Enlightenment, a *Weltanschauung* in which reason and experience held a central place. The natural sciences had opened new worlds by means of close observation and dispassionate reasoning, and politics and economics seemed to be subject to the same rules. Theoretically, it was possible to plan and understand the world. Human beings were by nature good; given

Artist unknown, *A Demonstration of Electricity in the Felix Meritis*, drawing (c. 1870).

good education and an honest society offering liberty and equality for all, a new world could be created, founded on logic and reason.

The Enlightenment, a movement hitherto almost unthinkable, was borne aloft on a wave of enthusiasm and optimism, and gained momentum in the midst of the inertia that characterized much of the century. Perhaps unsurprisingly, Amsterdam played the role of intermediary in the dissemination of the Enlightenment ideal. Here, after all, everything that was forbidden in other countries could be published, and the thinkers behind the movement were quick to avail themselves of this opportunity.

The great French philosopher of the Enlightenment, Voltaire, who visited Amsterdam seven times and had his work published here, remarked that it made no difference to the Dutch whether they traded in books or in textiles, and that it did not concern them one bit what was written in these books as long as they made money out of them. That aside, however, he saw the city as an inspiration, as an anticipation of the realization of the utopian spirit of the Enlightenment. "I met the Councillor-Pensionary," he wrote in 1722, "on foot, without lackeys, right among his people. One finds that nobody has to court anybody else. Here, nobody stands in the street in order to see a prince ride by. The people here know only work and moderation."[46] When the American colonists declared their independent republic in 1776, thereby for the first time making the principles of freedom and equality the foundation stones of a state, their Declaration of Independence contained phrases that had been borrowed straight from the document in which, in 1581, Dutch rebels had refused to recognize the power of King Philip II of Spain, and had instead proclaimed their own Republic.

Surprisingly, strong Christian traits were characteristic of the Dutch Enlightenment. People somehow managed to reconcile their pragmatism and their Calvinist principles with the reason and logic of the Enlightenment ideal. Many preachers, too, were able to establish connections between theology and modernity, thus rendering redundant atheism and deism, beliefs that were very much in vogue in other countries where the power of the Catholic Church was under attack. As a result, the movement towards this secularization and emancipation from the Church, that was such an important process in Europe throughout the eighteenth century, would gain ground in Holland only in the nineteenth and twentieth centuries.

Among the Dutch bourgeoisie the Enlightenment – which was first and foremost a bourgeois movement, rather than a populist one – precipitated a huge thirst for new scientific knowledge and empirical research. Full of bafflement, Jacob Bicker Raye describes a demonstration of a machine to show Galvani's theories of electrical impulses in muscles: "When someone else brought his finger close to my leg, there were sparks flying from my shins and through two pairs of socks, without my socks being singed or my feeling any pain." In Amsterdam, societies and clubs sprang up like mushrooms, bearing names like "Diligence is the Nursemaid of the Sciences", "For Edifying Entertainment", and "The Society for the Common Good", known as "The Good" for short.

The best-known society in the city was "*Felix Meritis*" or "Happiness through Achievement". In 1788 this moved into large premises of its own on the Keizersgracht. The building still stands, number 324, with a music room which was also used for scientific experiments, an auditorium for lectures, rooms for exhibitions, a blossoming department of drawings, and an astronomical observatory on the roof. Until well into the nineteenth century, *Felix Meritis* was a meeting point for the arts, for science and for technical innovations, a think-tank for a new age.

Felix Meritis was politically neutral. Those wishing to discuss the state of the country and the abolition of the governorship of the House of Orange could go to one of the countless coffee houses. As early as 1749, Bicker Raye notes the existence of a group called "Principled Patriots" which met regularly in a garden of the Plantage. Unfortunately their assembly was violently broken up by a bargee called Arie Falck and his companions.

In Amsterdam this patriotic movement consisted mainly of the educated middle classes, a segment of society which, rapidly gaining in confidence, understood that the time was ripe for a change in the distribtuion of power in the Republic. Among them were lawyers, doctors, petty merchants, and many Lutherans, Remonstrants, and Mennonites, who had always been excluded from holding high office in the city administration on account of their religion. All of these knew that only a transition of power could give them the place in society to which they had felt entitled for generations. They were joined by a section from among their natural opponents: younger members of the regent elite saw them as natural allies against the Orange dynasty, although this association quickly cooled when democratic demands became more radical.

The Orangist Party, on the other hand, was backed in the city by a significant section of workers and the "petite bourgeoisie", especially in the Kattenburg and the Jordaan areas, and was led by the conservative clergy. Increasingly some of the regents, too, began to support this block, after they had come to see that the aims of the patriots were at least as dangerous to their position as they were to the House of Orange.

Initially the struggle between the parties took place mainly around the coffee house tables, or in pamphlets and newspapers. Supporters of the two groups distinguished themselves from each other by special symbols: on one side, silver lapel pins and tobacco boxes with a patriotic symbol of the faithful *keeshond* (a Dutch breed of long-haired dog), on the other, orange cockades, portraits of the Governor and all sorts of trinkets bearing the Orange Tree symbol. When the Patriots went one step further and established their own militias, the so-called "free corps", the situation became more serious. The corps exercised publicly, and indulged in countless long-winded perorations about the Noble Blood of the Bataviers (although almost no Dutch person was descended from them), about the restoration of the Patriotic Civil Rights (although these had never existed in the first place), and about Batavian Liberty (although nobody knew the first thing about the Bataviers, which was probably just as well for the orators).

In the meantime it was an event taking place thousands of miles away that eventually precipitated matters at home: the American Declaration of Independence in 1776.

The insurrection of the colonists in North America against the British mother country was fed by European ideas of Liberty, Equality, and Fraternity, and like a mirror it cast back these Enlightenment ideals upon the democratic movements in Europe. The young American Republic now divided minds and nations, just as the young Soviet Union was to do at the beginning of the twentieth century.

France, Britain's old rival, moved quickly to recognize the new republic, but the Netherlands, in accordance with their traditions, attempted to remain neutral. Meanwhile, the revolutionaries across the ocean received weapons and ammunition from Amsterdam; every merchant wanted to do business, legally or otherwise, with such a significant new trading partner. Moreover, the enlightened bourgeoisie had great sympathy for the ideas of the American Revolution. It is not surprising, therefore, that no Amsterdam burgomaster even attempted to intervene when ships bound for America with illegal cargo appeared in the city harbour. The WIC was the first to salute an American ship, firing a cannon from the Fort Sint-Eustatius, and its American captain, Paul Jones, was cheered as a hero in Amsterdam's theatre, the schouburg, because he had captured a British ship. The Amsterdam banker Jean de Neufville even drafted a secret treaty with the American Ambassador, William Lee, with the full knowledge of the burgomasters.

Eventually, the British lost patience, declared war against the Republic (for the fourth time in one and a half centuries), and blockaded the coast of the Netherlands. The Dutch war fleet was in such a reduced state that it could do nothing, and trade, especially with the East Indiies, came to a virtual standstill.

In 1782, the United States was formally recognized by the Dutch Republic, after pressure from Amsterdam bankers. Its then ambassador, John Adams, could borrow as much as he liked on the city's capital market.

Two years later, peace was made between Britain and the Netherlands. The new and lucrative American market did not, however, turn towards the Netherlands but towards the motherland, Britain, while the blockade of the Dutch coast proved a heavy blow to commerce in Amsterdam.

Undoubtedly, the later French occupation contributed to the end of Amsterdam's trading power, but many other factors indicate that the city's commercial empire was already beginning to atrophy before 1795. When Amsterdam merchants redirected their attentions from India to America they had fatally manoeuvred themselves between the Devil and the deep blue sea. It was common knowledge that the West Indian Company was not performing well, and it was eventually dissolved in 1791. However, few people understood that the apparently solid United East India Company was also no longer able to honour its good name. Although throughout the eighteenth century the Company's wealth and reputation remained as solid as a rock, since 1737 it had already paid its generous royal dividends from monies it did not possess. Its grand name provided the VOC with as much credit as it wanted, so that it could simply borrow whatever was required.

Just how fragile this basis was became apparent during the Fourth English War, when the Company found itself unable to import anything from India for years. The VOC lost Siam and Malacca and numerous trading posts to the British, resulting in financial damage of eleven million guilders. For two years nothing was sold and nothing was earned. In order to keep up its payments, the VOC borrowed money from the state. On 24 May 1782, dividends were paid for the very last time.

An analysis of the disentanglement of the remains of this enormous multinational lies beyond the scope of this book; it is enough to say that it was reminiscent of the butchering of a whale: a stinking business that seemingly lasts for ever. Only at the beginning of the new century, on 1 January 1800, did this national adventure finally vanish from the history books for good.

Together with the WIC and the VOC, other old-established merchants retreated from the stage. They became more cautious and more parsimonious, or they simply went bankrupt. They relinquished their country estates. A certain Frederik Kaal, an adept speculator, bought up these houses and made a substantial profit by dismantling them, since the sale of stone, timber, and fertile soil was by then more lucrative than the cost of knocking them down. Of the scores of estates in the Watergrafsmeer and along the Amstel, only a handful were left when Kaal died in 1790.

Meanwhile, the opposition between the Patriots and the Prince's party had hardened. Representative of this, and also one of the most exciting documents from these times, is an anonymous pamphlet, *Aan het Volk van Nederland* (To the People of the Netherlands) which was distributed in September 1781, particularly in Holland and in Amsterdam. The author was unveiled only many years later: Joan Derk, Baron Van der Capellen tot de Poll, a nobleman from the Overijssel province, who maintained an intensive correspondence with John Adams and other American revolutionaries. The pamphlet contains a direct attack upon the British-minded Governor, William V, who was held responsible for the desolate state of the country. The Baron goes on to plead for direct elections of "a moderate number of good, virtuous, pious men", who would execute the will of the citizens in conjunction with the regents. He uses the people of America as an example of thoughtfulness, although at the same time he exhorts the citizens: "Arm yourselves, all of you. Elect for yourselves those whom you want to give the orders and go to work in everything with calm and moderation."[47]

The situation escalated. Backed by the Patriotic "free corps", Patriots gained power in several cities. In Amsterdam, too, there were increasingly wild debates at a number of inns. "There were between 200 and 300 people," wrote one young eyewitness, "half choked by pipe smoke and gin, screaming and giving vent to their feelings about affairs of state."[48]

On 21 April 1787, several "free corps" occupied the Dam, entered the Town Hall, and pushed nine of their members into positions on the Town Council. Governor William V felt impelled to act. He demanded that all Patriots relinquish their seats, but his intervention had the same effect as a red rag to a bull. It caused a revolution.

As soon as news of the Governor's intervention had spread, Patriots stormed the café Lands Welvaren on the Reguliersgracht and threw out the assembled customers who were loyal to Orange. In retaliation, the following day, the houses of Patriots were ransacked, especially on the islands, which regarded themselves as Orange strongholds. The bridges were drawn up to allow the plundering to take its course unhindered, thus transforming the territories of the *bijltjes* into fortresses.

The Patriot "free corps" could not leave this unavenged. On 30 May a small battle took place on the Kattenburgerbrug, and after one night's fighting the Patriots succeeded in lowering the bridge, although their gunner, Hendrik Hilmers, was killed in the process. On the invitation to his funeral were printed the following lines:

> Thus we honour Amstel's gunner
> Whose name now lives for ever.
> Thus we honour each Batavier
> Who perishes for Freedom.[49]

The rule of the Patriots did not last long. The King of Prussia, Frederick William II, whose sister Wilhelmina was married to Prince William V of Orange, came to the aid of his brother-in-law. At the beginning of September, the King crossed the border of the Netherlands with an army of 20,000 men. The House of Orange was helped back into the saddle, and within a month all Patriotic members of the Town Council had vanished and the old members had taken their places again.

The balance of power between Amsterdam and the House of Orange now swung to the other extreme. The city lost its grip on the government of the Republic; important decisions about trade were taken over the heads of the Amsterdam merchants, newspapers and other organs of public opinion were strictly censored, many Patriots, and among them many prominent citizens of Amsterdam, fled to France. The people of the city slowly began to gather up the discarded orange cockades.

It was not a wise course of action on the Governor's part. Amsterdam may have been in decline, but it was still a powerful trading city. When William found out just how short-sighted he had been to get the merchants and bankers up in arms against him, it was already too late. Eighty years later, when the French were at the borders and he needed to borrow money in order to defend his regime, he found Amsterdam's purses firmly closed. True, the old Republic was as ripe for picking as a pear, but its eventual downfall was caused by a simple lack of funds. The Amsterdam bankers had done their sums and, Orangist or not, they refused to donate a penny.[50]

The coldest winter of the eighteenth century was the one in 1763, but in December 1794, winter struck again, harsh and hard, and this time the city could no longer defend itself. Within its walls revolt was fermenting once more. The Patriots had regrouped in secret "reading societies", analogous to the French Comités Révolutionnaires, and were waiting impatiently for the day of the great overthrow. The troops of Revolutionary France, meanwhile, had marched up through the Southern Netherlands and were standing on the line of the great rivers.

In its frozen state, the Dutch water line, the Republic's last line of defence, was suddenly without value. The French moved across the ice of the Waal on 10 January 1795, occupying Utrecht on the 16th. Two days later, Prince William V of Orange fled to England from the icy beach at Scheveningen.

On the same day, the Amsterdam Comité Révolutionnaire held an assembly in a coffee house, Het Wapen van Embden, on the Nieuwedijk, where boxes of cockades stood ready; once issued, it was hoped they would allow the city to be handed over to the French brothers without bloodshed. In the afternoon, Doctor Krayenhoff, a Patriot Amsterdammer who had fled and was now fighting for the French under Brigadier Daendels, arrived at the Weesperpoort. He rode through the snowy city, to the quarters of the garrison commander, where he demanded to be given control over the city in the name of the revolutionaries. After being wined and dined, he found himself in command of Amsterdam by the evening.

The next morning saw dozens of Amsterdammers adorned with red-white-and-blue cocades, shivering miserably on the ice of the Amstel by the Hoge Sluis, ready to welcome the French hussars. At nine o'clock, the official revolution took place. The burgomasters and the old Council of 36 regents arrived in the freezing Town Hall, met for exactly one hour, called in the deputies of the Comité Révolutionnaire, and, together, all moved their chairs around the crackling fire.

The chairman of the Comité, Rutger Jan Schimmelpenninck, thanked the old administration in the politest possible terms for their services to the city, and then declared them, in the name of the citizens, relieved of all duties. Without any resistance, the regents left the Town Hall, and the population was informed of what had taken place. On the Dam there was a fruitless attempt at planting a fir tree, which the French had pinched from the Watergraafsmeer, in the frozen ground, and eventually there was a little dancing around a "Freedom Tree" held in fragile equilibrium by ropes.

Such, in all its folly, was the end of the old, glorious Amsterdam.

For once, figures speak louder than anything else. In 1794, the profit of the Amsterdam trading convoys had been 719,000 florins. A year later, the tally had more than halved to 321,000, a year after that and even that figure had been all but decimated, standing at just 55,000 florins. The assets of the bank of exchange had been in excess of 22 million florins in 1793, in 1795 it had dwindled to half of that. The British enemy put the Dutch colonies beyond reach; the ally France drained away capital and goods; the banks and other financial institutions of the old Republic lost trust, shops and businesses suffered declining turnovers, and slowly the Amsterdam money machine ground to a halt.

On 9 April 1808, the city gave away the famous Town Hall to the newly-created King of Holland, Louis Bonaparte, the brother of the Emperor Napoleon, for temporary use as palace. The decision was never to be reversed: after the return of the House of Orange in 1815 the bastion of the Republic remained firmly in royal hands. Louis Bonaparte's throne room was never again to serve as the Citizens' Hall. The city administration found shelter in the Prinsenhof on the Ouderzijds Voorburgwal (now the Grand Hotel), where it was to remain for more than 150 years.

The place of execution was moved from the Dam to the Nieuwmarkt. The Waag on the Dam had to be demolished because the King complained that the building spoilt his view. In the summer of 1808 the old, lively heart of the city was suddenly transformed into a dignified, stiff, and horribly boring square.

In 1810 Amsterdam was incorporated into the French Empire, along with the rest of the Netherlands. The glory was over.

Gerrit Lamberts, *The Gallow Fields*, drawing (1795).

Chapter Eight

The Fire Palace

"MIDNIGHT! SLOWLY THE CLOCK ON THE CHURCH TOWER TOLLS twelve times, its metal voice sounding solemn and heavy through the clear, calm winter night. I look out of my window. Everything is white. The ground is covered with a thick layer of fine, dry, firm snow, which creaks under the footfall of a few late passers-by. I am lying here, listening to the night: a carriage rolls by in the distance, I hear faraway singing, everything sounds louder and clearer through the freezing weather."

So begins one of the strangest stories by Justus van Maurik, a cigar manufacturer and journalist. It is a painstakingly accurate account of a sleepless night in nineteenth-century Amsterdam, in which he describes hardly anything apart from the sounds which reach him from the dark city beyond his study: the first farmers driving in with their milk, the cart of an early Jewish street trader, the hurried step of the lamplighter snuffing out the streetlamps.[1]

If one were to be catapulted back into the Amsterdam of the middle of the nineteenth century, one would probably notice, first and foremost, a new experience of sound and silence. The city of those days might have been more noisy than it is now, but tone and rhythm were entirely different, dominated by the tap of hoofs and rattling of carts and other vehicles, the shrieks of seagulls, the calls of the market traders, bells, voices and, especially, footsteps.

What else would one notice? Almost certainly the darkness, the absolute pitch blackness in which the city was cloaked after nightfall.[2] Even as late as a hundred years ago, the number of streetlamps was a fraction of what it is now, and at full moon they were not lit at all. Countless nineteenth-century paintings show the stars above the dark city, just as numerous, bright, and sparkling as in the most far-flung countryside. Many accidents happened in the dead of night: on a single misty December evening in 1893, 96 Amsterdammers fell into the canals. Two of them, a servant and a funeral orator, were drowned, and six were never found.

"Still and unmoving, black and threatening, like a chipped wall rising from the canal, the high houses of the Warmoesstraat stood against the lighter sky," Justus van Maurik wrote of the Damrak on a moonlit night, near the area of today's landing place for sightseeing boats. From the windows, a yellow-reddish light was cast upon the dark ships, their masts standing out starkly against the sky, and in their rigging several small lamps shining through the night, tinting pink the thin columns of smoke rising up from the cabins. And, in the distance, a red light glowed from the somewhat busier Dam.

In the small hours of the night, only the nightwatchman regularly made his rounds with his rattle – "Twelve is the hour! The hour is twelve!" – while on the towers another guard watched over the sleeping city. A description of the city dating from 1875 details his precise task: in case of fire he had to blow his horn and then hang his lantern, the sign of fire, on the side of the tower from which he had signalled the fire. A short time later the fire brigade would come tearing past: galloping horses, heavy men wearing helmets and holding red flaming torches, "a troupe of devils, riding up from the shadowy realms on Pluto's red wagon".

The third thing that one would notice on a trip back into the nineteenth century would almost certainly be smells or, more precisely, the stench. The smell in the quiet, picturesque Amsterdam of the mid-nineteenth century had become so bad that it seemed to choke and poison every activity. The same description of the city from 1875 records that "in autumn, the wooden parts of houses, especially in the Jordaan and also on the Prinsengracht, look as if blackened with pencils, a consequence of the chemical effect of stinking sulphuric vapours on the white lead in the paint." Another description tells of "disgusting heaps of rubbish, heaps of manure and similar things", and as late as 1866, a virulent cholera epidemic claimed 1,100 victims in the city. Eight per cent of the people in the city lived in cellars. Half of all children went to paupers' schools. The population statistics of nineteenth-century Amsterdam are similar to those of a third-world country today: extremely high birth rates matched by death rates at least as great. Only half of all boys reached the age of 35, and the life expectancy of simple labourers was hardly more than 30.

Finally, after the noise, the darkness, and the smell, the notion of time itself was of another order from that in our day. Anyone wanting to punt a barge from one end of the city to the other would spend a whole morning doing so; if one had to go to Utrecht one had to set aside an entire day; ships waiting to enter the harbour might sometimes wait a whole month. Idea and result, departure and arrival, which today are accomplished in hours, were separated by days and weeks. Time was not yet a scarce commodity; it was plentiful, like air and water. Life in the city had a delayed quality, an effect that was reinforced by the fact that the fast-paced existence of the former trading city was disappearing.

Ever since the French occupation of the city, no major changes had taken place in Amsterdam. The enormous depot of the former East India Company had collapsed one night in 1822 simply due to decay. In 1851 the *Algemeen Handelsblad* reported that nobody had dared to build a new representative town house for a century. "Stagnation has set in, it is a sleeping country," wrote the Parisian writing duo, the brothers de Goncourt, in 1861, during a visit to Amsterdam. "One enters a museum, and one meets the house or the canal exactly as one has seen it in a painting by Pieter de Hoogh."[3]

In some respects, the French occupation had blown through the Low Countries like a fresh breeze. There was a new system of administration, old privileges and oligarchic structures had finally been abolished, and in certain ways the Netherlands had been brought closer to the rest of Europe. For Amsterdam the trading city, however, French rule had proved fatal. The Continental System, by means of which Louis Napoleon Bonaparte, then King of Holland, banned all trade with Britain and had literally cut off French access to the sea, had also almost completely severed all of Amsterdam's connections with the colonies and with countless other business partners. Between 1795 and 1815, the city's population dwindled from 221,000 to 190,000. Houses stood empty all over the city; some were even demolished in order to save taxes. Of the 3,000 men who had worked on the wharves along the IJ, only 350 were left in 1811. Of 50 silk- and velvet-weaving workshops, an important part of Amsterdam's industrial production during the entire eighteenth century, only two survived the era of the French. The once burgeoning tobacco industry was finally brought to its knees.[4]

The grand ideological dreams had passed as well, to the vast disappointment of the Patriots. Despite the ideals of their so-called Batavian Republic, it had very quickly been established that government policy was to be decided over the heads of the citizens. For their part, those who had supported the House of Orange understood that the power of the regents was gone for good. Moreover, the pressure of French rule had brought together many former opponents.

People were by no means disoriented. Both parties remained children of the Enlightenment in their optimism and their emphasis on reason, believing that only through education would it be possible to elevate the people to a state in which they would be able to rule themselves. Meanwhile, it would be necessary for groups of educated men with good intentions, belonging to all churches, to take care of the people. The time for rhetoric was past, the polarization of Patriot and Orangist was forgotten, and a cautious sobriety set the tone of the debate.

After the French army had been disastrously beaten at Leipzig on 19 October 1813, the French occupation of Amsterdam quickly came to an end. On Sunday 14 November the military governor-general, Molitor, together with his entire garrison, left the city without fuss. The brawny Dutch sailor Job May, hearing of the quiet exodus, immediately came to this conclusion: "In that case, let's have a revolution." On the following Monday, market day, a small people's insurrection erupted. Orange banners appeared everywhere throughout the city, and the small French customs offices on the IJ went up in flames. When the hastily appointed commander, Falck, approached the Kattenburg with his troops he came upon a crowd preparing for a spot of pillaging. Falck himself relates the following dialogue in his memoirs.

"But captain," called one of the leaders, "it isn't that we want to plunder anything."

"What are you doing on the Kattenburg then, where you don't belong?"

"Just having a bit of fun, captain, getting the big bird down from the gate of the Landswerf."

"And then what?"

"Lighting a little fire, captain, there's a chill in the air."

The calls for the "big bird", the French Imperial eagle on the top of the Admiralty building, grew louder, and Falck wisely decided to hand over the carved wooden eagle. It was delivered to the mob and its wings and head were ceremoniously hacked to pieces, and when the flames began to engulf the remains there was no end to the cheering. By now it was four o'clock in the morning, and, as Falck remarks, "After the *auto-da-fé* of the imperial bird, the members of the crowd really did keep to their word and dispersed. The heavy shower of rain that followed meant that the revolution was postponed."[5]

A month later the new sovereign, King William I of Orange, rode into the city, to be cheered as no Orange had been before or has been since. All Amsterdam lay at his feet, and all the more so because he had resolved not to indulge in recriminations about the Patriotic rebellion, and proved himself ready to start with a clean slate as far as the Dutch were concerned. The potentially embarrassing experience of the Amsterdam notable Maurits van Hall is indicative of this new state of affairs. Once a prominent Patriot, he was invited to a dinner with the new King. According to his diary, he found himself on the settee next to Princess Wilhelmina, widow of the former Governor, William V. The old Princess salvaged the situation by saying "What a transformation in so few years", and then proceeded to sing the praises of Amsterdam's citizens.[6]

There was, however, one awkward question in the air between Amsterdam and the House of Orange: was the Dam to remain a palace, or was it to return to being the Town Hall? Initially, King William declared to the provisional city administration that he was willing to "cede" the palace to the citizens, "as a gesture of respect and affection for this important city". The only concession he sought was to be allowed to keep a few apartments in the building for his own use whenever he stayed in the city. That seemed logical: now that Amsterdam was no longer the royal residence, there was no reason to leave the enormous building on the Dam standing empty. On the other hand, the advisers to the King felt that it would be prudent to use Amsterdam as a residence for a substantial part of the year, and to cultivate a certain court atmosphere in the city. What everyone was anxious to avoid was a repetition of the open conflict between Amsterdam and the House of Orange. Eventually, an agreement was reached: Amsterdam was allowed to call itself the capital, the Town Hall was to remain a royal palace, and the House of Orange promised to stay in the city for a part of each year.[7] Of the last concession, little or nothing eventuated. For decades, the palace stood on the Dam as a dead block, used only for representative purposes, the very symbol of the almost permanent absence of the Oranges from the city. From having been a power without title, Amsterdam had become a capital without power.[8]

In his hilarious comedy of manners, De Geschiedenis van Wouterje Pieterse, the Dutch writer Eduard Douwes Dekker, born in 1820 and better known as Multatuli, describes the Amsterdam of his youth. It is a world full of small side streets, alcoves and backrooms, populated by characters such as Miss Pieterse, Master Pennewip, Miss Laps, the assistant teacher Miss Stoffel, the catechist, Van de Gracht, and the "ever so respectable" Van Halls.[9] It is only in the almost fairytale atmosphere of paths and bleaching fields does the eponymous Woutertje find some freedom, and it is also there that he encounters his love, Femke. The entire book takes place on the boundary between the city and the countryside, and Woutertje is in fact the child of a city that is ready to burst beyond its walls, but does not have the strength to do so.

After the French period the city remained an introverted community. From 1820 the large, picturesque city wall was demolished little by little, the Entrepotdok was built on the eastern side of the IJ, the connection to the sea was improved by driving a canal straight through North Holland, the legacy of the East India Company was picked up energetically by the new Nederlandse Handelmaatschappij (Dutch Trading Company). Mentally, however, Amsterdam remained within its old ramparts.

There were exceptions, of course. In 1816, all Amsterdam went to the IJ in order to see the miracle of a ship making way against the wind without oars or tugs. The small English steamer Defiance excited astonishment everywhere, but few would have understood that they were witnessing something that would eventually change the character of the city more than all the regents, palaces and treaties taken together. In 1825, Paul van Vlissingen established the Amsterdamse Stoombootmatschappij (Amsterdam Steamer Company), and offered regular services to London, Hamburg and a number of ports on the Zuiderzee. Initially, he ordered his ships from England, but he built his own smithy for repair work. This wharf quickly grew into an entire plant for machines and steam engines, and iron and steel began to flood the old timber wharves on the islands. In the city itself some businesses also began to use steam-driven machinery: a sugar refinery, and, of course, the diamond industry. These, however, were still exceptions.

Uncle Stastok, one of the main characters in the nineteenth-century moral panorama *Camera Obscura* (1839), a series of sketches of everyday Dutch life by Nicolaas Beets, who had an "insuperable aversion to steam engines", might have been a typical Amsterdam entrepreneur of his day. For most of them the very idea of progress was anything but natural. Having learned from bitter experience, the era of the Patriots having just passed, they preferred to stick to the working methods of their fathers and grandfathers. In early capitalist Amsterdam, very few businesses employed more than 40 workers; most had a handful of labourers and that was that. Innovations were adopted only when there was no other choice, and even then it was usually against the businessman's inclinations and without thanks. The advance of technology made people retreat into romanticism.

There was a curious culture of reaction in the city that flowed against the broad undercurrent of international progress: a mixture of conservatism, narrow-minded nationalism, romanticism, and religious revival. Amsterdam writers and poets such as Willem Bilderdijk and Da Costa inspired a movement called "Misgivings about the Spirit of the Age". Bilderdijk, especially, saw the Enlightenment and the French Revolution as a lapse of faith, a spiritual evil, a sin that had conjured up all the evils of modern times and let them loose on the world.

One of the sons of Maurits van Hall, Anne Maurits, a young and promising lawyer, joined this new movement. During the cholera epidemic of 1866 he tended to patients himself in one of the poorer districts, an experience which instigated in him a spiritual rebirth that led both him and Suze, his wife, to join a devout group of Calvinist Separatists, the Afgescheidenen (the Separated Ones), the precursors of today's Dutch Reformed Church. The Amsterdam elite perceived this as class treason, however. In vain did the old Patriot Maurits van Hall attempt to make his anti-revolutionary son change his mind. "There can be no compromise when it comes to religion and truth," he replied. Anne Maurits was expelled from his lawyer's chambers by his brother Floris, and thereafter the couple were avoided or harassed, until eventually they even had to be put under police protection. Shortly after this, Anne Maurits died of consumption. His wife, Suze, did not long outlive him, she too died of tuberculosis, only 27 years old. Their three children became wards of old Maurits van Hall and of their uncle, Floris, who had recently become Secretary of State for Finance.

A pencilled letter written by Suze to her children a month before her death has survived: "Farewell! Farewell! I can go on no longer. Almighty God, Thou knowest the struggle . . ." For her eldest son, Maurits, she wished her dead husband's reason and faith; she asked her daughter Johanna, a "dear, tender child", to give her heart to the Lord ("God may save you from false testimony and a loose tongue"); while her youngest son, Floris, was to become a preacher, a "servant of the Lord": "O, my consolation and my joy, often in my bitterest grief, how often have I made over your life to the Lord to be a Samuel . . ."

Maurits became an enormously wealthy banker, Johanna married a Secretary of State, and Floris Adrian ended his days a lonely, eccentric millionaire, in the largest palace of glass and steel the city ever was to see. The names of their parents, Suze and Maurits, however, were no longer mentioned in the canal house of the van Halls.[10]

The houses on the corner of the Leidsestraat and the Koningsplein which had collapsed at the beginning of the century had not been rebuilt 50 years later. The first Amsterdam water pipeline that runs through the dunes, opened in 1853, could only be built with English capital, and it was not until 1861 that the first pavement appeared in the city, in the Kalverstraat. Even as late as 1875 the Rembrandtplein was so quiet that the locals still kept chickens there, which scratched the ground all day long.[11]

While industrialization was marching swiftly forwards in other European cities, and factory chimneys began to darken their skylines, the cityscape of Amsterdam was to remain unchanged for decades. The opening of the first Dutch railway line, which ran between Amsterdam and Haarlem, on 20 September 1839 – an event which was to become a symbol for change – was reported by the *Algemeen Handelsblad* in no more than 20 lines. More important were a fire in the Kerkstraat, the opinions of the *Arnhemse Courant* about the nature of the Constitution, and the end-of-term celebrations of the Latin School.

"The plays are bad, some theatres are closed. Imagination and *esprit* do not exist here," wrote the young wife of King William III, Queen Sophie, to a friend after a visit to Amsterdam in 1850. "There are among the Amsterdammers some very intelligent and remarkable old gentlemen. As regards the ladies, although my reception was very well attended, I did not see a single beautiful or elegant one, apart from an exquisite Jewess. The people collect treasures, beautiful old cabinets, all manner of really magnificent show-pieces, but they never open their collection rooms and salons in order to take pleasure in them themselves."[12]

Even the revolutions of 1848, which set alight the capitals of France, Prussia and Austria – and which transformed the King at The Hague from a conservative to a liberal within a single night – hardly touched this burnt-out world city. There was a small group of activists in Amsterdam, however, mostly German craftsmen like the wood-turner Christian Gödecke and the apprentice tailor Karl Hanke, who were already seeking to adopt the precepts of the *Communist Manifesto*, which Marx and Engels published that year. Under the influence of the unrest elsewhere in Europe they had distributed a pamphlet encouraging the jobless of Amsterdam to congregate on the Dam on 24 March 1848, "so that there may be men there who represent their interests and who will take measures in order to improve their lot". When, on the day, thousands of people actually did turn up, the would-be revolutionaries almost died of shock. No member of the group could muster the courage to address the crowds and the people dispersed again, not much the wiser. To escape the authorities Gödecke and Hanke went underground but were arrested in due course and put on trial. Although there were demands that they should be sentenced to death, in the event they were acquitted. These events, too, largely passed the city by. Paradoxically, however, it was Amsterdam's very backwardness, its fear of progress, which was to rescue the old city for the future.

Slowly, Amsterdam merged with the water surrounding it. Even the most elegant houses were decaying in mud and dampness. An example was the almshouse on the Elandsgracht, now numbers 71–77, once the "fort" of the eighteenth-century master thief Shako. The journalist Justus van Maurik visited the building in its decay: there were windows broken in the façade, some of them had been replaced with paper, and at the back of the building there was not a single window pane intact. Seventeen families, more than a hundred people, lived in this "filthy and lightless den".

> In a small cellar at the back of the house, little more than a damp hole without light, at best a place to store coal or firewood, I came across an entire family: mother, father, eight children and an enormous dog.
>
> In the rooms above lived a few beggar women, who went around begging holding their small children in their arms. The dim and misty light that fell through the strangely slanted, half-obscured windows matched the dismal, miserable and dirty rooms that still bore a few traces of having seen better days.
>
> I was taken to a small room inhabited by an old bachelor. The alcove bed was falling apart. On a burnt and blackened chimney-piece stood a bottle with a candle stub, a broken mirror, an old tin of corned beef covered by a paternoster and a pair of rusty pince-nez.
>
> In a small room under the roof, pervaded with an abominably clammy, stinking atmosphere, I saw a woman washing the red baize underwear that her husband, a digger, had been wearing.
>
> In another room, a woman wearing no more than a few rags sat squatting near her neighbour's stove because she had no heating of her own. Her room contained no objects whatsoever.[13]

Among the Jewish community, the poverty was worse than among other Amsterdammers by several degrees. In spite of the fact that since the Batavian Revolution Jews had been allowed to work in any profession they chose, most kept to petty trade, even if some of them did manage to break out of the ghetto and become physicians and lawyers. After centuries of quasi-banishment, most professions seemed alien to them; they lived apart from other Amsterdammers in their own neighbourhoods, while their religion's proscription of work on Saturdays added to their practical problems.

Children were given into service or started to work as labourers at the age of twelve. In Amsterdam's wax candle factory, girls of this age had to carry boxes weighing 20 to 30 kilos, while boys sometimes worked from six o'clock in the morning until midnight for weeks on end. In 1886, a worker in the sugar refinery explained to a parliamentary commission that in the 19 years of his marriage, he and his wife had had 17 children, of whom only two were still alive.

Eduard Douwes Dekker, Dutch writer and government official, recorded the budget of the family of Klaas Ris, a sawmill worker.[14] Husband, wife and three children had to live on six guilders a week. Food, mainly bread and potatoes, took up two thirds of their money, leaving precisely 22½ cents for clothing, shoes, and medical help. When larger sums were required, Klaas would approach his employer for an advance, and for weeks afterwards the family would have to eat bread and potatoes with peas and salt, without butter or fat. When the writer asked, "Do you ever spend money on yourself, or to give pleasure to your wife and your children?" Ris answered, "I don't know how I could afford that."

Perhaps one of the most notable features of Amsterdam in the nineteenth century was its lack of monuments. While other European capitals competed with one another in building substantial urban palaces, tearing down old parts of the city and transforming them into imposing boulevards, and creating new streets and whole new districts of a hitherto unknown theatricality, Amsterdam contented itself with its "Naatje" on the Dam, a shabby statue representing Unity, which suffered the indignity of losing first an arm, then its head. The number of monumental buildings in Amsterdam dating from the nineteenth century can be counted on the fingers of one hand. Nowhere in the city was there anything comparable to a Regent Street or a Ringstrasse, there was never time, nor the municipal will, for the planning of a Place de la Concorde or a Boulevard Hausmann, much less an overall concept of city regeneration.

The few grand exceptions to this rule are the Rijksmuseum, the Central Station, the Concertgebouw and the Paleis voor Volksvlijt (Palace of People's Industry). The lack of monuments can be partly explained by the absence of an absolute and all-embracing princely rule, something necessary to effect the building of such large-scale projects. On the other hand, it was also a question of mentality. Grandiosity and gesture did not sit well with the character and outlook of the Dutch middle classes; besides, Holland had already been established for too long to feel the need for large national symbols. The monumental building which both expresses grandeur and at the same time creates it, did not in any way conform to the psychology of the city. It may be that the culture of compromise in Amsterdam was too strong for such gestures, perhaps, too, the city had been left too far behind to be able to participate on equal terms in the power play of modern industrial capitalism. Yet it may also have been due to another factor altogether: a lack of belief on the part of the sober Dutch in the value of the symbol, and the power of the immaterial.

It was a "stranger" who was to provide the city with its largest nineteenth-century building project, one of "the Old People" (as the Jews are called in the Netherlands), the son of a simple Jewish trader: the doctor, chemist, bread manufacturer and philanthropist Samuel Sarphati. Sarphati was a driven man, brilliant, full of ideas and initiative, convincing and energetic, a man of the kind that appears only once in every community, and that refuses to acknowledge the word "impossible". He woke the city from its slumbers with a number of initiatives: he established a rubbish collection, founded an abattoir, a society for land reclamation, a school of commerce, a school and a national mortgage bank. In order to stimulate the production of good and cheap food for the masses he set up on the Vijzelgracht Holland's first bread factory with a production of 90,000 cheap loaves a week. He established a new bank, the Credit Mobilier, especially for the newly emerging industry of the city. He seemed to be at home in all markets. In the municipal archive, I even found a little brochure he wrote about the miracle cloth Tarlatan, with the significant title "The Inflammation of Clothes and Means to Prevent It", which still contained between its pages a small piece of fabric printed with red polka dots.

The city patricians looked on Samuel Sarphati as a parvenu, a paria who was at best an amiable madman. This madman, however, tended to make whatever he founded or built work remarkably well, in some cases even down to the present day, be they hotels, factories, banks, or abattoirs. When, for instance, he built the Amstel Hotel outside the city, everyone declared him to have taken leave of his senses; but it is still there, one of the most prestigious hotels in Amsterdam.

Yet, significantly for Amsterdam's anti-monumentalism, Sarpharti found himself restrained by the city's bureaucracy, just at the time when he wanted to begin work on the surroundings of his hotel. Hoping to create more than just institutions and single projects, he had planned to build suburbs of grand villas to the east and west of the Amstel, with large gardens and parks, much like the area that was later built around the Vondelpark. Behind this, he had planned a spacious area for the lower middle classes and workers. This would have created a magnificent entry to the city on its south side. Sarpharti, however, died in 1866, and there was nobody of his stature to take over his role.

Even if there had been, all city planning schemes that were a little more ambitious than usual were routinely rejected by the municipal administration. Private initiative remained the one course of action, in the most limited sense of the word "action". The land alongside the Amstel and the orchards and sawmill yards were quickly redeveloped by people chasing a quick profit, once the green light had been given. Short-term gains were the main priority; the wood used was cheap, the stones of poor quality, the beams thin and the cement too sandy. In 1876, a building in the Ferdinand Bolstraat collapsed while it was being erected, and the same thing happened in 1900 in the Willibrordusstraat. One result of this practice was that the streets looked dilapidated after only a few years. "What do you feel when you see these high, monotonous houses?" asked the *Amsterdamsche Studentenalmanak* in 1882 after a visit to the new neighbourhood, Area YY, known as de Pijp. "You want to turn on your heel, don't you, and run away?"

Samuel Sarpharti did succeed in erecting one monumental building in Amsterdam, despite all opposition: the Palace of People's Industry on the Frederiksplein, now the site of today's Nederlandse Bank. It was a very modern and substantial building for its time, constructed in steel and glass, and modelled on London's Crystal Palace and the Palais de l'Industrie in Paris. Sarpharti wanted to give the palace to the city as a monumental building for commerce and exhibitions, and moreover as a symbol rising above the city, a sign of the modern times.

In September 1858, the first pile was driven into the ground by King William III himself, while Sarpharti apostrophized his monument as a "link in the chain of the great foundations which the human genius has erected in God's honour and for the benefit of the world". He also gave a speech which summed up the optimism of his century.

Photographer unknown, *View of the Paleis van Volksvlijt*, undated.

Six years later on 16 August 1864, after much strife, the city's new citizens' palace was formally opened by Prince Frederik Hendrik. For Sarphati, this was a day of triumph, the advent of modern times in Amsterdam. Tens of thousands of Amsterdammers had gathered there in order to look at the glass miracle, with its hundreds of arched windows, its vast hall and enormous glass cupola surmounted by a shining statue of a woman, De Faam (Fame), with a real torch in her hand which was visible at night from far away. In his speech, Samuel Sarphati addressed the Prince, telling him how many Amsterdammers had chipped in to put the building there: "Not one stone, not one nail has been given to us."[15] The orchestra came in and played the celebratory overture by von Weber. The Prince knighted the "stranger". The newspapers overflowed with lyricism:

> Where temples rise
> To truth and to light,
> We will sing our praises
> To the gift of the wise
> And the decent and bright.

In the evening fireworks exploded above the Amstel, while thousands of gaslights transformed the building into a fairytale palace. Poor Sarpharti was not to enjoy the glory of the building for long, however, for he died two years later, only 53-years-old.

"His" monument remained. But since the cost of maintaining the building was higher than the actual takings from exhibitions, the palace was also used for concerts, plays, and operas. Then a concert hall was built, and a gallery for exhibiting paintings, and before long the palace became a focal point for popular entertainment where people came in order to be seen. Masked balls, Oriental plays, fairs, balloon flights, Saint Nicholas celebrations for poor children – the Paleis van Volksvlijt was alive, though not perhaps in the way that Samuel Sarphati had envisaged. One image endured, however, one that he had seen in his dreams: the graceful lines of the palace with its cupola and rising above it the city, inspiring the surroundings with a harmony and a grace which, even today, still glows in the streets around the Amstel and the Frederiksplein.

World cities are tough institutions. Once a few enterprises have grown around the original core, be it a court, a market, or an industry, the whole acquires the dynamism of a piston. The attraction generated by such a system of activities is so great that the city is able to withstand considerable adversity. If not destroyed by terrible wars or some other overwhelming catastrophe, such a metropolis will rarely, if ever, be snuffed out once it has passed a certain threshold.

For this reason Amsterdam was eventually to catch up with the nineteenth century. This did not happen gradually, but abruptly, as if the Amsterdammers had been reluctantly seized by the scruff of their necks by an inescapable mechanism. In 1860, one could still hear a pin drop in the city. Barely 20 years later, however, in 1877, on an evening walk around the Damrak and the Kalverstraat, the Belgian writer Charles de Coster saw nothing but magnificently lit shops, spectacular jewellery, earrings, bright linen and a great many customers. "Illuminated cellars opened their entrances wide, and inside there were toy shops, piles of scarves and fabrics in all sorts of colours. The quays and canals were equally lively. Steamers with green lamps moved across the black, silent water in all directions. Omnibuses with people hanging on to them in droves and jumping off during the ride rattled across the echoing cobblestones. Street lamps in huge numbers were reflected in the water like large fiery snakes."[16] Suddenly, in barely two decades, Amsterdam was a waking city again, and even had a certain European air about it.

The causes of this economic miracle were many. In the first place there was the mighty neighbour, Germany, which was beginning to establish itself as an industrial power, dragging with it its satellites, including Amsterdam. Then there were the distant Dutch colonies in the Far East, which, after the opening of the Suez Canal and the adoption of a new system of agriculture, brought in so much revenue that within a short time it became possible to finance a number of railway lines, harbours, canals and other infrastructural projects.

Thus, in 1847, Amsterdam was linked to Rotterdam by rail, in 1856 to the German Rhine area, and in 1874 with Zwolle and the Dutch north. In Amsterdam, a large, wooden provisional station was built by the Droogbak, while bridges and viaducts brought rails further into the city.

As a result, another new phenomenon could be observed: mobility. All of a sudden Amsterdammers could be in Paris within a day, a journey which earlier would have taken them a week. Goods (and ideas) were distributed all over Europe, and the miracle of the steam train alone made the advent of modernity inevitable.

A crazy time began when diamonds were discovered in South Africa in 1869. This had an immediate effect on the city's diamond industry, then the most important branch of business in Amsterdam. With so much work coming in, the wages of the diamond workers climbed to hitherto unknown heights. For the dirt-poor Jewish proletariat, this was a small miracle. Almost a third of the city's working Jewish population were in "the business" as diamond splitters, cutters, or polishers. Now they became the elite of the working classes. They found that they could suddenly keep their children at school for longer, which improved the rest of the family as well. Others founded their own businesses or bought houses. The Weesperzijde, the Swammerdambuurt behind it and even a few "rich" parts of the Pijp still bear the marks of the sudden influx of wealth among the diamond workers of the time. In the event, their paradise lasted less than six years, at which point everything returned to "normal" poverty again. For many diamond workers, however, it had been the one push that had allowed

them to look beyond the narrow horizons of their existence. They would
never forget what they had glimpsed.

The great motor behind the modernization of Amsterdam was, however,
most of all the construction of the North Sea Canal. Begun in 1865 and
opened in 1876, this entirely new connection to the sea ran due west,
straight through the dunes from Amsterdam to the North Sea, suitable
for the largest and most modern ships. The city's harbours were enlarged
and renovated, new quays and islands were built, the first contours of
the Central Station (designed in 1876 and built between 1882 and 1889)
appeared on the IJ, and the city acquired a new face. Several years later, in
1892, Amsterdam gained a connection with the Rhine and the German
hinterland via the Merwede Channel. This channel was eventually to be
widened and deepened, and its course partially altered to become the
Amsterdam-Rhine Canal, but in principle the structure of the port of
Amsterdam was established now, serving partly as a final destination and
partly as a transit point, the second largest Dutch port after Rotterdam.

The economy was rejuvenated. The supply businesses gained full order-
books and on Amsterdam façades, countless inscriptions can still be seen
of businesses that started their existence then: cheese traders, makers of
harness leather, pump washers, glass blowers, coach builders, and steam
cutters for diamonds.

Thus the old city unfolded into the new Amsterdam, a city that was to
maintain its momentum for almost a century.

———

During those same years, Amsterdam was transformed from a city of water
into a landlocked city. In one of his stories Justus van Maurik describes
how he sat on a bench in front of the Yacht Harbour in the Nieuwe
Stadsherberg on the IJ one summer evening in 1872. It was at a time when
efforts were being made to clear away the last of the city's old water-
dominated landscapes. The Nieuwe Stadsherberg was to be demolished, and
the Yacht Harbour with its bizarrely shaped little houses and worm-eaten
jetties seemed destined to suffer the same fate to make way for the Central
Station, quays, and other harbour works that were to come in its place.
The people sitting on the little terrace were Amsterdammers who, as van

Maurik writes, had come by "to take another look across the IJ, irritated that the municipality was intent on spoiling it". "I could stay here for the entire night, it is so wonderfully calm and still," his neighbour said, an old man with a pipe, and they enjoyed one more summer's evening in the fresh, half-salty wind from the IJ, carrying the smells of grass and hay from the far side.[17]

The building of the Central Station was the largest construction project in nineteenth-century Amsterdam, and the city's greatest planning blunder ever. Originally the plan had been to site the main station either in the vicinity of the Leidseplein or by the Weesperpoortstation, today's Weesperplein. But the authorities in The Hague were convinced that the best place was right in front of the city, erected on three artificial islands. Almost all Amsterdam's own experts and others involved thought this to be a catastrophic plan, "the most disgusting possible attack on the beauty and glory of the capital". Nevertheless, the building of the Central Station in front of the open harbour was forced through by the railway department of the Ministry of Transport in The Hague, and the Home Secretary, Thorbecke. Finally, the plan made its way through the Amsterdam municipal council by a narrow majority.

The Amsterdam Chamber of Commerce warned that it would be an "eternal and irreversible mistake" if the station were to appear in the place in which it stands today, and listed several points of order. The wharves on the Kattenburg would be inaccessible to large ships, and the Chamber was especially worried by the position of the harbour which would be "forever and without salvation spoiled and unusable" because of the enormous island on which the station was to be built.[18] As it happened, the latter problem proved to be a minor one; the harbour developed elsewhere and became better and larger than would have ever been possible in its original location. Even though the architect of the station, P. J. H. Cuypers, produced a grand building, the fact remained that it cut off the city from the IJ in one fell swoop. The contrast between the bustling inner city and the spaciousness of the IJ, which must have lent Amsterdam an invigorating and liberating air, had vanished. The wonderful panorama of the city, the two miles of shimmering masts, spires and merchant houses, was destroyed for ever.[19]

The closing of the IJ spelled the end of Amsterdam as a typical water city,

as the Chamber of Commerce was only too well aware. The inner city had
been built or redeveloped with the three main means of transport of the
seventeenth century in mind: the sailing ship, the towing barge, and carts.
"The rumbling of the bridge chains merges with the rattling of the wagons,
the whistle of the steam boats drowns out the chimes from the bell tower;
the rigging of the ships blends into the leaves on the trees; the carriage rides
next to the barge; the shop is mirrored in the canal and the sails are reflected
by the shop windows," the young Italian Edmondo de Amicis wrote of
Amsterdam in 1873. "Life on land and on sea go hand in hand here . . . and
thus form a new and lively stage, a feast of peace and community."[20]

Not many years later this had all ended. Amsterdam had been transformed into a landlocked city within very few decades. The railway took
over the function of the waterways. Some canals were filled in for reasons of
public hygiene – the open sewer, for instance, called the Goudsbloemgracht
(Gold Flower Canal), today's Willemstraat – but mainly to make room for
the increasing volume of street traffic. This was not entirely unreasonable:
the countless steep bridges, pavements, fences, cellar holes and conserv-
atories were not especially suited to tramways, stage coaches, large carriages
and masses of pedestrians. In order to create an efficient tram link with
the new building developments in the west of the city, the Rozengracht
and the Warmoesgracht were filled in 1889 and 1895 respectively. In 1904,
the "enjoyable Overtoom canal" was filled in, followed in the 1930s by the
Vijzelgracht. A boulevard was even built in the narrow centre of Amsterdam
by closing another famous waterway, the Damrak and the Rokin.[21]

A total of 16 canals, small and large, vanished from the map during the
period between 1857 and 1895, and this landfill mania only abated around
the turn of the century. Amsterdam's elite began to acquire a feeling for
something that had not been a consideration at the time of the building of
the Central Station: the beauty of the city.

When the Nieuwezijds Voorburgwal, a canal with surprising little
squares, fine churches and historic sites, broad and narrow in parts, which
would have been one of the most beautiful in the city, was renovated into
a dull street, the measure was full. The newspapers protested against this
"shallow and characterless imitation of foreign cities". So, when it was
suggested, around 1901, that the Reguliersgracht and the Spiegelgracht
should be filled in, the lobbying of those who wanted to protect their

homes and of the historical societies was so strong, the plans were quickly shelved. Thus Amsterdam was saved the fate of, say, Paris or London, where the medieval and seventeenth-century city structure was almost entirely obliterated by large-scale nineteenth-century redevelopment.

Amsterdam's population was on the rise again, from 211,000 souls in 1840 (fewer than the 221,000 in 1795) to 243,000 in 1859 and 265,000 in 1869. A growing movement of people into the city, as the harbour and other large projects provided more work, eventually swelled into an immigration wave around the end of the century. Between 1880 and 1910, more than 130,000 migrants came from the poor rural areas of Friesland, Groningen and Overijssel and settled in the outskirts of Amsterdam. Countless Amsterdammers today only have to go back three or four generations to find this change from country to city in their own families. Just as in the seventeenth century, Amsterdam had become a city of newcomers again; by 1900, its population numbered more than half a million.

Artist unknown, *Panorama of Amsterdam from the Oosterkerk* (c. 1870).

Never before had the city been so large. First, in 1860, the former city walls were used as building land (the rows of flats in the Marnixstraat are remnants of this). For the affluent middle classes, the former Plantage was transformed into a beautiful neighbourhood, the first "modern" residential area to be built in nineteenth-century Amsterdam. For ordinary people, the Pijp was developed in 1868, and afterwards the Swammerdam area on

the other side of the Amstel. After 1880, the Dapper and Oosterpark areas
followed, and then the city slowly continued to spread east and west.

Urban planning hardly preoccupied the municipal administration at this
time. If a building company wanted to insert another street into the already
narrow back yards of a development there would be no opposition, and
this was the genesis of bizarre little lanes such as the Van Swindenstraat
in the Dapper area. Other builders did not even go to the trouble of
spreading a layer of sand on top of the boggy foundations. They built no
higher than polder water level, which is the reason why even today one
has to step a good yard lower around the Bellamystraat and the Kinker
area.[22]

Only the one part of the city escaped the blandness of most nineteenth-
century developments: the area around the Vondel Park. When the Plantage
recreation ground was swept away to make way for houses, members of
the Stock Exchange and bankers set up a fund for the establishment of a
large, new park. The Vondel Park would enable Amsterdam once again to
compete with other great cities. The founding fathers, however, had bought
far more land than was needed for the park, in order to finance it with
the profit from selling the unused ground. When this land was auctioned
off, the same restrictions were applied as during the building of the canal
belt: private individuals were permitted to use it as building ground,
as long as no worker's lodgings or factories were built on it. Thus, another
area of the city came into being, a spacious area of stately villas, intersected
by quiet, broad and shady avenues, the Vondelstraat and especially the
Willemsparkweg, the beginnings of what was to become Amsterdam
Oud-Zuid. Important institutions found their home in this semi-rural
environment: the Manege (1881), the Concertgebouw (1888), and the
Rijksmuseum (1885), this last being, quite literally, the gateway to another
world.[23]

During the nineteenth century, Amsterdam was not one but several cities,
which sometimes had very little to do with each other. Every living thing
between God and His angels in Heaven and the beetles and worms of
the earth was classified by rank and class. In Multatuli's satirical "moral

panorama", *De geschiedenis van Woutertje Pieterse*, a character called Master Pennewip has devised a scheme in order to determine where exactly in the social ranking the young hero, Woutertje, belongs – but one has to admit it is closer to the beetles than to Our Lord:

Bourgeois, Third Class, Seventh Sub-Division
Middle-class people living "in rooms".
a) Own front door. Three windows. Two floors with back rooms. The boys sleep by themselves, but get dressed with the girls. Folding screen. Learn French. [...] The girls are called Lena, sometimes Maria, but very rarely Louise. They do embroidery and are very polite. The boys work in an office. Keep maid, sewing mistress, and a "person for hard work". The washing hangs wet in the house. [...] Sundays smoked meat, clean linen, liqueurs and coffee. Religion and respectability.
b) Still three windows. One floor. [...] Leentje, Meitje, Louise very rare indeed. [...] Sleep in one room. Maid, "half sewing mistress", and a "person". Sundays cheese, no liqueurs, but other-wise religion and respectability as above.
c) Second floor. Two sash windows. Whole family sleeps in two beds. Boys are called Louw, Piet, or Gerrit, and become watch-makers or typesetters. Sometimes, rarely, trips to the seaside. [...] Otherwise religion as above. Know "very respectable people". No maid or person, but a sewing mistress for sixpence and a sandwich.

This lowest-class floor, in the eyes of Master Pennewip, is where Woutertje Pieterse belongs.

Until the mid-nineteenth century, the concept of class was all-important. One Amsterdam consisted of "gentlemen", the "better class", the bour-geoisie that still perceived itself as a unity. The other consisted of the great majority, "the people", or, since workers were seen mainly as needy consumers rather than as exploited producers, "the poor". Between these two Amsterdams there was a vague concept of a middle order, although its position was far from clear.

It was immediately obvious to which class one belonged. There was, for instance, a marked distinction between hat people and cap people; a gentleman wore a hat, black in winter, white in summer; a worker wore the same cap all year round. A worker wore a smock, a gentleman a long, formal coat. As far as the women were concerned, the crinoline and the hooped skirt made it clear that its wearer did not have to do paid work (which, incidentally, would have been impossible while wearing such a contraption), and that she was entitled to be addressed as "Mevrouw" (if married) or "Juffrouw" (if not).

In any community where there is little social mobility, it is only a matter of time before society ossifies, and that is precisely what happened in the Amsterdam of the first half of the nineteenth century. The rigidly hierarchical division of the world into classes ensured that the small upper echelon was insufficiently replenished and renewed from the groups beneath it. Climbing the social ladder was almost impossible for someone from the lower classes, and the only paths open to him were to seek his fortune in the colonies, or to become a teacher or church minister. Education in the Latin and French schools was open only to children from the upper classes.

With the modernization of the city, all this was slowly to change. Curiously, the lessening of class differences was most obvious from the clothes people wore on the street. By the late 1800s men from the "better" classes no longer wore colourful and expensive jackets, waistcoats and trousers. Often they contented themselves with a black cloth jacket and a black tie. Off-the-peg clothing, which was introduced after 1850, further helped to blur class distinctions. "Class" as a concept still existed (it had not even been superseded yet by that other yardstick "money"), but it was no longer a criterion applying to clearly and rigidly circumscribed groups.

Now, however, the new bourgeoisie began to conquer the city. There arose an army of civil servants, directors and engineers, who took part in the *de facto* government of business and State for rewards that were good, but not especially handsome. Yesterday's craftsmen became valuable skilled workers in large, modern factories, and because these manufacturing concerns no longer had direct contact with their customers, another large group sprang up in between, consisting primarily of retailers, cobblers, and small merchants. This process took place within one or, at the most, two generations, a breathtaking pace for the people involved.

In the literature of the time we frequently meet this new bourgeoisie, which tended to borrow its norms from an older "genteel" class as best it could, because it was not able to develop a stance of its own *vis à vis* its newly-found wealth in so short a space of time. The ceilings and mantelpieces of the new houses on the Weesperzijde, the Amsteldijk, the Stadhouderskade, the Binnenkant and the Plantage Middenlaan were more or less faithful copies of those in the large canal houses, only smaller and less lavish. Even the simple houses in de Pijp had a little ornamentation above the door and a bit of stucco on the ceiling, cheap and simple, but still sufficient to maintain the illusion of propriety and respectability.

The second half of the nineteenth century was thus a period of social change: fault lines shifted or vanished, new ones appeared, as though a volcano was making Amsterdam society tremble and tear.

People increasingly wanted to know about the world. Amsterdam became a city of newspapers, with its own "Fleet Street" on the Pijpenmarkt at the Nieuwezijds Voorburgwal. There was a newspaper for everybody. For the liberals there was the distinguished *Algemeen Handelsblad*, the first newspaper of the Netherlands, which had appeared daily since 1830 and was alluded to among journalists as "the Pope of the Pijpenmarkt". For the middle classes there were the more popular *Nieuws van de Dag*, *Het Nieuwsblad Nederland*, and later *De Echo*. Then there was *Het Geeltje*, a smaller revival of the old *Amsterdamse Courant*, which had lost its place to the *Handelsblad*, a journal printed on yellow paper. For lovers of scandal there was *Het Amsterdams Vliegend Blad*, a kind of tabloid, full of reports of fires and other sensations. For the "radicals" there was *De Amsterdammer*, originally a daily, which became the weekly *De Groene Amsterdammer*. The Protestants had *De Standaart*, the Catholics *De Tijd*. There was even a special paper for those who preferred not to read certain stories: *De Amsterdamsche Lantaren*, which appeared at irregular intervals containing scandalous news about prominent citizens and was sold close to the house of the concerned. "Buy, citizens, *De Amsterdamsche Lantaren*. Herein you can read about the adventures of a well-known Amsterdam slumlord, a young widow and her friend. The names and addresses are in there, too. The price is only three cents." It was usually not long before the victim got out his or her purse and bought up the entire edition, compensating the hawkers and editors handsomely.[24]

The discussions in the more serious papers mirrored the political debates in the city. The old-fashioned liberalism of the wealthy bourgeoisie was increasingly coming under pressure. On the right, Protestant and Catholic "ordinary people" set about their emancipation, a social development that largely took place within the closed, ideologically streamlined circle of schools, universities, unions, and political parties. One of the first demands was directed towards the reinforcement of their own ramparts: private schools should be funded with public money – after all, one also paid tax for State schools. Every Catholic had his own Catholic school, his own Catholic paper, his own Catholic politician and his own Catholic greengrocer – it was the same with the Protestants and later, in some respects, with the socialists. During the first half of the twentieth century this "compartmentalization" of society was to spread further: to radio stations, class organizations, children's crèches, in short, to virtually every aspect of life in the Netherlands.

On the left, the liberals (who were usually from the families of regents) were mainly attacked by a group of young citizens who sought an immediate end to the existing *laissez-faire* administration. To them, the wild growth of private horse-drawn trams or of gas and water companies was nothing less than evil. They understood that the modern age, with its large-scale developments, required different administrative structures from those of the years of barges and small shops. The most important representative of these "radicals", William Treub, described the existing liberalism as "an old maid who will never flame into passionate fire, however long one may stroke her". Together with P. L. Tak, later a socialist leader, he founded a union of voters, "Amsterdam", and at its meetings pleaded for universal suffrage, a social building programme, and the annexation by the municipality of the private gas and water companies and other utilities. For the radicals, some things were so important that they "cannot be established at all, or quickly enough, or cheaply enough, by private enterprise".

In 1893, Treub was successfully elected into the city magistracy. Meanwhile, suffrage had been widened considerably. He immediately began to de-privatize. He revoked the licences to the unpopular Imperial Continental Gas Association and fashioned it into a company owned by the municipality. The same happened with the water pipeline over the dunes and the Amsterdamse Omnibus Maatschappij (Amsterdam Omnibus Company), which had run a number of horse-drawn trams in the city since

1875. In doing all this, Treub instigated an evolutionary process that was to give a lasting social basis to city policy.

From the beginning, electricity was provided more or less by the municipality, but the licence for operating telephones was in the hands of the Nederlandsche Bell Telefoon Maatschappij. In 1896, the municipality began to establish its own telephone net, thereby causing a silent war to erupt between Bell and the city of Amsterdam. The network was still largely connected by overhead wires, with tall telephone towers here and there from which a chaos of lines emanated. One of these towers still stands near the Beurs van Berlage. It was therefore not difficult to cut the necessary wires during the night, and Bell even used a special boat with a tall mast to which a razor-sharp blade had been fixed so as to cut the wires suspended above canals. The fight between the two companies ended on 30 October 1896, when Bell gave up, threatened with a court case. On 1 November 1896 Amsterdam had its own municipal telephone company.

Photographer unknown, *The Uilenburgstraat* (c. 1900).

Things were also on the move in the working-class districts. The "other" Amsterdam had never been entirely docile in the past, but the social order had never been fundamentally challenged. Things were different now.

Already half way through the nineteenth century, the typesetters and diamond workers had founded their own unions, but now other groups began to stir as well. In 1872, not only the typesetters but also the cigar makers and the bakers went on strike. In the same year, Karl Marx spoke in Amsterdam before a circle of interested workers. On 7 July 1878 the city's first social-democratic society was established, led by H. Gerhard, the organizer of the First International. Six months later the first social-democratic newspaper appeared, *Recht voor Allen* (Rights for All), edited by the charismatic former preacher Ferdinand Domela Nieuwenhuis. The paper was widely distributed throughout all working-class areas and was to play an important role during the upheavals that rolled through Amsterdam in the next few years.

Socialism was little less than a faith for Amsterdam's workers, and Ferdinand Domela Nieuwenhuis was its prophet. A one-time preacher, he looked and behaved like an apostle, having abandoned his ministry in order to dedicate himself full-time to the working-class movement. In some districts the workers carried him on their shoulders, and there were skirmishes on some Amsterdam streets when he was given a prison sentence for lese-majesty, a crime which could hardly have been avoided, given the antics of the "Gorilla King" William III. On Sunday, 4 July 1886, he was celebrated as a martyr in a park outside the Raampoort. People sang the "Mariannenlied", a song popular with workers at the time:

> Your masters, low parasites,
> Demand of you: believe in God;
> That they may have all heav'nly rights
> And you a Hell of shame and rot.

Exactly three weeks later, the notorious "Eel Uprising" erupted in the Jordaan, eventually causing 26 deaths and scores of casualties. For the first time, a red flag flew above an Amsterdam barricade.

The uprising took its name from an old Dutch folk tradition: the so-called "eel pulling". A rope was strung across a canal or other waterway and a live eel, preferably smeared with green soap, was suspended from it. The participants had to pull the eel off the rope from a small boat, or to hang on to it so tightly that the head was torn off. Of course the fun was that most of those trying would fall into the water. The authorities had already forbidden this game years earlier, considering it "a cruel popular entertainment".

The Eel Uprising was a typical example of what is now called a police riot, a disturbance caused by the presence of police drafted in to prevent it. Many other factors played their part in the background, but the initial cause was trivial.

On a warm summer's day in 1886, the inhabitants of the Lindengracht, then still a working canal (it was later filled in), had organized a street party with sack races and similar entertainments. This had been such a success that it was decided to breathe new life into the dead folk tradition of eel pulling on the following Sunday, 25 July. Twenty Jordaan inhabitants each contributed half a guilder, a nice fat eel was bought, and there were still six guilders left over for the prize. The police got wind of the affair, however, and untied the rope which was had already been strung across the canal. There was a small commotion, during which one policeman was beaten with an umbrella and another was thrown down into a cellar. The police were not going to put up with this. A detachment of officers sent into the area was pelted with stones. Meanwhile, a meeting of socialists had taken place in the nearby Volkspark and the participants began to take part in the fights. Police officers used batons and sabres, some arrests were made and at ten o'clock things seemed quiet again.

On the following day, however, all hell broke lose. Probably inspired by the Commune revolution in Paris in 1871, barricades constructed from cobble-stones and planks were erected in the Lindenstraat and the Boomstraat. On the Zaterdagse Brug, over the Lindengracht, one red and one black flag flapped in the wind, but these were quickly pulled down by the sons of the very Orange-minded "burgomaster" of the Willemstraat, Ko Mens, better known as Bokkebek.

"At half-past four, an attack under a red flag was made on the police with stones," wrote Johan Geerke, city reporter of the daily De Amsterdammer.

It was raining stones. The police were pushed back up to the [police] station on the Noordermarkt. In the Lindenstraat and the streets that run off it, people broke up the paving and halved

the cobble stones in order to use them as weapons. Thirty policemen came in order to reinforce Section Five. A walk through the
Boomstraat and the Lindenstraat and behind the crowds showed us
that the stones used as projectiles were prepared by boys, who tore
them up out of the streets and broke them into the pieces with a
variety of instruments, and then brought them to the barricades in
baskets. It was impossible to ignore the fact that the attitude of the
people was, with some exceptions, overwhelmingly hostile. Among
other things, a woman railed against a boy on the Lindengracht
who had angrily thrown a stone into the water that he had been
unable to break up: "Are you stupid, boy? You can put that one to
better use against the lackeys!"

Military reinforcements were now brought in. The crowd was threatening
to storm the police headquarters on the Noordermarkt. At six o'clock in
the evening, live ammunition was fired. Many "ordinary" people were
wounded in their houses by stray bullets, as Johan Geerke reports:

> The salvos rang through the streets, the bullets flew everywhere,
> hitting the houses. The man who had flown the red flag on the
> barricades collapsed, hit by a bullet, and a horrifying spectacle
> of confusion arose. [. . .] Around nine o'clock the lanterns on the
> lock connecting the Prinsengracht and the Prinsenstraat were
> extinguished. In front of the Prinsenstraat, a barricade of cobble-
> stones had been erected. Forty police officers who had tried to
> take the barricade had to retreat under a hail of stones. Meanwhile
> a detachment of infantry had come to their aid and fired three
> salvos in the direction of the dark Prinsenstraat. We do not know
> whether there were any dead and wounded, but we assume so.[25]

On the following day, *Het Vliegend Blad* published a long list of those who
had been killed, including the name of the man with the red flag who had
refused to leave the barricades. He was called Hallee, and was a basket
weaver by profession.

The eel itself, with which all the trouble had started, resurfaced years
later. In February 1913, its brown, dried skin was sold as Lot 1324 by the
auction house Bom in the Warmoesstraat, complete with a declaration of

1. Het palingtrekken op de Lindengracht.
2. Aanval op het huis van den bakker.
3. Gewonden worden het bureau van politie binnen gedragen.
4. De roode vlag op een barricade.
5. Wachtpost in de Noorderkerk.
6. Begrafenis der slachtoffers

W. Streelink, *The Palingoproer*, etching (1886).

authenticity signed by a certain D. Nieuwenboer of Lindengracht, which claimed that this was the only true eel of the Eel Uprising "and the holes for the rope are still visible". It was sold for one guilder and seventy-five cents to a retired infantry lieutenant, and has since then vanished without a trace.[26]

There exists a photograph of the Amstelveenseweg taken in early spring, 1898, the same Amstelveenseweg that we know from old prints as a shady country lane. The roadway is still unpaved, the large trees are still standing, and in the foreground there is, as always, a farmer walking with a basket full of eggs or bread. The great difference between this scene and earlier depictions lies in something else, however: suddenly, there are cyclists on the path, a boy in a sailor's suit, a lady wearing a smart cycling skirt, a gentleman with a hat, and two other men – five cyclists on an old, narrow road.

These were the years of gaslit Amsterdam, that soft, humming light which was lit, lamp by lamp, along the canals; the years of new technology and old forms, of hesitating on the threshold of the new century.

Floris and Maurits van Hall, the children of the "Separated Ones" Suze and Anne Maurits van Hall, had grown up to become wealthy bankers. Their sister Hanna had died in 1884. Floris had a banking office in Utrecht, he was a valued member of the Utrecht council of magistrates, but after the death of his wife he had retreated to his old city, Amsterdam. His house in Utrecht stood empty for most of the time. It was known as "Hall's Haunted House", because of the secret passages and empty safes which he had installed to confuse burglars. He was President-Commissioner of the Paleis voor Volksvlijt, and he quickly moved into Het Paviljoen (The Pavilion), a building that had been incorporated into the palace itself, high up between the glass arches and steel beams.

Maurits van Hall had become a genuinely liberal banker in Amsterdam, an aristocratic patriarch with a large, dark beard, and the father of nine children. He was the founder and director of the Banque de Paris et de Pays Bas and a member of the Lower Chamber. He lived in one of the most beautiful houses in the famous "Goude Bocht" (Golden Curve) of the Herengracht, and from there walked every day to his office a little further along the quiet canal, silver-topped walking stick in hand, greeting his acquaintances amiably with a lift of his tall hat.

Amsterdam was prospering once more. In 1903, a new palace of trade was opened on a landfill site between the Warmoesstraat and the Damrak, the new Stock Exchange building by the progressive architect Berlage, virtually a city in itself, a vast complex of squares, halls, rooms and corridors.

The Amsterdam Atheneum Illustre had become a university in 1877, with laboratories and hospitals, and now the Reformed Protestants, the descendants of the "Separated Ones", founded their own university, the Vrije Universiteit (Free University). They had increasingly more confidence, these pious Protestant dissidents, because another charismatic leader had appeared among them, the Amsterdam preacher Abraham Kuyper, who had left the official Hervormde Kerk (Reformed Church) in 1886 with a large group of followers. They found that they had no place anymore in the old Reformed churches, even though Kuyper and his congregation had attempted to "squat" in the Nieuwe Kerk; nevertheless the Gereformeerd (Reformed) Protestants had soon built their own church, the Keizersgrachtkerk.

Amsterdam was bustling with life. By the 1890s, the first electric trams were screeching through the city, roughly along the route which is still followed by today's number 10 tram, and everyone thought that the sparrows who alighted on the wires would immediately be struck dead. On 21 July 1897, the *Algemeen Handelsblad* carried a report of a "peculiar vehicle" on the Nieuwezijds Voorburgwal: "The object, which was far from graceful, had the speed of a horse at a slow canter, and cannot be compared more accurately with anything but a box-bed on wheels." On the Rembrandtplein, legendary establishments blossomed: Mille Colonnes, De Kroon, Mast, Schiller. Then there was the Karseboom, a local hall with space for 1,400 patrons, offering 24 Wilhelmina billiard tables, two deafening orchestras, a ladies' and a gentlemen's band. When one stopped, another struck up. Everyone went there.

The Kalverstraat was full of glamorous shops, although between the hours of twelve and four o'clock in the afternoon it was effectively off limits for respectable ladies. During these hours, their menfolk went to the Stock Exchange, and only prostitutes were seen strutting on the Dam and the Kalverstraat.

As for the "Area YY" or de Pijp, it had by now become the bastion of bohemians, full of dreamers, poets, drunkards, and pioneers of the new century. In one simple little hall, the cellar of Quellijnstraat 64, the singer Eduard Jacobs introduced the Netherlands to the phenomenon that was cabaret, stunning his audience with his harsh, realist songs. The area was full of beer houses, lodging houses and other places of a more secret

Photographer unknown, *An Amsterdam Street* (c. 1910).

entertainment. There was, too, a special weekly published here called
Pst-Pst, and full of advertisements like these:

FOR RENT: A SPACIOUS SITTING- AND BEDROOM IN THE
PIJP. RENT 200 FLORINS A MONTH, INCLUDING USE OF GAS
LIGHT AND OF A CHARMING 18-YEAR-OLD LADY. LETTERS
UNDER NUMBER . . .

I NEED AN HEIR. MY HUSBAND IS NOT IN ANY STATE TO PROVIDE
ONE. WHO WILL DO SERVICE AS CREATOR ? LETTERS UNDER
"CREATOR" TO NUMBER . . .

MY HUSBAND IS TERRIBLY JEALOUS. I AM NOT ABLE TO
PROMOTE HIM TO CUCKOLD. WHO WOULD BE WILLING TO TAKE
UPON HIMSELF THE ROLE OF MANSERVANT IN MY HOUSE?
GENTLEMEN WITHOUT FORTUNE, AS LONG AS THEY ARE FROM
A GOOD HOUSE, CAN LAY CLAIM TO A LARGE SALARY. LETTERS
UNDER SERVANT TO NUMBER . . .

Hotbeds of chaotic talent appeared everywhere. The radicals around Treub assembled in the comfortable beer house Zur Batavia (Kalverstraat 165) and the Willemsen (Heiligeweg 26–28), while in Fricke's Bodega (Kalverstraat 234) a whole new literary movement developed, the so-called Tachtigers.

"Yes, all that 'gassing'," one of them was to write much later. "In all sorts of rooms in the Pijp, or in cafés, at Willemsen's, the Mast, Krasnapolsky, the Poort van Cleve, or in all the beer houses of Amsterdam. How we talked, and how I talked! New concepts of literature and other arts came into existence here: everything was fermenting." These years, however, were also destined to pass away.

Photographer unknown, *The New American Hotel* (c. 1910).

The writer Bordewijk once likened Amsterdam before the First World War to a dilapidated brothel, describing it as a great mass of stone, a Red Palace: "a heavy brick building, coloured brownish-red, the shutters closed in all its windows," a place from which the patricians kept away because the age of patricians was over.

In 1903, the determining conflict in Amsterdam was fought between the fast-growing workers' movement and the city's old elites. The workers, whose confidence had increased, demanded that their harbour employers should only take on personnel who were members of a union, as was already the case with their British colleagues.

These demands were not met, and on 9 January workers on the Blauwhoedenveem went on strike, and before long all Amsterdam's rail workers had followed their lead. Later the strikes were to spread to shunters, engineers, stokers, brakemen, watchmen and other railway employees throughout the Netherlands.

"Every wheel will stand quite still / If your strong arms show the will," the socialist posters triumphantly declared, posters that depicted a gigantic railway worker halting outgoing trains at Amsterdam Central Station with one hand imperiously raised. Encouraged by the railwaymen's success, Amsterdam's municipal workers also went on strike, and on 9 February they got their way.

Two weeks later, the government hit back. Led by the already mentioned anti-revolutionary Abraham Kuyper, it made illegal any strikes in public services, such as the railways, the "throttling laws". Another railway strike followed, but this proved to be a traumatic event for the still young workers' movement. Soldiers had been deployed on stations and in railyards everywhere, keeping the machinery running and protecting the non-strikers. Strikers were sacked and those willing to work were employed in their place. Years later, the daughter of one of the strike leaders was to recall that the strikers had one day suddenly heard the faraway whistle of a steam engine, and that her father had put his head in his hands and murmured "Now all is lost."

The First World War passed Amsterdam and Holland by. The Netherlands remained neutral, and the only thing that Amsterdam noticed was a collapse in trade, a brief panic in the banks, a stream of Belgian refugees, a handful of war profiteers, and hunger among the workers and their families. When, in 1917, there were no longer any potatoes to be had in the entire Jordaan, while ships full of potatoes were lying in the Prinsengracht, a small rebellion broke out. The ships were stormed, as were railway wagons in the Rietlanden. The Social Democrat Wibaut, then just elected, received a delegation of five women in the Town Hall and had his first taste of the dilemma faced by revolutionary leaders in power. "Did you know that there is rice enough for all?" he dared to suggest. "Good food, and cheap." The women departed furiously. The Communist daily *De Tribune* commented the next day: "Wibaut is trying to poison the workers."[27]

A more critical confrontation took place in November 1918, when the revolutionary movements in Germany and Russia threatened to erupt in the Netherlands as well. Soldiers who wanted to return home began a mutiny; there was some looting and even the Social Democrats declared that the time was ripe for radical change.

On 13 November, the revolution spread to Amsterdam – and immediately sank without a trace. In the evening, a recently established *Landelijk Revolutionair Comité* (National Revolutionary Committee) had organized a meeting in the Diamond Exchange on the Weesperplein, at which the prominent Socialists Henriette Ronald Holst, Domela Nieuwenhuis and David Wijnkoop were to speak. But the hall was so packed with people that the podium was obscured by thick clouds of tobacco smoke, and no speaker could be understood by anyone standing at a distance, as one eyewitness, the journalist-to-be, Maurits Dekker, recalled. After the close of the meeting the participants marched through the city, and when these demonstrators passed the Sarphatistraat Barracks, they shouted to the soldiers inside to join them. Maurits Dekker was to recall the details of what followed years later:

Upstairs [in the barracks], by the open windows, the soldiers stood laughing. Down below there was a floodlit gate and about ten metres in front of it an iron fence, the gates of which are locked with a thick chain. The papers later wrote that the crowd had wanted to attack the barracks and that someone had tried to force the gates with a hatchet. I did not see that. I only know that the light on the gates suddenly went out and that shortly afterwards I saw a row of fire flashes and heard the whistling of bullets. There was shouting, some of the demonstrators fled, while others threw themselves to the ground. I, too, had hit the ground. More salvos followed. [. . .] In the light of a lantern, the man who had been lying in the street next to me showed me something: a light-brown soft hat, on the rim of which there was a piece of greyish-pink fish liver, the size of a walnut. "A piece of my friend's brain," said the man.

Other defenceless demonstrators were struck down by this unexpected shooting. In total, three were killed and 18 wounded. However, the Dutch Revolution fizzled out almost immediately.

———

The liberal banker and patriarch Maurits van Hall had died at the end of the nineteenth century, but his brother, Floris Adriaan, who had once been "made over to the Lord as a Samuel", was still alive. He knew the world of the stage as no other, had travelled the Balkans during the Russo-Turkish War and had retreated from public life after a financial scandal. Bizarre stories made the rounds in the city about the schemes in which he had invested: a submarine railway link between Ireland and Newfoundland; an expedition to find the vanished Atlantis, after which gigantic tubes were to be sunk vertically into the sea-bed in order to make the fabled city visible again; and a plan to irrigate the Sahara.

He rarely if ever left his rooms in the immense Paleis van Volksvlijt, and for the most part lived in the eternal night of a windowless room. One door in his apartment led to a box in the Paleis Theatre, from which he could follow whatever was happening on stage.

Sometimes, during an opera performance, it would happen that all eyes would suddenly fix on the Director's box. There he would be, standing as though he had appeared out of thin air: an ancient, bent man, thin as a rake, with a pale, sharp bird-like face. "The figure bent forward out of the box, the trembling hand rested on the velvet rim, his mouth as though he was chewing", as a theatre critic described one of these interruptions. "This strange, almost ghostly figure looked into the theatre, wrapped up in a woollen smoking jacket, head covered with a small cloth cap, and held hundreds of visitors spellbound, distracted, staring at the peculiar apparition."

He died on 24 February 1929, aged 90, in his lonely palace apartment. Not two months later, flames suddenly sprang up in "his" palace, at the front and back, seemingly everywhere at once, fanned by a strong south-westerly wind. It seemed, as the newspapers were to record, as if the building was covered in oil, for the flames licked greedily up the façade and, before long, along the sides as well.

The walls of the palace, for a large part made out of corrugated iron sheets, literally curled up, glowing red. The burning doors of the Paleis Café flapped open and shut. At times it seemed as though a whole district was on fire, the flames reflected in every window around the Frederiksplein. For the last time, the clock on the Paleis struck three.

So intense was the heat that the members of the fire brigade attempted to protect their faces with pieces of zinc, and turned their helmets round to use the leather neck flaps at least to partly cover their faces. The oxygen cylinders in the Paleis Café periodically exploded, sending debris flying into the surrounding areas, in addition to the sparks raining down from the fire itself. The trees on the Frederiksplein looked like Christmas trees, decorated with bright sparks on every branch.

At a quarter to four, the roof of the restaurant, which had just been renovated and where, in all probability, the blaze began, caved in with a heavy sigh. The iron pillars bent like burning matchsticks. The flames were now beginning to reach the cupola, throwing light in fantastic colours around the square. The fire brigade could do little else apart from struggle to keep the houses on the Frederiksplein wet and to prevent the trees from catching fire. The fire was so hot that water from the hoses evaporated before it had even reached its centre.

At four o'clock came the moment for which everyone had been waiting, like an image in a horrifying feverish dream: The statue of Fame had remained visible amid the smoke and the yellow flames, and above it the ever-present advertisement for Haust Honingkoeken (Honey Biscuits). Now it fell. About a minute later, the cupola suddenly seemed to fold in upon itself. It hung, poised, for a moment, then the colossus crashed to earth. It was as though a battery gun had been fired. A pillar of flame shot right up into the dark air, a storm of sparks raced across the square, and a sound like a thunderclap, audible throughout the entire city, rolled through the silent night. It was all over in an hour.

Chapter Nine

The Last Stop of Train No 11537

DURING THE "ROARING TWENTIES" ALL OF INTELLECTUAL AMSTERDAM
was to be found on the Nieuwemarkt. Here, every Saturday evening, worlds
would be created and shattered, the air would be full of sparkling ideas,
like soap bubbles, and thoughts as strong as steel, while the hands of the
clock stopped for ever at five to twelve.

Janus, a figure as thin as a rake, mostly leant against a handcart when
he started to speak.[1] He prophesied the "Big Bang": bombs, barricades,
dynamite, violence against violence. He had a new thesis: "Burglars are
practical idealists."

> Up, men, who never rest
> Be aware of your own power
> All wheels will stay still . . .

"Hear the trumpets ringing, the weapons clanging, the clatter of hoofs,
the cries of murder," the Free Socialist Flip Bartels shouted from his corner.
"The Javanese are still being exploited . . . " Near the Waag, the evangelist
Griffioen climbed on a folding chair: "Children of Beelzebub, save your
souls, prepare for the last torment." Next to him, someone began to speak
about the need to abolish for ever the three Ks: "Kerk, Kroeg, en Kapitaal"
(church, pub, and capital). In another corner, people debated the question:
"Could one command a flower: scatter seed?" Elsewhere, the subject
was the rottenness of bourgeois morals and the topic: "Why natural
impulses are always pure." Teetotallers swarmed about the market with
piles of newspapers over their arm. They discussed whether a sober strike-
breaker was to be preferred to a drunken striker. Catholic hawkers stood
in a corner beside their stall, boldly marked: *Pope Leo XIII*. A number of

anarchists debated astronomy, gravitation, light and fire. The voices of the pamphlet hawkers rang out: "'The Purgatory of Revolution' – five cents!" "'Has Man got a Soul?' – 'Is Death the End?' – two cents!" "'The Last Contortions of Capitalism' – three cents!"

Universal suffrage had for the first time given all Amsterdammers the chance to elect whomsoever they wished, and of standing for election themselves, and they had seized it enthusiastically: at the local elections of 1923, 35 parties fielded candidates – even the large and the small laundry establishments put up separate lists of candidates. Some poked fun at the whole affair: surely the stupid masses would elect anyone, irrespective of what he or she did, as long as they were fed enough propaganda? One evening in the Uilenkelder, an unofficial artists' society on the Reguliersgracht, a group of anarchists, Free Socialists, and Dadaists decided to try out this "Berlusconism *avant-la-lettre*" on the Amsterdam public. At the interim elections of 1921 they established the Rapaille Partij (Scum Party), with a down-and-out called Nelis de Gelder, knicknamed "Hadjememaar" ("If-only-you-had"), as their candidate. De Gelder had got Hadjememaar's name from a popular song of the time, with which, on the instructions of the theatre director, he had advertised a new musical:

> If only you had a few quid,
> If only you had a lock on the side,
> If only you had what you hear and see,
> I would make love to you,
> But you won't get my pennies!

Hadjememaar had hit the bottle after the early death of his wife. He had been for a time a circus artiste and a bricklayer. These days, however, he usually ambled around the Rembrandtplein with his cigar box, begging for a little money and every now and then performing a little Red Indian dance occasionally punctuated by the battle cry *Hap*! Apart from these few facts, there is very little known about him.

His political agenda, if brief, was admirably lucid: lower prices, such as brandy for five cents, bread for eleven cents, and butter for 35 cents; the pissoir in the Rembrandtplein had to go; and there was to be free fishing in the Vondelpark. Having polled more than 14,000 votes he was duly elected to the City Council on 27 April 1921. Panic-stricken, the acting Burgomaster went to The Hague, where he was received the reassurance he sought: a small emergency law had already been prepared in order to halt the political advance of Hadjememaar. In the event, however, it proved unnecessary. A few days before the elections, he had been picked up in the streets, drunk as a Lord, and it took him several months to recover. Meanwhile, for the next two years, the hawker and former bottle cleaner Bertus Zuurbier was silently to collect Hadjememaar's attendance money at council sessions.

What is most noticeable about this political farce is not so much the person of Hadjememaar himself, but the campaign that was conducted around him. The posters of the Scum Party that have survived are extraordinarily professional, the newspapers ran an illustrated series concerning the popular beggar, and he became the talking point of the day. The Dadaist experiment had been more than successful: for the first time, the media had "made" a politician, and it was also to be the first time that an idea by the young anti-bourgeois poet Erich Wichman had achieved any sort of success. Wichman was a follower of Sorel's theory of living dangerously, a man who could remove his glass eye from its socket as though it were a hard-boiled egg.[2] He was also the first person in the city to propagate the ideology of those embittered Italian war veterans known as the Fasci di Combattimento, and better known as fascists.

In the Amsterdam of 1928, 1,660 incidents of public drunkenness were reported to the police, as well as 2,013 stolen bicycles. To read read the logbook entires of the different police stations is to see a kaleidoscope of life in Amsterdam, district by district, during the 1920s.

At the Stadhouderskade police station, the tone is set by trouble with domestic staff: crying servant girls who had been thrown out of the house of their employers; arrogant wealthy ladies who sailed into the station like five-masted ships; landladies complaining about tenants who had paid little or nothing of their rent. On the Ouderkerksplein, in contrast, the police had to intervene when prostitutes were beaten up by their pimps, the latter often receiving such a beating in turn from the officers that they had to go to hospital themselves.

In the Jordaan, in the Willemsstraat station, the cells were full of men who

Photographer unknown, *View of the back of houses on the Warmoesstraat* (c. 1920).

had been brought in to sleep off their drunkenness, and so-called "water divers", drunkards who had fallen into the filthy canals and who would then swim around for a while, joking with an audience of passers-by. In contrast to this, at the Jonas Daniel Meijerplein station in the Jewish quarter drunkenness was extremely rare: here the officers were kept busy by unresolvable, seemingly eternal conflicts between neighbours and family feuds.

Each quarter had its own face, its own tone, even its own language. Until the end of the nineteenth century, many of the older Amsterdammers rarely, if ever, left their own districts. There were people in Kattenburg who were proud never to have been near the Haarlemmerpoort. Their dialect was very different to that of the inhabitants of Haarlemmerpoort.

The historian Ter Gouw distinguished no fewer than 19 different dialects, among them "Kattenburgs", a sailor's argot that employed many Frisian, Norwegian, and Danish elements; the "Jodenhoeks", the language of the Jewish quarter, which introduced many Yiddish words into Amsterdam; the Zeedijk idiom, full of nautical jargon; the language of the Jordaan, of the Fransenpad (later the Willemstraat), a dialect influenced by gangster slang; the Haarlemmerdijk; the Kalverstraat; and the Duvelshoek (behind today's Tuschinsky Theatre), the language of the fairground people.

During the twentieth century, however, these district cultures slowly faded away. The young moved to newly built areas around the city, newcomers took their places. Moreover businesses, churches and political parties slowly established strong links between the districts. The centre around which people's thoughts and actions began to revolve was no longer the district but the party, the union, or the sports association.[3]

Even so, the "vanishing" of the districts proceeded at a slow pace. Many parties, especially the Communists, still had their "district bastions", and also sports associations were often organized by district. When, in 1930, the young Dutch sociologist Henk Dijkhuis moved in with a family on the Palmgracht "camouflaged" as a florist's apprentice, and from there began his study of life in the Jordaan, the legendary Baize-skirts of the Jordaan women had already vanished from the streets, but a girl still would not dare to become involved with a boy from another district, that was asking for trouble. The curious district feasts were still celebrated: the Hartjesdag, a kind of carnival at which many people wore drag, on the third Monday in August, and the Luilak, on the Saturday before Pentecost, during which youths made a tremendous noise early in the morning.[4]

The Jewish district also had a very special atmosphere.[5] More than half of all Dutch Jews were to be found in Amsterdam, in all more than 80,000, and most still lived practically on top of one another in the old district around the Jodenbreestraat, the Waterlooplein and the Uilenburgstraat. On Sundays the area became a gigantic market with stalls stretching from the Jodenbreestraat up to the Oude Schans. (The houses in the Nieuwe Uilenburgerstraat still have the large ground-floor rooms that were used as warehouses by the Jewish market traders.) While there was a great deal of singing and frolicking in the diamond workshops, the diamond industry was in recession. Increasingly, though, Jews were to find their way into other professions.

The socialist movement had a considerable influence on Amsterdam's Jewish community. During the nineteenth century Jews formed the poorest population group in the city, so that for them a man like Henri Polak, the founder of the Algemene Nederlandse Diamantenwerkersbond (ANDB, the General Dutch Diamond Workers' Association), appeared almost literally as a Moses, born to lead them to the Promised Land. Jewish workers had shown little enthusiasm for the revolution that had been preached by Ferdinand Domela Nieuwenhuis, but when Polak and his followers began to spread the gospel of a socialism without violence, of change through constitutional means, they went over to him in great numbers. Their union achieved things that would have been unthinkable only a few years earlier: health and accident insurance, grants for study, and holiday homes.

The politically active diamond workers had their headquarters at De Ijsbreker, a spacious, newly renovated coffee house (which can still be found on the Weesperzijde 23). Evening after evening the "left-wing" Marxists and the "right-wing" revisionists of the Social Democratic Workers' Party (SDAP) would be at each other's throats in endless heated debates. It was at a café table here that P. L. Tak, chief editor of the party newspaper Het Volk, would write his editorials and radicals like David Wijnkoop, the founder of the Dutch Communist Party, and Sam de Wolf were also regulars; here too the respectable wood merchant Wibout (later the first SDAP Deputy) would come to drink a glass of an evening.

The influence of the ANDB on other workers was enormous; indeed, it can be said that for years the union functioned as the engine of the infant social-democratic movement. Henri Polak, who was both a rabbi and a child of the Enlightenment, made education and intellectual development a priority. The task of the ANDB, he maintained, was to introduce workers to culture, and to that end he organized readings and discussion groups about art and literature. He also made an official plea for workers to wash their hands before taking their shift breaks, and he even meddled with the furnishing of people's living rooms: he opposed excessive decoration, and favoured instead quiet colours and solid furniture.[6] The diamond workers adored him almost as though he were a saint, and obediently followed his advice. In their homes, plush sofas and ornate easy chairs were replaced by divans and simple armchairs, while monochrome designs replaced the flowery wallpaper.[7]

Before long, socialist leaders had assumed the role formerly held by religious leaders within the Jewish community, with the important difference that Jews were now encouraged to acquaint themselves with the culture of life outside the ghetto. For Jewish workers new worlds were opening up: they read Multatuli and Émile Zola, admired the architect Hendrik Petrus Berlage, and the radical teacher Jacob P. Thijsse took the city's

Jewish youth on trips to the countryside for the first time. Young Jews found a new ideology in the Arbeiders Jeugd Centrale (AJC, the Workers' Youth Centre) and other organizations, as did young people from other cultural and religious backgrounds. Mixed marriages became increasingly common.

In a collection of interviews, *Herinnering aan Joods Amsterdam* (Memories of Jewish Amsterdam) the elderly rabbi Jacob Soetendorp recalls that he used to hear singing in the street on Friday evenings to welcome the Sabbath. The traders' carts stood upside-down on the streets, and people would sing Jewish songs, interspersed with socialist anthems; thus Psalm 126, introducing the prayer of thanks, Shir Hama'alot, might be followed by a song of socialist struggle.

If any single factor furthered the integration of Jews into Amsterdam society, it was the workers' movement. This process was accelerated as more and more Jews moved out of the original Jewish district. Those who were rich moved to the Plantage and later to the Plan-Zuid; the "modern" workers, as they were then called, moved to de Pijp and especially to the new workers' districts in East Amsterdam which were built behind the old Jewish area, first the Swammerdambuurt, then the Transvaalbuurt. Only the poorest remained in the old district, until that was renovated as well. This migration took some getting used to: many poor Jews had never operated a modern flushing WC, and the historian Jacques Presser would recall many years later how, cycling to school on Saturday afternoons, he would see lying on the street chicken bones that had been thrown out of windows, after the famous Friday Night chicken soup.

The Jews formed about 13 per cent of the population of Amsterdam. They felt safe in the city, although that is not to say that they were never discriminated against. In some cafés they were made to pay twice the normal price. The most prestigious and influential club in the city, the Grote Club, did not accept Jews as members, and neither did student fraternities. The Barlaeusgymnasium, a school association, had as its motto: "no prole-tarians, no girls, and no Jews."[8] The same was true of the distinguished rowing club, De Hoop. Throughout the districts there were constant fights among boys – that is, between "the Christians" and "the Jews".

In the ghetto, people lived mainly by protecting each other, as the textile merchant Mozes de Leeuw relates in the same collection of interviews. The same pattern was to continue in the new, expensive Amsterdam Zuid.

"As a Jew, you did not go to live in an area where there were no other Jews. [. . .] The whole Churchilllaan (Churchill Avenue) became at one time an expensive Jewish street, from the Waalstraat right up to the Victorieplein. Jewish doctors were here, and the entire Plotske family, and all my uncles. It was, again, a protected environment."

———

During these years, Amsterdam had the dynamism of a bustling harbour city, an air of rolled-up sleeves, of something in which you wanted to participate and of which you wanted to be a part. In the occasional Dutch film dating from the 1930s we can still glimpse the Amsterdam and the IJ of these years: worn-out freighters, a tug boat belching smoke as it tows a line of barges carrying cargo; ferries moving to and fro; a ship laden with ore, lying low in the water; the ferries for Kampen, Lemmer and Marken; and, in between, the brown sails of a *vrachttjalk*, a cargo sailing boat. The hero of the film might be standing on the deck of an outward-bound ocean steamer surrounded by tug boats, smoke everywhere, steam, life and activity.

The trade in part-finished goods from the West Indies was experiencing a boom. In addition, many products were processed directly in Amsterdam: the import of copra led to a blossoming margarine industry; cane sugar was converted into syrup; imported tobacco gave work to thousands of cigar manufacturers. Until the 1950s, the city was seen as the most important industrial base in the country, but it was an industry consisting of countless smaller ones. There was no single, all-dominating industry, as was the case in other cities. There were, for instance, two large breweries, a fast-growing confectionary industry centred around the Keizersgracht, and, until 1927, the city even had its own car industry, manufacturing the quintessentially Dutch Spijker.

There were grand plans for North Amsterdam, which was supposed to merge with Ijmuiden into one large industrial area. Fokker had an aircraft plant by the Papaverweg, and, until 1951, the planes were brought to Schiphol by barge in order to be fitted with their wings. Thousands of Amsterdammers were employed in the metal and shipbuilding industries. Werkspoor & Kromhout, which had emerged from the nineteenth-century wharf of Paul van Vlissingen, was among the largest European manufacturers of diesel engines, and in 1933 the Nederlandse Scheepsbouw Maatschappij (NSM) was the second-largest wharf in the world. The grass airfield on the Harlemmermeer, from where the KLM had started the world's first regular passenger service (the pilots navigated by following the railway lines on these flights to London) was transformed into the municipal airport, Schiphol, in 1926.

Moreover, the city was once more attracting people. In 1900 there were about 500,000 Amsterdammers, in 1925 more than 700,000, which is still roughly the size of the population today. The situation was reminiscent of that at the end of the sixteenth century: more and more new immigrants coming to a city that was already bursting at the seams with people.

Wibaut, who later became an alderman, was a member of the Municipal Commission for Public Health from 1907 to 1914, and his descriptions of inspection tours in his memoirs still make astonishing reading. Often he would find families with eight children crammed into one room in which they lived, cooked, slept, and did outwork for factories. The children, some as old as 17, slept in the same room, girls on one side, boys on the other. Wibaut asked a mother whether this arrangement always worked out. "Not always," she replied. "But if there is the smallest movement at night I get out of bed and give them a good hiding. That helps. I'm good at that." Another mother told a similar story. "Whoever moves is in for it as soon as I notice it – immediately, otherwise it won't work. One boy and one girl, their bums are always black and blue. They never have time to heal since they never give me any peace. The children all sleep in their underwear."[9]

Faced with explanations like these, Wibaut became convinced that, come what may, the municipality had to build flats that would be let at rents below commercial rates. This was now possible, for a new law on housing introduced in 1901 permitted the building of subsidized apartments. As soon as Wibaut became elected to the City Council, he set about implementing his idea with all his energy and enthusiasm.

Amsterdam's first social housing projects were built in 1918, in the Spaarndammerbuurt, among other areas. They took the form of a large number of well-designed blocks of flats built around courtyards, because the socialists believed that workers should be able to live in beautiful surroundings. Here and there, at the edge of the city, so-called "garden villages" were built, the best-known among them quickly acquiring the nickname "Betondorp" (Concrete Town), (it is the neighbourhood in which the soccer star Johan Cruijff was later to grow up). For years it served the social democrats as the model of their ideal society: good, fresh air, sober, decent flats, front and back gardens, good schools, a park and a community hall within reach, and a library reading room full of books dispensing lofty ideals. On 1 May each year the area was awash with red flags, the children had a day off school, "De Stem des Volks" ("The Voice of the People") was sung on Brink Square, and members of the AJC danced around a maypole on the nearby field. Today, this intimate suburb still looks like a backdrop for a 1 May parade, circa 1925.[10]

More needed to be done, however. As already mentioned, the city had not expanded beyond the boundaries that had existed around the year 1600. A completely new, large-scale expansion was necessary, and it was at least as necessary that the Town Council should have both the strength and the enthusiasm for the task.

As is often the case, however, this ambitious undertaking owed its realization largely to chance, in this instance to the presence of a number of visionary administrators who complemented each other wonderfully: the "soul" of the group, F. M. Wibaut, also known as "the Mighty One"; his right-hand man the Mayor Monne de Miranda; the Reformed building contractor William de Vlugt and the Director of Municipal Housing, the impassioned Arie Keppler. Luckily, the mood of the times was on their side.

In 1921 the Social Democrats achieved a great break-through in the municipal administration. In elections that year the SDAP won almost a third of the votes, and they had three men on the Town Council who could be relied upon to force through the social housing project: Wibaut, De Miranda and Vliegen.

In the same year, the area of the municipality of Amsterdam quadrupled by virtue of the incorporation of five surrounding boroughs. Suddenly cheap building land was available, the city was able to expand freely beyond its natural boundaries, and in quick succession the garden villages of Oostzaan, Nieuwendam and Buiksloot sprang up out of nowhere. Berlage designed a new area of the city on the south side, with broad avenues, squares, high streets, intimate side streets some of them Y-shaped, and beautiful views. At major crossings the architect aimed to accentuate this open effect with tall, indeed monumental buildings such as the "skyscraper" on the Victorieplein, although in the end little came of this plan.

To the south, Berlage broke with the concentric layout of the old Amsterdam and the enclosed cityscape of the nineteenth-century districts; instead, the new development was dominated by three avenues which ran through the area at odd angles. The plan had been conceived so clearly and intelligently that the district today is a wonderfully lively part of the city, despite having been designed in an entirely different era.

Berlage's plan had in fact been approved by the municipal council in 1917, but building only started during the 1920s. He himself did not design a single house in "his" district – all the new building followed the designs of the new "Amsterdam School". These young architects, who were considerably influenced by both Expressionism and Art Deco, saw a row of houses as a coherent whole, rather than as an agglomeration of individual façades. They did everything in brick: convex and concave curves, spherical shapes, windows that protruded oddly or at seemingly impossible angles, bizarre patterns, mighty front doors, bay windows, corner turrets – they simply kept on laying bricks until a modest monument had come into existence, "of regimented, disciplined beauty, fitted to the sense of order of the petty bourgeoisie".[11]

Berlage's development in the south extended as far as the new station which was built for the Olympic Games in 1928. The Olympiaplein also served as a training course. The participating athletes lived in hotels or in private houses throughout the city.

Most of the new flats were built by housing associations. The first of them, put up in 1909 by the Association of Tramway Workers, was called Rochdale, after the English town where the first workers' co-operative had been founded in 1844. These flats were revolutionary by the standards of the city: no more box-beds, but separate bedrooms and a lavatory off the hallway.

The municipality itself also remained very active. Under De Miranda's guidance, the redevelopment of the centuries-old quarters of the inner city was begun in 1929, an operation that, with interruptions, would take until well into the 1980s. First to be tackled were the worst parts of the Jewish quarter. Old buildings by the Lastageweg and the Montelbaanstraat were demolished and new ones built in their place, a measure that can still be clearly seen today. Shortly afterwards, the Uilenburgerstraat and the small back streets that ran off it were demolished and replaced by the Nieuwe Uilenburgerstraat.

It was a time of grand schemes when everything seemed possible. On the drawing boards of the new City Development Department, entire districts were planned and drawn up, even down to the balustrades on the balconies and complete with playing children, mothers clustered around bakers' carts, and well-rested, lively workers. The explanations were written in an unambiguous style. Concepts such as "chaos", "unpredictability" or "ungovernability" simply did not exist. With undiluted optimism, the civil servants, administrators and politicians determined the world of their children and grandchildren; the possibility of a city without mothers and bakers' carts simply did not occur to them.

In 1928 the planners finally took the plunge. They embarked upon a fascinating attempt to determine the development of the city for decades to come, to shape it and lead it down proper channels. A total plan had to be found that would be valid at least until the year 2000. On the basis of research, predictions were made about the requirements of the Amsterdam of the future. It was believed that the size of the average family on 1 January 1961 would be 3.34 persons, and this, together with factors such as immigration, led to an estimate of the city's population for the year 2000 of between 900,000 and 1,100,000.

The Algemeen Uitbreidingsplan (General Expansion Plan) that was presented in 1934 was to gain international fame because it was the first urban-expansion scheme to make use of target dates so systematically and backed up by so much research. Its creator, the eminent city planner Cornelis van Eesteren, distinguished four functions: living, working, relaxation, and traffic as a link between the other three. As a result, residential areas were designed to be relatively close to working areas, separated by relaxation zones. This division of functions was the thread running through the entire plan.

The Algemeene Uitbreidingsplan was to be entirely different from Berlage's earlier layout for the south of the city, which, with its closed, rather dark dwellings and lack of green spaces, was, according to his critics, still had one foot in the nineteenth century. Van Eesteren, on the other hand, with his philosophy of "light, air, and space" was entirely a child of the twentieth century.

A special characteristic of this plan were the so-called *stroken* (strips), the now well-known blocks of flats with their long walkways, and the large number of green areas, the parks and sports fields penetrating deeply into the districts, after the example of Greater Berlin. For the first time, relaxation and recreation were taken extremely seriously by the planners. The new districts were centred around an artificial lake (later the Sloterplas), a smart move as it turned out, since its construction provided the enormous quantities of sand necessary for the building project.

Close to this city of the future, an entire forest had been planned, the Amsterdamse Bos. Planted in 1934 under an employment scheme, it was equipped with an ingenious system of land drains and artificial ponds, since otherwise no tree would ever have consented to take root in the boggy terrain that had looked so pretty on the drawing board.

The *Algemeen Uitbreidingsplan* is still an astonishing piece of literature, especially when one realizes that it was written in a period of crisis and increasing international uncertainty, although it may have been this very uncertainty that made these reassuring drawings, explanations and plans so necessary.

After the catastrophe of the Second World War, when Amsterdam was in urgent need of a building programme, the visionary plans were already available and could be put into effect immediately. The city was saved, or almost saved, from those terribly sad and dire post-war residential areas that mark so many other cities. Even before the war the eastern districts of Bos and Lommer had been built, and afterwards Slotermeer, Slotervaart, Geuzenveld and Osdorp. Finally, in 1958, building was started on the area of Buitenveldert.

Not for nothing was Wibaut called "the Mighty". From photographs we can get an idea of the impression he must have made, with his grey tousled hair and his small, intellectual's glasses. He wanted to go much further than simply building good flats. In his vision, "democracy" was not something to which one paid lip service, but was to be "applied to the utmost limit possible within capitalism".[12] For Wibaut, socialist communal politics

meant that cities were test-beds for socialism itself, and in a place like
Amsterdam one had to actively test its possibilities within the margins of
capitalism. He had already tested these principles in the First World War,
when the city's food supply had almost broken down. It had been on his
initiative that the municipality had bought potatoes, bread, grain, clothing
and rice and had sold them in special shops at extremely low prices. In this
way the city administration had continued the tradition instituted by the
regents of the seventeenth century, even if its motive had been exclusively to
maintain public order. Wibaut and De Miranda, however, were determined
to push things further. The municipal shops remained open after the
war, selling, among other things, shoes, clothes, and furniture. De Miranda
considered opening canteens where people could eat at cost price, and the
municipality also began to concern itself with supplying milk and fish. It
was not long before shopkeepers and suppliers began to protest. During
one meeting the Liberal Conservative Walrave Boissevain sketched out a
future in which the administration of the city had been transformed into
one large cut-price shop: "If B. & W. wanted to buy out either Cloppenburg
or De Bijenkorf [the largest department stores in the city], the council
would be forced to approve this." De Miranda in particular had to take a
lot of flak. The establishment of a municipal dairy, one of his main projects,
was vetoed by the council,[13] although he did manage to see that a number
of public laundry houses were established. "A woman who has the vote,"
he said, "should not have to stand at a washtub." Swimming in the public
baths was free, and every borough tried to establish its own bathhouse.
From this originated the popular slogan of the social democrats during the
election campaign:

> If you want to bathe and swim –
> De Miranda, vote for him!

———

Six months after the Paleis voor Volksvlijt was consumed by flames, stock
exchanges around the world collapsed. A year later, the economic crisis
also hit Amsterdam. In 1932 there were four times as many people out of
work as in 1929, and in the years afterwards the number rose to 60,000,

either a fifth or a quarter of the city's population, depending on which estimate one uses.

Drawing the dole was a humiliating business. Unemployed workers who were in a union received 70 per cent of their last wages for a certain time; after that they became the victim of "a whole network of exclusions, delays, limiting qualifications, and debasing duties and controls", as the historian Roegholt put it. Fathers were often forced into labour camps, some of which were hours away from the city and their families. The basic benefit payment was just high enough to keep the jobless alive, and was adjusted for those with families. The subsidy was designed mainly for the purchase of food. Street hawkers, mostly poor Jews, were excluded because, according to the official explanation, "they are impossible to control and can therefore defraud the system more easily". Never before had Amsterdam suffered unemployment on such a massive scale and for so long. Looking for work was almost pointless. The average family of an unemployed man spent 19.30 florins a week, compared to 45.48 florins in comparable families with work. The jobless were often too ashamed to go outside, where everyone in the neighbourhood would see that they had no work. Their children came home crying, having been bullied on account of their free school clothes.

"It is difficult to know which was harder," Roegholt wrote, "the grey, monotonous minimal existence without money for newspapers or for a radio, for going out, for relaxation or hobbies, when even the postage for a application could grow into an insurmountable problem, or the realization that this was a life without a way out, the fruitless search for work, the stubborn adherence to a few norms of common propriety where children and neighbours were concerned, the struggle not to sink into poverty."[14]

So traumatic was the crisis of the 1930s that it was to determine the policies of the city's — and indeed the country's — administration until the 1980s: "never again" became a watchword. Many politicians of the 1950s and 1960s had been children during the Depression, and its effects were to mark their lives for ever. The post-war policies of the Netherlands, including Amsterdam, the dynamics of the rebuilding during the 1950s, the confusion of the 1960s, and the "soft" society of the 1970s, are incomprehensible unless seen against the backdrop of countless family tragedies during the 1930s.

*

In September 1933, the socialist members resigned from the City Council in protest at its refusal to lower the salaries of municipal employees. For two years, until the elections in 1935, a centre-right Council ruled over the city, adopting as its slogan a single word: "economize". On 1 July 1934, they lowered the allowance for the jobless by ten per cent. This meant that a family of nine received 14 guilders instead of 16.

A few days later, on a sultry Wednesday evening in July, another popular uprising erupted in the Jordaan. After a meeting of the Communist "War Against Unemployment" Committee, a number people took to the streets. When the police finally intervened, after having broken up an anti-NSB (Nationaal-Socialistische Beweging, the Dutch National Socialist Movement) demonstration on the Ambonplein, the officers quickly found stones and roof shingles whizzing around their ears. Streetlamps were pulled to the ground, and their lanterns shattered. The first barricades went up. Only late at night did peace return.

The following days were nothing short of civil war. The fighting in the Jordaan sparked unrest in the Spaarndammerbuurt and Amsterdam East and North. A strike broke out in the Timber Harbour. Shots were fired on the islands, and later in the Jordaan as well. The Communists called for new protests, while the Social Democrats warned workers not to let themselves be dragged along. Soviet flags flew on some of the barricades. Poems were written:

> They thought we would not hear the noble call
> That came from Russian Moscow, from afar,
> They thought that boredom might just kill us all
> In this swamp that reeks of boredom, stinks . . .

By Monday it was all over. Five people had died and 41 were wounded.[15]

The future was unimaginable. At the end of the year 1939 Monne de Miranda, a town councillor once more, expressed his desire to see "jobs for the jobless, good business for the middle class, loyalty to their city for the rich". To east Amsterdam he wished a final end to isolation, to the west a speedy building programme for the Bos and Lommer, for the south the completion of the building of the Rijksverzekeringsbank (National Assurance Bank), for the north a start to construction of the IJ tunnel, and finally "to the centre, the first spade in the ground for the new Town Hall".[16]

In reality, the tunnel and the Town Hall would only be built 30 and 40 years later respectively, and the Bos and the Lommer would be populated in the main by immigrants from Mediterranean countries. As for De Miranda, he would be brought down within the month. Less than four years after his Happy New Year message, he would be interned in a concentration camp near Amersfoort, where he was, in the words of one eyewitness, "carted across the central square in a wheelbarrow like a heap of misery, bloody and sullied with mud, slumped over, then thrown to the ground, like a heap of rubbish". This was what the unforeseeable, treacherous future actually held in store.

The rise of fascism in Italy and of National Socialism in Germany had not passed unnoticed in Amsterdam. Already in 1933, shortly after Hitler's ascent to power, there was a demonstration by anti-fascist youths on the Rembrandtplein, which was directed against the showing of *Morgenrood* (*Dawn*), the first German film with an overtly Nazi message. There were other protests. At one, in the Rembrandt Theatre, slogans were chanted, stink bombs thrown, and white mice and doves of peace released.[17] There were anti-fascists committees and exhibitions. In 1936, there was even one against the Olympic games in Berlin using the acronym DOOD (dead), short for "De Olympische Spelen Onder Dictatuur" ("The Olympic Games under Dictatorship").[18] Even the heiress to the throne, Princess Juliana of the Netherlands, visited the Joodse Invalide (Jewish Hospital) shortly after her marriage to the German Prince Bernhard, so as to demonstrate her contempt for Nazi anti-semitism.

Jewish refugees from Germany, and later from Austria, had meanwhile begun to arrive in Amsterdam in their thousands, and many established themselves in the spacious new areas of Berlage's Amsterdam South, particularly in the area around the Beethovenstraat. There was a relatively large number of writers and artists among these exiles, and their presence reawakened the Amsterdammers, who were especially taken by their cabaret and literature. It was a repetition, in miniature, of the situation during the seventeenth and eighteenth centuries, in that, for a brief period, the city became a kind of sanctuary. The Amsterdam publishers Allert de Lange and Querido began to publish émigré literature in the original language, and there was a special newspaper for emigrants with the German title Die Sammlung (The Collection).

Here and there, however, especially among the city's petty bourgeoisie and the upper middle classes, National Socialism also found favour. From time to time members of the Nationaal-Socialistische Beweging (NSB) would march in uniform through the streets and there were regular running battles between them and young socialists and communists. Sometimes they got out of hand. In April 1935 there was a violent brawl between NSB members and young Jewish liberals in the Concertgebouw, when the NSB attempted to disrupt an assembly of the Liberale Staatspartij under its chairman, Abraham Asscher. In the municipal elections of 1939 Amsterdam was the only city in the Netherlands in which the NSB fielded candidates. The party gained three seats.

Anti-semitism was raging elsewhere in Amsterdam, too. As early as the beginning of 1933, the Catholic North Dutch MP, J. Bomans, had made it known, with the support of the daily De Telegraaf, that he regarded the presence of four Jews in the Amsterdam City Council as "untactical". One of the first and most important victims of this silent "cleansing" was the short, optimistic, driven reformer Salomon "Monne" de Miranda.

Although Wibaut had been De Miranda's great mentor, their differences are more obvious than their similarities. Wibaut, originating from a bourgeois background, had attended high school and had then become a successful and wealthy businessman. De Miranda had been born into a poor Jewish area, went to school for only five years, and became a champion of the masses who continued to look up to "learned people" and who never sought to hide his modest origins. In the eyes of his political opponents, and despite his loyalty to the SDAP, Wibaut always remained the socially engaged magistrate. De Miranda was a party man of fierce emotional engagement, who did not shirk from using unparliamentary language in his public speeches and who made himself enemies by so doing. "Wibaut", writes De Miranda's biographer, G. W. B. Borrie, "was a Sunday's child of politics. De Miranda became the victim of anti-socialist propaganda with significant anti-semitic overtones. In this despicable affair he lacked the 'inner certainty' which his friend and party colleague Wibaut possessed in such large measure."

What exactly did happen to De Miranda, the great rebuilder of the city, the man of the bath houses and the co-operatives, who dreamt of a communal utopia?

The last chapters of Borrie's biography contain a detailed reconstruction of his political end. They provide more than that, however, for they can also be read as a case study in political character assassination. All the elements are there: the enemies, the motives, the protagonists' unguarded moment, the growing momentum, the press, the mixture of lies and truth, the final short-lived explosion and the long silent aftermath.

Let's start with the enemies. De Miranda's impulsiveness, which may have had its roots in a deep-seated insecurity, made him many foes. The Amsterdam middle classes would gladly have torn him limb from limb for his cheap housing programme and his persistent attempts to regulate the sale of basic necessities. During the period when he himself had not been a deputy, he had treated his successors in the Council very rudely, especially the already mentioned Walrave Boissevain, president of the Grote Club, who was related to the grandest Amsterdam families and was an important man in high society. Behind the scenes, De Miranda had also had serious differences with the powerful Administrator of Public Works, W. A. de Graaf. In addition to all this, however, he was a Jew and a socialist, a combination that was never going to make him very popular in certain circles.

After Wibaut's death, some of these ill-wishers saw their chance. On 6 January 1939, *De Telegraaf* started a vicious campaign under the title: ACCUSATIONS AGAINST DEPUTY DE MIRANDA AND COUNCILLOR GULDEN. The article reported a "broad investigation" by the police into the allocation of building land on a long-lease basis. Too often, it emerged, building plots were allocated to one particular group of contractors; moreover it was found that they had repeatedly been allocated to contractors who had no intention of building there, forcing bona-fide contractors to take over the plots at inflated prices. De Miranda's son, Bram, had been involved with at least one of these transactions and this had cast doubts over De Miranda himself.

The article struck home like a missile, and the ensuing series of reports in *De Telegraaf* and the NSB-friendly *Nationale Dagblad* spelled the end of De Miranda's political career. A special commission was set up by the municipality to investigate these claims, something unprecedented in the city's history; it was headed by Walrave Boissevain, but de Graaf also played an important role. Eventually it transpired that De Miranda was merely guilty of a having made number of management errors. Two Social Democrat council members and Bram, De Miranda's son, were indeed found to be not quite spotless, but De Miranda himself was cleared of any wrong-doing. With hindsight, none of *De Telegraaf's* allegations against him had been based on fact. He was, as the investigating attorney remarked at the time, "quite unblemished".

The damage had been done, however. Unequal to the barrage of accusations, De Miranda suffered a breakdown and was treated in psychiatric clinics for over six months. From the spa town Rheden, where he had been sent by his doctor because he would be unknown there, he wrote in despair: "Here everything is sheer luxury. A drawn-out dinner with individual service. The Burgomaster comes here every year. You can therefore get a pretty good idea what this pleasure will cost." Moreover, he only had one newspaper to read: *De Telegraaf*.

It remains difficult to explain how a high-ranking administrator with a record of exceptional good services to the city could have been damaged so swiftly and so fatally. One of the reasons, undoubtedly, is the fact that De Miranda lacked the mental strength to defend himself at a crucial moment in his fortunes. But more importantly, as a Jew from a working-class background, he was "exposed", he could not look for protection from the Amsterdam establishment, nor even from his own party, when he most needed it. With hindsight one can now see that De Miranda's fall was merely an indication of the fate that lay in store, on a much larger scale, for all of Amsterdam's Jews.

In the last years before the Second World War, Amsterdam and the entire country lived in an atmosphere of cheerful disbelief and deliberate self-deception. The Dutch population was very well informed about what was going on in Germany, but the more serious the situation became, the less the average citizen wanted to know about it. At eleven o'clock on the morning of 3 September 1939, war was declared between Germany, Britain, France, and Poland, but most Dutch people firmly believed in their country's neutrality. It was generally expected that their situation would be much the same as it was during the First World War: problems for trade, an influx of refugees, and food shortages, but otherwise nothing of any great importance.

It has to be remembered that the Netherlands had been on the political sidelines of Europe for centuries. Not a shot had been fired in anger for several generations. Almost all the wars that had ravaged the Continent had passed the Netherlands by, apart from a few minor skirmishes hardly worth mentioning. People had become so unused to the dangers of war that they no longer knew what they were.

Anyone who looks through the newspapers of this period will find that in the beginning, in 1933, 1934, and 1935, great concern was expressed about the Nazi pogroms in Germany, but as the situation grew worse in the succeeding years, these events ceased to hold centre-stage. The Dutch Jews, too, who had lived in peace for generations, could not believe that the situation was really all that bad in Germany. "I simply laughed at the first marches of the NSB," remarks one of the interviewees in *Herinnering aan Joods Amsterdam*. Another remembers how, in 1938, a certain Mr Gans, a lawyer in the city, leisurely packed his belongings, took his money and emigrated to America. Why? Fear. "We thought that he was both mad and a coward; that's how we talked about it. 'We are Dutch,' we would say, 'and we will stay in the Netherlands'." This inability to see danger, this long acceptance of peace and quiet, highlights the extent of the catastrophe that was to be visited upon the Dutch Jews a short time later.[19]

This head-in-the-sand atmosphere prevailed after the German occupation, even among the best-informed Amsterdammers. There is an extremely interesting report by an editor of the *Algemeen Handelsblad*, A. Ekker, about the experiences of the night shift tasked with preparing morning paper No. 37,104, the edition of the memorable night of 10 May 1940, which sums up the mood in the city.[20]

In the *Handelsblad*'s proud building on the Nieuwezijds Voorburgwal, the evening of 9 May had begun like any other: editors, stenographers, couriers, typesetters and layout artists streamed in and out; metre-long snakes of telex reports curled on the floor; contributors' copy, sent in by mail train, arrived from the Central Station; impatient correspondents telephoned their reports.

For more than a week the editors had been able to see that there was a serious danger of a German attack on the Netherlands. Every evening the editor-in-chief, the deputy editor and the foreign news editor had sat in their rooms, talking urgently on the phone to correspondents and business contacts in The Hague, and conferred with each other. What exactly they heard remained a secret, certainly their readers were unaware of it, but everyone in the building knew that something was wrong.

Curiously enough, this "crisis committee" did not surface on the evening of 9 May; the danger, they believed, had receded. As a result, on the front page of that night's edition there would be a small item for those in the know with the heading: TENSIONS DEFUSED. EXPECTED EVENTS NOT TO OCCUR. There was, however, also a report from the Associated Press, origi-nating from "very reliable sources", that two German panzer divisions from Bremen and Düsseldorf were moving in the direction of the Netherlands, "so quickly that they will reach the border very soon". The paper's Berlin correspondent, Max Blockzijl, had also wired perplexing reports about "preparations" and "counter-measures" against the putative violation of the neutrality of the Netherlands and of Belgium.

Then, towards the end of the evening, a whole series of strange reports from Maastricht, Venlo, Nijmegen, and Enschede, cities along the German border, reached the home-affairs desk which was staffed by the editor responsible, Hein van Wijk, later a lawyer and senator, the poet Ed Hoornik, and Ekker himself. Ekker takes up the tale:

> All the correspondents report strange noises that have been audible along the border since nightfall. The heavy droning of motors, explosions, and other noises harder to identify. Also angry barking, apparently from startled farm dogs, and the lowing of restless cattle.

The noise seemed to come from the other side of the border, but The Hague government was not informed of anything, and these observations were too vague to merit a report in that morning's paper.

Midnight. The first edition has gone to press. A break for the setters; the editors go off for a glass in the neighbouring cafés, Scheltema and Hedes.

1.30 a.m. The six pages of city news are being made ready. At this moment the ANP* telexes start rattling away, and the Air Control station also comes in with reports. Unknown aircraft are flying over Dutch territory. This is not unusual, but this time in very large numbers. The editorial staff become suspicious, particularly in the light of the curious reports from along the border. The night editor decides that nobody is to go home. The correspondents in Gelderland and Overijssel are called again: they report more noise. Only the correspondent in Maastricht seems to be suddenly unavailable. The Maastricht telephone exchange tells us, in a strange tone of voice, that they cannot connect us anymore.

3.15 a.m. The night editor decides to defer going to press for another hour. The typesetters, sensing the atmosphere, agree. Two editors remain, "just in case". The others can go home to bed.

3.55 a.m. I am standing with my key in my hand, about to open the cycle shed on the Cliostraat, when suddenly the silence of the sleeping city is torn apart by low-flying planes and then again the muffled sound of explosions and gunfire. Now there is no doubt. Enormous fires at Schiphol. A German fighter plane is tearing over the Bosplan with thunderous force, firing all its cannon. The sky is filled with violence.

So Amsterdam renewed its acquaintance with war, for the first time in almost four centuries. On Sunday 12 May a German plane dropped a bomb on the Blauwburgwal, on the corner of the Herengracht. The carnage was terrible, with 51 people killed. Otherwise the city was not severely damaged, apart from the harbours and Schiphol, which were heavily bombed. The tragedies were mostly human. Despite the wonderful weather, smoke could be seen issuing from some chimneys, as countless "dangerous" books and pamphlets were burned. In the Joodse Vluchtelingencomité

---

* Algemeen Nederlands Persbureau, a Dutch press agency.

(Jewish Refugee Council), volunteers had begun work incinerating dossiers in the central-heating furnace from 8 a.m. on 10 May.

Meanwhile, many thousands of Jews had fled to Ijmuiden, hoping to gain passage on a ship to England. While a panic-stricken crowd was moving along the North Sea Channel in cars and buses, and on bicycles, all laden with suitcases and bags, three stately ocean steamers, the *Johan de Witt*, the *Jan Pieterszoon Coen*, and the *Bodegraven*, steamed through the canal like a torment of Tantalus. The authorities, however, decided on Tuesday 14 May to close off the area around the Ijmuiden harbour "out of concern for public order". The *Johan de Witt*, the last ship to leave, sailed according to schedule for the Dutch East Indies, taking on board at the last minute a handful of Jewish families by means of a rope ladder. Save for a few Jewish orphans, the gigantic passenger ship *Bodegraven* set a course for England almost empty. The refugees saw the *Coen* pass by, a ship that could easily have accommodated almost all of them, but she was scuttled in order to block German access to the Ijmuiden piers.

Then the suicides began: Alderman Emanuel Boekman and his wife, the criminologist Professor Bonger, and about 150 others – Jews, known anti-fascists, stranded refugees, some of them alone, but also entire families. Walking through Amsterdam's Jewish cemeteries today one can still find them, the stones bearing the dates of 15 and 16 May 1940, some narrow, some much broader, so as to accommodate the names of an entire family, husband, wife and children.[21]

On the 15 May 1940, German troops entered the city, via the Weesperzijde and the Berlagebrug, watched by thousands of Amsterdammers.

The first phase of the German occupation of Amsterdam was marked by defencelessness and naïvety. The newspapers submitted to voluntary censorship, most political parties were declared illegal, the unions were incorporated into German organizations, German law was introduced, but despite these measures life went on much as usual. Because a speedy end to the war still seemed likely in 1940, the Germans adopted a two-pronged political approach to governing the Netherlands: on one hand, they bound the country firmly to the German Reich, both economically and militarily, on the other, they treated it as a more or less independent nation in order not to forfeit their claims on the rich Dutch East Indies during any peace negotiations that might follow the end of the war.

Things began to change in the autumn. On 26 October 1940, civil servants were confronted with their first moral dilemma. They were presented with a form headed "Declaration of Aryan Descent", which asked in great detail about possible Jewish forebears. It was the first official instance since the invasion of a line being drawn between Jews and non-Jews. The teachers of the Amsterdam Lyceum refused *en bloc* to sign, but their action remained an exception. The "cold pogrom" had started, as the first underground publication, *De Geus*, declared at the time.

Just a month later, on 23 November, all Jewish civil servants were dismissed, including teachers and university professors. A spontaneous strike broke out among pupils at the Vossius Gymnasium, but at the telephone exchange, Jewish employees were not even allowed to quickly return to their workplaces in order to say goodbye to their colleagues. Twenty-six of the lecturers at Amsterdam University were forced to leave, but, in stark contrast to the universities of Delft and Leiden, there was no demonstration of protest.

On 30 November, the Jewish members of the Municipal Council were dismissed. One of the historians already quoted, Roegholt, found that the minutes of their meetings contained not a word of disagreement when he came to examine these documents. When one Jewish councillor, Ben Sajet, attempted to raise the topic during the last meeting of the SDAP faction within the council, the chairman overruled him with the reply that he "did not want to be sentimental" about the dismissals. Two weeks later the council's leaders dotted their I's and crossed their T's with characteristic Dutch precision: it was suggested that the deposed Jewish council members should surrender their special season tickets to the theatre, "because they won't need them anyway". The council agreed that the former members concerned were to be informed.[22]

In January 1941 another step was taken. All Jewish businesses were required to be registered. Jewish shops were put under the authority of German "administrators", sometimes honest businessmen, sometimes incompetents, sometimes thieves. Jewish properties were confiscated and sold by a spurious bank.

Harassment now took to the streets. The NSB, the organization that most aspired to being the embodiment of the New Order, attempted to gain credit with its masters through street action. This was not so much intended to convince the city's population, but rather to consolidate its hegemony over the other National Socialist organisations. Groups of marching NSB members in uniform terrorized Jewish neighbourhoods, dragged Jews from trams and beat them, and burst their way into cafés in order to force their owners to put up the little notice: JEWS FORBIDDEN. This regularly led to street fights between the blackshirts and the cafés' furious clients.

Whereas the first measures initiated by the Germans had mainly met with little more than a wall of disbelief, coupled with irritation, the limit was definitely exceeded by these violent actions, which indirectly also struck at the non-Jewish population. As the historian Ben Sijes was later to recall:

> One knew these people face to face. One knew them as colleagues
> in factories and offices. They had been adopted into the circles
> of families and acquaintances. They had provided leaders in the
> political struggle. One felt that the Germans, with their decrees
> and notices "from official sources", intended to break bonds that
> one had either purposefully sought or had accepted, and which had
> been created by social interaction and human sympathy.[23]

Such sentiments were to drive the briefest-ever Amsterdam popular movement, later known as the "February Strike".

Amsterdam has never known a ghetto uprising such as that in Warsaw in 1944, a dramatic last outburst by those who stood with their backs to the wall. The process of deportation took place too gradually for there to be any coherent resistance, and the occupiers had understood too well how to mask their true intentions until it was far too late.

There was, too, another aspect. During the first half of the twentieth century, Amsterdam's Jewish neighbourhoods had undergone a development unheard-of in the rest of Western Europe: within a few years, a politically active Jewish workers' movement had been formed, and firm bonds had been forged with workers' organizations in other part of the city. As a result, the integration of the Jews into the city as a whole was mirrored in the February Strike. Non-Jewish workers downed tools in support of their Jewish colleagues. Young men from the Jordaan and the Islands fought NSB groups, alongside the gangs from the Jewish quarters. For a brief moment, it looked as though the city would resist the fascists.

Moreover the strike had a broader background than just the persecution of the Jews. For months there had been considerable unrest in the city: the cost of living had risen by a third since the occupation, Amsterdam's unemployed, still hovering around 40,000, were forced to accept work in Germany and metal workers were threatened with the prospect of being compelled to work for the German war machine.

The marches and other street actions of rival pro-Nazi groups were also a source of unrest. The WA ("Weerafdeling", the militant wing of the NSB) with its "soldier-like bearing", became an established part of the Amsterdam scene, which led to a great number of street fights and even running battles, especially on 8 and 9 February 1941, when the pro-Nazis went on the rampage. In the Jewish quarter, old Auntie Golly's orange cart was overturned; here and there houses were raided; the windows of De Kroon, a café-restaurant on the Rembrandtplein, were broken; there were constant running battles between the NSB and the police, and when the owner of the nearby café Alcazar, one of the few establishments still open to Jews, refused to put up the sign forbidding them entry the premises were stormed by some 60 armed NSB members who proceeded to wreck it completely. Meanwhile, there had also been fights between the Dutch police and German soldiers when a number of the NSB forced their way into De Kroon to "drum the Jews out". In the evening, 150 NSB members and German soldiers went to the Huize Bob on the Waterlooplein, a place where young men and women, Jews and non-Jews, went to dance. The unwanted visitors were badly beaten and thrown out of the dance hall. The destruction was terrible and only when the German military police arrived did the fighting stop.

Meanwhile, a number of young men who attended a Jewish boxing gym called Maccabi had come to the conclusion that things had gone far enough. They formed a fighting group "in order to thump back for once". One of the few survivors, the trainer Joel Cosman, would later describe how this first "commando" trained three times a week. "One of us built a sort of raiding vehicle, an old wagon with a hood and two benches inside. When we got a call telling us that Jews were being harassed somewhere, we went there to hit back."[24] They fought at De Kroon and later at the Jewish ice-cream parlour Koco, in the Rijnstraat, a typical little neighbourhood café where the locals had already established a defence system, complete with patrols, "look-outs" and first-aid posts. Maccabi also had good contacts with other boxing clubs, so that when there was trouble there would immediately be dozens of stocky men from the Jordaan and Kattenburg at hand.

Soon other Amsterdammers came to see that the National Socialists had to be opposed by force. In some factories across the IJ, for instance, the Verschure & Co. wharf, weapons were clandestinely machined from thick steel-clad cable.

On Tuesday 11 February there was renewed fighting around the Jewish quarter, as Joel Cosman recalls:

> Everyone who looked as though he could be a member of the NSB was knocked on the head. [. . .] It was a very misty evening and we hid in house doorways. It was about seven o'clock in the evening when we heard the NSB group arrive across the Blauwbrug, singing "Juden an die Wand" ("Jews to the Wall"). There was a playground on the Waterlooplein with a fence around it, and when the NSB approached it, the boys from the commando came out of their doorways and from the Nikkelsberg café to give them a terrible thrashing. They fled right and left, but there were a few who ran the wrong way in the mist, deeper into the Jewish quarter. The leader of the WA group was called Koot, and he ran into the arms of some of our boys. They gave him such a hiding that he fell unconscious. He was missed, and in the morning the NSB men came looking for him. He was brought into the Binnengasthuis hospital, and though he got out of there all right, he couldn't talk about it any more.

Three days later Koot died. The NSB now had a martyr and the Germans had a stick with which to beat the dog. The following morning, the Jewish quarter was closed off from the rest of the city. The bridges were hoisted up, and municipal workers started to put up posts for a substantial fence around the area. Moreover, on 22 February the occupiers decided to make a raid, aiming to take around 400 "hostages" from among the Jews. There now followed scenes that the peaceful Amsterdam had not seen before, as is recorded in the police reports: boys and men were knocked off their bicycles or pushed down steps; small children were torn from their fathers' arms amid terrifying cries; wailing women who leaned out of the windows were threatened with rifles; men who fell down were kicked until they no longer moved.

There was a similar raid the following day, only this time, because of the Sunday market, a large number of non-Jews were there to see the Nazis at work. Thousands of witnesses returned to their homes with the shouting of men and crying of women still ringing in their ears.

One of the factors that contributed strongly to the success of the February Strike was the degree of organization of the Communist Party of Holland, later the CPN. By 1941 the Communists already had a well-established illegal organization with some 1,200 active members in Amsterdam alone, divided into groups, sections, and cells. Nevertheless, it was ordinary members who often took the initiative: in the case of the February Strike, it was street worker William Kraan and Piet Nak, from the city cleaning division, who proved to be the driving force behind the action. Convinced that something had to be done to prevent the Jews being persecuted, they sounded out their fellow workers in the municipal services and on Monday 24 February held a clandestine meeting on the Noordermarkt, where they announced a protest strike for the following day. The intention was to bring all of the trams and the city cleaning and Public Works department to a standstill; if these ceased to operate, then the rest of the city would follow as well.

In the event things happened more quickly than anyone had expected. On the following morning, after a number of strikers had persuaded their colleagues in the Kromme Mijdrechtstraat tram depot not to drive out, the remainder of the tram service also ground to a halt. After that, the strike snowballed throughout the city.

DEMAND THE IMMEDIATE RELEASE OF THE ARRESTED JEWS! read one of the pamphlets:

DEMAND THE DISBANDING OF THE WA TERROR GROUPS!

ORGANIZE SELF-DEFENCE IN FACTORIES AND

NEIGHBOURHOODS!

REMOVE JEWISH CHILDREN FROM NAZI POWER —

TAKE THEM INTO YOUR FAMILIES!

BE OF ONE MIND, BE COURAGEOUS!

STRIKE! STRIKE! STRIKE!

Around 9 a.m. the strike had spread to the wharves and steel plants in the north. At the Fokker aircraft factory, groups of workers went through the halls enforcing the strike. Within ten minutes, 2,600 people, almost the entire workforce, stood in front of the main gate. Meanwhile, long queues of strikers had assembled by the ferries, wanting to be taken across to the city. To quote from Ben Sijes's detailed reconstruction of these days:

> Men and women, boys and girls were all cheering. The Internationale and other socialist strike songs were sung. In their elation, young men seized hold of working girls and lifted them up. Everyone was laughing. The captain and the ferry crew were cheered. One ferry went across the sunny IJ crammed with people. It was simply marvellous.

The Germans were taken completely by surprise by this wave of strikes, but they quickly regrouped. A German police battalion and two SS Totenkopf infantry regiments were drafted into the city, a curfew was declared, at night SS patrols were everywhere in the streets. Burgomaster De Vlugt, who would later have a shady avenue in the Geuzenveld named after him, threatened striking civil servants with all sorts of sanctions, including dismissal. Monne de Miranda, retired as a councillor but still a man of great influence, was asked to call the strikers to order. He refused. He was arrested and murdered shortly afterwards.

The intimidating attitude of the Germans, who on occasion would fire on the strikers, and their stranglehold on the civil service did the trick: the next day the trams were already beginning to run again, and, dragging their feet, other people went back to work as well. After two days, the strike was over.

Four strikers were executed by firing-squad and a further 22 sentenced to prison; 70 more were dismissed from public service. Moreover, the City of Amsterdam was forced to pay five million guilders in "reparations" to the Germans, while the Jewish community was forced to accept its "own" Jewish Council, made up of Jews prepared to collaborate with the Germans and even to organize the deportation of Jews. All but two of the Jews who had been arrested during the raids were sent to the Mauthausen concentration camp. Four days after their arrival, ten men jumped to their deaths in a deep stone quarry, holding one another by the hand. By the autumn of 1941, all of the others were dead as well.

In one sense, the February Strike was a battle lost, like ghetto uprisings elsewhere in Europe. Psychologically, however, that sunny February day in 1941 was of crucial importance in the war. A typical Amsterdam phenomenon – the neighbourhood – had opposed the administrative and military powers. The occupiers' anti-semitism, its subtle phases, and the exceptions to the rule that concealed it, was immediately revealed for what it was. The strike also crystallized an awareness in Amsterdam of what it meant to do "right" and "wrong" during Occupation; and even if only for a single day, there had been an atmosphere of unity and resistance. Moreover a standard had been set: the decent Amsterdammer had learned to stand up for the oppressed, and the oppressed of the day were the Jews. Above all, the Jews knew, if only for a moment, that they were not alone.

———

One feels somehow dishonest when writing about this period in Amsterdam's history, more so than with any other. It is because we know the outcome, whereas the people of Amsterdam did not. It is a difficult time to visualize. A permanent insecurity dominated life, and every decision had to be made against a background of rumours and confused assumptions. This was true not least for the Jewish community.

During the first phase of persecution, there was, among the Jews of Amsterdam, a widespread belief that they were facing hard times, somewhere beyond the Netherlands, with cold and general hardship, but almost nobody at this stage had any idea what was hanging over their heads. In May 1940, for instance, there was considerable pressure from various sides for the destruction of Jews' registration cards for safety's sake, but the Jewish community's leaders adamantly refused. Even as late as September 1941 the Jewish Council asked the Red Cross for the address of the Mauthausen concentration camp, and whether it was possible to correspond regularly with "persons staying there".[25]

Naïvety, innocence – are hardly the right words. People who have lived undisturbed for generations, who have not experienced a pogrom for centuries, simply lack the imagination with which to picture the sort of evil that lay in wait for them.

Nor can it be denied that the German occupiers displayed great cunning. What appeared at first to be little more than mild harassment turned out to have been but a prelude to the Final Solution. The displacement of Amsterdam's Jews was not achieved in a single action but by a process of uprooting, intimidation, marginalization and isolation that was established step by step. The chief means of this was not physical violence, but the insidious power of bureaucracy.

With their obfuscating use of language – "work deployment" was the euphemism for deportation to Auschwitz –the persecutors lulled their victims, and often themselves, into a false sense of security. The Germans and many of the Dutch collaborators saw themselves mainly as transport agents transferring a certain product, in this case Jews, from A to B. What happened afterwards was not their problem. Furthermore, everything happened in gradual stages, each of which seemed to suggest that it was the worst that would happen.

In his book *Ondergang*, the historian Jacques Presser documents this process of expulsion and extermination over more than a thousand pages. Some of his chapter titles give a precise idea of what happened: "Into Isolation" (May 1940–September 1941); "From Isolation to Deportation" (September 1941–July 1942); "The Deportations" (July 1941–September 1943). Let us follow Presser's data in more detail:

1 May 1941: Increasingly more professions are declared prohibited to Jews, for instance, those of doctor and chemist.

29 August 1941: Jewish pupils are expelled from schools. Special schools are set up.

15 September 1941: Jews are forbidden to take part in public events, artistic shows, concerts; to visit parks and zoos, cafés and restaurants; to use wagon-lits and restaurant cars in trains; to attend sports events, or visit swimming pools, public libraries, museums, markets, auctions and suchlike, as long as these are not held especially by and for Jews. "The newspaper with this report was brought to the café at five o'clock and at five minutes past the café was empty," the daughter of the landlord of the Ijsbreker was to recall. "That is how it went. We lost everything from one minute to the next. We never saw a single customer again."[26]

6 January 1942: All unemployed Jews are sent to labour camps in the countryside. A survivor remembered that "It was like a Russian winter. The snow lay metres deep on the tracks and froze over. To be there made one feel as though one was overwintering in Nova Zemlya."[27]

14 January 1942: Beginning of the ghettoization of all Jews from the Amsterdam province. Jews everywhere received instructions to be ready within three days with their luggage in order to move to their new Amsterdam quarters. The Jewish refugees from Germany were sent directly to the transit camp at Westerbork in Drente.

20 March 1942: Jews are forbidden to use private cars.

27 March 1942: Jews are forbidden to marry non-Jews or to have sexual relations with them.

29 April 1942: "As of Sunday next, a so-called 'Jewish Star' will have to be worn by every Jew. A maximum of four stars is available per person. The price of a star is four cents."

24 June 1942: Jews must remain indoors from 8 p.m. until 6 a.m. They are also forbidden to visit non-Jewish friends (this was in order to make raids easier later on, although at the time no one but the Germans were aware of this). Trams, buses and trains are also forbidden to them, subject to certain exceptions. "Only now can I see how wonderful a tram is, especially an open one, but that pleasure has been taken away from us Jews. For us, walking is good enough," wrote the 13-year-old Anne Frank in her new diary.

Two days after that last entry, the representatives of the Jewish Council were informed that Jewish men and women between the ages of 16 and 40 would be sent to work, "under police guard" in Germany. Until that moment, deportations had taken place only incidentally, as "punishment", usually for some "act of terror" that the wretched deportee had had no part in. After the end of June 1942, however, they began to happen systematically. On Sunday, 5 July, the first groups received their summonses by special post. All hell broke loose in the building of the Jewish Council in the Nieuwe Keizersgracht 58. Everyone hunted for rubber stamps and exemptions, everyone was suddenly found to be indispensable, everyone had been baptized or wounded or was an invalid; everyone queued up for doctor's certificates, letters from the church, Ausweise (passports); failing all these, a week's deferments were begged for. "The Jewish community would have had to consist of saints in order to prevent the explosion within it of corruption, nepotism, jumping-on-the-bandwagon and all the accompanying phenomena, which now occurred," writes Presser. He describes one end-of-term celebration at the Jewish Lyceum, where he himself was a teacher. Some of the pupils had received summonses in the post, girls of 15 or 16 years. The feeling of threat at the gathering was palpable, like a suffocating fog. People spoke and made music, beautiful and sensitively. Suddenly a girl from the highest class got to her feet. She and her sister had each received a summons. What should they do? Presser continues:

> There stood the girl, 17 years old, and with her final term report full of high marks, quite alone and unprotected, directly in front of the green board behind which the teachers were sitting. To this historian, it is as though he can still see her standing there, a kind, intelligent child, utterly decent; he can still hear her question, a question he will never forget: "Ladies and gentlemen, please tell us what we must do?" Nobody knew, nobody could help, and they were deported.[28]

14 July 1942: The transport for "work deployment" leaves Amsterdam at dead of night and arrives in Auschwitz [in German-occupied Poland] two days later. The first German raids are taking place. In the following weeks the summonses, raids and

transportation following each other in quick succession. A Jewish woman writes about a visit to her parents: "Shuddering with revulsion, Mother told how she sat in the dark in front of the window every evening while people were dragged away like animals, shivering with apprehension, because it could be her and father's turn at any moment; how large trucks brought in for the raids had waited there, loaded with people whimpering or shouting out loud with fear, of whom only a hopeless tangle of arms and legs had been visible."[29]

Most arrested Jews were billeted temporarily in the Hollandsche Schouwburg (the National Theatre) on the Plantage Middenlaan. Sometimes after a few hours, but generally after days or even weeks, they were taken to the Central Station by tram and from there by train to the transit camp at Westerbork. From there, with the help of the Resistance, a large number of small children were smuggled out, via a kindergarten across the road from the camp, in boxes, potato sacks, sometimes even in rucksacks. One of them was little Ed van Thijn, later to be Major of Amsterdam.

All through the winter of 1942–3 the arrests and deportations continued, but by then the shock had dissipated, just as, Presser says, the first tumbril on its way to the guillotine had been an event, whereas the tenth no longer attracted comment. In the advertisement pages of *Het Joodsche Weekblad* (The Jewish Weekly), marriages are announced; maids are sought; many Jews have "established themselves", especially as hairdressers and pedicurists; French conversation lessons are offered; "Not travelling? You can still keep in touch with your clients with good commercial letters"; and a manufacturer promises "for those who are sent to work in Germany, an important reduction on our rucksacks".

On the night of 10–11 November 1942, some 500 Amsterdam Jews were arrested. On the afternoon of the 11th, the entire Hollandia factory in Kattenburg was emptied of people, and almost 400 Jews were taken. On 24 November all Amsterdam Jews whose surnames began with the letters "K" and "S" were taken from their houses. On 27 November it was the turn of "L" and "P". At the end of that month, an internal memorandum notes that the arrested Jews have already been sent from Westerbork to Auschwitz. Presser's chronicle continues, relentlessly:

30–31 December 1942: Exuberant celebrations at the Jewish Council. The Chairman, Professor Cohen, is 60.

1 March 1943: From the modern building of De Joodse Invalide [the Jewish Hospital] on the Weesperplein, now the offices of the Amsterdam Health Authorities, three hundred patients are arrested by the SS, most of them old, sick, disabled, blind. The evacuation happened in terrifying silence. "There was no shouting or crying."

21 May 1943: Most exemptions [from deportation] accorded to Jewish Council personnel and their families are rescinded. The Council is allowed to determine who is to go. Finally, total panic breaks out: to evade the order, the employees must remove their names and those of their families from the register. People work throughout the weekend in the large, well-lit building. In the end, they just pull cards from the boxes at random. A boy who works as a courier brings documents from one room to the other, pulls out his own card. Panic-stricken, he runs from the building. As not enough Jews appear voluntarily, there is a big raid in the ghetto during which another 3,000 Jews are arrested.

20 July 1943: Another *Grossaktion* [Large Action] is held, at which a substantial remaining group of Jews from Amsterdam South and East are made *marschfertig* [ready to march]. They are assembled in the Sarphatipark [the part that is now the Victorieplein], the Polderweg, and the Olympiaplein. It is a beautiful Sunday, and on the Olympiaplein people continue with their games.

1 July 1943: Jews in "mixed" marriages are only permitted to stay if they let agree to be sterilized. [This measure was, incidentally, sabotaged by many doctors, including the German doctor in charge of the operation.]

29 September 1943: Of the 140,000 Dutch Jews, most have now been deported. Some thousands were able to escape persecution because of their mixed marriages; an estimated 20,000 have managed to go underground, and about the same number were able to obtain a "worker" stamp. Now this last category is to go as well.

From the camp at Westerbork people are quickly transported on to
unknown destinations in the east.

This is not all we know, however. Invariably, it was always the same train
going backwards and forwards, and when the deportees realized this they
hid letters and accounts of their journey in the carriages for those who were
left behind. A few of these few last documents have survived. One writer
writes that the carriage is crammed full with people and that it is stifling
inside. "The atmosphere is horrifying and everyone is picking fights with
everybody else." Another notes that: "Thanks to some funny remarks from a
true-born Amsterdammer, the mood was soon quite good, but the closer
we came to the border, the quieter people became." A woman writes that
there was such an "outstanding" atmosphere that a "cabaret" was organized
in her carriage on the evening of the first day. "One song shall always stay
with me, sung by a girl of 16 in the half-darkness of a paraffin lamp set
on the floor, namely 'Nederland'." From another account of these journeys
we learn that a barber cut the men's hair, and that a teacher "gave a wonderful lecture about Zionism, making us all forget the goal of our journey".
But always the last sentence of these notes is the same: "We have stopped at
Auschwitz. We have to get out. It is a large factory city, because you can
see a lot of chimneys." Or: "In the distance there is a building which is lit.
'Bye everyone, we'll be back soon."

Of the 80,000 Jews in Amsterdam, only 5,000 were alive at the time of the
Liberation in 1945. In total, 98 deportation trains with more than 100,000
people were able to leave the Netherlands without a single incident.

Shoah, the documentary film about the Holocaust directed by the
Frenchman Claude Lanzmann, features a number of "technicians" who
made the wheels of this gigantic death-machine go round: some of
them were guards, some workers, one is even the engineer of the train to
Auschwitz. One of the most notable of these figures is a certain Walter
Stier, a railway official who was in charge of organizing "special trains".
These were intended for large groups of people on holiday, but also for
Jews on their way to the camps – the "transport of the resettled", as he
calls them. Stier was ultimately the central figure in the entire system of

transports, but he had wanted to know nothing about them. As far as he was concerned, he was simply someone who co-ordinated the movements of "regular trains", "holiday trains", or "special trains". Treblinka and Auschwitz were to him final destinations, "accommodations". "I was simply an office worker," he protested afterwards.[30]

In the Netherlands, too, countless Walter Stiers aided the Germans in their discreet mass slaughter. Dutch Railways arranged, without the slightest objection, special night trains to Westerbork and to the German border, for which the bill was paid punctually by the occupiers: Train 11537, departure Amsterdam CS 2.16 a.m., arrival Hooghalen 5.48 a.m., with stops in Amersfoort and Zwolle, and, exactly 20 minutes later, the second train, the 11539, left following the same schedule. Amsterdam's Municipal Transport Office also collaborated perfectly. On nights when there were raids on the Jews, several trams, one from line 8, one from line 6, and two each from lines 16 and 24, would run between the assembly points and the Central Station. Not a single instance of refusal to work or any other protest was recorded.

Other municipal services also carried out the work as though nothing out of the ordinary was happening. Municipal clerks stamped Js on identity papers, impounded Jews' radios and bicycles, and sent the Jewish unemployed to labour camps. Almost everybody took great care to hand in his Declaration of Aryan Descent. Amsterdam University collaborated without protest by dismissing Jewish teaching staff and by asking students to sign a declaration of loyalty to the occupiers. After the war, a "cleansing commission" was to find very little to say in exoneration of the policy of the university's administration and faculties.[31]

On 20 January 1941, the German authorities requested the Civil Registry to make a colour-coded map showing the distribution of Jews throughout the city. By 29 January it was complete: a map with one stripe for every ten Jews. Not one civil servant so much as hesitated.

The Germans never posted more than 60 officers in Amsterdam, even at the height of the persecution of the Jews. The rest was done by the Dutch. Of the total number of men deployed in the big raids, about half were ordinary Dutch policemen. Moreover, after October 1942, the Dutch police were ordered to raid Jewish houses on their own, instead of under the leadership of the *Sicherheitspolizei* or the SS. The majority of these officers did just that, and more: they were so thorough that when they found Jews in a flat for which they did not have an arrest warrant, they took them anyway. "Concerning the Jewish Question, the Dutch police behave outstandingly and catch hundreds of Jews, day and night," the senior German police officer in Amsterdam, Rauter, wrote to his superior, Himmler, on 24 September 1942. His colleague, Willy Lages, was to admit after the war: "We would not have been able to arrest ten per cent of the Jews without their help." [32]

There were, of course, "good" policemen. Amsterdam officers found various ways of working against the raids that accompanied the February Strike, and some even did the exact opposite of what they had been ordered to do by letting everyone out of the ghetto and nobody in. [33] The successful raid later carried out by the Resistance against the office of the population register would not have been possible without a tip-off from the police. Everywhere eyes were closed, records of interviews falsified and dossiers "mislaid". A number of workers at the Amsterdam Municipal Employment offices became past masters at destroying registration cards, forging the results of tests and producing fictitious doctors' letters. Sometimes they even managed to send unemployed Jews as "Aryans" and under false names to a "normal" work deployment in German industry, where their chances of survival were far higher. Thousands of Amsterdammers were also involved in helping those who were in hiding. Yet for all these efforts, the city did not do enough.

The Shoah took place in Germany, but as far as Amsterdam is concerned, the supply lines of that gigantic abattoir began in the Polderweg, the Olympiaplein, the Nieuwe Keizersgracht, and the Elandsgracht. With some exceptions the attitude of the average Dutch non-Jew was little different from that of many of those interviewed in Claude Lanzmann's documentary: naïve, inert, cowardly, sometimes magnanimous, on occasion extraordinarily courageous. The Amsterdam tram drivers, police, and civil servants, particularly those in the population register office, oiled the wheels of the German machine of destruction. The parts such people played are varied, from service beyond the call of duty to outright sabotage, to obeying orders through gritted teeth.

A fragment from the diary of an Amsterdammer who went to the Betuwe for the day to pick cherries with his family on the Sunday of one of the biggest raids is indicative of the isolation into which the Jews had been manoeuvred. He complains that, due to the raids, some stations are inaccessible. "It is wonderful in the Betuwe. How beautiful life can be!" Back on the train, the family is "in a happy mood, because everyone has had a splendid day". On the Amstelstation, German troops and Dutch police are still busy with the Jews. "What a world. We can see a bit of it on the Ringdijk. House after house is being searched. And we are carrying our precious cargo home . . . 35 pounds of cherries! What happiness! At eleven o'clock we creep into our beds and fall asleep immediately." [34]

Did the average Amsterdammer understand what was happening? The full extent of the horror of this mass murder only became apparent after the war, but it is beyond doubt that, after the summer of 1942, it was understood in Amsterdam that not all was well with the "work-relocation transports" that ran so regularly to the east. Hardly any letters were answered; the fact that the sick and the old were taken to the "work camps" was highly suspicious, and besides these and other signs, rumours about what really happened had found their way back into the city. On 9 October 1942 Anne Frank wrote about the deported Jews in her diary: "We assume that they are killed. The English radio speaks of gassing. Perhaps that is the quickest method of dying. I am totally devastated." At that time, most Amsterdam's Jews had yet to be deported.

"The Netherlands has carried out the biggest public relations exercise to follow the Second World War by using the diary of Anne Frank to give the impression that the Jews were all in hiding here, and that the entire Dutch population was in the Resistance," one of the Jews who, as a child, had been smuggled out of Amsterdam was to declare before a congress of Holocaust survivors. [35] Some of the participants of the congress had emigrated intentionally, far away from the "respectable" Netherlands that had hidden its past so well behind clean façades and flowerpots. It is true, however, that the Dutch still have a tendency to talk up the extent of their resistance to almost mythical proportions. In reality, proportionally more Jews were deported from the Netherlands than from any other Western European country. As Adolf Eichman was to explain later, the persecution ran "like clockwork". After the war, an official investigation found that almost half a million Dutch men and women had collaborated with the occupying forces in one way or another.

As for the extent of the resistance, the numbers are unclear. Henk van Randwijk, one of the leading figures in the underground network, was later to say that, right up to the end of the war, one would always meet the same people in the Resistance, and that their number "did not exceed four figures". Furthermore, he maintained that resistance only really got under way when the Germans began to disturb Dutch families, as well as Jews, with their *Arbeitseinsatz* (work deployment), taking husbands away from their wives and children, removing them from their "fixed understanding of forms and norms" and thus forcing them into resistance.[36]

The Jews of Amsterdam received scarcely any support from abroad, either. Until the end of 1942, there was no one within the Dutch government-in-exile in London who was concerned with the plight of the deported Jews. Nothing concrete was done from London until June 1944. While more than ten per cent of the population of Amsterdam was being deported to extermination camps, the issue was not even mentioned in the minutes of the exiled Dutch government's Council of Ministers. After the war, its members would explain to an investigating committee that they had "underestimated the difficulties".

The war years were hard, the dilemmas sometimes almost irresolvable, and it befits generations that had no part in this period to be cautious in their judgement. It has to be said, however, that this phase of Amsterdam's history offers little scope for self-congratulation. Most Amsterdammers were anything but resistance fighters. With their families they tried to avoid the perils of occupation as far as possible, and that was all. "The commonly held notion that one does not retreat from violence but opposes it is from now, from afterwards, not from then," wrote Primo Levi, himself an Auschwitz survivor. "The imperative of resistance grew with the resistance and with the global tragedy of the Second World War; before that, it was a rare quality of rare individuals."[37] In this respect, too, the February Strike in Amsterdam was an isolated moment of courage and clarity.

The total number of Dutch Jews who did eventually manage to hide from the Nazis was around 25,000, of whom about 8,000 were still arrested, mostly after having been betrayed by other Dutch people. This means that in the Netherlands only one in five Jews had even the chance to go into hiding, or, as a preacher who served with the Resistance put it: "You can place ten [escaping] English pilots in one house, but in ten houses not one Jew."[38] Not infrequently the Jews' Dutch "helpers" also asked for large sums of money from their charges – 500, sometimes even 1,000 guilders a month. Presser records the case of a woman who, after a year in hiding, could no longer afford the money demanded by her hosts. She was cast into the street and ended up in Auschwitz.

It should be said, however, that some of those in hiding were capable of seriously abusing the situation, and, if arrested, would not hesitate to denounce their helpers: If I have to go, I will report you. Going into hiding was difficult for both parties, quite apart from the gigantic risks connected with it. It required great resolution and courage.

Even so, nobody who immerses himself or herself in this history can escape the conclusion of Presser and others: that despite the heroic work of some individuals, no form of resistance was such an abject failure as that against the deportation of the Jews. The motto which, since the war, Amsterdam has been permitted to adopt for its coat of arms – "Heroic, Decided, Merciful" – is more a reason for shame than for pride, since it was precisely these three qualities that were so singularly lacking during those years.

This passive guilt, the guilt felt by those who have allowed something terrible to happen, explains why the Dutch population developed such a vicious anger against everyone who had formally been "on the wrong side" during the war, while genuine collaborators were often ignored. The guilt of the idle spectator still hovers like a cloud over the entire city.

Chapter Ten

The Years of Moral Panic

I HEARD THE STORY MUCH LATER FROM ATTIE VAN HALL; THE STORY about probably the last time she saw her father. It was on a cold evening during what must have been the final winter of the war (she did not remember the date precisely), when Walraven van Hall, a man burned out after months of working himself to the bone, came sailing unexpectantly into the kitchen where his wife and children were. Better known as Van Tuyll, or sometimes also as Barends, he rarely came home any more during these months, it had become too dangerous. He had a rough journey behind him, from Amsterdam to Zaandam on a wooden-wheeled bicycle, and he was shattered. His wife attempted to warm him up, gave him something to eat. In the end, she resolutely climbed on a chair, and, from behind the kitchen chest took the last two lumps of sugar, carefully preserved for a case of extreme need. She was never to forget that simple act.

A short time later Attie's father was betrayed, arrested, and on 12 February he was shot near the Spaarne in Haarlem. He knew everything about the resistance group with which he worked, but had told his interrogators nothing. Attie van Hall remembered hearing her mother crying by the kitchen door. "She only told us when it had already happened." Attie also recalled how she felt during the Liberation celebrations shortly afterwards: "That muddle inside you. The enormous happiness, everyone on the street dancing and jumping, and you yourself just walking through it all, feeling only a sort of heaviness."

There is no history without heroes, and they too should appear in this account, by their thousands, minor and major ones, men and women who surpassed themselves under the pressure of the circumstances. They are too many to recall, so I will limit myself to two figures who were enormously important and yet are now almost forgotten: Walraven and Gijs van Hall, grandsons of the old banker Maurits van Hall, great-grandchildren of those two idealists, the Separatist Calvinists, Anne and Suze van Hall.

Walraven, or "Wallie" as he was mostly called, and his brother Gijs had both worked as bankers in America in the 1930s, and on their return to the Netherlands they had continued on the stock market and in banking. These two energetic Amsterdam businessmen exuded an air of progressiveness, placing their trust in the simple compass of goodwill and common sense.[1]

As was true of many people, they found themselves in the Resistance because of a fairly trivial matter. After the February Strike, Gijs van Hall became involved in a scheme to collect money for the strikers and the families of those who had been executed. Walraven van Hall found himself performing a similar task: he had to find money from among the business community for the so-called Zeemanspot (Sailors' Pot), a semi-legal fund that paid pensions to the wives and children of Dutch sailors who, since the German occupation, had taken jobs on Allied ships. It proved a laborious business, and soon Walraven van Hall conceived the idea of seeking only large sums, which were given to the fund as loans guaranteed by the Dutch government in London. The financiers were not issued with an ordinary receipt, but with shares in the Imperial Russian Railways or other worthless securities, to which was appended their true value. In this way, the van Hall brothers collected more than half a million guilders. Running into difficulties when the 1,000-guilder banknotes were suddenly declared invalid, they came into contact with a group of sympathetic tax inspectors who were to play a central role in this "paper Resistance". By means of forged tax-refund orders and other fiscal high-wire acts, they managed to channel millions of guilders' worth of tax moneys into the van Halls' funds.

Meanwhile, on 4 May 1943, the occupying powers ordered that all Dutch men between the ages of 18 and 35 had to register for placement in the German war industry. Raids were conducted, but countless men went underground or vanished in the countryside. Thus, in addition to the Jews, a second group of "illegal" people came into being. Whole networks and organizations developed to provide the refugees with places to stay, false papers and ration coupons. Armed commandos raided distribution offices. Little by little, Amsterdam emerged as the centre of this Resistance, with its own blossoming illegal press: Trouw (Faithful), Vrij Nederland (Free Netherlands), Het Parool (The Watchword), De Waareheid (The Truth). The names spoke for themselves.

Vast sums of money were needed to fund all of this, and especially for the people who had gone into hiding. The van Halls decided to broaden their activities to cover all those in hiding, and consequently established a special organization in addition to the "Zeemanspot", the "Landlubber Fund", later known by the more respectable title of "National Support Fund". At the start they borrowed money from banks – ten of Amsterdam's twelve major banks were part of the conspiracy. In dealing with the smaller banks and life insurance companies they recruited specialists, so-called "lending agents" who were also adept at illicitly freeing millions of guilders.

To handle the payment end of this support fund, the van Halls had meanwhile quietly established a huge country-wide organization which managed an ingenious system for getting the money to those in hiding. They had divided the country into 23 districts, each of which had a district head who oversaw local heads, "investigators" and "payment agents". In the end, the entire organization numbered almost 1,900 underground workers, each known only by a code name. Couriers kept up the connections. At the end of the war it was one of the largest financial institutions in the country.

Within a space of two years, the van Hall brothers had become central figures in the Dutch Resistance; indeed, Wallie was even spoken of as "Prime Minister of the Occupied Netherlands". This had much to do with his character. Few people knew his real identity. He usually operated under the name van Tuyll, but all who knew him during those years would later testify that he had had unique qualities, "a man who combined great gifts with great personal charm, and who took a warm personal interest in everybody". The leading Communist in the Resistance, Gerben Wagenaar, described Wallie van Hall as one of the rarest people he had ever met. "During our conversations I was unable to guess his profession – I assumed that he was an engineer or a machinist," Wagenaar told the historian Lou van Jong later. "He was a man of great insight and great tolerance. He had an incredible way with people. He was a stunning improviser, but he was also honest and upright. Nor did I think him conservative."

His daughter Attie, then ten years old, had no idea of her father's double life. True, he was seldom at home, but she mainly remembered the many people who visited the house in Zaandam during that period. To her, the well-known resister Gerrit van der Veen was not the man who had led the successful raid on the Civil Registry Offices on the Plantage Kerklaan, but a kindly artist who once came by for a meal and to whom Wallie gave, just like that, a precious half-cheese. Other resistance members were guests who were simply referred to as "Uncle Jaap", and who would tuck Attie into bed at night and tell her stories. Van Tuyll? – that was a different world.

In 1944, without the knowledge of the grassroots Resistance, an apparently insoluble problem arose at the top of the underground movement that threatened the lives of tens of thousands of people in hiding: cash was running out fast. The banks involved in the conspiracy were still willing to provide credit, but the National Bank blocked the distribution of banknotes. Moreover, it would have appeared very suspicious if ten Amsterdam banks had continued to bring money into circulation when by this stage in the war the entire west of the Netherlands was, as one German put it, "economically dead". It followed, therefore, that the money had to come from a single source – why then could that source not be the National Bank itself?

It was Gijs van Hall who conceived the idea of the largest banking fraud in Dutch history. During the 1930s when he was working for an American bank, a huge scandal had been raging around forged treasury bonds, certificates of government loans with dollar values equivalent to at least 100,000 guilders each. What the Americans can do, we can do as well, Gijs thought, and thereby set in motion an incredible coup. Through the Centre for Identity Cards, an underground printing workshop that specialized in forging official papers, good imitations of genuine bonds were painstakingly produced. These forgeries were not put into circulation, however, for that might have attracted attention; instead they were exchanged in the vaults of the National Bank for real ones by the bank's Chief Cashier, himself a member of the conspiracy. Since there was almost no electricity in Amsterdam any more all this took place in candlelight, and the false bonds easily passed muster. The real treasury bonds were then sold, their history explained with a complicated story, to five different banks. The revenue – 2,000,000 guilders a week, or five suitcases full of five-guilder notes – was distributed throughout by the country-wide organization. The total profit of this operation was then more than 50 million guilders, the equivalent of almost £80,000,000 today.[2]

The money came at just the right moment. After the Normandy landings in June 1944, the Allies reached Maastricht in September. In that same month a second landing took place near Arnhem. After a fierce battle, the Allies failed to capture the bridges at Arnhem and therefore were unable to liberate the western Netherlands. The Occupation, which Amsterdammers hoped would be over in September 1944, would continue throughout another winter, the terrible months of the so-called "Hunger Winter". Because the Allies had already taken South Limburg the normal supply of coal did not come into the city. In addition to this, the railway workers had gone on strike at the request of the London government. Together, these two factors brought the country's gas and electricity plants to a stand still. Amsterdam became a cold, dark city in which not a single tram was running. Schiphol and the harbours were destroyed by the Germans, who then proceeded to steal half of the city: wharves, buses, trains, machines, factory stock, tramway carriages, bicycles, textiles, everything that might be of some use was taken away. Neither post nor telephone worked any more, the rubbish collection was terminated and the sewers overflowed. Meanwhile, military patrols hunted for men between 17 and 50 years of age for the *Arbeitseinsatz* in Germany. In December, business life was almost at a standstill. Most Amsterdammers no longer worked, or if they did it was only for a few days a week. The schools were closed.

At the end of December, the frost came, ushering in a period of severe starvation. Until the beginning of February it remained savagely cold, and because the Ijsselmeer froze, the last supply routes for food were cut off. There was no fuel and the people of Amsterdam had to fend for them-selves. They cut down trees, lifted the wooden blocks that lay between the tram rails, and plundered the empty houses where, once, tens of thousands of deported Jews had lived. Floors, staircases, beams, everything that would burn was taken away, and eventually the walls slowly caved in as well. During the Hunger Winter, entire streets – the Jodenbreestraat, for instance – became little more than ruins. In total, this mass hunt for fuel resulted in the felling of 20,000 trees and the utter destruction of 4,600 houses.

Black markets flourished on the Zeedijk, the Nieuwmarkt and especially in the Jordaan: a loaf of bread cost 25 florins, a sack of potatoes 800 florins, and a packet of cigarettes 80 florins. Most Amsterdammers lived on sugar beets, tulip bulbs, even candle fat, and thin, indeterminate soup from communal kitchens.

In search of food, thousands of city dwellers walked – pushing rickety carts, prams and bicycles – across the cold, bare countryside, searching for a few potatoes or a cauliflower. If they were lucky enough to find something, they would exchange it for jewellery, antiques, watches, linen, and in some cases sexual favours. Towards spring, as the desperation increased, these hunger tours would sometimes last for weeks, taking some walkers as far as Friesland in the east of the Netherlands. Hundreds of Amsterdammers died from starvation and from the cold: about 1,200 in January 1945, in February, 1,400, and in March 1,600.[3]

During this time, Wallie van Hall was everywhere and nowhere. Wherever the machinery of resistance threatened to run dry he operated, in his own words, as "the oiler". He helped to establish what came to be called the Internal Defence Force, the "official" arm of the Resistance. He co-ordinated the financing of the railway strike. Most of all, he took care that whatever problems the Resistance might face, it would never lack for one thing: money.

"When Wallie came into a room, everyone was happy within five minutes," a secretary of the Internal Defence Force was to recall. "He could always make people laugh with a joke, even in the most miserable circumstances. It was a catastrophe during that winter, I remember, if an emergency stove could not be made to burn properly. Lots of people didn't know how to operate them. Wallie would mess around with it a little and it would suddenly work again. I did think, though, that he began to look worse and worse, very emaciated, with large rings under his eyes."

One of the chief problems facing van Hall during these months was the question of the vacuum of power that would inevitably come about after the liberation of the capital. For years there had been an organization, the Ordedienst (Order Service), which was concerned not with resistance activities, but with power. It was a society of mostly demobilized military men who intended to support the Allies during the Liberation, not least

Emmy Andriesse, *Small child during the Hunger Winter* (1945).

because they planned to take over the military authority in order to "prevent a popular uprising". They had access to influential circles, and there was no ignoring them. Opposing them were a number of Resistance groups, among them the groups centred around the underground papers *Het Parool* and *Vrij Nederland*, which wanted as swift a return as possible to a parliamentary government. In addition to these there were the members of the commandos, Communists, often from Reformed Protestant backgrounds. Finally, there were the armed resistance groups of the Raad van Verzet (Resistance Council), led by another Communist, Gerben Wagenaar. Wallie van Hall managed to bring about a form of collaboration between these disparate elements, which resulted in the Delta Committee. He co-ordinated the office staff, supplied safe addresses for meetings, and arranged access to the clandestine telephone network. There remained large differences between the groups, however, especially between the Ordedienst and the organizations actively involved in the Resistance, and it was obvious there would be trouble.

It seems bizarre now, but this is how it happened. While a dark Amsterdam died of hunger and cold, while the German occupiers demonstrated their presence on every street corner, in a house on the Leidsegracht the leaders of each faction were fighting it out over three very simple questions: Who would become Burgomaster of the city after the war? Who would become Chief of Police? Who would become leader of the armed resistance in the capital? All of which could be summed up in a single question: Who would be boss of Amsterdam?

As far as the Burgomaster was concerned, there was little controversy after the London government had been consulted. The purposeful shipowner Feike de Boer was to become interim Burgomaster, and in the autumn of 1944, in the strictest secrecy, he went about his task with great energy. Next, after a good deal of "oiling" by Wallie van Hall, a stockbroker C. F. Overhoff, one of the more moderate Ordedienst members, was accepted by all as leader of the armed resistance. The nomination of a Chief of Police, however, posed problems.[4] The Amsterdam police had been one of the most important accomplices of the occupying authorities, especially during the last years of the war. Now, the "good" officers demanded a Chief who would clean up the service with an iron hand. The collaborationist officers, however, feared that a turning tide might cost them their lives. This struggle for power behind the scenes would persist throughout the Hunger Winter.

The preferred candidate of the first group was Commissioner W. H. Schreuder, an officer determined to make the police into a modern, democratically-minded organization. In May 1940 he had been Commissioner of the Warmoesstraat district, but his actions and attitudes had got him into so much trouble with the Germans that he was eventually demoted. Unknown to them, however, he had been an adviser for years.

The candidate of the second group was K. H. Broekhoff, who, until 1942, had been Deputy Chief Commissioner, and before the war had been Head of the Political Information Service of the Amsterdam police. He was in favour of a military-style police force, and deplored the fact that there was no procedure for fast trials in the Netherlands. He despised the NSB and in every respect was the man of the Ordedienst. He had agreed to accept its military authority after the war, with the condition that the police force be allowed to clean itself up.

Initially, Schreuder had far and away the best chance of being chosen: he had the support of most Resistance groups. At the beginning of 1944, the London government confirmed his nomination. Then, however, he was injured in a traffic accident which took him out of circulation for two months, during which time Broekhoff continued his incessant lobbying. The Ordedienst was concerned that it might draw the short straw if Schreuder were appointed, the upper echelons of the police and many of its ordinary members were dead against a thorough cleaning-up of the service, and Broekhoff himself threatened to resign. Together these three elements exerted so much pressure on the Delta Committee that its members changed their minds. The nomination of Schreuder, they now decided, would cause "too much confusion", especially in the police force. London, of course, did not want to give in; the British Secret Service had strong reasons to suspect that Broekhoff had himself been "on the wrong side" during the Occupation, but eventually even they turned, and Broekhoff became Chief of Police. Schreuder was dismissed in February 1945 by senior police officers.

It was therefore arranged, even before the end of the war, that the Amsterdam police force, the single most important instrument of the German extermination machine in the city, would never be called to account. The cards had been shuffled and dealt out a hand that would largely determine Amsterdam politics and Amsterdam business for the next two decades.

The Resistance had grown more and more brazen during the Hunger Winter. In May 1944 there had been an unsuccessful attempt to free

Resistance members in an armed raid on the prison in the Weteringschans. Gerrit van der Veen was wounded, and though he managed to hide for a few days, he was eventually arrested and executed. A month later the Resistance tried again, but the commando, which was led by Johannes Post, was betrayed, fell into a German trap and all of them were killed. Other actions succeeded, however. Several senior Germans and a number of traitors were killed, and military targets were sabotaged.

Wallie van Hall was closely involved in these activities. He travelled across the country like lightning, and was not afraid to do some of the most dangerous work himself, whether entering a suspect house, or helping a British pilot escape.

The Germans, meanwhile, continued to harass the Resistance wherever they could, carrying out raids, and intimidating the city with random executions. On 6 January 1945, 26 Amsterdammers were shot in reprisals for an attack on the Arbeitseinsatz offices in the Spiegelschool on the Marnixstraat. On the following day five citizens were executed on the Muiderstraatweg near the train viaduct; on 8 March, 51 people were killed by the Rozenoord; on 31 March, another six in the same place, and a further eight on 14 April. On 12 March, an agent of the Sicherheitsdients (SD), the German Security Service, had been liquidated on the Stadhouderskade by the Resistance. In revenge, 30 Resistance prisoners were shot on the Weteringplatsoen. Passers-by were forced to look on, and it was ordered that the corpses were to remain lying where they had fallen, until some courageous Amsterdammers covered them up with a Dutch flag. Even on 7 May, two days after the capitulation, drunken German marines caused a bloodbath by shooting into the celebrating crowd on the Dam from the windows of the Grote Club. Gijs van Hall was an eyewitness to the incident and would describe it later:

> Within a few moments the Dam was empty, apart from some tens of dead and wounded who were still lying there. After some minutes, a boy in a Scout uniform suddenly came riding into the square with a white flag tied to his bicycle. He cycled on to the Dam and managed to rescue one or two of the casualties. We held our breath.[5]

For Wallie van Hall, however, the end had come months earlier, in January 1945, brought about because of a stupid love affair between a young man and woman. A young, decent, married man called van Arkel had fallen in love with one of the couriers for Het Parool, whom he had met because he, too, did "something" in the Resistance: he was a legal expert at the negotiations between the various Resistance groups. When the young woman was arrested, her lover made a visit to the SD in order to rescue her. He was put under pressure by the SD, who threatened to tell his wife know about his affair, and who therefore managed to extract from him times and locations of a number of secret meetings. Arrests followed. The girl was freed. A notice about the next meeting at the end of January was found on one of those arrested, who told his interrogators the address, believing that everybody in the Resistance was aware that he had been detained. Most of those involved had indeed been warned, but Wallie van Hall and some others had been unavailable. Thus, van Tuyll was arrested. The Germans, who had only a vague idea of the existence of such a person, never knew whom they had in their hands.

Young van Arkel fled. Together with his lover he went into hiding, but was eventually found by a Resistance commando. At the beginning of March he was picked up on the street by four members of the Communist Party and taken to an illicit meeting. There he was questioned by two Resistance leaders, and admitted in tears that he had betrayed them. His account was taken down and then read back to him, after which he signed it and put his fingerprint next to the signature. He was given a cup of tea, and with it, a cyanide pill. Since the pill did not fully dissolve, however, he did not die. One of the Communists finished him off with a pistol. His widow was informed.

Much later, a signature was found among countless others scratched into the wall in a corner cell in the Huis van Bewaring, the main prison: W. VAN HALL.

The story of Commissioner Broekhoff remains to be told. He was appointed Chief of Amsterdam's Police after the Liberation, but at the beginning of July 1945 he fell into a coma and died three days later. A brain tumour, his family said. It was later to transpire, largely from the research of Lou de Jong, that the collaboration between the Dutch police, and especially Broekhoff's Information Service, and the German Sicherheitspolizei (Security Police) had been very close.[6] At the beginning of 1935, for instance, Broekhoff had been invited to Berlin – with, incidentally, the knowledge of the Dutch government – in order to talk about the dangers of the "Communists" who, being refugees from Germany, wanted to transfer their activities to the Netherlands. There is a report by the Dutch Information Service claiming that Broekhoff assisted German spies before the war, but it was only in 1994 that a researcher found the key to his secret in a Russian war archive.[7] Among the old Gestapo files he came across records of a secret agreement in which Broekhoff, under the code-name "David", had promised to give information to the Gestapo. Attached to the dossier was a list of names and addresses of political refugees. If they stayed in Amsterdam illegally, they could be sent back to Germany without any problems. As for the others on the list, the Germans knew what to do with them after 10 May 1940.

It was, however, this same Broekhoff who, during the February Strike – and on later occasions as well – had duped the Nazis in all sorts of ways. Years after his death, tenacious rumours persisted that he had been poisoned by the British with a pouch of tobacco he had been sent. There has never been any kind of evidence for this and, moreover, Broekhof didn't smoke.

———

One of the most eloquent photographs of the Liberation does not show Canadians, girls, or tanks, but three simple Amsterdam urchins beside a canal. They are not wearing shoes, and have only a few rags on their bodies; thin as rakes with eyes full of hunger, they have a little drum, made from an empty tin, and they proudly raise an old piece of cloth on which is written *Je maintiendrai* (the motto of the Dutch kings) and *Nederland zal herrijzen!* (*The Netherlands will rise again!*).

Shortly after the Liberation, these children would have had the summer of their lives, celebrating, scrounging from British and Canadian soldiers – and their Dutch girlfriends – whose pockets were full of heavenly things: cigarettes, chewing gum, chocolate, packets of wine gums. On posters all over the city the "Liberation Burgomaster" had proudly announced what had been achieved in only a few months: "The bread ration has increased six times. The telephone connections are entirely restored. There is radio reception for 30,000 families. A hundred aeroplanes have landed at Schiphol. Eleven tram lines have been put back into operation." The summer had been like this since the end of the war in Europe in May, with big celebrations in whole districts and in the streets; parties for no particular purpose, relentless Liberation celebrations that seemed destined never to end.

"Everyone got pissed and fucked around . . . " was the general opinion – and there was increasing concern in the editorial offices of the newspapers and in the studies of religious ministers. Weren't the city's youth getting out of control? Had not the population lost every semblance of order since the German occupation – I quote editorials from this period – were they not now lazy, in decline, lying and cheating, using violence, in short, "living solely in accord with their most primitive sensual instincts"? "The war", someone wrote, "violently awakened a slumbering sexual desire and set it free. Like a reckless ice-breaker it broke through the ice of our sexual morals, and now the dikes are groaning with the breaking ice."[8] These are the first indications that a new moral crusade was about to begin, without parallel in the history of Amsterdam. In brochures and newspaper articles – printed on precious paper, which was still in short supply – there was an outcry against what was regarded as the "unlawfulness of our youth", an "unwillingness to work", "immorality", and "anti-social behaviour" in general. All this boiled down to a single question: How can we impose control on a city without rules?

After the Liberation, a war about power and morality began. It raged under the skin of Amsterdam, as Herman de Liagre Böhl and Guus Meershoek put it, two historians who studied the mentality of this period. They even speak of a "moral panic". The unemployed were "disciplined", that is, seduced with increased benefits, but they had to be at the beck and call of potential employers. It was usually forgotten that "unwillingness to work" was more often a the result of material hardship rather than laziness, after all, how were you supposed to dig a new harbour if you had neither shoes nor ships? The same was true of the "unlawfulness" of the youth. Most of the poor children, like those in the photograph, were forced to remain barefoot until the autumn, so they had every reason for using the self-help techniques they had perfected during the Hunger Winter.

Photographer unknown, *Dancing couples in front of a Gracht
with street organ* (1945).

There were, of course, the "flirts", the "birds", the "chickens who would cackle with pleasure at every feather that was plucked from them", that is, the Amsterdam women and girls who befriended the Canadians. "During this 'weird and wonderful summer' of 1945, there probably was a short-lived – but in Dutch life, unheard-of – explosion of extra-marital sex," our two historians soberly conclude. The priests spoke of women who were "throwing themselves away" for a little soup and a packet of cigarettes;

but no Dutch man dared consider the real motive: that their woman went with the Canadians because they simply enjoyed doing so. As a Canadian soldier was to recount later: "I was overwhelmed by the most tempting offers from the most tempting women. Sometimes their husbands would stand nearby, a little confused, their suits too big for them now, looking thin, their legs a little shaky."[9]

Amsterdam sought to impose some order on all this. There was indeed a moral problem, but it did not lie with the young or with the girls. If one simply considers the statistics, it is simply a miracle that so few Amsterdammers perished during the Hunger Winter. The reason is simple: during the last months of the war, the people of Amsterdam cheated, deceived and stole on a grand scale. They pillaged and participated in the black market. In order to survive, even the most respectable citizens had to do things that they would rather not remember. They had overstepped their own norms of decent behaviour, and more than that, they had betrayed their neighbours and had looked the other way when the most horrific injustices had occurred under their very noses. Entire districts were now silent. In the summer of 1945, only a few Jewish survivors walked among the ruins of the empty and plundered houses of the Weesperstraat and the Jodenbreestraat.

The "moral panic" of the summer of 1945 turned out to be an excellent weapon in the hands of those who wanted to restore the old order as quickly as possible and who wanted nothing to do with the anarchy that had been developing during the last two years of the war. They also distanced themselves from the Resistance. About 6,000 collaborators had been arrested and were interned in six sheds belonging to the KNSM, the Royal Dutch Shipping Company on the Levantkade, but the clean-up operation, of which those in the Resistance had expected so much before the war, ended in an ugly compromise. Most of the "technicians" of the Amsterdam Holocaust remained in their posts. They were a necessary part of Amsterdam's reconstruction programme, and, after all, too much of an upheaval might have destroyed the delicate balance of power in the city. Things were even taken a step further. In some administrative circles it was felt that the characters of Resistance members, by defini-tion, were troublesome and "anti-social". In certain contexts, a Resistance background quickly became a minus rather than a plus point.

A similar process took place in city politics. When, during the Great Liberation rally, Prime Minister Gerbrandy was confronted by several thousand people waving red flags, he murmured, "Amsterdam has become – very red." At the first elections to the City Council, the Social Democrats and the Communists received almost two thirds of the votes. But despite the flags and the radical language, there was little opportunity to actively alter the politics of the Council. The "wild" ideas of the "boys" and "girls" of the Resistance were quickly forgotten. The post-war city administrators were in fact merely moderate reformers, and they were only too ready to involve the pre-war elites in their activities: the "moral crisis" had to be controlled; the rebuilding of the city was a priority, the rest would follow. That is not to say that the war did not cause a rupture in Amsterdam's history. In terms of civil infrastructure, business life, social care and other material matters, the city thoroughly embraced modernity. But the culture of its government and its political codes of conduct remained stuck in the year 1939, and this would be the case for at least another 20 years. Those who had been forced into hiding during the Occupation, such as the dock-workers and the Resistance couriers, were ceremoniously remembered every year, but their dreams and ideals were swept under the carpet.

What followed were the years of rolled-up shirtsleeves, of clearing rubble and drawing straight lines into the future. The harbour was enlarged enormously, moved from the east to the far west, and out of sight of the city. A large new connection to the German hinterland was built, the Amsterdam-Rhine channel, but for the most part, the city was busy reconstructing itself and was turned into an enormous building site.

There was a serious shortage of living space. This was partly due to the fact that most building programmes had stagnated during the war, but after the Liberation there were new factors concerning living space that had not been anticipated: young adults wanted to live on their own; people were marrying much later in life; the economy was beginning to pick up. In addition to this, there was another phenomenon, the so-called "thinning out". After the war, city dwellers gradually began to ask for more and more space for themselves. The elderly no longer moved in with their children; sons and daughters left home earlier (the latter before they were married), and the divorce rate was slowly on the increase. In 1917, four or more people lived in one Amsterdam flat; by the 1950s it was only three; and at the end of the century the number had dropped to two. This means that, towards the end of the twentieth century, twice as many flats will be required to house the same number of people.

Lots of living space was created during the 1950s and 1960s, especially in the areas of the Slotervaart, the Geuzenveld, the Osdorp, the Bos, and the Lommer. These flats were built in one flamboyant gesture, following the principles of what was then called the New Pragmatism, which, according to the architects, befitted the modern way of life of the 1950s: active, airy, open, fresh, simply-designed furniture, light rooms, thin curtains, bright colours. In practice, however, what Amsterdam ended up with were long rows of standardized blocks of flats, because almost all ornamentation and variation had been rationalized away during those harsh times.

Slowly but surely, a certain amount of wealth returned to the city, the most obviopus consequence of which was a new mobility. Many Amsterdammers bought cheap, motorized bicycles, and roads in the 1950s would be characterized by the leather-clad couple on their Zündapp scooter, perhaps with a child crying in the sidecar. More and more cars appeared on the streets, and the curious phenomenon of roadside recreation emerged: Amsterdammers drove some miles out of the city and then sat in their thousands by the side of the road, talking and looking at the other cars – or at cycles, motorcycles, scooters, and three-wheelers – just as they had done from the pavement of their districts some years before.

The 1950s mentality is typified by the solution which a certain Kaasjager, then Chief of Police, came up with to solve the traffic congestion that had developed in the narrow roads of the inner city. In October 1954 he took a map of Amsterdam and proposed that no fewer than 15 canals should be filled in: the Open Havenfront in front of the Central Station; the Singel; the last extant waters of the Rokin; a part of the Amstel; the Klovieniersburgwal; the Geldersekade; the Raamgracht; and a part of the Lijnbaansgracht. The entire Singel would then become a main road, and, via the Amstel and the Kloveniersburgwal, there would be a broad ring road around the old inner city. The Raamgracht and the Lijnbaansgracht were to serve as parking spaces.

The plan did not meet with universal approval. As one would expect, those responsible for protecting the city's historical monuments were far from happy. Nevertheless, what is more significant are the hundreds of people who greeted Kaasjager's plan as symbolic of a brave new era. I quote from some letters: "Every large metropolis is a mixture of old and new, but Amsterdam wants to remain old and decayed, stuck in the seventeenth century . . . come on!!!" Another writer wanted a concrete tunnel built just underneath the waterline of the canals to enable the trams to ride through them: "In times of emergency, these tunnels would provide excellent shelter for the population." There were also proposals to build a "parking palace" in glass on the Rokin, "in order to preserve the cleanliness of the city as far as possible". Someone else thought that Kaasjager should go further: "If the Kloveniersburgwal and the Geldersekade are to be filled in, the Waag and the Schreierstoren remain simply in the way. The Paleis, too, is an eyesore. It stands right in the axis of the Raadhuisstraat." The Chief Commissioner of Rotterdam remarked that "We in Rotterdam know from experience that traffic demands space. I once said during a lecture that Rotterdam had the 'privilege' to have been bombed." A woman asked herself whether the filling in was really worth it, when "in 20 years' time we will all float in the air in nuclear aeroplanes. Then roads will no longer be necessary." Yet another correspondent suggests pumping all of the water out of the canals and letting the traffic drive on the dry beds: "The walls of the canals can easily be smartened up and, if necessary, planted with lawn." Another: "Amsterdam has to make a choice: to be a museum with pretty façades and canals from the seventeenth century, or a modern business city where one can park one's car and where twentieth-century life will finally be given a chance."[10]

The Kaasjager plan very quickly vanished from the drawing boards, but the fight between the "museum" and the "modern business city" was to dominate the political agenda for decades to come.

In 1956, Gijs van Hall, Wallie's brother, became Burgomaster of Amsterdam. He was one of the very few bank directors to also be a member of the PVDA, the newly founded socialist party. He applied himself with great energy to the building projects of his predecessors; realized a further enlargement of the harbour in the west; added grain transfer and container cargo; managed the incorporation of the Bijlermeer; found the necessary funds for the IJ tunnel; grasped the chance to sort out the much-needed extension to the university; made preparations for the building of the gigantic Polder Hospital; and would probably have entered the history books as one of the best burgomasters the city had ever had, had he not been tripped up by an unexpected problem.

———

Of the 1960s, the American cultural sociologist Philip Slater once wrote that every revolution is not so much a renewal as the blossoming of latent alternatives that have lain dormant for years.[11] This could certainly be said of the movement that was to bring turmoil to Amsterdam and was to signal the beginning of what came to be known as The Twenty-Year Civil War. In Amsterdam it began exactly as Slater prognosed: "Suddenly the environment changed; the tolerated madman became a prophet; the clown a dancing master; the puppet an idol; the idol a puppet. The elements themselves did not change, but their relations with each other did."

One of the dancing masters was Rob Stolk, a printer's apprentice and rebel. His wedding on a white bicycle during the 1960s was so sensational that he was seen in photographs in every newspaper throughout the Western world.

"A new age dawned for us when a white car drove down our street, one day," he was to recall later. "A bunch of girls were sitting inside and they were handing out samples of a new kind of soup – Royco soup, from a packet. That was unheard of. People got soup just like that in order to taste it, something that they would have had to queue up for only a year earlier. All of a sudden the people were being taken seriously as consumers. That was the beginning. For my parents, a job was holy, it was security, but me and my friends began to talk about work more casually, because at the beginning of the 1960s there were lots of jobs. We had a record player in the house. Sometimes there would be meat on the table. For lunch we had a fried egg on bread. Here and there, televisions appeared, and the pictures came in hard and fast. Suddenly, everything you saw made you think that you weren't some bumpkin but a citizen of the world. And what was happening in the world was far worse than you had ever imagined. You could not buy that off with a few tenners contribution to the PVDA. We thought we had the right to be involved in everything."[12]

Rob Stolk was an idol and a dancing master, but the real prophet of this strange new movement was Robert Jasper Grootvelt. A little man with piercingly blue eyes, he claimed to have been cleaning the windows on the Hirschgebouw for five years. When he had finished cleaning the last window, he would start again with the first one.[13]

For one obscure reason or another, Grootveld had begun a virulent anti-smoking campaign aimed at the "enslaved consumer". This started in the spring of 1962, at a series of magical meetings in a derelict garage in the Korte Leidsedwarsstraat, number 29. He himself preferred to smoke something more consciousness enhancing than tobacco, but that was not, as yet, discussed. The building was baptised the Anti-Smoking Temple or Temple K, where, dressed as a kind of shaman, Grootveld carried out various rituals as the self-appointed "anti-smoking magician". He saw "advertising columns as the totem poles of the Western concrete jungle", and Amsterdam as a city "full of refrigerators and food mixers" ruled by a "sickening middle class"; after which diatribe his followers would add the chorus (incomprehensible to the layman): "Bram, bram, uche uche, bram, bram, uche, uche, at night I smoke my pipe, you understand." Johnny van Doorn, who was later to become a writer, was also a regular at Temple K. He had the nickname Johnny the Selfkicker, because he was able to bring himself into a state of trance through no other means than by producing a veritable Niagara of sentences. A certain Bart Huges attempted to reach a state of eternal widening of consciousness by drilling a hole in his forehead, thus creating a "third eye". On the streets, mysterious graffiti began to appear: "Gnot", "K", "Klaas comes", "Warning".

Magic had a magnetic appeal in a city that was so busy with practical matters, building flats and ramming poles into the ground. Throughout the 1950s, underneath this unified culture of reconstruction, small groups of students, writers and artists had kept the old torches burning and had even lit new ones. Something was blowing in the wind, and the rickety garage-Temple was full every week and Grootveld made sure that he got the publicity he wanted. Months later the Temple burned down, but it was

not long before the gatherings resurfaced around the Lievertje, the statue
of an Amsterdam urchin, that had been erected on the Spui as a bequest
from a wealthy cigarette manufacturer. When a graduate student introduced
the word "provo" – derived from "provoke" – into his dissertation on
disaffected young, it was immediately adopted as a *geuzen* name, a rebel
name, and a new jargon was associated with it: *vogel* (boy), *chick* (girl), *hip*,
blowen (to smoke a joint), *te gek* (crazy), *kip* (policeman).

Cor Jaring, *Burning Lievertje* (1965).

From the summer of 1965 onwards there were "happenings" almost every weekend around the Lievertje, and these always followed the same pattern: at first, the "Provos" and the police would keep at a wary distance; then Grootveld, painted like a tribal chief, would try to get to the statue while a cordon of police kept him at bay. The Provos began to move in and then what everybody had been waiting for would happen: the police got out their batons and sabres and began beating everything in sight. The crowd would call out more or less incomprehensible slogans such as "Republic!" or "Gnot!", "Image, Image!" and "Smurf the ones who smurf the smurfs!" The police would chase the youths between the cars, strike out at unsuspecting passers-by, and even detained a girl in a cell for days because she had distributed currants. The behaviour of the police only made things better for the Provos, who made several new recruits each time. "I found these riots wonderfully violent," an older officer would recount a quarter of a century later. "Back then you were at least allowed to give someone a decent hiding without fear of being reprimanded."[14] Rob Stolk: "The Lievertje ritual became a sort of maelstrom that sucked the entire city into its centre." Meanwhile, safe behind the windows of the cafés – Scheltema on the Nieuwezijds Voorburgwal and Hoppe on the Spuy – progressive journalists and intellectuals were busy sabotaging the old order: they established a new party, Democrats 66, and formed a new radical left grouping within the PVDA called Ten Past Red.

The Provos were a very small group with at most some ten or so active participants, but their influence on the rest of the city was enormous. Their success was largely due to the manner in which they presented themselves. They had a perfect feeling for images and symbols, and that was gratefully recognized by the new medium of television, which only served to multiply the effect of their actions. While they demonstrated, dressed in white and carrying a white banner, the police could be seen in the background waiting to beat them up. The authoritarian and brutal appearance of the police stood in stark contrast to the playful innocence of the Provos. It was a case of the old versus the new, the 1930s versus the 1960s. It was as if these "happenings" were a last flowering of the Resistance, a delayed reaction to the Liberation. Twenty years after the war, something was really about to change.

All this was only partly due to a conflict between generations. Of course there was a feeling among some that these "spoiled" youngsters "didn't know the meaning of work", but many of the older people also harboured sympathies for these rebellious boys and girls. The Provos were doing things they could not even begin to understand, but they seemed to have achieved a liberation that had eluded an older generation in 1945. The Provos even managed to put forward candidates in the council elections. They only got one seat, but it is significant that more than half of the people who voted for them were over 35.

Intuitively, the Provos had the genius to bet on two horses. They pointed out the impossibility of a situation in which wealth and opportunities for personal development were rapidly increasing, while the moral attitude supporting this remained as parsimonious, prudish and authoritarian as it had been in the 1930s. At the same time, however, they also poked fun at the "cream-whipping masses", tapping into the anti-progressive cultural undercurrent. This situated them exactly at the crossroads of two distinct developments that were extremely topical during the 1960s: on the one hand, they were the catalysts of progress, and on the other they were the romantic conscience of the nation.[15]

Their "White Plans", and many of the ideas that informed them, were to become common currency. Their White Bicycle Plan advocated a car-free inner city for the first time. In their White Chimney Plan the problem of air pollution was put on the political agenda. The White Women Plan signalled the beginning of a revival of the women's movement. The Buro de Kaker or Squatting Office, would anticipate the more recent squatters' movement. The White Kip Plan wanted to turn policemen on the beat into social workers: "He carries matches and contraceptives and also oranges and chicken drumsticks for the hungry provotariat."

The youth of the 1960s, however, also needed its martyrs and its enemies in order to act out the play of war and liberation. For this the "SS men" of the police were ideal, as were the "fascist" newspaper the *Telegraaf*, "the authorities" and last but by no means least the top boss in the city, the inflexible world-rebuilding Burgomaster, Gijs van Hall. It was a tragic situation. The new generation saw in van Hall nothing but a second Broekhoff, an embodiment of inflexible authority, without knowing, and without wanting to know, about his courageous anti-authoritarian stance at a time when war was a much more serious business. This inversion of values was difficult for Gijs van Hall to digest. He could not understand what was going on, made some ill-judged comments, and soon developed into the Provos favourite whipping boy.

The unrest in the city escalated anew, after almost two centuries of relative civil peace, around the House of Orange. Crown Princess Beatrix had fallen in love with a friendly diplomat, Claus von Amsberg, who had unfortunately served briefly in the German *Wehrmacht* during his youth, although it was quickly established that he had not hurt a fly during this time. Princess Beatrix wanted the wedding to take place in Amsterdam, precisely because she hoped to reinforce Amsterdam's position as the capital. This gesture of reconciliation towards the city, however, only added fuel to the already raging fire. "How dare she! In the city of the February Strike!" was the general response (for the younger generation had long since overcome the shame of Amsterdam's past and only remembered its heroes). Moreover, many older people declared themselves "hurt" – a simple word that works a peculiar magic in Amsterdam and makes any authority take notice.

Burgomaster Gijs van Hall belonged to the few who really did have a right to speak on this matter, and he made some attempts to convince the government that the capital was not the best choice. On 31 October, a meeting was organized between representatives of the three Jewish communities in the city and the engaged royal couple, after which Princess Beatrix explained that she was quite happy for the wedding to take place in Baarn. The government, however, refused to make concessions to a "small minority", and Amsterdam it was. The negotiations were an undignified tussle for prestige between The Hague and "troublesome" Amsterdam, and neither the royal wedding nor the feelings of the people of Amsterdam entered into the equation.

Preparations were being made on both sides. "Each day brought anew loud laughs or aggravation," one of the opponents to the plan was to write much later. The city was made into something resembling a bastion. In addition to thousands of men from the municipal police, there would be 1,700 national police, 1,300 military police and 4,000 soldiers in the city on that 10 March. It was proposed that the police coffee stall should be set up in – of all places – the Anne Frank House. As part of the festivities, women could pay to contribute a knot to the national carpet; money was collected for a national wedding gift, consisting of silver cutlery and enough crockery for half an orphanage. At the same time, miscellaneous presents came in from the public, ranging from dozens of oven gloves (many of them crocheted in orange cotton) to a tin of baby powder.

The opponents were equally busy. "Amsterdam is known as a troublesome city and the Amsterdammers are troublesome people, but perhaps that's why the heart of the Netherlands is beating most strongly in Amsterdam," Burgomaster Gijs van Hall had said, without exaggerating, during the royal engagement. For the Provos, the wedding represented everything they were fighting against: rulers, Churches, monarchy, and authority. One of the leaders of the actions, Luud Schimmelpennik, would later admit to me that he wanted the "action for the action's sake". "We attacked everything in order to break through the unimaginable sluggishness of these years, in order to win back the streets. The monarchy and the wedding were of course perfect occasions for that."

For the first time there was a firm coalition between the Provos and the students, two groups that had operated quite separately in the past. During the meetings for a special wedding edition of the student paper Propria Cures, one diabolical plan after another was concocted. They planned to make the horses shy using lion's dung; to frighten the police by playing the sound of machine-gun fire from loudspeakers; a small technical modification would result in the church organ piping out laughing gas; the drinking water was to be spiked with LSD; and a diver was to pump stinking gas into the church via the sewer system.

Of all these imaginative plans, only the smoke bombs were to see action. About 100 small, light aluminium foil balls to be tossed on to the street, plus a few heavy ones which could be put into a handbag, were manufactured on a houseboat in the Kattenburgergrach. The curve of the Raadhuisstraat was chosen as the most strategical place to create a large curtain of smoke.

Those responsible for guarding the stables, by the way, were least surprised by the actions. When some of the Provos had let it be known that they planned to throw fire crackers, the stable master trained his horses to get used to them weeks in advance. First they shied and kicked out, but soon they ceased to take any notice.

On the morning of the wedding day, hundreds of students, former resistance fighters and others laid flowers at the monument of the February Strike, The Dock Worker. Meanwhile, standing on the Raadhuisstraat, the Provos were faced with a genuine problem: not enough people had turned up to see the procession. As Luud Schimmelpenninck recalls: "We were completely conspicuous. Even we could not anticipate that the royalists would hide at such a crucial moment!"

There was a reason for the poor turn out. It was the first time that a national celebration had been televised. People sat at home on 10 March 1966 and watched the royal coach ride back along the Raadhuisstraat after the wedding ceremony and then – their screens suddenly went white. A smoke bomb! Out on the street, events took their customary course: shouting, charging, running.

There was another bizarre incident. Part of the ceremony required "ordinary" guests to walk from the Westerkerk to the Palace on the Dam. The ladies stumbled along in their high heels and sophisticated finery, while the general public mocked them shouting "Gnot!", "Klaas komt!" and "Republiek!". To increase the misery it began to rain. "I felt like the representative of some ancien régime on my way to the guillotine," one of the editors of the NRC, who was among the people walking along, would write on the following day. The marijuana expert, Kees Hoekert, even managed to throw a live chicken at the golden state coach. He had convinced the security men that the bird was called Eibertje Vos and that it wanted to have a look at the queen.

For the royal family, it was not a day of celebration. Queen Juliana had seen nothing, or had wanted to see nothing, but the fact that she wore her festive hat back to front made clear how nervous she was. The relationship between the city and the House of Orange was to cool even further during the Coronation of Queen Beatrix, on 30 April 1980. After the ceremony on the Dam, it was noticeable that, rather than the customary cheering, there was whistling, which was only amplified by the acoustics of the square. An explosion of riots, barricades and plundering, followed, a collective rampage of such proportions that the Tenants' Uprising, the Eel Uprising and the wedding pale into insignificance.

*

It remained, as the newspapers put it rather euphemistically, "restless" in the city. Three months after the wedding another riot broke out. It began on the warm evening of 13 June 1966, when workers on the Marnixplantsoen protested over the provision of holiday pay. A disturbance broke out, which involved brief running battles with the police. During one of these, a builder called Jan Weggelaar suddenly dropped dead from a heart attack, it was later discovered. The daily *De Telegraaf*, however, reported on the following morning that he had been hit by a stone thrown by his own colleagues. Angrily, several hundred builders went to the building of *De Telegraaf* on the Nieuwezijds Voorburgwal, to hurl stones and set cars alight. The disturbance continued throughout the day. Everywhere around the Dam there was fighting and destruction. The city authorities panicked. Ministers Smallenbroek and Samkalden came to Amsterdam to re-establish order, the city was occupied by more than 1,400 national and military police from outside. A state of emergency was declared and there were even plans to prepare the Olympic Stadium to accommodate large numbers of internees. After one day, however, the street fights were over. Chief of Police, Van der Molen, who had failed to contain the riots, was dismissed. An investigation established just how corrupt the Amsterdam police had become, and how insular and hostile the organization had been since the war. Increasingly the slogan "Van Hall to fall!" was heard. Almost a year after the rioting, in April 1967, Gijs van Hall was removed from his position by the government. As a parting gift from the city he received a medal and an outboard motor.

In 1967 the Provo movement celebrated in the Vondelpark. New movements had sprung up along with the motto "Better Long-haired than Short-sighted". Students began what they called democratization actions. Several hundred of them occupied the Maagdenhis on the Spui in 1969, and were finally forcibly evicted by the police. Internationally, Amsterdam was seen as the centre of this activity, the Dam was full of young, joint-smoking tourists, and in the newspapers the "hurt" middle classes whined about the desecration of "their" national monument. That the designers had built it for people to relax in was conveniently forgotten. The Paradiso and Fantasia centres were crammed full every weekend: pop bands, strip shows and screenings of the film *Queen Juliana visits Zierikzee* in the background. In 1970 the Provo ideologue Roel van Duijn established the Oranjevrijstaat (Orange Free State), an "alternative" city within the city. His Kabouterstad (Dwarf City) Party got no less than five seats on the Amsterdam council. Morals were relaxed, and the city's feminist movement flexed its muscles. The feminist writer Anja Meulenbelt sent the entire canal belt into uproar with her *roman-à-clef*, *De schammte voorbij* (*Shame Past*), in which she exposed the personal lives of members of the City Council, publishers and others. All this was constantly shot through by unrest over the American war in Vietnam, by demonstrations, and by television images which for the first time brought the reality of war into living rooms and student flats every evening.

In this respect Amsterdam did not differ greatly from other cities in Germany, France, Britain, and America during those years, when, with hindsight, there was no single movement in the city but at least five or six, connected with each another by the tenuous thread of the new "pop" music. There were long-haired hippies and Marxist bookworms, utopians and budding politicians who now wanted power for themselves, and thousands of girls in Indian flowery skirts.

A revolution cannot appear *ex nihilo*. Many of the so-called "radical innovations" were nothing more than the coming to power of a new generation. At the same time the 1960s were golden years of political creativity, originality, open-mindedness and genuine idealism. Imagination was power. But with hindsight, this power appeared far more fragile and transient than anyone had expected at the time. The revolution of the 1960s was in some respects no more than a dreamy Gulf Stream of light megalomania. But the city had rid itself of its pre-war mentality and had finally opened itself to new possibilities.

Meanwhile, in the shadow of political and cultural violence, a process was taking shape the consequences of which were apparent to very few at the time. The inner city of Amsterdam was running on empty. The power of the city had always been contained at the centre, in discreet offices by minor canals, or in a little business somewhere in the lower ground floor of a building in the Nieuwmarktbuurt or in the Jordaan, but now both were vanishing. In 1969 Amsterdam had only about 100 businesses with more than 1,000 employees, but almost 12,000 businesses employed fewer than ten. Only a decade later, most of these had vanished from the canal belt. Many businesses moved to the residential parts around the old city centre, some went further still.

This migration from the centre was partly to do with the expansion of businesses and the increased traffic – an historic city centre is simply more difficult to access than a purpose-built suburb – but it was also the indirect consequence of two catastrophes that had hit the city. Both had taken place just after the war, but the effects were only slowly noticeable.

The first catastrophe was the loss of the Jewish population. This was not only a human tragedy but a hard blow for the city as an organism. Previously lively neighbourhoods were now lying derelict, and more-over the emancipated Jewish population had played an important role in Amsterdam's economic and scientific achievements, as well as in the political life of the city.

The second catastrophe was the breaking of the centuries-old bond with Indonesia. Since 1600 Amsterdam had acted as the European outlet for trade with this rich archipelago, and the city's economy was built around it to a large extent. It was suddenly over when these connections were severed in 1956. While industry in the rest of the Netherlands increased its employment base by six per cent between 1950 and 1960, in Amsterdam employment fell by twelve per cent during the same period. The tobacco auctions in the Nes – the European centre of the tobacco trade – vanished. It was quieter in the harbours, the Steamship Company Nederland lost its voluminous passenger traffic to Indonesia, railway stock was rusting on industrial estates, and at the end of the 1960s the harbour facilities were finally closed.

For Amsterdam these were more than catastrophes, they were enormous cultural upheavals. During the 1970s there was another: de Bijlmer.

In the optimistic 1960s, Amsterdam had decided to build "a city of the future" in the Bijlmer, to the south-east of the city. It was hailed as a "significant landmark in the history of city planning", and was to consist of spacious, bright houses surrounded by plenty of green spaces. It was to be characterized by high-rise blocks, with the division of functions taken to an extreme, separate traffic streams geared towards the new car culture, large scale and uniform, a "honey comb structure" that looked very handsome on the drawing board and from the air. It was expected that the area would have a "very strong character", and that there would be new types of collective facilities. One did not want to build "slums of the future" anymore, but "apartments with future value".[16] In theory it was, and still is, an extraordinarily interesting project, a paragon of the building technology of the 1960s and of city planning informed by numerous surveys that had been carefully considered for a long time, the crowning moment in a series of city development plans – from Berlage to the General Expansion Plan – that had bestowed international fame on Amsterdam.

It all worked out quite differently. With the Bijlermeer Project, the city was suddenly confronted by unplanned and uncontrollable forces. Those behind the project were rudely awakened from the dreams of "total planning" that they had had since the 1930s.

When the first apartment blocks were inaugurated in 1970, it was immediately obvious that the area was indeed green and quiet, that the flats were spacious and comfortable, but that most of their inhabitants felt swamped by the vast size and anonymity of the area. The parking garages became breeding grounds for criminal activity, the collective facilities in the blocks created numerous quarrels rather than a "newly emerging feeling of community". While the area had originally been intended for the inhabitants of those neighbourhoods that were to be redeveloped, it was in reality many newcomers who came to settle there, people who had come from the countryside to the city and who could not find a house anywhere else; foreigners in the main, and especially immigrants from Surinam. The old colony had become independent exactly at this moment, and many of its inhabitants, choosing security, took up Dutch citizenship. The flight route that catered for this exodus was dubbed the "Bijlmer Express".

Bijlmer indeed gained a reputation, but it was a far cry from what the planners had imagined. The percentage of unemployed and poor people was high, as it was for crime. Some parts of the development were regarded as no-go areas. Many of the flats in the Bijlmer remained empty almost ten years after it opened, and a quarter of a century later the first blocks were already being pulled down.

The débâcle of the Bijlmer was a calamity for the planners, the politicians, and anyone who sought to think on a large scale. It is true that this unfortunate chain of events could hardly have been foreseen, nevertheless, terrible mistakes had been made by the city planners. In contrast to the General Expansion Plan, for instance, those behind the Bijlmer Project had never properly researched the preferences of the Amsterdammers. The fact that even then most people preferred low buildings rather than multi-storey complexes was completely overlooked. Warning signs from Sweden and Great Britain that these sorts of buildings had severe problems were similarly ignored. As the architect Hazewinkel wrote in June 1965, Amsterdam's town planners had attempted to build "a city for the year 2000, using the building philosophy of 1930 and the technology of 1965".

Much later, the city developer Maarten Menzel studied how this planning disaster had occurred. He found that the Bijlmer Project could be classified as one of those historical mistakes attributable to what he calls "groupthink", when a small group of policy makers, who regard themselves as all-powerful, refuse to accept that there might be a problem with their plans and ignore all reports that run contrary to their view of the world.

The same arrogant attitude was also prevalent in plans for the development other areas of the city. The once cosy and narrow Weesperstraat was three times proposed for demolition: for the construction of the IJ tunnel; for a large traffic corridor through the Nieuwmarkt area; and for the building of a subway from the Central Station to the new Bijlermeer.[18] Around 1960, all of the houses there were demolished and replaced by imposing architecture designed to impress – a barren strip of desert right through the inner city. A large part of the former Jewish quarter vanished for the IJ tunnel.

The Jordaan was to be largely torn down and then rebuilt according to new plans. Some of the roads were to be broadened, the Rozengracht was to become a large avenue, and to the south of the Elandsgracht grand office buildings were supposed to be erected. A similar plan was made for Kattenburg and Wittenburg and was carried out (in contrast to the Jordaan). The nineteenth-century working-class neighbourhoods – such as the Pijp and the Dapperbuurt – were also to be torn down and blocks of flats put up in their place, while broad roads opened up the area for the ever-increasing volume of traffic.

The Nieuwmarktbuurt, too, was to be transformed in this way. The Sint-Antoniesstraat and Jodenbreestraat were to become four-lane motorways in order to create an easy connection from the IJ tunnel to the Central Station; followed by new hotels and office buildings, plus a multi-storey car park for thousands of cars. In addition to this, the planners drew a broad line on the map where a subway would be built, for which dozens of houses would have to be demolished. This was the beginning of the famous Nieuwmarkt question which was to monopolize the political debate of the city for much of the 1970s.

These large-scale municipal plans were fiercely defended by the deputy, the former radical Ten Past Red follower Han Lammers. He was concerned that the Bijlmer was doomed to become a ghetto unless it had a quick subway link. Against him stood the Nieuwmarkt Residents Association, which fought for the idea of a "compact city", an idea that was only to be adopted by the city councillors at the end of the 1970s. A graffitto on a Nieumarkt wall sums up this idea: "We want a city with neighbourhoods where living, playing, working, learning and shopping take place close to one another, and where the old and the young live in harmony."

To some extent, the Nieuwmarkt movement was born from the old Provo movement, and it was, incidentally, to give birth in its turn to the squatters' movement. The Provos had had a plan to make the then derelict Nieuwmarkt area into a so-called "play-street", a safe street for children and others. As the residents at the time were afraid that people would be having sex and taking drugs on their very doorstep the project was quickly shelved, but the interest of a number of Provos in this area was to be reawakened. After 1968, more and more of the houses had been occupied by squatters and more or less renovated, and the Provos did not want to lose them to the bulldozers.

The rest of the city began to make noise as well. The architects Apon, Van Eyck, and Hertzberger, who had initially developed the Nieuwmarktplan, now refused to co-operate any further in its implementation, because they agreed with the protesting residents. Together with some of his colleagues, Hertzberger developed an alternative subway route that avoided cutting through Nieuwmarkt but went instead through the Oude Schans.

The first important success of the Nieuwmarkt residents was the reassurance by the City Council that the so-called De Pinto house was to remain standing. As this old patrician house stood right in the middle of the proposed road, it spelled the end of any plans for a motorway through the area. Instead the road went in front of the Sint-Antoniessluis, a reminder of this change of heart for years to come. Later the municipality back-peddled further: the Nieuwmarkt was to remain a residential area and would, after the building of the subway, be restored and redeveloped as quickly as possible.

The Nieuwmarkt squatters began to prepare themselves for a final confrontation with the authorities as though it were a matter of life and death. They made improvised shields, turned diving masks into primitive gas masks, had an internal telephone line installed, and on one of the roofs a siren announced meetings and emergencies. There was a special radio station, Radio Sirene, and the protest's leaders had an old van transformed into an armoured vehicle. A hanging bridge had been built out of ropes and canvas across the Recht Boomsloot, which served as a look-out post and emergency escape route.

Council politics, meanwhile, had descended into chaos, along the lines of a classic right-left opposition. The Communists, who had a lot of weight at the time, were an important factor in the balance of power in the city. They stood squarely behind the original plans of motorway, demolition, and rebuilding, because it "was good for employment". There was an outcry when the main candidate of the pacifists, Huib Riethof, who had campaigned energetically against the subway, all of a sudden appeared to be in favour of the scheme, and was immediately deposed as deputy. Within the PVDA there was a virulent conflict between the party faithful and those who had strong links with Nieuwmarkt and the student movement.

The political opposition reached its climax when an extreme right organization planted a bomb by the Bijlmer subway station on the eve of a large anti-subway demonstration. In an official statement the City Council alleged that this was the work of the Nieuwmarkt activists, without having any proof for this. Finally, on 24 March 1975, the police attempted to clear the Nieuwmarkt. A fierce battle ensued that involved water cannon, tear-gas, paving stones, primitive fire bombs and fire crackers, and numerous assults on the police. In the end, it was the weaker party that won.

*

In the years that followed, the Nieuwmarkt area, like other old areas in the city, was thoroughly redeveloped, but all attempts to impose large-scale plans on Amsterdam were consigned to the dustbin of history. At its opening on 10 October 1980, the much-hated Nieuwmarkt subway station appeared to have been rebuilt as a monument to the actions that had previously sought to prevent it; a high point in Dutch duplicity.

A second Wibaut rose up, alderman Jan Schaefer, who, under the motto "You Cannot Live on Bullshit" put in motion the renovation, demolition, rebuilding, polishing, and smoothing over of district after district. There was still enough money during these years to do such things, and although Amsterdammers continued to whine about it long afterwards, the city was in better shape than ever before. Towards the end of the 1980s, however, the money had run out and the future problem areas, the hastily constructed blocks of the 1950s and 1960s, hardly benefited from any renovation.

Meanwhile an entire youth culture had developed around many of the empty houses; less playful and theoretical than those of the 1960s and 1970s, and also less all-embracing, though practical, concrete, and down-to-earth. The goal was no longer to go on the offensive – the World Revolution that was proposed by the Provos – but to be defensive: all that was demanded was a place of one's own, and the right to live there exactly as one wished. "We have already started by living the sort of life that suits us – we don't take much notice of their petty laws and regulations." That was the bottom line. Many squats were breeding grounds for political activities, for the assistance of refugees and the homeless and for new art forms, although at the same time any abstract theorizing was taboo. Not words but objects were their ideas: bed springs, stones, opened electricity meters, cheques from the social services, illegal telephone lines to connect up neighbours. The clothes were no longer colourful but black, sexless and ragged. "Apart from the short real-leather jackets, the squatters' costume was no different from the street fashion of the metropolitan drug-and-drink addicts," some former squatters were to write later. "Our clothes were covered in disgusting stains, we wore PLO scarves, parachute boots, and bikers' jackets, and this ensemble was complemented by the pungent smell of petrol, sweat, and beer."[19] This was the generation that had grown up in the affluent 1970s, and which, after having been promised more and more, had been confronted by the crisis of the 1980s.

In the autumn of 1979 a number of squats were cleared with an iron hand. The squatters defended themselves and were on their guard for several months. Six houses in the Keizersgracht were barricaded like medieval castles. Fridges, washing machines and other heavy appliances were hauled up to the roof to be thrown down on the bailiffs. In the end the city capitulated and bought up the entire block.

One Friday afternoon some months later, on 29 February 1980, a house in the Vondelstraat, number 72, which had been cleared by the police, was reconquered by several hundred youngsters in a mass action. The squatters had learned from experience: they now wore helmets and carried iron bars; one of them looked like a helmeted Greek warrior with his punk hair sticking up like a plume. After the police had been chased away, only the sound of breaking tiles and falling stones could be heard: the first barricades had been erected. For three days there was a sort of nervous Free State waiting on the crossing of the Eerste Constantijn Huygensstraat and the Vondelstraat and the Overtoom. The barricades grew higher and higher: containers, rubbish, wood, gutters, all sorts of objects were piled up.

The demands of the squatters, meanwhile, remained unclear: the house had to be bought, but another important point was the freeing of someone called Nanda. Most of the youngsters, however, quietly sat around their fires at night and waited for whatever was going to happen.

On the following Sunday evening, it looked as though most of the demands of the squatters had been accepted and that the barricades would be voluntarily taken down in the morning. Many of the occupiers went home to get some sleep. At 6 a.m. those who had stayed behind suddenly saw the lights of a row of tanks appearing. The Burgomaster, Wim Polak, had pamphlets distributed: THE COLUMN, ONCE ON THE MOVE, CANNOT BE STOPPED. The squatters did not resist, but they felt totally betrayed.

The mood of the movement hardened after this. Many people were involved in battles with the police over houses on the Prins Hendrikkade, the Herengracht, the Weteringschans, the Bilderdijkstraat and the Jan Lykenstraat. During the latter conflict, a tram was set alight. The squatters stood by and cheered, unaware that they had forfeited the last scrap of sympathy that the Amsterdam majority had had for them – because the city is very fond of its trams.

The Staatsliedenbuurt, where several flats were empty, became the headquarters of the squatters' movement where the radicals held sway. The City Council was the enemy, it should be building houses for the youth of today, who had declared open war on the predatory city "speculators". It was in the Staatsliedenbuurt that the only fatality occurred, the squatter Hans Kok, having been arrested during a violent clearing in the Schaepmanstraat, suffered a miserable death in a police cell after swallowing several methadone tablets.[20] No guard had looked in on him, no doctor had been called. On the following day, the squatters, hearing of his death, wanted to reconquer the house in the Schaepmanstraat. It was a matter of principle. One of those present was to recall how they had heard of Kok's death on the radio during a lull in the fighting: "It was as if a bomb had fallen in the square," he wrote, "at first everyone stood close, listening, then they all went away and finally it was Piet standing there alone with the radio above his head."

Hans Kok immediately became a martyr, even though he had not been popular because of his drug-induced tantrums. His death, however, fitted the "no future" heroism of the movement perfectly. To the squatters, he was not the latest victim of an ever-increasing repression, but the most radical protester. He had taken the momentum of the movement to its logical extreme.

Eventually the squatters' movement was so spellbound by violence and counter violence that it destroyed itself. The last squatters mainly fought among each other; they fought for power in the neighbourhood, in their houses and especially in the squatters' cafés. Others allowed themselves to be corrupted, they sold "their" flats for a lot of money or were bought out for a few thousand guilders. The most radical leader of the Staatsliedenbuurt managed to sell his flat for a comfortable sum and went to the Dutch Antilles. The remaining squatters were pacified and bought out, the municipality providing them with nicely renovated flats. Others, but only a few, stayed faithful to their ideals.

That is how The Twenty-Year War in the city ended. It had begun on 12 July 1965, when the first issue of the newspaper *Provo* was sold on the streets, and had ended on 21 December 1984, when the squatters spat at the newly appointed Burgomaster, Ed van Thijn, on a working visit to the

Staadsliedenbuurt. They managed to chase him away, and in so doing they manoeuvred themselves into total political isolation. One might argue about this final date, but it certainly marked a symbolic cut-off point.

The Twenty-Year War was in a sense one continuous period of unrest, even if the names, the culture, and the clothing of the main protagonists kept changing. Despite their differences, the Provos and their successors, the "dwarfs", the Nieuwmarkters and the squatters were typically urban social movements.[21] All four groups held the same cluster of opinions: self-government rather than bureaucracy; quality of life versus economic growth; large-scale demolition versus the rebuilding; the preservation of what was already there rather than mass culture; a vision, often nostalgic, of a neighbourhood culture; and against increased traffic congestion, easy access to all essential services by pedestrians.

According to the social geographer Virginie Mamadouh in her study of this explosive period in the city's history, this ongoing battle was in principle a confrontation between the "romanticism" and "functionalism". Functionalism regarded the city as an organism that had to fulfil certain goals. The romantic ideal considered the city as an ensemble of citizens, a collective, with a distinct history and personality. Mamadouh's research allows us to reconstruct how this happened. In the first place there were the consequences of the baby boom generation. In the mid-1960s, Amsterdam became a typical youth city. The post-war generation wanted to live on their own, in the heart of the city, women's emancipation and the contraceptive pill allowed them to delay starting a family, and thus a group of "older youth" developed, for whom the open spaces of the city became a second home. It was also the generation that had known little or no material deprivation during their youth and who therefore placed more emphasis on immaterial goods than their parents had.

In addition to this, there was an "ignition mechanism": Amsterdam itself. During the 1960s, the city's buildings were in need of thorough renovation and restructuring. Many of them were on the point of collapse; apartments were small and hard to come by; the streets and canals were full of parked cars and cars waiting for parking spaces. Something had to happen, and until this rebellious era burst onto the scene, the choices made by the City Council had been purely functional. It was asssumed that Amsterdam could be renewed by demolishing most of its older districts, by building motorways everywhere, by replacing the Nieuwmarkt with an office complex, and the Jordaan with a sort of modern garden city.

It is only to be expected that many people opposed these plans, especially the younger citizens, and that their actions were effective can be seen by anyone who walks through the city centre today. It testifies to a huge change in orientation in Amsterdam, thanks mainly to a broad group of sympathizers who gathered around the Provo movement, along with the "dwarfs" and the Nieuwmarkters, and also the sheer scope and intensity of all sorts of peaceful (and less peaceful) street actions led by the squatters.

Meanwhile Amsterdam was gliding into the 1980s. The canals became quieter; herons, moorhens, great crested grebes, and coots came to nest in the confines of the city. A fourth cultural rupture occurred, perhaps the most profound of them all, although it went largely unnoticed.

The great exodus of ordinary Amsterdammers had begun during the 1970s. It was not a spectacular event, but happened gradually and without fuss, its consequences only becoming clear later on. Within less than 20 years, between 1965 and 1984, at least 400,000 Amsterdammers left the city for good. Despite the influx of new immigrants, the population fell to 200,000, a quarter of the original number. The old Amsterdammers had moved to Alkmaar, Purmerend, Almere, Lelystad, Weesp, Enkhuizen, and Hoorn. Old district communities, such as Kattenburg and the Islands, were left empty and destroyed within a decade.

At the end of the 1960s, the Hartjesdag feast day was already extinct, but Luilak was still celebrated with gusto and the annual fair on the Palmgracht remained the climax of the year. The Jordaan was still a typical workers' district with "Auntie" Riek and "Uncle" Piet, although the first "nephews" and "nieces" had already moved to Purmerend and Slotermeer. Just under 15 years later, at the beginning of the 1980s, the district had been thoroughly renovated, although its inhabitants had changed beyond recognition. Instead of workers, there were teachers, journalists, doctors and young bankers living here, and most of the little shops and greengrocers had been converted into cafés and restaurants. The Palmgracht fair petered out. In the Pijp, also largely rebuilt, a similar process had taken place, and the same was true for the Nieuwmarkt. Amsterdam's city centre had changed within a decade from production to consumption. It was now a luxury area for recreation and entertainment. The city had lost its innocence.

The Jenever, with which the Jordaan's heavy drinkers (known as "water divers") had drowned their sorrows was substituted by much stronger things. Drugs, and the crime that accompanied them, were poisoning the city.

The silent emigrants were mostly working families with children, the motor of Amsterdam's economy. In the garden cities in the east and west their places were mostly taken by immigrants from Surinam, the Dutch Antilles, Turkey, and Morocco. When the industry that had attracted them to the city had largely disappeared, they were left unemployed. During the last decade of the twentieth century this group of relative newcomers accounted for a quarter of the population. In some areas, built according to the utopian ideals of Wibaut and De Miranda, the exotic eastern culture of the immigrants began to gain the upper hand, as the Jews had before. A vibrant and unique community developed, especially in the Bijlmer. The original inhabitants of these blocks remained, here and there: small islands of dissatisfaction in a city that was changing rapidly. Thus, compared with other European cities, Amsterdam managed to preserve a relatively mild climate of cohabitation between its old and its new populations.

Meanwhile, the last large wharf in north Amsterdam, the ADM – the Amsterdam Dry-Dock Company – had closed, and the city administrators began to worry about the building of the Channel Tunnel. It was feared that the main European traffic would pass by the Netherlands and especially Amsterdam in the south. The opening of the east European borders also shifted the priorities. The Amsterdam Rhine Canal was broadened and deepened, but the traditional harbour industry had vanished, even if Amsterdam still remained the fifth largest harbour in Europe. Nevertheless the city retained its central position for culture, education and tourism.

Schiphol took over to a certain extent the function of the old harbour. It grew into one of the most important airports in Europe, and a new centre of activity was born in the broad, shiny silver ring of modern offices and trading places that connected the old city and the new centre. After 1984, the population was finally on the increase once more. The administration of the municipality of Amsterdam was decentralized into so-called "partial councils": 16 small municipalities, each the size of a large city district. 16 times as many people talked about 16 times as many issues; the Xerox machines were going day and night and the district – rather than the city in its entirety – came to be a focus for party politics. Attention to the day-to-day administration of Amsterdam noticeably improved, but at the same time the power of the Central Council was weakened by this fragmentation. A prestigious project to transform the empty harbour area on the banks of the IJ into a European prime location was a dismal failure.

In the summer of 1994, the municipal council decided – together with the surrounding districts – to work towards a new structure of conurbation which would have made redundant the administration of the old city. Amsterdam would, after almost 800 years, vanish from the map as an administrative unit. Just one year later a referendum called a halt to these plans. Nine out of ten Amsterdammers who had stepped into a voting booth voted against the total dissolution of their city into 13 independent municipalities that were to have formed a new city province, together with the surrounding municipalities. The districts at the edge of the city, especially, responded with an overwhelmingly "No!". The Amsterdammers obviously wanted to remain part of Amsterdam at any cost, even if they lived in villas and apartment blocks from which, for many years, they had not been able to see the towers of the old city. The outcome of the referendum was a slap in the face for those who came up with the plan. They had underestimated the role of emotion in politics. It also was a vote of no confidence in the paper tigers of the district councils, and it was especially a case of the populus running amok – a familiar sight in Amsterdam by now – a paper revolt against civil servants, politicians, all those in authority, and anyone else who tried to straitjacket the city.

The average Amsterdammer continued living and working as if a city province were already a reality, while the administrators quietly looked for new ways of adapting to the situation. Amsterdam was not officially dissolved, it did not fall apart, but it was, as it were, spread out across the region like a slowly melting piece of cheese.

The city is moving into the twenty-first century, from its gallow fields, through the waterscape, the church towers and markets, outwardly wealthy, internally uncertain and in turmoil. The seagulls are shrieking, a foghorn is lowing, the water is lapping at Amsterdam's shores as it always has done, unmoved and dull, without ever thinking of rest or sleep.

Notes

Prologue

1 Donald Olsen, *Die Stadt als Kunstwerk: London, Paris, Wien*. (Frankfurt and New York, 1988), p. 25.

Chapter One: *The Beautifully Constructed House*

1 Jan M. Baart, in *Ons Amsterdam*, No 43, p. 105.
2 Taken from the series by M. G. Emeis Jr. about the origin and growth of the city, *Ons Amsterdam*.
3 H. Brugmans, p. 21 ff.
4 Until February 1994, the scientific consensus was that the castle of the van Amstels was in Ouderkerk. As this had been the site of the first parish church, it was assumed that the legal and administrative centre was located there as well. The steward was living there, still or again, around 1306, because he employed a deputy sheriff for Amsterdam. Never has a trace of a castle been found in Ouderkerk. Old descriptions, however, do emphasize the existence of fortifications. In 1500, at the back of a volume by the learned Pontanus, an anonymous author describes the site of the castle almost exactly in the place where it has now been excavated by the city archeologists. A certain Cornelis Haemrode wrote that in the year 1564 the foundations of towers were found when an Amsterdam property owner wanted to dig a sewage pit there. Pontanus also records, around 1610, that "underground heaps of rubble had been found which suggest that there had been a building covering a great area, as the elderly can still relate" on the west side of the Damrak. The fact that in 1304 Jan van Aemstel chose Amsterdam rather than Ouderkerk as the centre for his rebellion also indicates the central position of the city even then. When enormous slabs of stone were found during the building of a cinema in 1920, the city historian 't Hooft concluded that a castle must have been situated there. He was politely laughed out of court: the archives did not say anything about a castle and the archives were sacred. Moreover, the castle was an obvious centre of a feudal past that had no place in the self-image of modern Amsterdammers. For more details of the excavations, see J. M. Baart in *Ons Amsterdam*, no. 46.

5 Apart from the cog, the city had another coat of arms, the familiar three St Andrew's crosses, which were eventually to replace the cog. It is certain that the St Andrew's Cross was already in use in the area. The van Aemstel family, too, had such a cross on their coat of arms. It is assumed that the burghers of the emerging settlement took over this sign because of its simple pattern and clearly recognizable colours. When Amsterdam grew bigger and began to need its own coat of arms, the cog was adopted. The three crosses, however, would always remain the symbol of Amsterdam.

6 Until recently it was thought that the dam in the Amstel was built during the second half of the thirteenth century. Following the marine engineer Fockema Andreae, the influential city historian Brugmans in his *Geschiedenis van Amsterdam* dates the building of the dam to around 1265. According to him, the building of dikes in a certain area is not necessarily connected to the damming in of the rivers streaming within it, especially if the river dikes are of good quality. Moreover, a document from the time records the agreement of the villages of Kalslagen and Nieuwveen with the landowner concerning the drainage of the villages. As long as the Amstel was open towards the sea, there was not a single reason to regulate the drainage. As soon as a dam was built, however, it became urgent. The document dates from about 1265, indicating that the dam was built not much earlier. According to recent hypotheses, however, the dam is about 100 years older. It seems much more logical that it was built around 1180, along with other water regulation projects. Moreover, there are indications that the site opposite the castle had already been built on during the twelfth century, which means that there must have been a dam allowing people to cross from one side to the other. Excavations by the dam will shed further light on the matter.

7 See, among others, J. M. Baart, *Een Hollandse stad in de dertiende eeuw*, and the inventories of the finds of the archeological service of the municipality of Amsterdam.

Chapter Two: *Bread and Stones*

1 Fernand Braudel, vol. 1, p. 472.

2 The following is taken from J. M. Baart, 1987.

3 J. M. Baart, *Ceramic Consumption and Supply in Early Modern Amsterdam*.

4 These facts are taken from, among others, T. Levie and H. Zantkuyl.

5 The following is mainly taken from Emeis Jr., ibid., p. 66, and from Roelof van Gelder and Renée Kistenmaker.

6 Until 1850 the inhabitants of the Bierkaai pointed out with some pride that their ancestors had never lived anywhere but there. It was an incredibly fit group of people who lived around the Oude Kerk.

7 See also: J. C. van der Dues, et al.

8 Ibid., p. 33 ff.

9 The following is taken from Brugmans, p. 210 ff, and from Clé Lesger, *Ach Lieve Tijd. Zeven eeuwen Amsterdam. De Amsterdammers en hun handel en scheepvaart.*

10 M. G. de Boer, p. 47.

Chapter Three: The Enemy

1 J. Huizinga, *The Autumn of the Middle Ages,* translated by Rodney J. Payton and Ulrich Mammitzsch (Chicago University Press, 1996).

2 Walich Sywaertsz; De Boer, p. 93.

3 Quoted in J. F. M. Sterck.

4 Quoted in Sterck, ibid.

5 Quoted in Huizinga, ibid.

6 Jan Wagenaar, p. 950 ff. Wagenaar was the first officially employed city historian. In order to conduct his research, he was given access to secret city archives, a remarkable fact for the time.

Chapter Four: Towards a New Jerusalem

1 Lesger, "Tussen stagnatie en expansie, economische ontwikkeling en levensstandaard tussen 1500 en 1600", in *Woelige tijden.*

2 Taken from Emeis Jr. p. 98 ff, also the next quotation.

3 Braudel, vol. 1, p. 506 ff.

4 See among others I. H. van Eeghen, 1959.

5 Wagenaar; J. G. van Dillen, quoted in Emeis Jr.

6 Anonymous, *Chronik van 1477–1534,* Koninklijke Bibliotheek Den Haar, quoted in Sterck.

7 J. A Grote, quoted in Emeis Jr. p. 130.

8 Wagenaar, p. 245.

Chapter Five: The Joy of God's Wrath

1 From *Brabbeling*, 1614, taken from H. van der Bijl et al.
2 Van Eeghen, 1959.
3 Zbigniew Herbert.
4 Brugmans, vol 1, p. 25 ff.
5 Ibid., p. 23.
6 Emeis Jr. p. 103. The same duplicitous attitude can also be observed towards excessive, extravagant and noisy funeral meals, christenings and wedding celebrations. In this strict city, these events had to keep to prescribed limits and the city decrees threatened a hefty fine for any infringement. Still, nobody observed the prohibition and the fee functioned in reality as an unofficial celebration tax. Even worse: the higher the fine, the higher the status of the celebration.
7 Ibid. p. 101.
8 H. Brugmans, *Middeleeuwen*, vol. 1, p. 283. Egbert Gerbrandszoon, probably the man in the portrait of a couple discussed earlier, also belonged to this strict Catholic faction. He was elected Burgomaster no fewer than three times.
9 Emeis Jr., the following passages are also taken from him.
10 Quoted after J. M. Fuchs and W. J. Simons *Nou hoor he jet eens van een ander, buitenlanders over Amsterdam*, Den Haag, 1975, p. 9.
11 Taken from Van Gelder et al.
12 An interesting illustration of the change in clothing over the generations is the painting by Dirck Santvoort from the year 1634, portraying the family of Burgomaster Dirck Bas. Dirck Bas himself is solemly seated, still dressed in simple and sober Amsterdam style, next to his wife Grietje Snoeck. Their five sons and daughters, however, look much more elegant, especially the eldest son: he wears a gold-coloured suit, splendid Spanish golden buckles and a magnificent lace collar and cuffs. See also: van Gelder and Kistenmaker, p. 224.
13 Taken from Els ten Napel and Benno Tilburg.

Chapter Six: Insiders and Outsiders

1 Van Eeghen, in Maandblad Amstelodamum, no 56, pp 73–78. Art historians always believed the drawings of the girl on the place of execution to belong to an earlier period. In this case, however, it was quite easy to establish the true date of the works, as they related to a historical event.

2 Simon Schama, p. 478. Schama here also mentions the "sleep woman" Mari Potters, who ran a house in the Boomsslooten. The girls, one of them 17, one 18 and one 20, were despatched to the Spinhaus without pardon.

3 Research by S. Hart, taken from Ed Taverne.

4 During the entire seventeenth century no fewer than 51,591 immigrants came from Germany, from East Prussia and Silesia, into a city of 200,000 inhabitants. During the eighteenth century even more made this journey: 66,681. During the same time, there were from Belgium 8,617 and 2,374 immigrants respectively, 7,784 and 4,085 from Norway, 5,382 and 3,228 from France, 4,331 and 1,087 from England and Ireland, and 3,458 and 3,589 from Denmark. During the period 1601–1800 174,874 immigrants came to Amsterdam from European countries, and 153,490 from the Dutch provinces. Quoted by S. Hart, former municipal archivist of Amsterdam.

5 Quoted in Taco Looijen.

6 Even the famous admiral Michiel Adriaensz. de Ruyter lived there. The present address of the house is Prins Hendrikkade No 131.

7 Mark Girouard.

8 Filips von Zesen, quoted in Girouard.

9 The sculptures from the old Stadthuis, symbol of the authority of the nobility during the Middle Ages, have miraculously survived. They can still be seen at the Amsterdams Historisch Museum.

10 Taverne, ibidem.

11 Henri Méchoulan, p. 79.

12 Van Gelder, et al. p. 148.

13 Gary Schwartz.

14 Other painters and art dealers were, among others, Jacques Saverij and his brother Roeland, Joos van Meerle, David Vingboons, Dirck Santvoort (in the first part), Jan Tengnagel, Adriaen van Nieulant, and Pieter Isaacszoon.

15 The Bloemstraat was popularly known as Weversstraat, because all kinds of luxury items were produced there. The Elandsstraat was the centre of the chamois-leather producers, who did not only make clothes and book covers, but also the famous gold leather wall hangings of the canal houses. Other tanners lived in the Huidenstraat, the Harten (read: Herten-) straat and the Berenstraat.

16 The tax records of this time make it clear how small this group really was. While, in 1585, ten per cent of Amsterdam citizens were subject to the wealth tax, the so-called Capitale Impositie, in 1631

not even four per cent fell into this bracket, 4,300 of the 116,000 Amsterdammers to be precise.

17 Taverne, p. 143.

18 Especially the spiritual father of the half-moon plan, the "Fabrikmeester" Frans Hendrickszoon Oetghens, made a considerable profit out of this project. Oetghens, who was burgomaster ten times between 1599 and 1624, knew from the beginning where the main spread of the development would be. Very quietly he bought up the relevant properties together with his brother-in-law, and later resold them to the city at extortionate prices. According to the former Burgomaster Cornelis Pieterszoon Hooft, the two brothers-in-law had "gain as their pole star and greed as their compass."

19 Taverne, p. 173.

20 Andries Pels, *Gebruik en misbruik des toneels*, quoted in Houbraken, ibid.

21 See also Schwartz, p. 193.

22 Dudok van Heel, p. 39.

23 The Rembrandt Research Project reached the surprising conclusion that even several famous "Rembrandts", such as the *Polish Rider* (New York), the *Man with the Gold Helmet* (Berlin) and *Saul and David* (The Hague) were not from the hand of the master.

24 Svetlana Alpers, p. 201.

25 *The Night Watch* probably represents the platoon of area number eleven, which was responsible for keeping watch over the Haarlemmerpoort during the famous visit to Amsterdam of Maria de' Medici. Of the 200 men in the platoon, only 16 were willing to fork out 100 guilders apiece for the privilege of letting themselves be immortalized.

26 See also Alpers, ibid.

27 Van Eeghen, ibid. p. 73.

28 See J. E. Elias.

29 A total of 175,000 slaves were shipped to America during this period. Dutch merchants were responsible for half of this mass deportation. During the following 25 years, this number was doubled. Van Gelder, et al., p. 82. See also: Lesger, *Zeven eeuwen Amsterdam, de Amsterdammers en hun handel en scheepvaart*.

30 Méchoulan, p. 96.

31 See also: Schama, p. 176.

32 Rembrandt's pupils Govert Flinck and Ferdinand Bol also made good matches: Flinck married the daughter of one of the administrators of the VOC.

33 Dudok van Heel, ibid. The story about the sitters of *The Night Watch* being unhappy with the painting is a romantic invention that cannot be corroborated by any contemporary source.

34 Typical north Holland seamen's cities were Ransdorp and De Rijp, from whence came several of Willem Barentsz's crews.

35 Immanuel Wallerstein, pp. 31 passim.

36 Quoted in Schama, p. 230.

37 Schama, p. 265.

38 Méchoulan, p. 115.

39 See also Méchoulan, p. 138.

40 See also J. L. Price.

41 Dudok van Heel, ibid.

42 Also other sources indicate Rembrandt's wealth. In 1647 he was still thought to be worth 40,000 guilders.

43 Alpers, p. 187.

44 Dudok van Heel, p. 36.

45 For more, at length, on this topic, see Schwartz, p. 245.

46 See also Dudok van Heel, ibid. p. 60.

47 Alpers, p. 193.

48 Dudok van Heel, p. 55.

49 Ibid. p. 61.

50 Magdalena Stockmans in a letter to a friend during the plague of 1655. Cited in B. J. Speet, *Zeven Euwen Amsterdam, de Amsterdammers en hun zieken.*

51 Wagenaar, p. 606.

Chapter Seven: *The Ice Age Explained*

1   A. M. Vaz Dias, in *De Telegraaf.*

2   See: Jan Stoutenbeek and Paul Vigeveno.

3   Schama, p. 274.

4   Ibid., p. 283.

5   Brugmans, vol. 4, p. 191.

6   Ibid., p. 202.

7   Van Eeghen, in *Tijdschrift Genootschap Amstelodamum.*

8   See also Van Deursen.

9   See also Méchoulan, p. 63 ff.

10 See also Schama, p. 291.

11 Brugmans, p. 112.

12 Quoted in Méchoulan, p. 153.

13 Ibid. p. 168.

14 Schama, p. 193.

15 Van Gelder et al., p. 208.

16 Brugmans, p. 130.

17 Renier Vinkeles, *De Amstel bij de Berebijt*, 1762. Municipal Archive, Amsterdam, collection van Eeghen.

18 Fr. Beijerink and M. G. de Boer. A number of quotations are taken from this edition of the diary, others from the original, which is in the Amsterdam Municipal Archive.

19 On this, see also Noé van Hulst and Ingrid Dillo, in NRC *Handelsblad*. Both authors maintain that the competitive advantage of the Netherlands during the seventeenth century was based not so much on low wage costs and low taxation but on the technological superiority of the country. According to them, the Dutch domination of the oceans can also be explained in this way. During the eighteenth century, the situation became inverted: when technology stood still, the economy went into recession as well. According to the authors, the Netherlands around the end of the twentieth century show a strong similarity to the situation two centuries earlier: the distribution of welfare, then carried out by different governmental departments, was and still is central, and welfare was taken for granted and not perceived as something that had to be fought over anew every day. The State rested on the laurels of the seventeenth century, and although the external surroundings had changed dramatically it reacted insufficiently or not at all. The country had rigidified in self-satisfaction, inertia, endless decision-making processes, and conservatism.

20 Brugmans, p. 48.

21 See also, ibid., p. 281.

22 Herbert, p. 57.

23 Shako's fortress was situated on the Elandsgracht 71–77; exhaustively on this: Justus van Maurik, 1886.

24 Stoutenbeek, et al.; Philo Bregstein and Salvador Bloemgarten; Speet, *Zeven eeuwen Amsterdam, de Amsterdammers en hun nijverheid*.

25 Edmondo de Amicis.

26 Anonymous, *De ongelukkige levensbeschrijving van een Amsterdammer*; first printed in 1775. It is thought, by the way, that Herman Koning, the rebellious publisher of this pamphlet, is also its author.

27 Quoted in Lesger *Zeven eeuwen Amsterdam, de Amsterdammers en hun handel en scheepvaart*.

28 J. M. Fuchs, et al., p. 94.

29 Casanova.

30 Original manuscript, dated 28 January 1763.

31 Schama, p. 475.

32 Ibid, p. 479.

33 A large number of homosexual brothels were raided in 1730. The participants were sentenced and most of them executed. In July 1764, Bicker Raye mentions a new hunt on homosexuals. Ten Amsterdammers were put in chains on charges of sodomy, while hundreds of others fled. Several homosexuals who were unable to flee because they lacked the funds and connections, committed suicide "by hanging, drowning, and cutting their own throats". One of the men arrested, a birdseller, attempted to kill himself by swallowing a serrated three-guilders piece, but the coin got stuck half-way down his gullet and resurfaced again after three days of vomiting. On 18 August of the same year, four of the ten "sodomites"– a grain dealer, a water carrier, a wig maker, and the birdseller – were garrotted and thrown into the IJ with weights attached to their bodies.

34 De ongelukkige levensbeschiving, p. 109 ff.

35 Van Eeghen, in Maandblad Amstelodamum, pp. 60–75; Geert Mak, 1987, p. 16.

36 E. E. de Jong-Keesing; Emeis Jr., p. 319.

37 Fuchs, p. 38. In 1765 it was proposed to make the stinking canal water circulate more in order to cleanse it. More than 3,300 Amsterdam cleaners reacted angrily to this. In a letter to the City Council they wrote that there were "20,000 houses in the city that had to be cleaned completely on account of the stench and the damp". Clean canals would cause a total loss in earning of about 36,000 guilders, "not counting two or three days polishing of copper, pewter, silver and the like". Moreover, according to the cleaners, the dealers in pumice stone, Brussels sand, potash, paint, scrubbing brushes, wooden clogs and fresh water would all suffer. "Even the Guild of Painters and Glaziers will have a cut in earnings, as the scrubbing of the façades usually causes several window panes to break and most of the paint is scrubbed away."

38 Van Gelder/Kistenmaker, p. 86.

39 See also: A. de Swaan, p. 56, ff. Another opinion is held by Schama, p. 570.

40 The first Amsterdam prison, which opened its doors in 1595 on the site of the old Clarissenklooster by the Hieligeweg, was based on the ideas of Dirk Volckertszoon Coornhert and Jan Laurenszoon Spieghel. Spieghel's plan was very modern for its time. He attempted to strike

a balance between discipline and moral re-education. The identity of the prisoners had to remain secret (a demand that was never taken very seriously) in order to prevent prisoners from being stigmatized when they were released back into society. The food had to be simple, but offer enough variation to make incarceration with water and bread seem like a punishment. It consisted of grey bread, porridge, peas, beans, and a piece of fish or meat once or twice a week. During their rest periods, the prisoners had to exercise by playing ball games or engaging in similar activities. See Schama, p. 29.

41 The story of the drowning cell features time and again in contemporary travel accounts, but it not borne out by any piece of documentary evidence from the prison itself. The historian Jan Wagenaar, who detailed all punishments in Amsterdam between 1760 and 1770, dismisses the existence of such a cell as mere rumour. City historians of our day also see it as an urban myth. Simon Schama (p. 35) however, assumes that these stories are unlikely to be totally unfounded and points out that some of the descriptions are extraordinarily detailed. Using a report from 1705, he assumes that the drowning cell had not been used since the seventeenth century, after a particularly stubborn "villain" had preferred drowning to pumping. However, in April 1747, Bicker Raye (p. 169) reports the sentencing of a carpenter to eight days of "water cellar", but he managed to escape from his chilly abode.

42 Fuchs, et al., p. 123.

43 Van Gelder, et al., p. 199.

44 Chaim Braatbard, p. 59. For more details of the tentants' revolt, see Wagenaar, vol. 4.

45 Brugmans, p. 71.

46 Van Gelder, et al., p. 220; Fuchs, et al., p. 232.

47 Quoted in Van Gelder et al, p. 232.

48 A. R. Falck, *Gedenkschriften*, quoted in Brugmans, vol. 5, p. 11.

49 Fuchs, p. 39.

50 Brugmans, vol 4, p. 257.

Chapter Eight: The Fire Palace

1 Van Maurik, in *Amsterdam bij dag en nacht*.

2 The following contains some fragments from an earlier article which I wrote together with Marjo van Soest in the collection *Als de dag van gisteren*.

3   Edmond and Jules de Goncourt.

4   Brugmans, vol 5, pp. 73–76.

5   Quoted in Brugmans, p. 91.

6   M. C. van Hall.

7   Exhaustively on the Town Hall question, see Brugmans, p. 108, ff.

8   The palace remained a delicate subject in relations between Amsterdam, the Royal family and their court. Amsterdam itself did not have a really suitable Town Hall, while the building which was so eminently suited to this function was standing empty for most of the year. In May 1930, a commission of legal experts came to the conclusion that the city had never legally ceded the building to the Crown. The Crown offered to take over the building formally in return for a payment of 15 million guilders, then a sizeable sum, to enable the city to build a new Town Hall. Many Amsterdammers, however, preferred to have their old city hall back. In 1934 it appeared, after further investigation, that the seventeenth-century palace/Town Hall was no longer suitable as the administrative centre of a modern city. In 1935, the municipal council accepted the Crown's offer and decided to build a new Town Hall. After this, the war intervened, followed by years of rebuilding, and it was not until the 1960s that the new Town Hall was on the agenda again. Twenty years of planning and discussions ensued. In 1988 the new building on the Waterlooplein was ready.

9   The "ever so respectable" Van Halls pop up so regularly in *Woutertje Pieterse* that they have almost become a Dutch literary concept. Their name is indeed borrowed from the famous Van Hall family and probably from M. C. Van Hall, who, with Douwes Dekker and other friends, established a beer society in 1861.

10 When Hester Boissevain, the daughter of the director and editor-in-chief of the Algemeen Handelsblad, got engaged to Jan van Hall, the son of Maurits, in 1893, the engagement was a major social event on the sweeping Herengracht, where the van Halls lived at number 475. When Hester, however, harmlessly asked her future mother-in-law about Jans grandparents, the "Seperated Ones", Anne Maurits and Suze van hall, an embarrassing silence followed. "Hester," her new mother-in-law said, "those people are never discussed in this house." When she tried her luck with the children she was not any the wiser. "They were in prison," they whispered. "Perhaps they were alcoholics or something like that." See Van Hall, p. 63; Suze van Hall's Testament, p. 54.

11 According to the personal reminiscences of L. C. Schade van Westrum, p. 22.

12 Hella Haasse en S. W. Jackman, p. 105.

13 Van Maurik, 1886, p. 81, ff.

14 Multatuli, Ideeën, second collection, p. 100.

15 Gerrit Osnowicz, p. 66.

16 J. M. Fuchs, et al., p. 9.

17 Van Maurik, Stille menschen. Later in the text, the old man next to him turned out to be the last Amsterdam hangman – but that is a different story.

18 Brugmans, p. 109. Also: H. Polak, p. 26.

19 In his standard work Amsterdam na 1900 (p. 87) the city historian Richter Roegholt discusses in detail the consequences of other railway routes. If the Central Station had been built in the south, the centre would have degenerated, or so he believes, to a "muddled complex of sheds and warehouses, a picture of silos, rows of cranes, switchyards, wharves and docks." The city would have been dislocated. The present location strengthened the inner city. However, it has to be acknowledged that many large European cities have their main station outside of the historical city centre without loosing the qualities of the centre. These maintained their dynamism, while independent centres developed around the stations, consisting of small hotels, restaurants, and shops. Roegholt, too, comes to the conclusion that the Central Station in its present location had a decisive influence on the city. The station necessarily became a focal point for traffic, leading to traffic problems because of the vulnerability of the nearby city centre.

20 De Amicis.

21 The smaller canals were emptied mainly for public health reasons. It was hoped that this would rid the city of the cholera epidemics that visited Amsterdam regularly during the nineteenth century. This proved to be a success. In 1857 the Goudsbloemgracht was dried (now the Willemsstraat), in 1861 the Ajeliersgracht (Westerstraat), in 1867 the Nieuwezijds Achterburgwal (Spuistraat), 1864 Bagijnesloot, 1870 a part of the Achtergracht (Falckstraat), in 1873 the Roetersburgwal (Roeterstraat), 1874 the Houtgracht and the Leprozengracht (Waterlooplein), 1881 the Zaagmolensloot (Albert Cuypstraat), 1882 the Spui, 1891 the Elandsgracht, 1892 Paulus Potterkade (Paulus Potterstraat), and in 1895 the Palmgracht and the Lindengracht.

22   See Ben Speet and Michiel Wagenaar, Zeven eeuwen Amsterdam, de Amsterdammers en hun stadsbeeld.

23   The Manege and the Concertgebouw were designed by the architect A. L. van Gendt, the Rijksmuseum by the architect who is also responsible for the Central Station, P. J. H. Cuypers. Nevertheless, it was not until after the beginning of our century that the Amsterdam elite would leave the canal belt. The guest list of the enthronement of Queen Wilhelmina contains just about the entire higher echelon of Amsterdam society. There were not enough hotels available, so the guests had to lodge in the "first houses" of the city. The long list shows that far and away most of them lived on the Herengracht and the Keizersgracht, only four around the Paleis voor Volskvlijt, and a single one in the Vondelstraat.

24   Schade van Westum, p. 117.

25   Johan Geerke, in De Amsterdammer, quoted in Mak, 1991.

26   For more details, see Fuchs, p. 83 ff.

27   F. M. Wibaut, p. 187. Also: Osnowicz, p. 14.

Chapter Nine: The Last Stop of Train 11537

1   The description of the Nieuwmarkt as a "Speakers' Corner" is largely taken from the memoirs of the Amsterdam journalist Gerrit Oznowicz, p. 51 ff.

2   Roegholt, p. 123 ff.

3   In 1859 for instance a quarter of Amsterdammers were living in the Jordaan, but 50 years later about 10 per cent, and 100 years later a mere 3 per cent. Around the turn of the century 77,000 people were still living there, in the same area now inhabited by 4,000 people.

4   Nobody knows the origin of the Amsterdam popular feast of Hartjesdag. Perhaps it is a remnant of Easter celebrations. According to the Amsterdam journalist Maurits Dekker (Amsterdam bij gaslicht, p. 70) the feast was celebrated in the following way around the turn of the century: in the morning of the Hartjesdag, the children went around the houses begging and singing, their faces coloured with charcoal and chalk, the girls wearing bowler hats, long trousers and jackets, the boys in old skirts and blouses, their chests stuffed with newspapers. They would collect money in a tin for fireworks and Bengal fire. In the evening, fires were lit along the way. The Dapperbuurt and especially the Pontanusstraat were notorious because of the fires on Hartjesdag.

5 A number of facts and quotations below are taken from Bregstein et al.
6 Roegholt, p. 71.
7 Henri Polak had worked in England for some time and had witnessed the activities of the already powerful unions there. On the basis of this model he established in 1894 the Algemeen Nederlandse Diamantwerkersbond (the General Netherlands Diamond Workers Association) with a strike fund and compulsory membership. In 1902 he was elected to the municipal council as the first social democrat.
8 Bregstein et al., p. 198.
9 Wibaut, p. 134.
10 Wibaut financed the Betondorp and other building projects largely with loans. In 1924 Amsterdam bankers did not want to cooperate any longer: they gave Wibaut to understand that they no longer had confidence in his financial administration. Just as in the previous century, London bankers were less concerned and gave the city all the credit it wanted. Wibaut, a passionate realist, was not to be scuppered by this sort of opposition. "That at least is standing already," he would say while walking through the Betondorp of the Spaarndammerbuurt. "Let them try to tear that down."
11 Maurits Dekker, 1931 / 1958, p. 12.
12 Wibaut, p. 387.
13 G. W. B. Borrie, p. 147.
14 Roegholt, p. 82.
15 Fuchs, p. 133.
16 What follows is largely taken from Borrie.
17 The unrest in the Jordaan also originated in an anti-fascist action. On the swelteringly hot evening of the outbreak of the rebellion, tens of youngsters had gone to the Indische Buurt in order to disrupt an NSB meeting on the Ambonplein. When this meeting did not take place they decided to have a little stroll in town instead, their minds set on trouble.
18 One of the most prominent committees against the nascent fascism was the Comité van Waaksaamheid (Committee of Watchfulness), established in January 1936 by a number of people associated with the University of Amsterdam. As with other groups, the committee ultimately broke up due to tensions between the Communists and Social Democrats. When Hitler and Stalin signed the non-aggression pact of 1939, many of the communists were unsure what to do. Richter Roegholt describes the irresolvable conflict between the watchfulness

against fascism and loyalty to the Soviet Union which ultimately broke apart the Committee. See Roegholt, p. 125 ff.

19 Bregstein en Bloemgarten, p. 295 ff.

20 This report is taken from: Mak (collection), p. 245.

21 J. Presser, vol. 1, p. 14 ff. Also: Roegholt, p. 136; Bregstein et al., p. 309.

22 Roegholt, p. 137.

23 B. A. Sijes, p. 18.

24 Bregstein, et al., p. 312.

25 Presser, vol 1, pp. 91 and 163.

26 Mak, 1987, p. 53.

27 D. C. A. Bout, quoted in Presser, vol. 1, p. 185.

28 Ibid. p. 253 ff.

29 Ibid. p. 281.

30 Lanzmann, p. 158.

31 Mindful of the difficulties of Occupation, the post-war Minister for Education, Prof. G. van der Leeuw, concluded that the position of Amsterdam Univeristy during the war was indefensible. Jewish students and teachers were removed, teachers dismissed, students sent to Germany and forced to sign a declaration of loyalty, all without so much as a breath of protest. The university had tolerated measures "quite incompatible with its value as a Dutch cultural institution". See Roegholt, p. 182.

32 H. de Liagre Böhl en G. Meershoek, p. 29; Presser, vol 1, xerox p. 180.

33 Sijes, p. 107.

34 Presser, vol. 1, p. 377.

35 Max Arian, in De Groene Amsterdammer; Sylvian Ephimenco, in Trouw.

36 H. M. van Randwijk, p. 274.

37 The afterword by Primo Levi in Presser, 1957.

38 Investigating commission, Vol 7, C, p. 262, quoted in Presser, vol 2, p. 255.

Chapter Ten: The Years of Moral Panic

1 The following is based on research which I carried out with Steven Adolf, and which was published in the NRC Handelsblad. See also Van Hall, p. 91 ff, L. de Jong, Vol. 7, second part, p. 782 ff, and Vol. 10b, p. 532 ff.

2 The Dutch Bank has never been very proud of this Resistance stunt. Even though the Chief Cashier, C. W. Ritter, was later honoured for

his part in the affair, the bank itself never publicized it. "For years it was swept under the carpet," Ritter was to tell us later. "The bank was somewhat embarrassed that such a thing was possible. It was felt that publication would only result in more trouble."

3   De Liagre Böhl et al., p. 32 ff.

4   For more details on this, see De Liagre Böhl et al., p. 55 ff.

5   G. van Hall, p. 95.

6   L. de Jong, vol 1, p. 494.

7   See HP/De Tijd, 18 May 1994.

8   A. Bouman, quoted in De Liagre Böhl et al., p. 88 ff.

9   Gerard Rutten, quoted in De Liagre Böhl et al., p. 83.

10   Mak, in Ons Amsterdam.

11   Philip Slater.

12   NRC Handelsblad, 6 June 1991.

13   D. van Reeuwijk, p. 12.

14   NRC Handelsblad, 14 June 1991.

15   Ruud Abma, 1990. Also in NRC Handelsblad.

16   Maarten Menzel. Also: Roegholt, p. 270 ff.

17   Quoted in Roegholt, p. 338.

18   Roegholt, p. 323 ff.

19   Bilwet, Bewegingsleer, p. 7.

20   Ibid., pp. 172 and 173.

21   There is still a shroud of mystery about the true number of participants in the Twenty Year Civil War. In her study, Virginie Mamadouh tried to ascertain the numbers. An indication of the public support for the Provo movement is the result of the council elections on 1 June 1966, in which the Provo List 12 attracted more than 3,000 votes. The number of the truly active Provos, however, was small, some hundreds at most. The number of squatters is even less clear, especially since there were "wild" squatters, as well as "silent" ones, who were not part of the movement. Only the print run of the squatter newspaper Bluf! gives an indication of the true numbers: 2,500 at the zenith of the movement. The hard core, however, was significantly smaller.

Bibliography

Abma, R., "Bij provo ging het niet om een generatieconflict", in NRC Handelsblad, 8 June 1991.

Abma, R., Jeugd en tegencultuur, Utrecht, 1990.

Ach lieve tijd, zeven eeuwen Amsterdam en de Amsterdammers, Zwolle 1988–90.

Adolf, S., "Bakier van het vertzet", in NRC Handelsblad, 2 May 1990.

Ailly, A. E. d', Historische gids van Amsterdam, ed. B. Rebel and G. Vermeer, Den Haag, 1992.

Alpers, S., De firma Rembrandt, Amsterdam, 1989.

Als de dag van gisteren, honderd jaar Amsterdam en de Amsterdammers, Zwolle 1990–92.

Amicis, E. de, Nederland en zijn bewoners, original Italian ed. 1876, Dutch trans. Utrecht/Antwerpen, 1985.

Anoniem, Chronijk van 1477–1534, Koninklijke Bibliotheek Den Haag.

Anoniem, De ongelukkige levensbeschrijving van een Amsterdammer, 1775 by Harmanus Koning, new ed. with an introduction by Maurits Dekker, Amsterdam, 1965.

Arian, M., "Nederland deportatieland", in De Groene Amsterdammer, 10 December 1992.

Baart. J. M. Ceramic consumption and supply in early modern Amsterdam.

Baart, J. M. Een Hollandse stad in de dertiende eeuw, Muiderberg-symposium, 25–26 September 1987.

Baart, J. M. "Het kasteel van Aemstel", in Ons Amsterdam, year 46, pp. 113–161.

Baart, J. M., "Romeinen aan de Amstel?", in Ons Amsterdam, year 43, p. 105.

Bakker, B., "De stadsuitleg van 1610 en het ideaal van de 'volcomen Stadt'", in Jaarboek Genootschap Amstelodamum, No. 87, p. 71, Amsterdam, 1995.

Beijerink, Fr. and M. G. de Boer, Het dagboek van Jacob Bicker Raye, 1732–72, Amsterdam, n.d.

Bijl, H. van der e.a., Amsterdam bezongen, Amsterdam, 1947/1959.

Bilwet, Bewegingsleer, kraken aan gene zijde van de media, Amsterdam, 1990.

Boer, M. G. de, Een wandeling door Oud-Amsterdam 1544, Amsterdam, 1952.

Borrie, G. W. B. Monne de Miranda, Den Haag, 1993.

Bouman, A., "Welke uitwerking had de oorlog op de seksuele moraliteit vans ons volk?", in Maandblad Geestelijke Volksgezondheid, year 1, 1946, 98.

Bout, D. C. A., In de strijd om ons volksbestaan, Den Haag, 1947.

Braatbard, Ch., De zeven provincien in beroering, hoofdstukken uit een jiddische kronick, ed. J. L. Fuks, Amsterdam, 1960.

Braudel, F., De structuur van het dagelijks leven, vol, 1, Amsterdam, 1987.

Bregstein, P. and S. Bloemgarten, Herinnering aan joods Amsterdam, Amsterdam, 1978.

Brown C., Kelch and P. van Thiel, Rembrandt, de meester en zijn werkplaats, Amsterdam/Zwolle, 1991.

Brugmans, H., Geschiedenis van Amsterdam, six vols, Utrecht, 1972–73.

Casanova, Hollands avontuur, ed. Frans Denissen, Amsterdam, 1991.

Daan, J. C., *Hij ziet wat! Grepen uit de Amsterdamse volkstaal*, Amsterdam, 1948.

Dapper, O., *Historische beschrijving der stadt Amsterdam*, Amsterdam, 1663.

Dekker, M., *Amsterdam*, Amsterdam, 1931/1958.

Dekker, M., *Amsterdam bij gaslicht*, Amsterdam, n.d.

Deursen, A. Th. van, "Rembrandt en zijn tijd: het leven van een Amsterdams Burgerman", in Brown et al.

Dillen. J. G. van, *Bronnen tot de geschiedenis van het bedrijfsleven en het gildewezen van Amsterdam*, vol, I, app. 1. Den Haag, 1929.

Does, J. C., van der et al. "De historische ontwikkeling van Amsterdam", in *Ons Amsterdam*, 1948.

Drion, H., "De rode draad in de burgerlijke cultuur", in *Denken zonder Diploma*, Amsterdam, 1986.

Dudok van Heel, S. A. C., *Dossier Rembrandt*, Amsterdam, 1987.

Dudok van Heel, S. A. C., "Rembrandt van Rijn, een veranderend schildersportret", in Brown et al.

Eeghen, I. H. van, "Elsje Christiaens en de kunsthistorici", in *Maandblad Amstelodamum*, 56 (1969), pp. 73–78.

Eeghen, I. H. van, "De Ijsbreker" in *Maandblad Amstelodamum*, 1954, pp. 60–75.

Eeghen, I. H. van, *Uit het dagboek van broeder Wouter Jacobszh*, Groningen, 1959.

Eeghen, I. H., van, "Coenraad van Beuningen", in *Tijdschirft Genootschap Amsteldodamum*, 1970, p. 107.

Elias, J. E., *De vroedschap van Amsterdam*, 1578–1795, two vols., Haarlem 1903–05.

Emeis, M. G., *Amsterdam buiten de grachten*, Amsterdam, 1983.

Emeis. Jr., M. G., serie over het ontstaan en de groei van Amsterdam in *Ons Amsterdam*, year 27, pp. 34, 66, 98, 130, 162 and 318.

Ephimenco, S., "Nederland liegt", in *Trouw*, 19 March 1994.

Fuchs, J. M., *Amsterdam, een lastige stad*, Baarn, 1970.

Fuchs, J. M., and W. J. Simons, *Nou hoor je het eens van ander, buitenlanders over Amsterdam*, Den Haag, 1975.

Gelder, R., van and R. Kistemaker, *Amsterdam 1275–1795, de ontwikkeling van een handelsmetropool*, Milaan/Amsterdam, 1982/1983.

Girouard, M. *Steden in groei en bloei*, Den Haag, 1988.

Goncourt, E., and J. de, *Dagboek*, Parijs 1956/Amsterdam.

Gouw, J. ter, *Geschiedenis van Amsterdam*, Amsterdam, 1879–93.

Grothe, J. A., *Merkwaardige vonnissen uit den tijd der geloofsvervolging*, Kronijk Historisch Genootschap, Utrecht, 1856.

Günther, R., *Amsterdam*, Hamburg, 1982.

Haasse, H. and S. W. Jackman (bew.), *Een vreemdelinge in Den Hagg, uit de brieven van koningin Sophie der Nederlanden aan lady Malet*, Amsterdam, 1984.

Hall, G. van, *Ervaringen van een Amsterdammer*, Amsterdam, 1976.

Hall, M. C., van, *Drie eeuwen, kroniek van een Nederlandse familie*, Amsterdam, 1961.

Heijdra, T., *De Pijp, een monument van een wijk*, Amsterdam, 1989.

Herbert, Z., De bittere geur van tulpen, Holland in de Gouden Eeuw, Amsterdam, 1993.

Houbraken, A., De grote schouburgh der Nederlandtsche konstschilders en schilderessen, Amsterdam, 1718/1719, Maastricht, 1943.

Huizinga, J. Herfsttij der middeleeuwen, Groningen, 1919.

Hulst, N. van and I. Dillo, "Nederland moet lering trekken uit lessen verleden" in NRC Handelsblad, 15 June 1994.

Jaarboek Amstelodamum, Jaarboek van het genootschap Amstelodamum, 1902 – today.

Jong. L. de, Het Koninkrijk der Nederlanden in de Tweede Wereldoorlog, vol. I, Den Haag, 1969.

Jong L. de, Het Koninkrijk der Nederlanden in de Tweede Wereldoorlog, vol 7, Den Haag, 1976.

Jong, L. de, Het Koninkrijk der Nederlanden in de Tweede Wereldoorlog, vol 10b, Den Haag, 1981.

Jong-Keesing, E. E. de, De economische crisis van 1763, Amsterdam, 1939.

Lanzmann, C., Shoah, Amsterdam, 1985.

Lesger, Cl., Ach lieve tijd. Zeven eeuwen Amsterdam, de Amsterdammers en hun handel en scheepvaart, Zwolle, 1990.

Lesger, Cl., "Tussen stagnatie en expansie, economische ontwikkeling en levensstandaard tussen 1500 en 1600", in Woelige tijden.

Levie, T. and H. Zantkuyl, Wonen in Amsterdam, Amsterdam, 1980.

Liagre Böhl, H. de and G.Meershoek, De bevrijding van Amsterdam, Zwolle, 1989.

Looijen, T., Ieder is hier vervuld van zijn voordeel, Amsterdam, 1981.

Maandblad Amstelodamum, Orgaan van het genottschap Amsteldodamum, 1914 – today.

Mak. G., The Amsterdam dream, Amsterdam, 1986.

Mak. G., Een bres in de stad, de geschiedenis van de IJsbreker, Amsterdam, 1987.

Mak. G., "Commotie rond het plan Kaasjager" in Ons Amsterdam, jrg. 43, No. 1, January 1991.

Mak, G., De engel van Amsterdam, Amsterdam, 1992.

Mak, G., (ed.), Reportages uit Nederland, Amsterdam, 1991.

Mak, G., and M, van Soest, in Als de dag van gisteren, honderd jaar Amsterdam, de Amsterdammers en hun stad, Zwolle, 1990.

Mamadouh, V., De stad in eigen hand, provo's, kabouters en krakers als stedelijke sociale beweging, Amsterdam, 1992.

Maurik, J. van, "'t ontwakend Amsterdam", in Amsterdam bij dag en nacht, Amsterdam, 1880.

Maurik, J. van, Stille menschen, Amsterdam, n.d.

Maurik. J. van, Toen ik nog jong was, het fort van Jaco, Amsterdam, 1886.

Méchoulan, H., Amsterdam ten tijde van Spinoza, geld en vrijheid, Amsterdam, 1990.

Menzel, M., De Bijlmer als grensverleggend ideaal, Delft, 1989.

Mulisch, H., Bericht aan de rattenkoning, Amsterdam, 1966.

Multatuli, Ideeën, two vols.

Napel, E. ten and B. van Tilburg, Amsterdamse sinjoren, Amsterdam, 1993.

Olsen, D., De stad als kunstwerk, Amsterdam, 1991.

Ons Amderstam, monthly, Amsterdam 1949 – today.

Oznowicz, G., Amsterdam uit Naatjes tijd, Amsterdam, 1961.

Polak, H., *Amsterdam, die grote stad*, Amsterdam, 1936.

Presser, J., *Ondergang*, two vols., Den Haag, 1965.

Presser, J., *De nacht der Girondijnen*, Amsterdam, 1957.

Price, J. L., *Holland and the Dutch Republic in the Seventeenth Century*, Oxford, 1994.

Randwijk, H. M., van, *In de schaduw van gisteren*, Den Haag/Amsterdam, 1976.

Reeuwijk, D. van, *Amsterdamse extremisten*, Amsterdam, 1965.

Roegholt R., *Amsterdam na 1900*, Den Haag, 1993.

Romein, J., *Op het breukvlak van twee eeuwen*, Amsterdam, 1967.

Roon, G. van, "Spion voor de Gestapo", in *HP/De Tijd*, 3 June 1994.

Schade, van Westrum, L.C. *Amsterdam per vigilante*, Utrecht, 1963.

Schama, S., *Overvloed en onbehagen*, Amsterdam, 1987.

Schwartz, G., *Rembrandt, zijn leven, zijn schilderijen*, Maarssen, 1984.

Sijes, B. A., *De Februaristaking*, Amsterdam, 1954.

Slater, Ph., *The Pursuit of Loneliness*, Boston, 1970.

Speet, B. J., *Zeven eeuwen Amsterdam, de Amsterdammers en hun zieken*, Zwolle, 1989.

Speet, B. J., and M. Wagenaar, *Zeven eeuwen Amsterdam, de Amsterdammers en hun stadsbeeld*, Zwolle, 1989.

Sterck, J. F. M., *De Heilige Stede te Amsterdam*, Hilversum, 1938.

Sterck, J. F. M., *Uit de geschiedenis der heilige stede*, Amsterdam, 1898.

Stoutenbeek, J. and P. Vigeveno, *Wandelingen door joods Amsterdam*, Weesp, 1985.

Swaan, A., de, *Zorg en de staat*. Amsterdam, 1988.

Sywaertsz, W., *Roomsche mysteriën ontdekt*, Amsterdam, 1604.

Taverne, E., *In 't land van belofte; in de nieue stadt*, Maarssen, 1978.

Vaz Dias, A. M., "Het huis met de bloedvlekken", in *De Telegraaf*, 21 August 1937.

Verkerk, C. L., "De burcht van de heren van Amstel is nog niet gevonden", in *NRC Handelsblad*, 21 March 1994.

Waganaar, J., *Amsterdam in zijne opkomst, aanwas, geschiedenissen, voorregten, koophandel, gebouwen, kerkenstaat, schoolen, schutterijen, gilden en regeeringe, beschreeven*, Amsterdam, 1760–68.

Wallerstein, I., *Het Moderne wereldsyteem*, vol. 11, *Mercantilisme en de consolidatie van de Europese wereldeconomie 1600–1750*, Weesp, 1983.

Wibaut, F. M., *Levensbouw, memoires*, Amsterdam, 1936.

Zahn, E., *Das unbekannte Holland*, Berlin, 1984.

Zantkuyl, H. J. *Bouwen in Amsterdam*, Amsterdam, 1993.

Zesen, Filip von, *Beschreibung der Stadt Amsterdam*, Amsterdam, 1662.

Index of Proper Names

Index of Places